Even the Women Are Leaving

Even the Women Are Leaving

MIGRANTS MAKING MEXICAN
AMERICA, 1890–1965

Larisa L. Veloz

UNIVERSITY OF CALIFORNIA PRESS

University of California Press
Oakland, California

© 2023 by Larisa L. Veloz

Library of Congress Cataloging-in-Publication Data

Names: Veloz, Larisa L., author.
Title: Even the women are leaving : migrants making Mexican America,
    1890–1965 / Larisa L. Veloz.
Description: Oakland, California : University of California Press, [2023] |
    Includes bibliographical references and index.
Identifiers: LCCN 2022040248 (print) | LCCN 2022040249 (ebook) |
    ISBN 9780520392694 (cloth) | ISBN 9780520392700 (paperback) | ISBN
    9780520392724 (ebook)
Subjects: LCSH: Women immigrants—Mexico—20th century. | Immigrant
    families—Mexico—20th century. | Mexico—Emigration and
    immigration—20th century.
Classification: LCC JV7408 .V45 2023 (print) | LCC JV7408 (ebook) | DDC
    305.48/4120972—dc23/eng/20221110
LC record available at https://lccn.loc.gov/2022040248
LC ebook record available at https://lccn.loc.gov/2022040249

32   31   30   29   28   27   26   25   24   23
10   9   8   7   6   5   4   3   2   1

For my grandparents:
Aurora and Jésus López
&
María and Roberto Veloz

CONTENTS

LIST OF FIGURES AND MAPS

FIGURES

MAPS

ACKNOWLEDGMENTS

The seeds for this project started out as stories told around my grandmothers' kitchen tables. What began as memories recounted to me in my childhood by various family members eventually inspired my curiosity about migration experiences in particular. The majority of my parents' siblings were shuttled back and forth across the border at various points in their lives, carrying with them the memories and histories of two nations that they passed on to me as I got older. I have many people to thank for the support they've shown me in this endeavor, but I would like to start by thanking the López and Veloz families for providing me with a history that I could have only learned from them.

I wouldn't have truly pursued this project during my doctorate at Georgetown University if not for John Tutino's wise intervention and gentle but persistent direction. When I wanted to delve into history of Mexico's nineteenth century, he assured me that the story of binational and early twentieth century family and female migration needed to be told, and he recognized that I had the passion and the persistence to take it on. I could never say enough about a mentor and advisor who always makes time to answer your questions, always challenges you to think in new ways, and who is always kind. John, thank you for your guidance at every step of this process.

I also want to thank Katherine Benton-Cohen, who fundamentally shaped my thinking on gender and migration, served as an incredible mentor at Georgetown, and continues to share her insights with me. Thanks also to Bryan McCann—the third member of my advisor dream team. Classes and conversations with Alison Games, Chandra Manning, Adam Rothman, Erik Langer, Amy Leonard, Meredith McKittrick, and Marcia Chatelain shaped me as a writer and scholar. I am also thankful to a supportive group of peers at Georgetown University for reading early drafts of the project. When I first visited Georgetown and met fellow Mexicanists Fernando Pérez Montesinos, Rodolfo Fernández, and Luis Fernando Granados, I knew I belonged there. The memories and knowledge gained from impassioned conversations about Mexico's past and present will stay with me forever. I was fortunate to receive important feedback and vital encouragement from Luis Fernando right before the world shut down in March of 2020 and it carried me to through the conclusion of this project. My friend, you are dearly missed.

Grants from the Franklin and Eleanor Roosevelt Institute and the Cosmos Club as well as the Irene Ledesma prize from the Coalition for Western Women's History supported US-based research. Research in Mexico was critically supported by the Fulbright Garcia-Robles Scholarship, and Robert Curley Alvarez facilitated an institutional home for me at the Universidad de Guadalajara, while Julia Young connected me to scholars and archivists throughout Guadalajara. I am grateful to archivists at the Archivo General de La Nación, the Acervo Histórico Diplomático, the Archivo Público del Estado de Jalisco, and the National Archives Record Administration in Washington, DC and College Park, Maryland. In Mexico City I was fortunate to find adventure in the archives and beyond with Vanessa Freije, Diana Schwartz, Maru Balandrán, and Tore Olson. Thank you for the enriching conversation and for navigating the city streets and cafes alongside me.

Colleagues and graduate students at the University of Texas at El Paso have been incredibly supportive, and special thanks go to Leslie Waters, Susan Stanfield, and Yolanda Chávez Leyva for listening to my endless meanderings and providing valuable feedback on ideas and finishing touches for the book.

I want to thank my friends and family. Your emotional and intellectual support held me up in the best and most challenging times. To Nicole Riggs and the Bivings, Yale, Imel, Ramos, and González families, thank you for asking me year after year to read drafts of my work and for always showing confidence in me and my project. Molly Imel, thank you for cheering me on down the homestretch of writing this book.

Lastly, I extend the most heartfelt thanks to my family members who doubled as research assistants. Lupe Luján took notes, flagged documents to photograph, read up on historiography, and made friends with archivists. She also did all the other things that tías do, like make me food, counsel me personally and intellectually, and accompany me to museums and bookstores. To my mom, dad and brother—Rosalina Veloz, Armando Veloz, and Alejandro Veloz—my words of gratitude and admiration could fill the pages of another book. Your imprints are on every page of this one. You gave me edits, and hugs, and encouragement, and love, and I simply could not have written this book without you.

Introduction

Dear President of the USA

I am a girl that pass all my childhood hear in California. I came to America
when I was only three year old. And we when to Mexico when I was 14 year
old. And as soon as we got in Mexico my father daid. And we are having a
very hard time to get along. We have no work to do. But if there was work
we don't like to live in Mexico 4 of my sister are born hear in California
and thay are allways sick because in Mexico the time is different for them. I
am married, But I Married a very poor men and like we live in a very little
Ranch there is no work to do. And he says he loves to come to America. All
day long I on toking to my husband about my dear Calif. And he says that
if you help us to come over hear that he will work the very best he can. And
us that when to school and study the dear lesson of this lovely Book, Are
wishing to come again to our dear America that we love so much.[1]

ON APRIL 20, 1939, Rosie Garcia sent a letter to President Roosevelt from
Arandas, Jalisco to request passports for herself, her mother, her husband,
and her six siblings. After opening her letter with a narrative of the hard time
that befell her family upon their return to Mexico from the United States in
1932, she went on to apologize for her writing, stating that she had not read
English-language books in seven years. She told the president, "Do your very
best to send for us. Answer my letter as soon as you can."

At the time of Rosie's writing, nearly forty years of regular, circular, binational migrations had been taking place across the US-Mexico border. Rosie
first arrived in the United States in 1921 at the age of three, at the dawn of a
migration boom fueled by growing population pressures in Mexico, the need
for temporary and low-paid labor in the United States, and the desire of
families to reunite with relatives across the border. Boom-era migrations

were critically sustained and made possible by family networks that had been created throughout the first decades of the twentieth century. Rosie was a Mexican citizen, but her siblings, like so many other children born to Mexican migrants in the 1920s, were US citizens. Two years into the Great Depression, they were shuttled to a country they had never known. And although Rosie had been born in Mexico, grown up in two countries, and married a Mexican citizen, it is clear from her letter that President Roosevelt was very much her president. She was one of thousands, if not hundreds of thousands, of binational migrants living in an era that experienced the coerced return of hundreds of thousands of Mexicans back to Mexico, along with the hardening of a border that had at one time permitted multiple crossings and re-crossings.

Much of the history of Mexican immigration is told through parallel histories of shifting US immigration policy, economic contractions, and the demand for overwhelmingly male Mexican laborers in the US Southwest. These histories so often dominate what is known of Mexican immigrants to the United States that contemporary understanding and political debates are still framed within these channels. But there is another story that has often faded into the background, centring on family migration and the migration of Mexican women. In recent years, as family separation along the border has garnered more attention, policies regarding the US-Mexico border and its power to demarcate "legal" and "illegal" bodies have been increasingly questioned. More than just an entry point for necessary or excess laborers, the US-Mexico border should be recognized as a gateway for family migrations that have intertwined the histories and fates of the United States and Mexico for the past 150 years.

The typical Mexican migrant of the period from 1890 to 1965 is imagined to be young, male, single, and from a rural community, and yet both men and women of all ages, coming from various socioeconomic, political, and religious backgrounds, pioneered early migration routes. All were involved in the making of Mexican America by mid-century. Families pioneering early multidirectional and multigenerational migrations provided the foundations for generations of binational families. One of the central arguments of this book is that while factors driving migration were wide-ranging and changed over time, one constant held: migrants crossed borders to be with families. Despite changes in immigration policies, fortifications along the border, and attempts to restrict the permanent settlement of families in the United States, family-centered migration persisted. I define family-centered migration as that migration which is motivated by family reunion and family labor recruitment, and facilitated by family networks through the exchange of information, contacts, transportation, accommodation, and labor contacts. The historical depiction of Mexican migration through the lens of male labor migration, the paucity of sources pertaining to migrant women in traditional archives, and the US and Mexican governments' attempt to restrict family migration during the bracero era from 1942–1964 has resulted in an erasure of continuous and sustained family migration and particularly of the women and children who embarked on cross-border journeys. While excellent studies have shed light on post-1965 Mexican migration inclusive of women, fewer studies tell the story of migrant women and transnational Mexican migrant families in the early decades of the twentieth century.[2]

This book recovers a history of Mexican women, children, and families in particular, who crossed the US-Mexico border in the first half of the twentieth century—a history that is a vital part of the national history of the United States as well as Mexico. An exploration into Mexican and US archives, as well into how Mexico responded to the emigration of millions of Mexican families, provides a transnational lens from which to better understand migration and diasporas. I argue that extended families, including women, children, and the elderly, regularly embarked on cross-border journeys in the first decades of the twentieth century, and that they did so for familial and not just economic reasons. Migration across the US-Mexico border was always diverse, always driven by multiple factors, and was often circuitous, multidirectional and at times circular. The presence of women and families, however, has been rendered invisible because of gendered expectations regarding migration. I argue that women, in particular, were undocumented and as a result undercounted in the history of Mexican migration, especially in the first half of the twentieth century. In fact, frequently women and families were undocumented twice over—once entering the United States and once exiting.

The history of Mexican migration did not begin in the 1890s. Arguably it began in the 1830s when Mexicans, having found the border crossing them, left the new US territory on their own or were forced off their lands to return South. Demographic shifts, displacement and violence, and sometimes negotiation and cooperation describe the Mexican experience in the shifting US-Mexico borderlands of the mid-nineteenth century.[3] Yet by the 1890s, as immigrants from all around the world were arriving to the western and eastern shores of the United States in high numbers, Mexican migrants, compelled to travel long distances to cross a figurative border (with the exception of a few custom collections outposts), were beginning to establish the foundational migration routes and social and familial networks that would firmly take hold over the next century. Mexican families, including women and children, were also crucially significant in building up northern Mexican borderland communities from Baja California to Tamaulipas. These communities would witness both an influx of migrants from throughout Mexico and the circulation of migrants across the US-Mexico border.[4]

Work, adventure, opportunity, and security drew early migrants to the United States, but plenty of factors continuously propelled migration out of Mexico. Demographic pressure in regions that were being parceled out through a combination of inheritance and land maneuvers, especially in places like Jalisco and Michoacán, may have first driven men, but quickly spurred families, across the dividing line. Families settled in boxcar communities and near railyards throughout the United States drew more family members. By the time revolution hit Mexico in 1910, Mexicans from the western and northern states had already been migrating back and forth to the United States to reunite with family and play an ever-increasing role in US ranching, agriculture, and rail maintenance, especially throughout the Southwest. This chapter of Mexican migration, but one piece of a larger history of immigration to the United States, has often been told through the lens of labor migrations, and understandably so. With greater resources, increased capital, new irrigation systems, and industrializing technologies taking hold of the US Southwest, Mexican laborers became central to the maintenance of railroads and commercial cultivation. When viewed from Mexico, however, this period was not just marked by male laborers exiting, but by entire families leaving the fold of the nation.

Sending regions in Mexico witnessed the exodus of extended families, including women, children, and even the elderly. Mexico lost workers, yes, but Mexican communities lost families as well. In Los Altos de Jalisco, observers noted the exit of migrants to the United States at the turn of the century, predating the Mexican Revolution, the Cristero Rebellion, and the bracero program—major events and processes that would come to further engulf that region throughout the twentieth century. Members of extended families also came back and forth to Mexico as livelihoods, families, and communities were extended across borders early on. Mexican and Mexican-American communities in the United States, explored in important works such as George Sanchez's *Becoming Mexican American* or Mario García's

Desert Immigrants, were towns made up of families of men, women and children, creating community with binational roots.[5] Beyond the fields and railroads, and beyond the Southwest, we find traces of Mexican migrants in shops, schools, churches, dancehalls, and mutual aid societies.

During the 1920s and 1930s, academics and policymakers including Paul S. Taylor, Manuel Gamio, and Carey McWilliams conducted studies in order to better understand how Mexican migrants lived and worked, and specifically how they fit within the existing labor systems of the United States.[6] While their field notes included information on a range of migrant experiences and migrant interviews, published works showed mostly laboring men in migration. These studies reflected then-prevailing preoccupations. Whereas Mexican migrant arrival during the first part of the 1920s signaled a welcome relief for some employers who sought to keep pace with the expanding needs of commercial agriculture, by mid-decade politicians began voicing concerns about the accompanying "social problems" that might arise from permanent settlement. Labor representatives had long deployed a portrayal of Mexican labor as temporary in order to justify the continued demand for Mexican migrants in agriculture, but immigration restrictionists gathered momentum in the late 1920s when it became clear that Mexicans would not simply return home to Mexico.[7]

Championed in part by labor organizers, and in part by nativists, restriction efforts zeroed in on arguments about Mexican labor as a threat to wages and Mexican families as a threat to citizenry based on fears of a foreign and racially different Other. To quell concerns of permanent settlement, employers repeated a refrain represented most clearly in an oft-cited passage by California labor representative S. P. Frisselle.

> There is also in the minds of many the thought that the Mexican is an immigrant. My experience of the Mexican is that he is a 'homer.' Like the pigeon he goes back to roost. He is not a man that comes into this country for anything except our dollars and our work; and the railroads, and all of us, have been unsuccessful in keeping him here because he is a 'homer.' Those who know the Mexican know that is a fact.[8]

According to Frisselle, "the Mexican" was in the United States for dollars and work, not to make community. Migrant lives beyond work were rendered invisible. Despite his acknowledgment of the difficulties that emerged with migrant schooling and vaguely referencing other "social problems," Frisselle's testimony maintained a strong commitment to the idea that

Mexicans were not immigrants. Yet we know that Mexicans were both immigrants and migrants. Tucked into Frisselle's testimony was another equally important claim that would go on not only to complicate his argument but also to reveal what became a challenge for US policymakers, an opportunity for Mexican migrant families, and a reminder to future historians: "The one we want is the family Mexican, and we are dependent on him for the harvesting of our crops before school opens, because the men and their wives and children all work in the grape harvest and the Mexicans earn from $4 to $6 a day, with the family." Family and labor were inextricably tied in the history of Mexican migration.[9]

Family and labor are, accordingly, best viewed as overlapping concepts within the larger conceptual map of migration patterns, migrant motives, and Mexican and Mexican-American lives. Not all migration journeys incorporated family, but not all migration journeys incorporated labor either, and except for specific instances of labor recruitment, we know that families followed families and friends followed friends. In their work on migration to the United States from Western Mexico, Douglas Massey, Rafael Alarcón, Jorge Durand, and Humberto González suggest that while structural changes within sending and receiving countries might generate migration, "once begun, this migration eventually develops a social infrastructure that enables movement on a mass basis. Over time, the number of social ties between sending and receiving areas grows, creating a social network that progressively reduces the costs of international movement." These scholars also recognize that lifecycle changes shape family migration strategies, that networks of migration are sustained by return migration and by migrants who eventually settle more permanently in receiving communities, and that at individual and community levels, migration is likely to encourage repeated migrations.[10]

Social and familial relationships were critical to driving and sustaining Mexican migration during the twentieth century and were the foundation for Mexican-American communities in the United States. Mexican women were central to early community-building in the United States in both productive and reproductive ways. Broadening an analysis of early Mexican migration to include social and familial networks reveals the importance of women in the history of Mexican migration, and yet it would be a mistake to think that women only crossed for family reasons and not for education, work, adventure, or escape. Relatedly, it's worth emphasizing that migrant men, while being almost exclusively depicted as laborers seeking labor only, were also driven in their migrations by family-centered motivations.

Examining migration through the lens of social relationships reveals much about men, as well as women. Family-centered motivations include those which conditioned men to provide for their families through patriarchal compacts, as well as those which drove sons, brothers, uncles, and fathers to reunify with their family members in the United States for support, affection, and stability. Relationships were central to male migrations. Beyond dollars and labor, men and women built families and communities in the United States, and across borders.

Migrant networks expanded with every family member who crossed the border and when new migration routes were initiated within a family or community, more migrations were sure to follow. Responding to larger events that pushed and pulled at them, but also to very personal, relational and sometimes intimate factors, migrants continued to cross the US-Mexico border, and did so in both directions throughout the 1920s. Men and women went back and forth, often with families in tow. They became familiar with the routes, with the processes of migration, and with state officials along the way. For some binational living was a strategy, just as, for others who both wanted to and could, it was a strategy to establish residency and own a house in the United States. A vast diversity of migrant lives and communities existed across the Southwest and increasingly in the Midwest as well. Cross-border migrants became domestic migrants, fanning out across the country from winter homes in Texas to take up jobs in factories, construction, railyards, and agriculture. This movement occurred alongside cross-border migrations by professionals, students, and business owners, and even priests fleeing the Cristero conflict.[11] Growing Mexican *colonias* would steadily welcome newcomers throughout the twentieth century.

Births, marriages, celebrations, illness, death—expected and unexpected—could lead to return migration, and so too could national and global events. The Great Depression came down with stifling force along the border, stopping migrant families in their tracks. Xenophobic campaigns to "send Mexicans back to Mexico" resulted in expulsions, and in some cases provided the opportunity for migrants and immigrants alike to re-examine how viable their futures were in the United States. More than half a million Mexicans, including US-born Mexican children, went south in the largest wave of return migration up to that point, with some of them abruptly and callously uprooted from their lives, homes, and families. It would take a decade for the pendulum of mass migration to swing back. Months into a global war, the United States and Mexico found an opportunity to spark and reformat the migratory process, to re-envision the diverse and many border crossings of the 1920s into a massive endeavor of continental labor redistribution. Families were left out of this political dealmaking. And yet all throughout the 1930s they had carried forward in their migrations, fighting hard to continue their binational living. Rosie Garcia was just one of many migrants writing to President Franklin D. Roosevelt, while hundreds of letters were written to Mexican President Lázaro Cárdenas as well. Consuls, welfare officials, migration agents, family members, municipal presidents, and even national presidents were brought into a web of correspondence that would serve to manage and mediate exigent passages and frustrated migrations. Families with mixed citizenship status, or those who had been separated in the lean years, identified their intercessors and sent out their petitions to reclaim their chances at migration.

Prior to the bracero-era reformulation of cross-border migration, decades of crossings had led to thousands, if not hundreds of thousands, of binational families. Families were made binational in two ways. First, migration patterns intersected with national and personal events in such a way that families were made up of both US and Mexican citizens. Take for example the *familia* Baltazar, who were repatriated to Mexico through Nogales in 1931. The father and mother were born in Pénjamo, Guanajuato, at the turn of the century, then after having migrated to Denver, Colorado, they had their first child in 1919. Their second child was born in Pénjamo five years later, after which the family moved back to the United States, first to Santa Rita, New Mexico, where they had their third child, and then to Simons, California, where they had their fourth child in 1929. By the time the family was repatriated, they had moved at least four times, including three times across the international border, creating a binational mixed-citizenship-status family in the process. Mixed-status families faced a different set of logistical challenges since they were not easily classified as either Mexican or American, thereby implicitly and unintentionally defying strict concepts of national identity that were taking hold across the globe at the time. On the US-Mexico border, nationality was reified and imposed through unwavering migration fees, more rigid exclusions, stricter border enforcement, and added criminal penalties for those who crossed illegally. Migrations for all, but for border-crossing families with multiple citizenships in particular, became harder to navigate.

Then there was the binationalism, or biculturalism, that emerged simply through the experience of having lived in two countries. Repeated and circular migrations meant that Mexican-born and US-born border-crossers experienced dynamic eras of history within both the United States and Mexico.[12] Children like William Nuñez, widowed grandmothers like Angela Moreno, and diverse others all lived parts of their lives in both countries during some of the most dynamic and difficult periods of their history. Catalina Hidalgo suffered personal tragedy and fled Mexico during the Revolution only to have the specter of her experiences hang over her son's legitimacy and identity as he tried to naturalize in the United States. Francisco Pérez campaigned for Mexican President Avila Camacho before he journeyed north as a bracero. Charles Hinojosa had multiple Great Depression experiences, working for Roosevelt's Works Progress Administration before he boarded a repatriation train back to Mexico. Some who would cross south to Mexico during the tumultuous 1930s would even make their way back to the United States during the 1940s. They did so alongside hundreds of thousands of braceros who would be entering for the first time on wartime labor contracts. All the while, Mexican-American families continued to move and settle along migratory circuits throughout and beyond the borderlands.[13]

Binational lives could happen by forceful dislocation or by happenstance, but they could also happen by design. Families migrated together and strategized their migrations specifically as part of a broad plan to chart out binational livelihoods. Mexican seasonal and cyclical migrations are evidence of capitalist economies that challenged the possibility of subsistence farming or even one-wage households, but they are also a result of migrant choice, especially for those who aspired to acquire capital in one country and use it to supplement their livelihoods or the livelihoods of their family members in another. The bracero era reveals this most clearly, but the program did not initiate binational living, only grafted itself onto a pattern of migration that had existed for decades.

Throughout the 1940s, tens of millions of men left their hometowns on temporary work contracts. Both governments inserted themselves into a process formerly dictated and dominated by social networks. As governments attempted to formalize, regulate, and reformulate mobility, families were left out, and so were men who fell outside the desired migrant ideal. The single, the agriculturally experienced, the non-*ejidatario,* the male, and above all else, the temporary, were welcomed to participate in the program.[14] But many more clamored to take part in a program that would subsidize their travel north *and* south and, in theory, ensure them much-needed wages.

The bracero program, stunning in its scale, is also revelatory because of its documentation. Mass migration, for the most part, was documented, as were the pleas of those who aspired to join the program's ranks. Among the ephemera left behind by program participants are letters written to officials not only capturing the appeal of the bracero program but also providing snapshots of mid-century Mexico and insight into a generation of providers who put their families' livelihoods at the center of their petitions to government officials. Scholars have shown the intricacies of the bracero program and have illuminated incredibly varied bracero lives through a close reading of government documents, interviews, and the use of oral histories. Bracero contracts could provide a vital lifeline to struggling rural communities in Mexico but could also prove to be an exploitative and humiliating experience. Some braceros came back from their contracts with nothing, while others returned with gifts for their family members and much needed capital to invest in plots of land or business ventures.[15] The continuation of the program until 1964 signaled to those laborers who did not receive the coveted contracts, those tired of the lengthy process and the political favoritism or victimized by corrupt schemes, that jobs were still to be had if they could only successfully cross the border. Thousands circumvented contracting centers altogether.

Millions of migrants left Mexico in the very years that were characterized as the Mexican Miracle. The agrarian reform ushered through most forcefully during the Cárdenas administration had parceled out land to campesinos, but without equipment and capital even those with land looked to the United States for a quick infusion of resources. The many others who weren't beneficiaries of land were caught out in Mexico's shift toward industrialization and they also looked north to bridge them through uneasy times. Entire families undertook cross-border migrations in response, but these crossings were less perceptible than their 1920s counterparts, overshadowed by the formal bracero migration and underestimated in the parallel, informal, and undocumented migration that also characterized much of the 1960s and 1970s. The exodus of hundreds of thousands of migrants recasts our understanding of the benefits of Mexican agrarian reform and the economic progress achieved during the Mexican Miracle.

If the exodus of the 1920s reflected the dislocations of the Mexican Revolution and a transformed countryside, the exodus of the 1940s and 1950s reflected further transformations in agriculture, a marked shift toward industrialization, and an end to Revolution-era commitments that promised redistributive gains. Demands in the Mexican countryside continued to be met with violence as the Cold War dawned. Mexico was not immune to the dislocations and violence of the era; it just looked different than in other parts of the world.[16] Widening an analytical lens to incorporate not only temporary and male migrations but rather a vast array of migrations offers another reflection on the relationship between people and the state in post-revolutionary Mexico. If some supported and submitted to the state, and others performed defiant acts of resistance, while still others negotiated with the state and consequently played a role in shaping state policies, a large number of people simply left.[17]

What might be easier to generalize at a community level is more difficult to generalize at a personal or familial level, especially considering that over the course of a person's life they could support, resist, negotiate and leave the nation's territory throughout the state-making project. The families that migrated throughout the first decades of the twentieth century left traces of their interactions with state actors through their correspondence with government officials. These letters also provide details of personal and intimate negotiations within households that stretched across borders. Such households were built on the negotiation of gendered roles that conditioned men to provide and women to tend to the home and contribute to family in their reproductive roles as mothers.[18] In this patriarchal household, the center, this negotiation of gendered roles, did not always hold, especially when men could not provide for their families. Households suffered multiple assaults due to changing land patterns in Mexico, violence, dislocation, and even governmental intervention in the revolutionary family.[19] While some patriarchal families ruptured, others stretched across borders, and by the time the bracero program came along the gendered expectation that men would leave their families in order to provide became part of the negotiation of patriarchal households. Many families, however, challenged the acceptability of males as absent providers and contrary to the desire of both nations, reasserted their place in binational migration.

A larger aim of this book is to not only uncover forgotten histories, forgotten voices and forgotten experiences of migration, but also to bring Mexican migrants and immigrants in from the margins of US and Mexican national histories. Rather than viewing Mexican migrants as living their lives within liminal spaces in each country during the first half of the twentieth century, it is important to recognize that Mexican migrants and Mexican migration played integral roles in the intersecting national formations of both countries. Migrants created social networks, bicultural livelihoods, and binational families that combined to integrate cross-border communities in an era when an emphasis on nationalism in both countries attempted to segregate neighboring nations and their often-inseparable communities.

Incorporating women and families more forcefully into our narratives of historical Mexican migration not only challenges national narratives of Mexico but of the United States in important ways. Immigration policy and border fortification in the last fifty years has been defined by the United States's power to expel, reject, and deport border-crossers. The nearly constant attention towards issues of the border and immigration within the US political landscape has created a recency bias that obscures a very important century-long undercurrent of *invitation*. The language of labor demand reduces people to labor inputs in the inherent logic of a capitalist system. It covers up the cruelty of a system that has invited and then rejected foreign labor based strictly on the needs of the host country. With the exception of the 1930s when Mexican migrants felt the cumulative effects of coercive strategies to push them out of the United States, employers have long played a key role in welcoming and inviting migrants *and* their families. The "Mexican Problem" or "social problem" accompanying labor migration was created and constructed by the expectation that Mexicans would want nothing but dollars and work—not belonging, or access to social institutions, or a decent standard of living for their families or citizenship. The invitation was conditional, contingent on maintaining foreignness with a guarantee of return, or Americanizing with a guarantee of permanent settlement. Binational lives defied the nationalist sentiments of the time. In fact, it would take until the end of the twentieth century before Mexicans were technically allowed to keep both nationalities.

There were, of course, spaces where binationality has thrived and even driven policy in the United States, especially within the US-Mexico borderlands.[20] For as much as the border authorities have sought to order, borderland communities have pushed for gateways that looked more like revolving doors than barbed-wire-topped chain-link fences. Scholars have traced out how policies and border-regulating agencies have adjusted to local circumstances over the course of the twentieth century while still ultimately being imbued with the power to criminalize.[21] Through such studies we are afforded a view of how the border has been contested throughout the US-Mexico borderlands. Numbers of Mexican migrant and immigrant entries into the United States have been historically and notoriously difficult to estimate, while estimations regarding migrant exits are even harder to get a sense of. Throughout the 1940s and 1950s a blind eye was turned to undocumented border-crossers, and while some laborers were even legalized after the fact as braceros, their families who had accompanied them were not. They were taken quietly across the border and with no trace of their entry or their return, much less their stay, it was like they were never there. When migrant men were caught, during the border patrol campaigns of the 1950s such as "Operation Wetback," they were held in federal prison, county jails, and detention centers, and thus often "counted." Women and children, especially those caught throughout the borderlands were taken to the border, where they might "voluntarily" return.

Gendered notions shaped detainment, detention and deportation procedures, and while every male was assumed to have the capacity to become a "repeater," women and children were viewed with less suspicion. Gendered precepts at the border were deeply grounded in gendered notions of labor migration and specifically on the assumption of women and children's inability to provide for themselves. Throughout the first half of the twentieth century agents scrutinized women's appearance, demanded proof that a male family member could support them if needed, and were particularly vigilant about women's morality. Moral decency and good behavior were a requirement for entry, with women's sexual morality consistently being questioned and policed. Men faced similar judgments, but assumptions that men could easily get work and thus were less likely to depend on public charity protected them from the primary exclusionary measures applied to women.[22] Patriarchy and gendered norms of sexuality operated at the border as well as in sending and receiving communities. Despite the progressive measures such as the legalization of divorce which were introduced as a consequence of the Mexican Revolution, the 1928 Mexican Civil Code still assigned housework and the maintenance of the home to wives. It also required wives to live where their husbands decided.[23] A modernization of patriarchy in the 1930s "sought to remake the family—men, women, and children—in the interests of nation building and development. It rested upon a restructuring of male productive practices and sociability, a mobilization of children for patriotic development and the rationalization of domesticity."[24] Mexico's modernization of patriarchy broadly meant that the federal state, rather than regional, patriarchies would govern domestic relations in service of a more modern nation, but for women patriarchal prerogatives still ruled in households and would shape migrant families and their migrations abroad.

In the United States where "Mexican" and "laborer" were synonyms, and laborers were interpreted as male, gendered labor assumptions obscured women's actual presence in the United States and in the history of migration. Women were often assumed to be visiting for temporary purposes and thus considered non-immigrants. In the 1920s, Frisselle admitted to preferring "family men"—and their families—for work in the grape harvests. Employers in cotton, sugar beets, and citrus also preferred families, and families worked in several other crop harvests.[25] Still, many large-scale agricultural outfits never truly provided for family units, as evidenced by limited housing options increasingly made up mostly of barracks for the preferred unattached male at mid-century. Women were invariably seen as dependents (and of course many were) in Mexico, at the border, and in the United States. Gendered assumptions about labor and expectations of women's dependence coincided to render women less visible in overall migrations. The scarcity of overall documentation for migrants and paucity of sources for those who constructed binational lives has resulted in even more untold stories.

As more historians combine histories of women and gender with histories of labor, and as more community histories emerge, the undeniable presence of women in Mexican migration and in binational communities has been revealed. However, the participation of women in the early generations of Mexican migration remains understudied.[26] The chapters in this book add to this emerging history but center women and their border-crossing experiences as well as the difficulties that emerged as a flexible border hardened over the course of the twentieth century. By searching to recover the female voices and experiences in fragments scattered throughout the archives I was led to discover the overall importance of binational families. Women and families are not synonymous, of course, just as labor and men are not synonymous; however, by following women in their border experiences in the first decades of the twentieth century, social and familial relationships, networks, and motivations are uncovered. Scholars have done much to disclose the importance of Mexicans and Mexican Americans in the making of the United States.[27] This book builds upon that idea to advance the argument that however binational and however temporary border-crossing migrants have been, they remain critical to the national histories of both Mexico and the United States and especially illuminate what a central role familial and social foundations play with regards to current migrations—one hundred years after family migrations first took hold in the Southwest.

Despite more than a century of border-making and immigration policies applied to the US southern border, migrants and immigrants have had to negotiate the intimate and personal spaces and aspects of cross-border migration in the absence of any kind of effective state approach or binational infrastructure to deal with binational lives and legacies. Binational families well-settled on either side of the border and families newly strained by unforgiving border policies still face such negotiations on a daily basis. The following chapters will bring to light forgotten histories of family and female migration and contribute to a more comprehensive understanding of who migrants were, why they migrated, and how family networks sustained bidirectional migrations.

CHAPTER OVERVIEW

This book explores pioneering journeys from the 1890s through the Mexican migration boom of the 1920s, the traumatic repatriations of the 1930s, the attempted reorganization of Mexican migration patterns during the bracero program, and the persisting family migrations and growth of undocumented migrations throughout the 1950s and 60s. The first two chapters examine the conditions in Mexico and the United States that led to high levels of Mexican migration to the United States during the early twentieth century and explore how and why families used migration as a crucial economic survival strategy during trying times, and how migration during this era created binational families. The next two chapters illustrate how the worldwide depression uprooted and often split immigrant and migrant families, and how women, and mothers in particular, coped with family separation. The final two chapters show how binational labor agreements in the 1940s dramatically gendered migration patterns to facilitate legal migration for Mexican men and empower them as household providers, while simultaneously denying women status as productive immigrant laborers, at least initially.

Chapter 1 describes conditions that led to the emigration of hundreds of thousands of Mexicans beginning with the construction of railroads connecting Mexico to the United States, especially in the central-west of Mexico. Shifting land tenure patterns resulting from increasingly commercialized agriculture, population pressures, and land privatization schemes led displaced workers to venture farther from home, first pulling together economic livelihoods through internal migration and then crossing the US-Mexico border. Revolution, the threat of violence, and the disruption of family and community personal and economic security spurred even more migration, resulting in hundreds of thousands of refugees streaming into border cities.

The Mexican Revolution, paired with World War I and the United States's need for agricultural laborers, ushered in a new era of migration characterized by the exodus of entire and extended families.

To illustrate the presence, significance, and growth of family migration during this pioneering wave of Mexican migration to the United States, this first chapter analyzes passport applications filed in 1920 by aspiring migrants from the state of Jalisco. They overwhelmingly listed family-centered reasons for migrating to the United States and reveal the extent to which migrants were already going to join relatives in the United States. By 1920 migrants were relying heavily on their family members across borders to assist them in their journeys. Family members began to pass on lessons from their own migration experiences, as well as employment connections and resources, to their relatives, thus creating 1) robust family networks and 2) family and community legacies of migration. In the aftermath of revolution and in the early days of state-making, Mexican observers grew increasingly concerned by the exodus of migrants from local communities.

Chapter 2 examines the 1920s as a boom era for Mexican family migration. New opportunities in the United States facilitated permanent immigration as well as seasonal migration. Whereas chapter 1 asks readers to consider the importance of family centered migration, and the reunification of family members as a major motivation for migration to the United States, chapter 2 emphasizes the important intersection of family and labor in Mexican migration and the inclusion of families in labor recruitment for commercialized crops such as cotton and sugar beets. The 1920s also brought US immigration legislation and restriction more forcefully to the border, with Mexico and migrants who had been in the habit of crossing back and forth forced to adjust. Reaching out to migration officials as well as diplomatic officials, migrants had to formalize their border crossings and learn how to navigate new realities at the border.

Following the establishment of foundational family networks, as described in chapter 1, chapter 2 asserts that families gained experiences across borders and experienced life transnationally, demonstrating that continued family migration led to an increase of mixed-citizenship families. The more that families moved back and forth across the border, the increased likelihood that some, if not all, children would be born in the United States. Mixed-status families had to negotiate border crossings differently. They would also have different experiences with settlement and return migration, and possible repatriation, in the years ahead. Members of the same family with different citizenships would experience privileges, opportunities, and identities differently as the rigidity of border enforcement shifted. Increased fees, restrictions, and vigilance at the border meant that family networks were more important than ever in helping to facilitate circular migration.

The worldwide economic crisis that struck in the 1930s had a profound impact on Mexican migrants, dramatically interrupting and changing migration patterns. Chapter 3 examines migrant letters to show how the economic crisis impacted migrant families in particular and how families separated by the US-Mexico border struggled to stay afloat. Migrant poverty led to family separation and abandonment, and migrants and binational families reached out to welfare and other state officials during times of crisis. Steep unemployment in the United States and an environment of growing intolerance to foreigners led to an episode of the largest return migration that Mexico had ever witnessed. Some migrants were removed forcibly through coerced repatriation and deportation; others returned willingly, sometimes through subsidized travel provided by the Mexican and US governments. In addition to migrant letters, chapter 3 takes an in-depth look at biographical data of 577 migrants returning to Mexico through Laredo, Ciudad Juárez, and Nogales in 1931. Manifests from repatriation trains include ages, gender breakdowns, family composition, labor status, and return destinations of migrants, enabling me to develop a geography of migrations just prior to the Great Depression and repatriations back to Mexico. The multiple paths and migrations of families reveals the breadth of mobility within the United States and confirms the presence of Mexican communities far beyond the border.

The dislocations of migrants and their families during the Great Depression resulted in particularly challenging separations. While family reunification had been a goal of aspiring migrants, as illustrated in chapter 2, family separation and reunification took on different dimensions in the 1930s chapter 4 delves deeper into family separations caused by the paralyzing effects of economic crisis. Furthermore, while chapter 2 presents a seemingly harmonious case for family migration and networks, the experiences related in chapter 4 show how economic crisis challenged patriarchy, strained families, and led to emotional and physical abandonment and abuse. Migrants shared intimate details of their personal lives through letters to US and Mexican Presidents and consular officials. US social workers looking to get migrants resettled across the border with their families (and off of public assistance) also revealed intimate details about spousal and family discord to other government officials. An ad hoc migration bureaucracy emerged, unprepared and without resources to truly contend with the human dimensions of migration.

At the onset of World War II, after a decade of pressing Mexican immigrants and many of their US citizen children back to Mexico, the demands of wartime created the conditions for migratory flow to swing back once more in a northerly direction. Chapter 5 shows how the bracero program sought to order a migration that for several decades had evolved according to economic as well as life cycles beyond the control of either government. The goal was a controlled movement of male workers from Mexico, with the effect of altogether excluding women. The desired control, however, was only partially achieved. The bracero program had the effect of resetting migration patterns. The state stepped into a role that had formerly been occupied by family contacts who had been integral to arranging contracts, facilitating transportation, and providing financial support. For the sake of keeping migration temporary, both governments tried to leave families outside of the process. Chapter 5, however, presents letters from bracero family members and shows how families interacted with the state in efforts to try to accompany their relatives, claim savings on behalf of their bracero family members, and explain their circumstances to the government. As the bracero program evolved and then was slowly dismantled, one legacy remained: the dual-state creation of an ideal migrant as able bodied, temporary and male. Those falling outside of this category were suspect and had less claim to legality, but they still crossed the border. A major consequence of the bracero program was an increase in *illegal,* or undocumented, migration.

In the waning years of the bracero program a number of parallel migration trends emerged. Extralegal migration increased due to the continued demand for laborers and the continued exclusionary legalization for certain migrants. Deportation efforts increased as a response to continuing immigration, and critically, female and family migration also increased. Despite the fact that Mexican migrants brought in as part of the temporary labor program were depicted as single men, women and children were migrating in more numbers to join their bracero relatives. While men were airlifted, buslifted, and "hot foot" lifted back to Mexico through deterrent schemes, women and children were more quietly removed across the border. The idea that bracero men were *solos* was a myth that had come to be deployed in service of US labor demands, which required large numbers of mobile workers during times of peak harvest, over the demands of families and communities in Mexico that preferred men to stay in Mexico if at all possible. In Mexico, the continued exodus of migrant families, similar to the 1920s, reflected a domestic situation always in want of an un- and under-employment safety valve. The migrations of the 1960s, grounded in the migrations of earlier decades, would portend the greatest levels of emigration in coming decades. Single women were now migrating in droves, not only to cities in Mexico but north, with border-industrializing programs drawing them to Tijuana and Ciudad Juárez and finally across the border. The national containers of the first decades of the twentieth century, holding within them the hopes for continued patriarchal family structures and Mexican miracles, burst and overflowed. Undeniably, publicly, and irreversibly, the national experiments were exposed for what they were: an early-twentieth-century ideal grafted onto a continent and a borderland that had always been connected.

CONFRONTING ERASURE

There are, to be sure, many erasures in the record of the Mexican experience in the United States. Historians are actively trying to address these erasures by uncovering lost histories of everything: the participation of Mexican nationals and Mexican Americans in US wars, educational segregation targeting Mexicans, anti-Mexican lynchings and violence, racialized public health campaigns, the incarceration and policing of Mexicans, political mobilizations, contributions of Mexican-American communities, and as ever and always the experiences of Mexican and Mexican Americans as laborers in the United States. A new geography of migration and diaspora is revealing migrant pathways beyond the southwest borderlands, finding that "new" southern migration has hundred-year-old roots, that regions like the Pacific Northwest also had Mexican *colonias*, that Mexicans weren't only limited to *colonias* across the country, that places previously assumed to be homogenous *barrios* were also diverse loci for democratic solidarity, and that against many obstacles, Mexican Americans succeeded in creating their own suburbs.[28]

Studies seeking to "recover" and unearth the Mexican, Mexican-American, and Chicanx experiences now abound and provide an invaluable and necessary corrective to histories of the United States. New histories reveal the astounding resilience of communities composed of both permanent and temporary residents; however, they also reveal the continued efforts that employers and public officials took throughout the twentieth century to keep Mexican communities temporary—an erasure having to do with non-permanence. Racial violence consisting of intimidation, coercive exile, dismemberment, and even death led to social, economic, and political displacement. However, erasure of long-standing Mexican communities, early binational histories, and family crossings has also been a result of exploitative labor systems, anti-immigrant sentiment, and demographic shifts, alongside displacing migrations, seasonal labor patterns, and socio-economic hierarchies that cast Mexicans as something foreign to the body politic of the United States. There are deep histories even where communities were transitory. Migrants could come in and out, perhaps without leaving any formal trace, as with those laboring women who never made it into observers' views of labor or of community.

As more oral histories and family stories emerge, the process of recovering historical memory and the historical memory of place continues.[29] Without such efforts histories easily remain forgotten, and with forgotten histories come foundational myths that lead to a form of historical gaslighting or a collective questioning of belonging that has lasted well into the twenty-first century. The chapters that follow attempt to rectify a deep and broad erasure resulting from the overall mobility of Mexican migrants in the United States. The letters written to government officials drawn upon for this study provide stepping stones in projecting a broader binational history and give insight into the everyday experience of migrants through their own voices. Temporary migrations were employed as strategies for migrants who could cross borders and see the possibility of making their worlds in two nations. Migrations of short duration, or cyclical migrations, that defied national borders and nationality containers are apt to yield a fleeting presence in the historical record, but not in the memories of border-crossers whose migrations were formative to their life experiences no matter on which side of the border they might have eventually remained.

Lastly, and most importantly, this book seeks to confront the compounded gendered erasure that has rendered the early-twentieth-century migrations of Mexican women for the most part invisible. To do this without conflating women with "family," as Camille Guerín-Gonzales warned nearly twenty-five years, ago is a challenging task.[30] At the risk of doing so, I aim to provide a family-centered history of early Mexican migration emphasizing the binational mobility of women and children so that we might clearly see Mexican family migration as integral to the evolution of communities in both the United States and Mexico.

PART I

———

The First Wave

SEEKING WORK AND FAMILY ACROSS OPEN BORDERS

CHAPTER ONE

"And They Go Silently"

PIONEERING FAMILY MIGRATIONS, 1890–1920

IN 1920, ELENA G. VIUDA DE ARROYO, a fifty-year-old housewife from Tamazula de Gordiano, Jalisco, petitioned the state governor for a passport to join her adult children in San Antonio, Texas. When asked for the objective of her journey, she stated that her children had been residing in the United States for eight years and that her intention was to reunite with them. Elena's children had gone to a city north of the border only two years after the outbreak of the civil unrest and violence that would come to be known as the Mexican Revolution, and she was now intent on joining them.[1] Twenty-year-old Rodolfo de Luna stated in his passport application in July of that same year that he also intended to go to San Antonio, Texas. Like Elena, he listed his desire to reunite with his family as his motivation. Unable to travel with his family on their journey to the United States due to business matters, he was now ready to join them, stating, "I have found myself here completely alone, and as is *only natural,* I find myself needing my family to care for me and for me to help them as well."[2]

Micaela Carranza also applied for a passport in 1920 before setting out for Exeter, a small agricultural town in the San Joaquin Valley of California. As part of her application, she attached a letter of support from her employer, the Compañia Galletería, attesting to her good character. Also included in her application packet was a letter from her mother giving Micaela permission to leave Mexico, a curious addition, considering that Micaela was over the age of twenty-one and not considered a minor. The letter from her mother, Leocadia Ruiz, was perhaps used to substantiate her intentions, her character, and convey to officials that a single woman seeking work in the United States was deserving of a passport and, importantly, that she had community and family approval to migrate.[3] For unknown reasons, passport pictures and supporting documents were given back to Micaela, the young single woman, and Rodolfo, the businessman, indicating that they failed in obtaining a passport. Elena Arroyo seemed to have better luck in securing a provisional passport to the United States, the first of many steps to crossing the border in the 1920s.

Each of these examples provide critical details about how and why Mexican migrants crossed into the United States during a period yielding few testimonies about the everyday experience of migration. Tucked in between histories of the Mexican and Spanish displacement that occurred after the Treaty of Guadalupe Hidalgo and the much larger waves of Mexican migration that occurred in the middle of the twentieth century, the foundational and pioneering migrations of the late nineteenth and early twentieth centuries illustrate how Mexican and Mexican-American communities in the United States grew by successive circular migrations. Migration during this era would establish long-lasting and multigenerational transnational ties and create binational families and communities. While we know about border crossings through the lens of the Mexican migrant settlement in the United States, we know less about how early migrations actually took place and the specific identities and experiences of those who left Mexico.

This chapter reconstructs a history of the first wave of Mexican migration that is inclusive of families and women, and examines how Mexican officials and communities reacted to the growing exodus of migrants. By 1920, Mexican migration was as much about family as it was about labor, and transnational family networks created in the first decades of the twentieth century spurred Mexican migration for the rest of the century.[4]

I argue that women were central to Mexican communities in the United States and to the migrations of their families, but that their migrations during this pioneering era have often been obscured by a stress on formal wage labor and thus on male migrants. In order to bring women back into focus, this chapter relies on early scholarship of Mexican migration that points to the presence of women; Mexican passport applications from the state of Jalisco; and local observations found in early-twentieth-century Mexican newspapers. This evidence shows that Mexicans migrated not just for labor but for family. A focus on the center-west region of Mexico, especially the states of Jalisco, Guanajuato, and Michoacán, reveals that Mexican officials grew increasingly concerned at the exodus of families.

Migrants, in their own words to government officials, tell us of an era of family migration that occurred prior to the more often recognized bracero migrations. Despite the gendered challenges that women faced at the border during this era, guided by expectations that women would migrate only in the company of their male relatives, women also struck out independently on journeys to the United States.[5] With the exception of the work conducted in the 1920s by Mexican anthropologist Manuel Gamio and US economist Paul Schuster Taylor, who interviewed Mexicans about their early migrations, we have few sources to access migrant testimonies.[6] The passport applications I study here are a rich source, which further reveal that men, who were also subject to gendered expectations for their migrations, migrated just as much, if not more so, for emotional connection and family reunification as for economic opportunity.

Elena's story brings attention to revolutionary-era transformations that initiated family migrations, pointing us in particular to the experiences of mothers and fathers who followed their adult children across the US-Mexico border. Without knowing exactly what drove her sons' initial migrations—whether they left for social, political, or economic reasons—we know that they joined a pioneering exodus out of Jalisco during an era of revolution. Eight years later, Elena, a fifty-year-old widow, would attempt travel to the United States for the first time, leaving her friends, family, hometown, and language in order to be with her sons. Would her sons be there to pick her up at the border, or had they returned to Jalisco to accompany her on her trek? Would she face border officials alone, or maybe she had friends offering her pointers about the process? Her sons had been in San Antonio now for eight years, and perhaps they had made a home there that would ease her transition and appealed far more to her than staying behind without her boys or a means of living.

Rodolfo's stated objective is so compelling because of his explicit invocation of the need to be with his family. A young man with enough prospects to stay behind and attend to business while his family went on to the United States, Rodolfo hadn't felt the need to leave until compelled ultimately by longing for his family. Other aspiring migrants would strike out to take their businesses north of the border, but Rodolfo explicitly pointed out the "natural" desire to be close to family. Rodolfo stood out from other applicants because, for this twenty-year-old young man, life across the border meant first and foremost that he would be cared for. Defying gendered stereotypes, he expressed affective and social, rather than economic, reasons for leaving his hometown. Importantly, Rodolfo and Elena's passport requests show us that family networks established in the United States in the first decades of the twentieth century were already leading to mass migration out of central-west Mexico.

Micaela's story is different. While she might have had family or friends in California, she made it clear that her intention was to work. That Micaela specifically identified the town of Exeter, a growing but nonetheless small farming community in Tulare County in the San Joaquin Valley, suggests that she would have likely heard about job opportunities for single young women by word of mouth. Would her journey have looked different from Rodolfo's due to her gender? What challenges might she have faced at the border and in her travel, either by ship up the coast, or overland across Texas to Arizona and then up to Exeter? The Governor's office rejected her request, but a border-crossing card for 1926 matching her name, age, and birthplace suggests that despite being rejected for a provisional passport she persevered and eventually entered the United States. Years after first submitting a pass- port application, Micaela made her way to Ciudad Juárez, established her residence first before attempting to cross the border, demonstrated that she was able to read and write, and successfully obtained a border-crossing card for the first time. She entered alone, without family members. She paid her own head tax, giving added proof against a standard assumption of immigra- tion officials that she might be likely to become a public charge. Letters of support from years earlier would have been helpful in attesting to her honor- able character, and warding off any suspicions of moral turpitude—another common reason for excluding single women at the border.[7] Six years would have made a difference; 1926 marked the height of a boom era for Mexican family and female migration. Whatever the case, or her specific strategy, Micaela finally entered the United States.

The aspiring migrants mentioned here are just three out of at least three hundred Jalisciences who applied for a provisional passport to the United States in the year 1920. They are but a fraction of those who attempted to cross into the United States and we know of them only because they attempted a legal migration during a period of time when the US-Mexico border was unevenly regulated. By the time Elena, Micaela, and Rodolfo were seeking passports, migrants had been crossing the border to make bina- tional lives for thirty years. 1920 marked the end of the first wave of migra- tion but would lead to an increase in familial and social networks that would proliferate throughout the 1920s, arguably one of the most important dec- ades for family migration throughout the twentieth century.

After briefly detailing the important features of migration during the Porfiriato and the revolutionary decade to follow, I will describe the condi- tions in Mexico and the United States which produced the mass migration of both genders and all ages, and established the foundation for binational family networks and later twentieth-century migrations. Migrants would carve out their journeys based on social factors and livelihood considerations, all the while being attentive to an ever-changing US border policy. Motivations were complicated, experiences were varied, and migrant journeys were hardly predictable. Local leaders were forced to piece together ad hoc policies in order to prevent mass migration as well as develop ad hoc solutions to deal with groups of migrants who had already committed to leaving their homes. The migration of thousands of Mexicans back and forth across a largely unpoliced border created families of mixed citizenship statuses and made for a jurisdictional mess. Migration officials and local observers were witnessing the beginning of a movement that would never be regulated, much less governable.

Written sources from this early period of Mexican migration detail the structural features of migration, highlighting mostly employer and government actions. Migrant testimonies are conversely scarce, resulting in a partial picture of what it would have taken for migrants to embark on journeys across the border, what it would have been like to move entire families to new regions, as well as how multiple migrations were constructed. Yet there are archival and testimonial traces of early migrations that are deeply revelatory of a complex era of migration, binational living, and making families across borders. The extant testimonies of Mexican migrants and aspiring migrants, told in their own words to a degree but almost always mediated through government documents and officials, provide a wide-ranging portrayal of migrant and immigrant life. Migrant words testify to the world that shaped them, the landscapes they left, the contours of migration corridors, the multiple journeys that they negotiated, and the multiple spaces that they inhabited. The majority of Mexicans stayed put, but many migrated to Mexican cities, and some, like Elena, Rodolfo and Micaela found reasons to venture north.

PIONEER MIGRANTS

A growing capitalist and industrialist economy in the US-Mexico borderlands, in conjunction with changes in the Mexican countryside during Porfirio Díaz's rule, sparked the migration of landless peasants to other urban areas in Mexico, northern Mexico, and the United States. This was the case, for example, in Jalisco and Michoacán, where changing land tenure

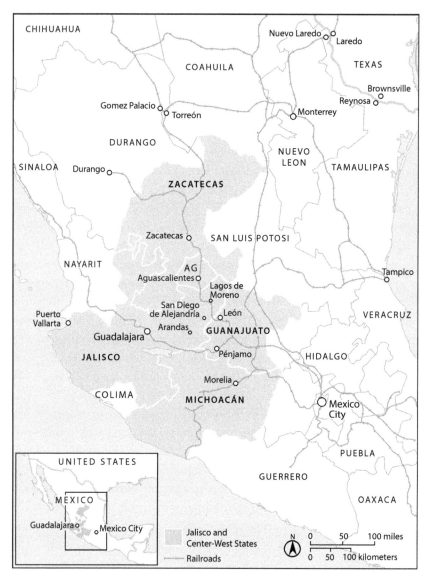

MAP 1. Jalisco and center-west States of Mexico. Map: Ben Pease.

patterns and an increased inclination toward commercial agriculture turned seasonal migrations between harvests into longer migrations that took laborers farther away from their hometowns. In Jalisco, a switch in agricultural production from basic foodstuffs to maguey and sugar, with an increasing concentration of land among fewer owners, resulted in urbanization, starvation in the countryside, and "Bracerismo." As early as 1899, community leaders in Lagos de Moreno in Los Altos de Jalisco petitioned the governor to create a law preventing labor recruiters from coming into their community. Concern over the exodus of migrants was thus developing even at the turn of the century. A comparison of census data from 1900 to 1910 reveals a gender imbalance in Los Altos de Jalisco; women clearly outnumbered men, suggesting that male laborer-led emigration was indeed already under way.[8] Similar patterns of increasing landlessness existed in indigenous towns like Naranja, Michoacán, where land privatization during the Porfiriato and ensuing ecological changes forced an increasing number of mostly men, but also their families, to migrate and sell their labor elsewhere, either in a neighboring state or north of the border.[9] Whether to the North or to the United States, emigration became an established characteristic of communities in Los Altos and Michoacán within the last decade of the nineteenth century, well before the Mexican Revolution.

Demographic pressure and the intensification of commercialized agriculture for export drove migrants first to nearby cities in Mexico before driving hundreds of thousands across the international border. For example, in Michoacán, peasants living in rural areas near Zamora and Purépero migrated to those cities first, and when they could not be absorbed into an increasingly industrial labor market they went further north.[10] Michoacanos also traveled to Veracruz, Campeche, and Chiapas as contract laborers. In some cases, men were specifically required to bring their families as a condition of their labor contracts, a requirement designed to keep migrants from leaving their work easily or prematurely.[11] Seasonal migrations within Mexico transformed into more prolonged migrations northward as railroads provided critical means of transportations for the landless, unemployed, and underemployed masses who faced increasingly dire circumstances toward the end of the Porfiriato.

Large-scale cotton production in northern Mexico drew migrants north. At the turn of the century irrigation and the arrival of railroads connecting northern Mexico to the United States transformed La Laguna, Coahuila, into the cotton center of Mexico. Between 1880 and 1910 the population of rural inhabitants grew from twenty thousand to two hundred thousand, with between ten and fifty thousand migrants arriving annually to the region.[12] While some workers would have returned to their homes in the interior of Mexico after working the harvest, many others would join groups heading even further north across the border for other seasonal opportunities, especially in railroad construction and maintenance throughout the US Southwest and the north of Mexico. Migrants lacking opportunities in the central-western states could rely on Mexican employers and even on the Mexican government to pay for their transportation to jobs in northern Mexico in hopes of parlaying a domestic labor contract into a contract that could earn them higher wages on the other side of the border.[13] As Casey Walsh points out, "by 1910 the Laguna had become just one stop on international labor circuits that included the cotton harvest of Texas and the harvest of California."[14] While cotton was a boon for elite landholders in La Laguna, peasants who previously provided for themselves on subsistence plots on hacienda grounds were pushed out to marginal land, barely able to provide for themselves even with a combination of wage labor. As John Tutino points out these deepening insecurities and losses of autonomy led to growing discontent between 1880 and 1900.[15] The borderlands would go on to become a hotbed of insurrection, and a thoroughfare for migrants working the railroads going north. Migrants out of the central-western highlands, together with those leaving Mexico's northern borderlands, would make up the first major wave of Mexican families into the United States.

They would join Mexican and Mexican-American communities that had remained in what was formerly Mexico. Located in the United States since the Mexican-American War redrew the border, these communities had lived through a transition from Spanish and Mexican landownership to Anglo-American incursion and settlement. In his classic work on Mexicans in Santa Barbara and Southern California at the turn of the twentieth century, Chicano historian Albert Camarillo details how Mexican communities transformed in the wake of Anglo settlement, environmental disaster, and political displacement. The combining factors, particularly in Santa Barbara, with parallels in other Southern California communities, transformed a pastoral economic system into a capitalist agricultural economy. The most obvious impact of such changes was that large Spanish and Mexican ranches were broken up and sold off to newly arrived migrants from the US Midwest and East. Mexican laborers who had previously found employment as sheepherders or in other ranching employment lost their jobs, and while many of them returned to Mexico, many also stayed in the United States and became wage laborers within a new occupational structure. Camarillo notes that by the mid-1870s, Mexicans were engaged in a pattern of employment that persisted for much of the twentieth century: "part-time, seasonal, migratory work."[16]

Importantly, Camarillo also points out that the temporary migrations of Mexican heads of household would lead to the incorporation of Mexican women and children into wage labor in order to supplement household earnings. In Santa Barbara in particular, Spanish-surnamed women were increasingly listed as domestic servants. Albeit a small community sample size, these findings are indicative of how gender roles transformed within new occupational structures and shows this shift even prior to the large influx of Mexican families that came into the Southwestern United States as a result of railroad work. Camarillo cites the incorporation of Mexican women into the labor force by referencing the 1880 census, a source which ultimately does not fully capture the informal labor carried out by Mexican women or the full dimensions of an increasingly mobile Mexican population within California.[17] These Mexican families who were caught in the transition between ranching occupations and seasonal and migratory labor, and whose presence is not always fully documented in the historical record, would nevertheless serve as the foundation for Mexican *colonias* throughout the twentieth century.

The Mexican communities that remained in the US Southwest were very quickly transformed by the influx of pioneering Mexican families who moved north with the rails. The railroad played a critical role in Mexican migration beginning in the 1880s. Importantly, the connection of the trunk lines of the Mexican Central, a Santa Fe subsidiary, with the Santa Fe and South Pacific railroads in the US Southwest, laid the foundational networks of Mexican migration.[18] Mexican laborers composed the majority of track labor in the desert sections of the South Pacific and Santa Fe Railroad lines, especially after Chinese laborers were excluded from the United States as immigrants in 1882.[19] In Santa Barbara the first large influx of Mexican section-gang workers replaced Chinese workers after 1890.[20] Active recruitment of Mexican laborers in border cities such as El Paso began in 1900 and peaked in 1910. From El Paso workers would be sent throughout the Southwest, numbering as many as 4500 in 1900 in California, while in 1908, 16,000 Mexican laborers were reportedly recruited in El Paso.[21] By 1909, Mexican workers were responsible for the majority of railroad maintenance work in California, Arizona, New Mexico, and Nevada.[22]

The development of mining throughout the US Southwest made railroad construction, as well as its maintenance, critical in the first decades of the 1900s as metals such as copper were more easily transported between mines and smelters.[23] Along with increased irrigation leading to commercialized agriculture and continued ranching economies, the advent of rail and industrializing technologies in the US-Mexico borderlands encouraged patterns of temporary migration on both sides of the border. Mexican cities such as

FIGURE 1. Rand McNally Company, "The Santa Fé Route and Connections," 1888. Photo: Library of Congress Geography and Map Division. https://www.loc.gov/item/98688797.

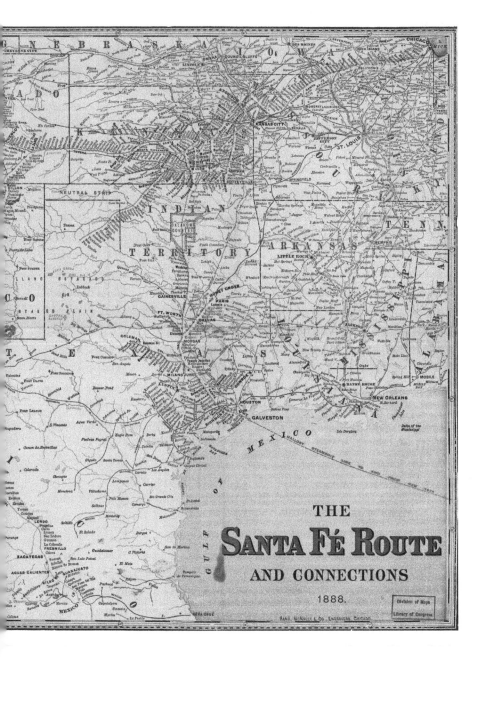

THE
SANTA FÉ ROUTE
AND CONNECTIONS
1888.

RAND, McNALLY & CO. ENGRAVERS, CHICAGO

Ciudad Juárez, Nogales, and Mexicali developed alongside their twin cities on the US side of the boundary line and labor, goods, consumers and vice moved back and forth rather freely up until the second decade of the twentieth century.[24] Mexicans and US Americans of different socioeconomic backgrounds flocked to cities on and near the border. The population in San Antonio doubled between 1890 and 1910; Tucson doubled between 1900 and 1920. San Antonio merchants advertised to middle-class and elite Mexicans while labor contracting agencies attracted Mexican laborers, placing them in jobs throughout the Midwest.[25] The population of El Paso more than tripled between 1890 and 1910, with as many as two thousand Mexican immigrants admitted monthly beginning in 1901, climbing to six thousand by 1907.[26]

While railroads specifically contracted Mexican men to work on the tracks, families accompanied their male relatives and either continued to live with them in boxcar settlements throughout the United States or made homes in towns and cities on the northern side of the border. More than half of male rail laborers were accompanied by their wives between 1907 and 1909, while US and Mexican officials in El Paso confirmed that men, women, and children were taken to railroad grading camps as early as 1902.[27] According to Cleofas Calleros, male railroad workers were given passes to visit their families for three to four weeks at a time and by the time that he began to work for the Santa Fe Railroad in 1912, old boxcars were given out to families who had accompanied male laborers. "They were called bunk houses, and the railroad usually had them in isolated whistle stops. They had anywhere from 10 to 20 box cars used by 10 or 20 families. One family was given a box car."[28] Calleros attributed the beginnings of towns like Vado and Rincón, New Mexico, to the boxcar communities, as well as those spreading along the rail lines to the West Coast through Deming, New Mexico, and onto Los Angeles. Once a week a commissary railcar would reach the families to leave provisions, while Calleros noted that for "those who didn't have a family, they hired some woman from around the little community there. She used to cook for 10, 20, or 30 cents; the meals were 25 cents per meal."[29] Mexican-American communities grew out of rail camps throughout the Southwest and beyond. By 1916, with the pressures of World War I on domestic production, recruiters began to bring Mexicans to Chicago railyards, where many would skip on their contracts and then end up in the steel industry.[30] By 1928, according to Carey McWilliams, "the boxcar labor camps of the railroads housed 469 Mexican men, 155 women, and 372 children in Chicago."[31]

The rail-facilitated exodus in the last decades of the nineteenth century would prove difficult for the government of Mexico to stop. Recruiters from US railroad outfits were persistent and persuasive as they toured the Mexican heartland with offers of high wages. Recruiters, or *enganchadores,* also promised free rail travel to draw people away from their communities to work sites across the border. But *enganchador* comes from the verb "to hook," and workers were frequently indebted into contract labor in the migration process.[32] As previously mentioned, migration to northern Mexico from the interior states was well underway by 1900 as jobs in mining and commercialized agriculture attracted many Mexicans to industrializing centers in the last two decades of the nineteenth century. But the new manner of transportation was crucial in initiating the first large movements of Mexican migrants and also critical in integrating the US Southwest with northern and central Mexico. The railroad facilitated the exchange of goods by connecting labor to mining and ranching economies but also had the power to displace and disrupt old trade networks, thereby putting muleteers and cargo carriers in places like Michoacán out of work.[33] Mostly, however, railroads stimulated job growth, not only because of the labor that rail construction and maintenance required but also because goods were able to reach more distant markets. Aside from integrating an industrializing economy throughout the borderlands, and providing economic opportunities for displaced migrants, the railroads were simply the most efficient means of exodus for Mexicans who faced threats to security and autonomy during Porfirio Díaz's rule.

Mexican government officials grew concerned regarding the volume of Mexican laborers going to work on US railroads as early as 1884.[34] In 1904, officials from the Secretarías de Gobernación and Relaciones Exteriores began to send out circulars to Mexican state governors that described abusive conditions for Mexican workers in the United States and pled with state officials to encourage migrants to remain in Mexico. In some regions, even *hacendados* began to complain to government officials about the lack of laborers.[35] The situation became especially concerning when officials realized that the problem extended beyond the industrializing north and into interior agricultural heartlands. However, little could be done by the federal government, let alone state governments, to combat the forces unleashed by unchecked land privatization, poor harvests, new technologies oriented toward capitalist production, and scrupulous labor recruiters.

As much as railroads led to booming industrialization in northern Mexico and the US Southwest—resulting in more developed and integrated mining, cotton, and ranching economies—foreign capital driving such development also tied Mexico's economic fate more closely to that of the United States. Northern Mexican elites benefitted during boom times and could survive periods of recession like that which followed the panic of 1907, but rural Mexicans struggling for sustenance on marginal land could not; migrants fled to the United States in greater numbers after agricultural crises occurred in Mexico between 1905 and 1907. They were then forced to retreat after losing rail and agricultural work when economic panic gripped the United States in 1907.[36] The repatriations and deportations of Mexican laborers to Mexico between 1907 and 1909 captured the attention of Porfirio Díaz, who made a point of speaking to congress in 1907 about the hundreds of Mexican workers returning from the United States.[37] Could Díaz have foreseen that the return of hundreds, or even thousands, of Mexicans into the already economically fragile and politically volatile north would contribute to the breakdown of his regime?[38] The Mexican Ministry of Labor was created in 1911 to attend to general labor issues and address the northward exodus of labor; however, by then it was too late. Díaz was deposed, and the revolution had begun.[39] If during the late nineteenth century economic transformations throughout the borderlands, spurred on by the railroad, brought a wave of Mexican migrants across to the United States where they would join remnant communities from a pastoral past, the revolutionary violence that gripped Mexico and the disruptions of World War I would ensure a steady stream of Mexican migrants throughout the next decades.[40]

MIGRATION DURING THE WAR YEARS

As a series of civil wars broke out around the country, the old Porfirian guard was left scrambling to retain some measure of federal control. Violence and disruption led to mass internal migration. Women in particular, who had been increasingly migrating for industrial job opportunities in Mexico City during the Porifiato, also fled there during revolutionary violence.[41] Despite initial interruptions to rail service, passenger travel on railroads increased 7 percent in 1913 when Mexicans traveled either to less violent parts of the country or to the United States. The following year, as the mining sector contracted, Mexican miners also emigrated to the United States.[42] As fighters for various factions moved throughout the countryside, families fled to urban centers to escape rural violence and banditry. While some migrants feared death as a

FIGURE 2. Mexican Revolution Refugees, c. 1910–20. Photo: El Paso Public Library, Border Heritage Center, Otis A. Aultman Collection.

result of either targeted or wanton violence, political refugees also fled to the US-Mexican borderlands. Especially as the war dragged on, Mexicans fled across the border as an alternative to conscription.[43] Refuge was sought across the border, then, not just for those embroiled in revolutionary conflicts, but also by those wanting nothing to do with war. Groups of migrants with varying interests, whether pacifists or revolutionaries, joined the rail and agricultural braceros who had already been traveling migrant paths.

Women had other reasons to flee the violence unleashed by the Mexican Revolution. In a letter to President Cárdenas in 1940 detailing an assault suffered during the Mexican Revolution, Leonor Salazar recounted:

> The year 1914, on the third of November, living in the company of my elderly grandparents, my house was assaulted by armed men who held my grandfather prisoner and who beat us, and I was the victim of a criminal assault. This was born out of ruinous vengeance because relatives of mine belonged to one party and them to another. They threatened to give death to all of us should we let the authorities know, for that reason we did not. Nine months later I had a son. That son is for whom I'm asking with all my soul that you study our case and help whenever convenient. My son was born in Mexico and registered as an *hijo natural*. Since [then] it was impossible to stay in Mexico.[44]

During the Mexican Revolution women faced the threat of being raped or stolen by government and revolutionary factions.[45] The threat alone could have caused families to migrate to protect their female family members, but in Leonor's case she sought migration after having been violated because of the social stigma that would have shaped both her and her son's life.

Revolutionary and counterrevolutionary activities were often a family affair and women and children followed federal and revolutionary factions to keep families together, help with provisions and vital services, and simply to save themselves from a worse fate that could befall them if left behind. So, when battles ensued near the US-Mexico border and retreat took Mexicans into US territory, and then to internment in military camps, women and children stood alongside their male relatives and companions. One such instance occurred as a result of Pancho Villa's assault on Ojinaga on January 10, 1914, when 5,019 Mexicans crossed the Rio Grande into Texas. Camp administrators were responsible for "provisioning and otherwise caring for this motley aggregation of some 5000 men, women, and children, wet, cold and half-starved, together with one thousand seven hundred and eighty odd animals on the verge of starvation."[46] The group included 1,081 women and 533 children and would be transferred to Fort Bliss from Presidio, Texas, just days later. They were followed by others claiming to be relatives of soldiers and seeking entrance into camp. The group was fenced in at Fort Bliss as a means of alleviating local fears of the spread of disease and possible retaliation attempts by Villa.[47]

At a national level, US observers were more concerned with the spreading of violence in the borderlands and with the safeguarding of US interests and financial investments. At a local level, communities in the Southwest began to notice the impact of the war and the newcomers it brought into their ranks. In February 1915, the *Los Angeles Times* reported, "100 babies have been born at the Mexican refugee detention camp near Ft. Rosecrans since the refugees arrived a number of months ago. The military authorities are worried and so are the fathers and mothers. The babies are American born but the parents are prisoners of war and can't return to Mexico, while the babies are free to do [so] as American citizens and may return to Mexico or may give their allegiance to the American flag."[48] As this article suggests, the influx of war refugees inspired concern beyond the sheer logistical challenges of accommodating war refugees. The birth of children complicated the citizenship status and rights of Mexican families by yielding mixed-status families. The article explicitly alluded to the potential danger of families being separated along national lines, but it also revealed implicit anxieties about the increased settlement of Mexicans in the United States and the growth of Mexican-American communities. The legal complications posed and encountered by binational families, and anxieties over permanent settlement, would persist through the century and into the present.

Whereas the importation of temporary Mexican contract workers to help replace "less desirable" immigrant groups was seen as acceptable, or was not as widely noticed, the permanent settlement of entire Mexican families, many of them destitute from their journeys north, provoked questions regarding assimilation and the ideal Mexican immigrant as one who stayed only temporarily. Mexican migrants were perceived as a public health threat, as evidenced by a series of nested headlines over a 1916 *Los Angeles Times* article. Under the section "Social Puzzle," the headlines read: "Refugee Horde Called Danger: Supervisors Discuss Steps to Expel Mexican Indigents. Thousands Considered Menace to Health and Morals. Inter-County Meeting to Grip Problem is Planned." Concern over the number of newly arriving Mexicans extended beyond the confines of the refugee camps and into conversations about public resources and public safety. "The reason for the agitation against the immigrants is that a great number of them have become charity wards shortly since their arrival here. According to reports of the County Health Officer, at least half the arrivals are afflicted with disease, many with a loathsome and practically incurable malady. More than 25 percent of the patients at the County Hospital are recent Mexican immigrants."[49] Rhetoric and fear coalesced around Mexican migrants and problematic citizenship, overuse of public resources, and worse still: the perceived invasion of a potentially diseased other.[50]

Restored rail lines and a lessening of bloodshed in late 1915 fueled US expectations that refugees would return home. J. Blaine Gwin, the secretary of the Associated Charities in El Paso, noted that "a fairly steady stream" of Mexicans had returned to Mexico since 1915.[51] Although some migrants returned home, consecutive years of economic and political instability fueled new migrants across the international border. For example, Fernando Saúl Alanís Enciso points out that despite the improvement of working conditions in Matehuala, San Luis Potosí, beginning in 1915 and 1916, laborers and middle-class Potosinos continued to migrate. The reopening of Mexican factories after violence had subsided could only partially resolved the issue of unemployment.[52]

Sustained migration from all sectors of Mexican society, including political refugees, small landowners in the nascent middle class, skilled and unskilled laborers, indigenous and mestizo, migrated back and forth across the border between 1910 and 1920. Mexicans were no longer generally viewed as migrant "peons" who returned to their villages for the harvest or the elite politicians and businessmen who partnered with American entrepreneurs and bought luxury goods in the borderlands. Migrant families and refugees who survived difficult circumstances but emerged from revolutionary conflicts poverty-stricken, in poor health, and with few options for a peaceful return to their hometowns remained in the United States. For refugees who remained in the north after revolutionary conflict subsided, perhaps to raise their children in the land of their birth, or for laborers who went on temporary sojourns prior to the outbreak of revolution and chose to stay in the United States rather than return to a war-torn Mexico, immigration of a permanent kind may have never been intended. But as railroads stitched the two countries more closely together when both nations were facing cyclical economic contractions, the number of border crossers entering either as political refugees, prisoners of war, migrants, and/or immigrants increased.

Just as revolutionary violence diminished in some regions of Mexico, American involvement in World War I led to another more intense and logistically muddled era of migration. Mark Reisler and Lawrence Cardoso detail how growers in the Southwest pressured the US government into exempting Mexican workers from provisions of the 1917 Immigration Act, namely those rules governing contract laborers such as literacy tests and head taxes. Alanís Enciso describes how employers, consuls, and government officials nearly organized a temporary worker program. However, a bilateral agreement at the federal level was hardly possible considering that the Carrancista government was tasked with several other national priorities including the achievement of economic stability, political consolidation of the country, and limited social reform.[53]

Emigration, did however, garner enough attention to warrant a section of article 127 of the Mexican Constitution dedicated to protecting emigrant contract laborers. It specified that the municipal president of the sending town and a foreign consul were required to approve an emigrant labor contract and that the employer should provide enough money for the eventual repatriation of the employee.[54] It said nothing of non-contract labor emigrants or emigrant family members. The measure fell in line with the nationalist framework of the Constitution and responded to the only set of problems that the federal government could actually mediate from a diplomatic standpoint—the abuse of laborers in the United States. The burden of preventing contract labor fell largely to local Mexican authorities, but hundreds of families had already been recruited to work in US agriculture and were crossing the border without approved contracts.

The revolutionary government was too new and contested, misinformed, or uninterested to regulate the exodus. Individual employers, state officials, and eventually federal officials in the United States negotiated with Mexican consuls, rather than the Mexican ministries of Government and Labor. Mexican officials trying to prevent the exodus issued their directives to Mexican state governors and municipal presidents. Dialogue, ideas, and resolutions regarding emigration and immigration were disparate, scattered, and loosely connected at best. The different, and even competing, frames of reference and expectations held by government officials within and between both countries left migrants vulnerable to abuses and misinformed about the requirements and risks involved in taking jobs or joining family north of the border. Mexicans interested in going to the United States faced a barrage of mixed messages. Employer announcements in borderland newspapers advertised the need for Mexican workers and their families, while Mexican newspapers often highlighted worker abuses in an attempt to dissuade migrants from leaving. Aside from a small section in the Constitution and newspaper propaganda, Mexican officials did little to curtail, control, or even accurately assess emigration and repatriation sparked by World War I US labor demands.[55]

Wartime production in the United States and the expansion of sugar and cotton production required cheap labor and both governments were made to reconcile with the large group of Mexican immigrants migrating to the United States and those returning back to Mexico. In March of 1918, the *El Paso Herald Post* reported that two hundred and fifty Mexican families from the interior of Mexico had arrived in Idaho by way of El Paso to work in the sugar beet fields and "help increase the output of several sugar factories in Southeast Idaho."[56] On June 30th, 1918, a letter written by the municipal president of Jalisco's capital Guadalajara, Jose Rivera Rosas, was published in the city's newspaper *El Informador*. It was published again on July 2nd, 4th, and 7th, which indicates both its importance and its necessary distribution as a public document. The municipal president included an excerpt of a letter from the Secretaría de Relaciones Exteriores to the state governors warning that they should do whatever possible to prevent the exit of laborers from their states, since migrants were often being left stranded at the border for failing to have proper immigration documents. The reminder was sent out because the municipal presidents of Jalisco had been informed that, "With each passing day, our workers who are contracted to work in the United States increasingly suffer abuses."[57] The letter also served as a warning to would-be crossers that they might be stranded at the border by broken promises made by *enganchadores*. The messages were sent out to the general public *and* labor contractors to prevent the northward exodus. The scenario was not so unlike the concern over labor exodus and the warnings to workers issued in 1906 and 1907. The important difference was that within the context of World War I a balance of national needs and diplomacy shaped approaches to migration. Mexico needed workers to rebuild the nation, at least according to rhetoric, and US officials had to prevent the entry of unsuitable and dangerous immigrants while at the same time bending to the demands of a war-induced labor shortage.

While newspapers spread messages from officials who aimed to prevent emigration, migrants also found evidence of a high demand for labor throughout the columns of Mexican newspapers. In October of 1920, *El Informador* reported a message from the Mexican consul in San Antonio stating that migrants seeking work in the United States should accept no less than three-dollar-a-day contracts, reporting that in some mineral industries, workers were earning up to six or seven dollars. Mexican consuls who were tasked with attending to Mexican concerns in the United States, and who witnessed the arrival of thousands of Mexicans, sought to prepare migrants who crossed the border despite the repeated warnings made by other government officials about the hardships of life once in the United States.[58] In another article on August 30, 1920, the main headline reads: "The Mexicans who emigrate have become victims of American exploiters." The first subheading explains that the Mexican consul in Laredo reported the news, while the second subheading reads: "A company solicits 15,000 Braceros." The article goes on to also mention that a "well organized group is crossing them as 'contraband' eluding the [American] law that prohibits the emigration of illiterates to our northern republic, and after exploiting them, they abandon them. Many emigrants who have crossed in that manner have been found in Texan deserts dead from starvation; in other occasions, just as it's going well for the ignorant migrants, they're returned to Mexico by the US authorities." The next paragraph reports that the consul at Laredo was advocating for Mexico to accept the offers made by a powerful cotton company, that would not only assure all guarantees to workers and but would have the Mexican consulate name agents to ensure that contracts were kept. The company would be requesting fifteen thousand braceros.[59] What would grab the aspiring migrant's attention most and how would they respond to it—death by starvation after abandonment by smugglers, or the promise of all guarantees and the knowledge that one powerful company needed at least thousands of workers? The next steps would depend on the calculus of individuals and families, but if they sought and could afford to begin the legal process, they had to obtain a passport.

IMMIGRATION CONTROLS

On April 9, 1918, *El Informador* reprinted a notice from American consul John R. Silliman summarizing the key passport requirements issued by the American consular service in November of 1917 following the Immigration Act of 1917. While the notice contained a fairly basic summary noting the requirement and procedure for obtaining a passport, most of the column space was dedicated to outlining the requirements for the entry of minors to the United States. Children under the age of sixteen would be allowed into the country only "when immigration officials found that: 1) the child was healthy and strong, 2) that while the child was abroad they would not be subject to public charity, 3) that they were going to live or visit with close family members who were able to, and agreed to, support and provide appropriate care for them, 4) that it was the intention of those relatives to send the child to (day) school until he or she is sixteen years of age, 5) that the child would not be made to engage in work inappropriate for their age."[60]

In comparison to the text of the actual Immigration Act of 1917, Silliman's focus regarding the legal requirements for children is disproportionate. While the subject of children takes up the bulk of announcement reprinted in the Guadalajara newspaper, it takes relatively little space in the actual text of the law where more attention is given to excludable categories, contract workers, the punishments for importation of illegal immigrants, and the ban on immigrants from the "Asiatic Barred Zone." The consul's increased emphasis on the migration of minors is significant and revealing of the migration patterns that were beginning to emerge in the central-western states. The conditions laid out in the announcement were meant to apply to those parties specifically traveling with children who were not their own but perhaps belonged to a brother or sister or another close relative. Further instructions were given to these adults reminding them to have a letter of consent signed by either the mother or father of the child. Family members were traveling together to cross the border but not always in nuclear family units, and both female and male children crossed regularly enough to warrant the added consideration of American immigration officials and added emphasis in the local paper.[61]

Growers in the American Southwest demanded Mexican laborers and exemptions to immigration requirements after the armistice and up until 1921, and President Carranza sanctioned the emigration of laborers.[62] The literacy requirement introduced by the Immigration Act of 1917 was by far the most restrictive policy potentially impacting Mexican migrants crossing the US-Mexico border, but US employers succeeded in pressuring immigration officials to issue waivers for Mexican migrants seeking labor. A view from Guadalajara through one of the regional newspapers offers insight into the familial dimensions of this labor migration—a dynamic and diverse movement including those without formal labor contracts, those of both genders, of varying ages, and varying abilities, whose migrations were facilitated by binational familial and social networks.

It is easy, as it was at the time, to focus on the macro-structural economic and political push and pull factors, including the Mexican Revolution and World War I, to explain Mexican migration in the 1910s; however, social and familial linkages established prior to and during this turbulent decade were also responsible for fostering, encouraging, and sustaining migration. Messages to sending regions illustrate the importance of family and child migration during the war years. The public notice's emphasis on minors also reveals a glimpse of how the process of migration was shaped by a person's age and gender. Male adolescents over the age of sixteen were expected to file a separate passport for themselves and could not be included in one of their parents' passport applications, whereas female children were included in their parents' passports up until the age of twenty-one unless they were already married. Young women would be spared the cost for a separate passport application, but presumably those between the age of sixteen (the minimum age of entry) and twenty-one would be considered by migration officials as subject to their parents' protection, wishes, and control. Patriarchy governed at the border as well and a young woman's ability to independently enter the United States was limited and made more difficult because she faced extra pressure to prove that she, or more likely a relative, would be able to support her economically in a morally-approved manner. Border officials knew that young women, as opposed to their male counterparts of a similar age, would have much less opportunity for remunerative employment in the United States.[63]

A key pattern emerged during the decade of revolution and civil war: whereas solo male migrants stretched their sojourns northward in the face of economic insecurity during the waning years of the Porfiriato, economic insecurity paired with threats of violence sparked the migration of entire families. The building of railroads had facilitated pioneering migrations in the first decade of the twentieth century, but the disruptions caused by revolution also prevented the arrival of much needed remittances to family members in Mexico. Mexican migration between 1900 and 1920 skyrocketed due to the interlocking of a number of phenomena and so too did family migration. Aside from the general factors causing Mexicans to leave Mexico, in the United States families were able to work alongside each other in agriculture, and contracts, even if they were intended to attract male laborers for temporary work stints, incidentally drew women and children into the booming war and post-war economy of the United States.

In addition to interviews such as those conducted by Manuel Gamio and Paul Taylor, we are also able to glean partial understandings of migrant paths and motivations from Mexican passport applications. The additional requirements of the Passport Act of 1918 would have added yet more steps into what was becoming a more laborious crossing process, but if families, especially those who were journeying from deep in Mexico's interior, wanted to ensure a successful border crossing, it was a necessary step. Letters offered by migrants as part of their passport applications provide insight into the multiple and overlapping motivations of migration, and also reveal the mature, as opposed to developing, social, familial, and economic networks that had facilitated and sustained family migration prior to the 1920s.

Mexican immigrants and especially regular border crossers protested the US Passport Act of 1918 as a significant barrier to their daily movement. During the World War I era, when waivers were extended to agricultural workers entering the United States, passport controls were relaxed enough to allow for certain temporary laborers to enter the United States. However, passports became ever more important when waivers ended, especially for Mexicans migrating from the interior who needed a visaed passport to guarantee against exclusion at the border.[64] Newspapers often published announcements regarding passport requirements when US laws changed or following government reports of stranded migrants at the border. Local officials would relay passport regulation reminders in the press throughout the 1920s, while accompanying articles continued to discourage widespread emigration by describing the misfortunes of Mexicans on the other side of the border.[65]

Migrants would either go straight to the border, or attempt to secure the necessary documents for crossing near their hometowns. The choice would have been shaped by several factors and would largely depend on the migrant's general knowledge about the border-crossing process. Personal connections

to friends and family who had already made the trip yielded critical information about routes and crossing points. Migrants would often make their first
trip alongside an experienced border-crosser to ensure a smooth journey.[66]
Passing information from one migrant to another had worked well enough
prior to the Immigration Act of 1917 and Passport Act of 1918, but even experienced migrants encountered setbacks during an era of increasing immigration restriction.

The process of obtaining a passport proved cumbersome, especially for
rural migrants whose migration preparation would require an extra journey,
meaning added travel costs and extra time, to the state capital or another
major city. After being issued a passport by the state governor, it was necessary to have it endorsed by the American consul nearest to the sending region
from which the migrant was leaving. This measure was in place to prevent
migrants from overwhelming the American consulates that dotted the
Mexico-US border, and to ensure that migrants had at least fulfilled the most
basic and important requirement before journeying far from home. For
example, migrants in the northeastern part of Jalisco, generally known as Los
Altos de Jalisco, would have to travel in the opposite direction to Guadalajara
before doubling back to go northeast for entry through El Paso. The mapping
of bureaucratic requirements onto a landscape of migrant mobility led to
gaps in information about the scope and magnitude of emigration problems,
which then led to erratic and idiosyncratic solutions. Many migrants didn't
learn of formal procedures until it was too late; The cost and effort increasingly associated with legal crossings led many migrants to arrive at the border
without documents.

Meanwhile, officials along the border witnessed the gravity and trends of
regional migration before those in the sending regions did. In a dynamic that
would continue for the rest of the century, border officials and municipal
presidents complained to each other about the number of emigrants leaving
a community. The governors of Jalisco and Michoacán were alerted by officials in Ciudad Juárez about migrants failing to get approved documents
from US consuls, resulting in their being denied entry into the United States
and stranded in the city.[67] Despite continued warnings in the press, migrants
kept finding themselves in this situation, some even falling victim to scam
artists offering to arrange required documents at exorbitant costs.[68]

Provisional passport applications from 1920 reveal insight into the motives,
processes and strategies taken by Mexicans who did take the exhaustive measures to seek legal entry to the United States.[69] They represent but a fraction of

migrants leaving Jalisco, and are likely to disproportionately represent migrants with means: those who could spare enough money to purchase photographs, perhaps employ the services of a notary or lawyer to prepare the letter of request, and solicit letters of support from acquaintances and employers. In 1926, a Mexican immigration inspector reported that in comparison to first-class passengers, most second-class passengers arriving at Matamoros from the interior of Mexico had not obtained a passport first.[70] Despite these limitations, reading passport applications filed for the year 1920 from the state of Jalisco reveals a multitude of objectives for migrant travel including work, education, and business interests. A surprisingly key motivation for migration to the United States stood out from all the rest: family.

OBTAINING A PASSPORT

Although the process to obtain passports could take considerable time and money, and despite the many unpatrolled points along the border, this step would be especially crucial for families in which multiple family members crossed the border. Of three hundred passport applications filed on behalf of five hundred people sampled for the year 1920, 21 percent of applicants were traveling with family members, and 64 percent of passport applicants listed family-centered motives as the reason for their migration. Migrants would have been motivated to get a passport to avoid deportation and to provide a legal route for crossing so as to not jeopardize future entry and reentry.

Along with letters of support, birth certificates, and photos, migrants included letters to the governor stating their objectives for travel, their intended destinations, and the ages of those traveling, along with other details such as occupational status. Recommendation writers attested to a migrant's good character but also regularly and emphatically stated that the aspiring migrant had absolutely no involvement in political affairs—an indication of the still tenuous political atmosphere amid continued revolutionary and counter-revolutionary strife. Honor, politics, and money were all at play in the first step of legal migration across the Mexico-US border. In short, migrants faced a series of requirements and hurdles as soon as they began their journey, aside from any challenges they might encounter along the way or at the border. Few applications indicate whether passports were given or whether requests were rejected; nevertheless, the information contained within the applications revealed surprising insight about migrant family life and the process of migration. They also shed light on the diverse paths that migrants took from their sending communities.

As might be expected, cities in California and Texas were listed as top cities of destination.[71] Los Angeles was cited fifty-three times as the intended destination, while San Francisco was listed twenty-nine times, and twenty-eight aspiring migrants stated that they wanted to go to San Antonio. The top destinations were also some of the US cities with the largest population of Mexicans during this period. By 1920, 41,500 Mexicans lived in San Antonio, and Mexican-born Mexicans made up 68 percent of this population. 30,000 Mexicans lived in Los Angeles by 1920, with 54 percent of the overall Mexican population being Mexican-born.[72] Notably, the top three cities cited were in the interior of the United States and not near points of entry along the border, illustrating that migrant journeys stretched well into the United States. El Paso (seventeen) and Laredo (fourteen) in Texas round out the top five cities.[73] Migrants also listed midwestern destinations such as Toledo, Ohio, and Chicago, Illinois, and broaden the dimensions of our understanding of Mexican diaspora in the first decades of the twentieth century.[74] Applicants of all ages leaving from urban areas like Guadalajara, but also more rural regions of Jalisco like La Barca, Ocotlán, and Arandas, sought to go north.

Passport applicants wanted to go to the United States for a variety of reasons, but the majority wanted to go for family reasons. Hilario and Tomasa Garcia intended to go to Toledo to reunite with family members but also intended to seek out work. Twenty-year-old Rafael Reynosa from Atotonilco el Alto wanted to go to Chicago to study medicine, but he also sought to join part of his family who lived there, and Dámos Pérez went to join his two older sons in San Antonio, bringing his youngest son along to be educated in the United States.[75] Some planned to go the United States for only work or business, but the overwhelming majority of applicants stated that they were reuniting with family north of the border. They wanted to live with, visit, and help sick relatives. Sometimes their statements were vague and yet still family-centered, stating that their main objective was to "*arreglar asuntos de familia*," "arrange family affairs." Even when family was not explicitly cited as a reason for migrating, letters of support from family members and the presence of multiple family members embarking on migrations together show that by 1920 migration to the United States from Jalisco was already a family matter. Mexicans migrating between 1890 and 1920 created linkages between communities across the US-Mexico border and were becoming the basis for subsequent family migrations and migrant support networks.

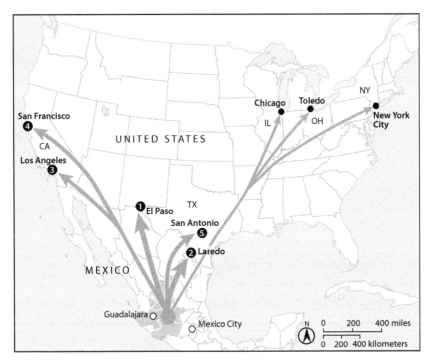

MAP 2. Top destinations for passport applicants. Map: Ben Pease.

While much of the petition language was formulaic, migrants stating their intentions in their own words provide a perspective that isn't immediately made clear when examining government statistics. Rodolfo de Luna, whose story was mentioned at the outset of this chapter, was not the only young man to express the necessity to be with his relatives as the main reason for his migration and to invoke the naturalness of being with one's family. Twenty-one-year-old Gregorio Ortega, a butcher originally from Jalpa, Zacatecas, requested a passport to go to San Antonio. He began, "Having my parents and brothers and sisters living in San Antonio, Texas, USA, I strongly desire to live with them and for that just motive." In the words of these young men, family unity and support were natural and just reasons for male migration. Valentin Flores, a twenty-year-old cart driver, requested to go to El Paso, Texas, "being that my brothers and uncles are living in El Paso, Texas and I haven't been able to continue here in a complete state, only lacking the care of my family." Flores's mother was still in Jalisco and presented herself to the governor's office in person to give permission for her son to leave. Not knowing how to write or provide a signature on a letter of support, she gave her verbal assent for her son to join the rest of the family in El Paso.

Aside from challenging our gendered assumptions about male motivations for migration across the US-Mexico border during the first half of the twentieth century, it is clear from passport applications that by 1920, migration from the center-west of Mexico was developing into an enduring pattern. The social dimension of this migration would have the power to sustain future migration, binational families, and community connections, and would combine with economic motivations to keep the center-west region as one of the primary sending regions throughout the twentieth century. These early migrations would leave an indelible impact on small towns and large cities, which became shaped more and more by migrant remittances and cross-border connections with each subsequent generation of migrants who left and by the many who returned.[76]

The fact that 64 percent of applicants had family-centered motivations is all the more surprising considering that only 10 percent of applicants explicitly stated that their intention was to work in the United States, with another 10 percent listing "commercial interests" as their main objective. Considering that male applicants outnumbered women applicants, the percentages are still more significant because they suggest that the primary motivation for male migrants traveling alone during this period was not strictly related to job opportunities and higher wages. Sixty-three percent of men requesting a passport on behalf of themselves only specified that they were traveling for family related reasons, and 65 percent of those men, or 41 percent of total male applicants, specifically stated that their objective was to live with family members in the United States.[77] Additionally, 21 percent of total passport requests indicate that families, including spouses and children, were also traveling together to reunite with family members on the other side of the border. By 1920 family migration, and family chain migration, facilitated by binational family networks, was a preferred strategy of migration.

The majority of those with family-centered passport requests specifically stated that they were going to "reunite" with family members living in the United States (40 percent of the total number of applicants). These were men and women of all ages, married, single or widowed. Brothers or sisters often went in groups, sometimes taking nephews or nieces with them. Some indicated that they were going only for a temporary period—there were those migrants going for recreation or specifically to buy certain goods and tools—while others implied they were going to take up residence in the United

States without indicating the duration. The passport applications, after all, contained only plans and guesses about what would come next. The forty-year-old widow Teresa Brizuela Allende wanted to cross the border to attend her daughter in St. Louis, Missouri, who was severely ill, and Antonio Silva went in search of sick family members in Arizona, not knowing what he would find. A mutualist group of restaurant workers writing on behalf of Silva wrote, "he fears that they are sick, and without resources, and maybe even dead."[78] Silva made sure to provide a letter confirming the veracity of his own statements about seeking out his sick family members. He was not the only applicant who desired a passport for such reasons, but he was one of the few who explicitly conveyed such a level of anxiety. And while it's true that some migrants might have employed dramatic pleas to the governor as strategy, the overall applications bear out a strong concentration on family-centered motives. In the era of the *enganche* and the period defined most as one of labor emigration, passport requests strikingly suggest that family was of utmost importance.[79]

GENDERED MIGRATIONS

Women have often been considered "dependent" or "associational" migrants while men, especially when traveling to the United States alone (regardless of marital status) or without any apparent dependents, are considered independent. Pierrette Hondagneu-Sotelo suggests labeling those instances in which women and children also migrate, even if at a later date than their male family members, "family stage" migration.[80] Her typology offers "family unit" migration as the best term to define instances in which family migrate together. Hondagneu-Sotelo acknowledges that "independent" female migration exists during her period of focus, particularly in the post-World War II era, as does other scholarship focusing on gendered patterns of migration.[81] However, research on early twentieth century Mexican migrations typically overlooks "independent" female migration in the early twentieth century. Passport applications provide details into how families might have organized separate or joint migrations, making them an invaluable resource in puzzling together the trends for non-head of household migrants. Multiple dependents could be listed on a family passport depending on specific criteria, defined by expectations of normative gender roles and based on models of nuclear family relations.

Even "family stage" migrations in which a woman traveled with her children to join her husband or other family members is an understudied phenomenon of the period. Of the 16 percent of women who initiated their own passport requests, nearly half of them intended to bring family (children, siblings, and cousins) along with them, but notably, more than half did not. This has important implications for understanding the logistical challenges of migrating and how they changed over time, particularly with regard to different family members. Quirina Gómez, a thirty-eight-year-old housewife, applied for a passport to join her husband in Pueblo, Colorado in October of 1920. Her husband, J. Concepción Gómez, who had made two failed attempts at obtaining a passport for himself and his son earlier in the year, had most likely entered the United States illegally sometime after May. In October of that year Quirina succeeded in obtaining a passport for herself and five of her young children, while her eldest son, eighteen-year-old Jose, after previously being denied, was also successful in obtaining his passport. Whereas her husband and son had failed to obtain passports earlier in the year, Quirina, even with five young children, was able to secure passports for herself and her family. In this instance, family migration, even as stage migration where the male "provider" was not accompanying the family, was not only sanctioned but succeeded where an attempt at legal independent male migration did not. Family migration was privileged, perhaps because it encouraged reunification, but the Gómez migration strategy also evolved over time. The first passport application in April by J. Concepción Gómez did not specify where in the United States he and his son intended to go, but only stated that their objective was to see family and bring back some merchandise. The second passport attempt, in May, identified Pueblo, Colorado as the destination and the objective was slightly modified to indicate that they would be reuniting with family. This attempt, less than a month later, was also unsuccessful and led to another strategy. The head of the household would try his luck by himself; meanwhile, Quirina would hold down the home front on her own. After her male partner was established on the other side, she would initiate her own passport request in October, with a clear destination specified.[82]

While Quirina's decision to migrate was likely very much linked to her husband's, she clearly interacted with state officials and took on the challenges and negotiations of her own migration, and so did forty-eight other Jalisco women who requested passports that year. The passport requests of women who went through the bureaucratic processes of migration during this early period, along with requests of men who either traveled with family members, sought to reunite with relatives, and depended on other family members to successfully cross the border, challenge gendered assumptions about independent and dependent migration. While many male migrants prior to 1920 left to the United States presumably on their own, and might be considered independent, when taking into consideration broader family networks and connections, they could just as easily be considered dependent migrants when following their brothers, fathers, uncles, or female family members. Equally significant is the fact that women like Micaela Carranza seem to have migrated entirely independently. Because she was subject to more stringent inspection at the border, and due to potential safety threats, her migration and the independent migrations of other women illustrate the determination of women crossing by themselves.

Family-centered motivations in combination with a desire for better wage opportunities drove pre-bracero migration. Mexican officials were aware of the extensiveness of family networks and had come to expect such migrations. They also knew that family and social networks likely bolstered a migrant's ability to withstand the challenges of binational migration.[83] US border officials would also have noted the families coming across the border. However, border crossing cards and manifests, as well as numerical tallies offered by border officials for the era, only indicate who succeeded in crossing the border, who might have paid their passage, where they were headed, and perhaps a note on physical features. They do not capture the broader contours of families nor the aspirations of would-be migrants. Letters written to secure passports, however, reveal motivations as well as details about the logistical processes, the financial concerns involved with getting photographs taken, paying fees, hiring a notary, and the wider social networks behind migration in the early twentieth century. Tucked into the files of passport applications are the pictures and stories about men, women, and children hoping to go north. Rather than a generic and stereotypic image of male Mexican migrants striking north for riches or adventure, we see a diverse array of historical actors. We see entire families crossing borders. Local observers at the time began to notice the trend also.

"EVEN THE WOMEN ARE LEAVING": REACTION AND RESPONSE

By 1920 the scale of exodus from Jalisco to the United States was noticeable to government officials and casual observers alike. Since 1918, when the wartime demand for Mexican labor greatly increased, Mexican officials at both the national and local level had become concerned with the increasing exodus of migrants. Of particular concern was the possibility that local harvests would not be gathered if agricultural workers were headed to harvests in the United States. In order to keep workers from leaving the country, offices were set up to inform underemployed and unemployed workers where they might find jobs within the state. The lists were dependent upon municipal presidents reporting their needs or excesses to their state office. In May 1918, a list published for the state of Jalisco cited the names of three towns that were in need of laborers, and twelve towns or cities that had extra workers. Aside from efforts at redistributing labor within Mexico in order to prevent outmigration, other efforts were made to stem the tide of emigration, including the opening up of jobs at the Cananea mine in northern Mexico. There were also rumors that investors were seeking to open up large tracts of land with the specific purpose of employing agricultural workers who would otherwise go to the United States. Still, word of US labor demand from relatives abroad propelled continued migration.[84]

Community responses to the emigration of men, women, and children from Jalisco's rural and urban spaces were reflected in one of the leading newspapers of the region, *El Informador*. Much editorial ink was spilled pondering the causes and impacts of Mexican emigration, especially in the 1920s. News from the municipality of Atotonilco El Alto characterized the number of migrants leaving to the United States as "truly shocking."[85] The departure of eighty-four migrants from the small town of San Diego de Alejandría during just one week in late February was highlighted as a sign that "the agriculture and industry of Jalisco was in grave danger of lacking sufficient braceros."[86] As reports came in about the increasing numbers of migrants leaving Mexico, the tone of editorials on the subject changed. Concern, which was initially expressed through questions about what could be done to prevent the exodus, quickly turned into anger, confusion, and partisanship. Agrarianism, the failings of the revolution, and flawed policies made at the national level were all blamed for the labor exodus.

Editorials, in particular, evidenced an attack on "reformers" tied to the constitutionalist leaders of Jalisco who had taken power during Carranza and then Obregón's national leadership. In the state of Jalisco, where ranches and small industry dominated the region, there was much less of a demand for land redistribution. To many, revolutionary land redistribution posed more of a threat than a promise.[87] Jalisco did see a degree of early, although limited, land redistribution under Carrancista Governor Diéguez's administration up through 1919 and again under Governor Luis Castellanos y Tapia. Governor Zuno's radical zeal for land redistribution beginning in 1923 would elicit even more opposition from conservative interests in the area.[88] Critics of "bolshevik agrarianism" began to specifically blame the federal government's economic policies for widespread emigration.[89] In a section titled "commentaries of the day" the author suggested that all of the efforts to contain emigration had been in vain and that the means by which "agraristas" and "obreristas" were carrying out their goals were pushing workers out of the country. For this commentator, the Obregón administration had gone too far in favoring the more radical revolutionary demands. He stated, "the war on capital was ruining all factories and businesses," and concluded that the dispossession of *hacendados* had led to unemployment. The impact on emigration was clear: "In a country that is being ruined more every day, what can these people without work do? Steal or emigrate. Most aim to emigrate to the United States where they are lynched. They go because they cannot live in their country."[90]

The argument was especially compelling because the commentator referred to the long history of injustice and the terror foisted upon Mexican immigrants and Mexican-American communities in the United States.[91] But emigration was seen as a direct result of attempts at land redistribution rather than the increasing demand and targeted recruitment of Mexicans for US agricultural and rail work or the parcelization of land through inheritance, the rise in landless and increasingly mobile workers, and the proliferation of familial and social networks facilitating migration that had started the century before in Jalisco and other center-west states like Guanajuato. The economic contractions, violence, and protracted political instability during and after the Mexican Revolution caused a number of dislocations, but observers trying to establish a logic or place blame for the exodus found a convenient excuse for emigration in the reformist policies that emanated from the Mexico's center. Despite President Obregón's rhetoric, his minimal land redistribution specifically targeted Zapatista strongholds in the south, and Jalisco wouldn't see more concerted efforts at agrarianism until the presidential administration of Lázaro Cárdenas.

How did officials in Mexico City respond to the hundreds of thousands of Mexicans who left for the United States? During his campaign in 1919, future president Álvaro Obregón acknowledged the increasing emigration and offered a general solution by emphasizing the need for giving guarantees to capital, for if not, he stated that capital would "remain inside the safe deposit box, or outside our borders, and then our workers will continue to have to leave the country, in hungry peregrinations, to look for bread in other countries where capital enjoys the sort of guarantees that it cannot find here."[92] People at the center of power were paying attention to the unfolding emigration crisis. Obregón's response provided hints to how he would rule as president, privileging stability above all else. In July of 1920, President Obregón declared to the press that while he lamented the emigration of Mexican braceros, the Mexican government could do nothing to stop the free movement of its people. He reported that six thousand families had left in the prior month and that fifteen thousand had left during the course of the year.[93] That Obregón specifically mentioned families leaving is important. Mexican officials and observers from sending communities were quick to realize that entire families were crossing the border, whereas US officials, looking at Mexican migration almost exclusively through the lens of labor, tended to view migration as mostly a male phenomenon.

The author of an editorial in *El Informador* expressed his alarm about the increasing emigration of women as well as men from the state of Jalisco in an article titled "Pueblo Vacio," or empty town. He first lamented that "the strongest men who work the fields" were emigrating by the hundreds and leaving emptied haciendas and ranches behind. But his most vociferous complaints were directed toward the markedly dire situation indicated by the fact that women were now leaving as well. He cited the example of female emigrants from a small town in Los Altos de Jalisco, stating almost incredulously, "even the women were leaving." An emphatic "Que se vayan!" effectively bid the women migrants of Jalisco good riddance, showing that his concern had turned into disdain.[94] The fact that women were leaving was especially significant in a post-revolutionary context. Men had been leaving Mexico for the United States for the past forty years. That women and entire families were leaving was particularly jarring for a nation that was trying to rebuild.

The federal government would have to deal with the thousands of emigrating families again in 1922 after the economic recession of 1921 and 1922 brought hardship to thousands of Mexican migrants in the United States. Mexican newspapers reported on the dismal conditions affecting migrant workers and the steps taken by government officials to try and both prevent the exodus of more workers and help facilitate the repatriation of others. For example, in November of 1921, President Obregón bolstered contract labor laws by mandating that laborers and contractors deposit enough money to cover the full fare of a round-trip ticket for each contract laborer.[95] The measure was supposed to prevent the Mexican government from having to foot the bill for the expenses of repatriation. Nevertheless, by the end of 1922 the Obregón government had indeed facilitated the repatriation of thousands of destitute Mexicans.[96] In fact, the government felt the need to warn repatriated migrants that should they cross into the United States again, their further repatriation would not be provided for.[97] The warning indicated that migrants might have come to expect repeated assistance from the Mexican government, and it also would have had the effect of keeping migrants close to the border to more easily facilitate repeated migrations. Measurable gains in political and economic stability since the Revolution would have prompted some migrants who had left in the previous two decades to return, but protracted political violence and economic crisis would persist throughout the 1920s when Cristero wars gripped communities and again drove Mexicans north.

Despite the public concern over emigration illustrated through newspaper reports, and the government's interaction with migrants in its efforts to prevent them from leaving, we hear very little from migrants themselves. Whereas passport requests provide a window from which historians can look through to glean motivations, sketch out family migration patterns, and find the voices of the many who left, the actual experiences of many migrants eluded their contemporaries. In fact, in one of the editorials written at the height of emigrant exodus from Jalisco, the author wrote, "they leave silently, with a suitcase of rags on their back and a bag full of tortillas, without saying what they see and what they know; but resolved, with or without a passport, with recruiters or on their own, but they leave, they leave. . . ."[98]

Those going north, according to this author, were the silent poor who kept their heads down but went forward determined to leave by any means necessary. The observation was right to a certain point, with two key exceptions. First, it was not only the poor who left. Second, those leaving were not always silent. Their hopes and even their disappointments can be found in the plainly stated objectives contained in passport requests. And if the author of the editorial saw a silent mass of Mexicans turning their backs on their hometowns, the next decade would see them continue to build vibrant transnational communities, moving back and forth across the border until the end of the decade, when Mexican government officials up to and including the president would bear witness to the very vocal return of their compatriots. Many Mexican families would come to know two countries and raise their families in each—in some way forced to the margins by each nation and yet critically central to the saga of both.

CHAPTER TWO

From Revolution to Exodus

GOING NORTH IN TIMES OF CONFLICT, 1915–1929

También los otros muchachos
que bienen atras piscando
vienen muy apuraditos
ya nos vienen alcanzando

Y mi tía Josefita
que viene también piscando
ya toditos la largaron
también agarró su paso.

También mi Tío Juanito
y que es muy buen piscador
las muchachas lo largaron
con cien libras de algodón.

En las piscas de algodón
nadie lo puede negar
que toditos a lo menos quiere
sus 100 libras piscar.

CORRIDO DE ROBESTOWN,
EUSEBIO GONZALEZ

AFTER THE ECONOMIC RECESSION OF 1920–1921, booming Southwestern US agriculture and continued insecurity and violence in Mexico led hundreds of thousands of Mexicans to cross the US-Mexico border in search of opportunity, family, and stability. While some regions were more peaceful than others, benefitting from the order brought by the centralizing governments of Obregón and Calles, the center-west region of Mexico was plagued by mid-decade violence spurred on by the armed conflict between the Mexican federal government and the Catholic Church known as the Cristero War.[1] Emigration out of Mexico from pre-revolutionary sending areas (the emigration heartland of Guanajuato, Michocán, and Jalisco) soared to new heights and it also became a new and enduring feature for other communities. Setting out for jobs in the north became an increasingly viable option in those regions where the Revolution caused disruptions and rebuilding was slow and limited. Migrants journeyed north to reunite with family in a land of growing opportunity and newly bustling Mexican communities.

Mexican *colonias* grew in American cities and hosted their own Mexican markets, mutual assistance societies, and pool halls. Schools and churches would sweep in toward the end of the decade along with the missionary zeal of Americanization campaigns.[2] Groups of Mexican migrants and immigrants were also traveling beyond the borderlands to work in family units and follow the harvests. The *corrido* excerpt that is the epigraph of this chapter, describing cotton work in Texas, captures how the labor landscape was changing in the United States. It not only reflects the role that migrants would play in that labor system, but also shows how Mexican family labor became central to commercial agriculture during the 1920s. The lyrics depict Mexican men and women in agriculture as well as extended families working alongside each other. It exalts quick-working family members, and beckons those nearby to work faster. It is decidedly upbeat for a song about picking cotton, a rally cry more than a lament. It reminds listeners subtly that piece-work equals profit when you work fast enough, and it rhymes to a catchy tune that migrants could carry with them across harvests and across borders.

This chapter will examine the 1920s as a booming decade of migration. In the first section I will describe how new opportunities and labor diversification in the United States attracted seasonal and permanent Mexican immigration to the United States, requiring more families—including women and children—to migrate at unprecedented levels. The second section will explore how US immigration legislation and evolving practices of the Mexican government transformed the border and the nature of border crossing. Lastly, I will sketch out how Mexicans responded to the exodus northward and what ongoing migration revealed to Mexican observers about the nature of state formation in post-revolutionary Mexico. Understanding the 1920s as a boom era of Mexican migration is critical to understanding future migration patterns, the development of social and familial networks for migration, the intersection between labor and family as motivating factors for migration, how the categorizations of "legal and illegal" emerged to define Mexican migrants, and why migration from this point on would be intimately connected to community

MAP 3. Major ports of entry along the US-Mexico border, 1923. Map: Ben Pease.

transformations and revolutionary policies on the Mexican side of the border. During the 1920s Mexican migration became more visible, debated, and derided in Mexico. Hundreds of thousands of Mexican families made new homes in the United States and in the process became binational and bicultural. These families wove a tapestry that connected the two nations together and built networks that sustained future migrations.

MEXICAN *COLONIAS* AND THE SOUTHWESTERN AGRICULTURE BOOM

The influx of Mexicans into the United States after the recession of 1921 and 1922 signaled a growing and sustained phenomenon of migration that could no longer be attributed simply to the dislocations of the Mexican Revolution and the labor demands initiated by World War I. Migration and immigration north was now deeply tied to family reunification and escaping poverty. According to most estimates, more than double the number of Mexican immigrants arrived in the United States between 1920 and 1930 as in the previous decade.[3] The aftermath of violence was as displacing as the revolution itself. It caused the migration of those like Juana Martinez, who, after being recently divorced and having just lost her father, decided to migrate to Los Angeles from Mazatlán in 1924 along with her mother and two sisters. Moving to the United States would protect them from devastating poverty in Mexico.[4] The lure of higher wages persisted in the 1920s. In 1923 a laborer could earn forty cents a day in Mexico, compared to twenty-five cents per hour on US railroads.[5] Isabel González went north after trying to keep his late parents' cattle ranching business profitable in Jalisco. After making some money as a track worker in California, he sent for his two siblings.[6] In the 1920s migration to the United States, especially from the center-west of Mexico, had not only become a viable option when faced with economic and social insecurity, it had become a way of life.

Binational social and familial networks facilitated migrations of other family members more easily and regularly in the 1920s. Family-centered migrations happened alongside and in combination with those facilitated by *enganche*, "hooking," the active recruitment by labor contractors that characterized Mexican migrations before the Mexican Revolution. Contracting for railroad and mining interests continued, but diverse labor opportunities and social networks provided new opportunities for migrants. Mexican men, women, and children migrated seasonally and labored for growing US agribusiness in the rural and semi-rural southwest, while year-round city jobs drew migrants to cities, encouraging permanent settlement, especially as children born to Mexican parents began to attend US schools.

With long-established Mexican communities, the Mexican population in cities such as San Antonio and Los Angeles skyrocketed, while cities in the Midwest also witnessed growing Mexican populations.[7] Mexican immigrants also settled in cities far from the US-Mexican border like Chicago, living in rail camps and becoming integrated into industrialized labor environments such as meat-packing plants and steel factories.[8] Male laborers were the majority, but train manifests from the 1930s documenting the great wave of return migration to Mexico suggest that women made up to 24 percent of the adult population returning from places like Indiana Harbor, Kansas City, and Chicago. Children made up another 27 percent of return migrants.[9] Family settlement was promoted by the fact that seasonal agricultural labor could be supplemented with income from nearby industries and informal labor opportunities. In Los Angeles, for example, where the expanding city was surrounded by irrigated farmland, migrants and migrant families worked in seasonal agriculture during harvest seasons and could take clerical, construction, and service jobs during non-harvest times.[10]

The development of *colonias* and the opening of service jobs was critical to the establishment of semi-permanent and permanent Mexican communities, as families weren't automatically subjected to seasonal incomes, non-permanent housing, interrupted education, and unstable work environments. Businesses catering to Spanish speakers provided security to Mexican migrants in times of need, while commercial businesses led to much-needed capital for some migrants and a burgeoning Mexican consumer class.[11] These developments made for a more hospitable environment to mitigate some of the challenges of racism and segregation.

Permanent and semi-permanent settlement in growing cities also meant that gender and age did not predetermine migration to the same degree that it had before. Opportunities beyond back-breaking manual labor provided additional spaces for women, children, and the elderly to build their lives. Mexican children and adolescents attended schools and worked, and Mexican women also found employment opportunities beyond domestic service or as laundresses.[12] In fact, Mexican women outnumbered Mexican men in the cities of San Antonio and El Paso. George Sanchez describes these cities as "clearinghouse cities" where male laborers would be contracted for work elsewhere, while their families remained.[13] Similar to patterns of migration and labor in late-1890s Santa Barbara, as described by Albert Camarillo, women remained in cities while male laborers journeyed to outlying areas for short trips away from their families. That families would cobble together livelihoods through this combination of strategies signaled a growing preference for some families to locate permanently on the US side of the border.

When interviewed by Manuel Gamio's team of interviewers, Señora Cruz Loera de Torres, who lived in San Antonio for at least a decade, explained that everyone in her family, including her ten-year-old granddaughter, picked during cotton season. The family, however, did not solely rely on the cotton harvest for wages. In fact, if not for her husband signing their family up for the cotton harvest the previous season, they had planned to skip working the cotton season altogether. Unfortunately, the family's luck ran out when they arrived to a fallow cotton field and were deceived into buying food on credit that was impossible to repay. The family recovered well enough as the señora's two daughters, ages nineteen and sixteen, managed to get jobs in a pecan-shelling factory. In addition to working, her daughters attended classes provided by the Cruz Azul, a local mutual aid society.[14] The Torres family thus participated in agricultural harvests, agriculture-related factory work, and attended reading classes in the city, taking advantage of the combination of rural and semi-urban opportunities afforded to them while living in San Antonio. When Señora Torres's husband died a couple of years later, the Torres daughters were able to maintain their family's residence in San Antonio through their work at the pecan factory.

The opportunity for mixed work, agricultural and urban, skilled and unskilled, expanded greatly for Mexican migrants during the 1920s as a result of a boom in Southwestern agriculture, federal immigration legislation in 1921 and 1924 restricting the entry of European immigrants, and the Great Migration of African Americans to northern industrial jobs. Just as Mexican labor had begun to replace Chinese labor on the railroads and other ethnic immigrant labor in truck crops in the first decades of the twentieth century, Mexican migrants became tenant farmers and sharecroppers in cotton and sugar beets.[15] After the importation of Mexican contract laborers during World War I had secured profits for US agribusiness, the combination of single Mexicans and migrant families became the dominant labor force for many agricultural harvests.

In addition to growing the Mexican communities in urban regions of Texas and California, along with Chicago, the expansion of large-scale agriculture was very significant in facilitating diverse family migrations. Family members in the United States would ask those in Mexico to join them by journeying north, but letters and remittances also indirectly enticed new migrants as proof of prosperity. Employers also began to encourage, welcome, and prefer the migration of entire families, making it possible for migrant family groups to stay together. The potential for family members to work and live as a unit could provide more stability and offer a more appealing option than having to endure long separations. After decades of land tenure disruptions and violence in Mexico, US Southwestern agricultural expansion provided an avenue for families to work land together once again. And even if the land was not their own, the wages were, and these multiplied when migrant groups and families worked together.

A number of shifts led to agricultural expansion in the 1920s, to the demand for Mexican laborers, and to increased migrant family crossings. The most notable developments related to agriculture and the use of Mexican labor occurred in California, but a significant increase in sugar beet production in the Midwestern states and Colorado and the continued use of Mexican labor in Texas also promoted sustained employment of Mexicans in agriculture. In the 1920s, California truck crops increased by 50 percent, fruits and nuts by 30 percent, and cotton by 400 percent.[16] Intensified irrigation, a pattern of continued large landholding extending from the era of large Mexican land grants, and a ban on Japanese landholding led to this surge of production in California.[17] The resulting pattern of production required intensive manual labor in a much more demanding manner than before and relied on an abundance of unskilled labor at peak harvest times. The scale and the types of crops required more labor, with, for example a crop like lettuce needing ten times the hours of labor per acre as compared to wheat.[18]

Cotton production expanded in the Imperial Valley of California and was then followed by expansion in California's San Joaquin Valley. In 1920, cotton acreage in California increased from 61,217 to 126,081 acres.[19] In 1924, due in part to the creation of a new superior strain of cotton (with increased market value) and the strong encouragement of business and government leaders, large landholders and small landholders alike began to specialize in cotton. Specializing to a time-sensitive-harvest crop with three pickings over a six-month period required large inputs of temporary labor.[20] Whereas cotton had ranked eleventh in importance in 1924, by 1929 it was "the fourth most valuable crop in the state, accounting for an annual return of $24 million."[21] Just as Mexicans were a crucial source of labor for cotton growers in Texas, migrants became a significant labor pool in California cotton as well.

Post-World War I acreage in sugar beet cultivation also increased greatly in places like Colorado and the Red River Valley in North Dakota and Minnesota.[22] In Northeastern Colorado in particular, sugar beet acreage more than doubled between 1909 and 1927 and accounted for 85 percent of sugar production in the state. Mexicans increased from 9.4 percent to 59 percent of the labor pool during the same period, reaching 14,313 in 1927 compared to 1,002 in 1909. The increased acreage accounted for the population increase, as did the decline of Japanese, German, and Russian laborers working in sugar beets. A ban on Japanese immigration in 1907 and restrictions to European immigration in 1921 and 1924 created spaces for Mexican laborers who were recruited from Mexico and contracted from Texas.[23] As illustrated in chapter 1, employers had already come to prefer Mexican workers before changes in immigration.[24] After demographic labor shifts spurred by World War I—which included American (ethnic white) men going off to fight, African Americans migrating to industrial jobs, Asian migrants being banned and forbidden from owning and leasing land, and the restriction of migrants from any part of the Eastern hemisphere by numeric quotas—the largest ethnic minority group remaining to occupy positions in unskilled poorly-paid agricultural work were Mexicans and Mexican-Americans.

Employers didn't come to just prefer Mexican labor, but preferred Mexican *family* labor for the largest and most demanding crops of the agricultural boom of the 1920s. Employers preferred family units in cotton, sugar beet, and some fruit and vegetable production (onions in Texas, citrus in southern California).[25] The increased preference for family labor units over *solos* was a stark contrast to earlier decades of migration patterns which had reflected labor preferences for single men. The boom in agriculture thus induced a pre-World War II peak of Mexican family migration.

Agricultural labor demands in the 1920s required both families who labored together as a unit and married male laborers who were accompanied by their families. The distinction between the explicit preference for family labor and a preference for male laborers who were married is an important one, as it reveals the multiple paths for Mexican migrant family incorporation into US labor systems and society. In northeastern Colorado, Mexican families became the preferred source of labor on sugar beet farms starting in 1920. Cross-border "shipments" of families came from Mexico and then from the reserve pool of laborers on the US side of the border in San Antonio and El Paso throughout the rest of the decade.[26] The labor commissioner for the Great Western Sugar Company revealed that 90 percent of migrants in "each shipment" should be composed of family labor.[27] Even though transportation cost more per family and families did not necessarily ensure more efficient labor, labor bureaus switched to family labor for many reasons. Paul Taylor explained quite simply at the time that the policy had changed because "The families are more stable." Employers found single laborers to be more lawless and "apt to be more shifting in residence."[28] Rather than gang labor, each family became its own contractor as a result of family model preference. Sugar beet companies also preferred resident labor so as to limit the recruitment and transportation costs of bringing in laborers every harvest. Taylor found that "in six years the number of families has increased an average of 258 families per year, or 288 per cent greater than the number resident in 1921."[29] Additionally, the presence of families could potentially defray the costs of prepared food for migrants and shift the burden of raising and preparing of food as well as the cost of housing upkeep from men's employers to their families. For example, a bilingual worker's manual published by the American Beet Sugar Company encouraged women and children to contribute to the preparation of food provisions to sustain families toward winter months, saying, "The wife who learns how to preserve fruits and vegetables will confer great benefits on her family." It published the names of women who had canned the most fruits and vegetables the previous year.[30]

Family labor also became a mainstay for cotton farming. As the *corrido* at the opening of the chapter describes, cotton picking was largely a family affair. As difficult as the backbreaking labor involved in sugar beets and cotton was, there were some advantages. Long seasons allowed for semi-permanent laboring and living conditions and prevented migrants from having to follow shorter harvest seasons for other crops. Women and children contributed to wages, and the family could be concentrated in one area working together, stabilizing migration patterns and reducing labor uncertainty.[31]

Although a preference for family labor expanded opportunities for families to stay together and could lead to increased economic gains, entire families were also subject to exploitative working conditions. Some employers might have certainly believed that family presence could domesticate male laborers, but it is likely that employers such as cotton growers in Texas favored families because children could pick cotton right alongside their parents and perhaps pick just as much.[32] Employers benefitted from patriarchal family structures where fathers acted as the foreman for the family and women and children were expected to help in the fields.

The Arizona Cotton Growers Association recruited, transported, and organized the importation of laborers from Mexico to Arizona and California, and even sponsored the border crossing of women in addition to many male laborers.[33] An "Alien Laborer's Identification Card" for Dolores Torres, age thirty-eight, showed that she entered the United States through Nogales accompanied by her husband, fifteen-year-old daughter, and eight-year-old son in 1919. Her destination was Tempe, Arizona, and her card was stamped "Arizona Cotton Growers Association". Dolores's card did not include a return date, but cards for two other women indicated that they returned to Mexico six months after their arrival, presumably following the conclusion of the harvest. The identification cards speak to the fact that entire families were sponsored by labor bureaus and grower associations. A different variant of family labor can be found in the citrus business of southern California described by Matt Garcia. Employers preferred married men as opposed to *solos* or single men.[34] The logic of this preference was similar to that governing sugar beet labor: marriage and children were seen as domesticating forces that inculcated more worker discipline overall. Married men were considered to travel less, be more mature, thriftier with their earnings and less likely to risk their jobs and family livelihoods by engaging in worker strikes.[35]

The incentives that drew migrant families to work together in agriculture proved beneficial to employers. Whether to furnish a more domesticated labor force, establish semi-permanent or resident labor colonies, cut down on recruitment and transportation costs, or generate overall labor stability with hopes of increasing production, employers in US agriculture welcomed family labor. This led to the opening of critical spaces for women and children not just to work or support a head of household, but also to improve housing environments, reduce transportation costs for cross-border travel and, in some cases, provide a less itinerant labor pool. In such cases, the social consequences for long term settlement were irrelevant; short-term labor security was paramount for employers.

Beyond facilitating migrant family labor, the employment of Mexicans in agriculture changed the diasporic landscape of Mexican communities in the United States and migrant mobility. Mexican and Mexican Americans were still mostly concentrated in the US borderlands, but resident communities began to dot the northern states beyond the industrial communities in Chicago. More migrants, whether newly arrived or already having worked in the borderlands throughout South Texas and Southern California, migrated specifically to agriculture-intensive regions and states which led them far into the interior. In California, this led to increased internal migration throughout the central valleys. As mentioned before, Mexican migrants also participated in Midwestern sugar beet harvesting. Mexican workers made up 75 to 90 percent of sugar beet workers in areas such as Michigan, Ohio and Minnesota.[36] In a 1932 study of a municipality in Los Altos de Jalisco, Paul Taylor found that emigrants had gone to as many as twenty-four different states from that town alone.[37]

The need for Mexican labor in agriculture also led to the constant over-recruitment of Mexican migrants and their families to provide sufficient low-wage labor during harvest periods.[38] Domestic farm laborers would consistently ask for higher farm wages only to be undercut by foreign labor and this dynamic would play out in the 1920s and again throughout the 1940s, 1950s, and 1960s. Over-recruitment certainly worked to large growers' advantage, but it would contribute to a massive social problem toward the end of the decade. By the time the Great Depression arrived, unemployed workers streaming out of cities in crisis would try their hand at rural agricultural work. Rural areas would simply not be able to absorb un- and under-employed Mexican laborers, and migrants could not afford to pay the transportation costs of seasonal interstate and binational migration.

While US agricultural demands played a large role in sparking mass family migration and thus perpetuating permanent and semi-permanent settlement, it is, of course, critical to point out that there were still many Mexican agricultural laborers that did not work in family units. Women worked in canneries and packing houses as well, but this auxiliary agricultural work was not contracted on the basis of family labor. Women made up 90 percent of Mexican cannery workers in Los Angeles by 1928 and were subject to the same inconsistent employment conditions created by seasonal agricultural harvests.[39] Men and women also worked in a variety of occupations beyond the fields and packing houses, in manufacturing and other industries. In El Paso, for example, women worked in garment factories, laundries, and as daily and live-in domestic servants.[40] Men worked in construction, railroads, and other industries, all of which still paid higher wages than could be earned in Mexico.[41] Mexican laborers made up 16.4 percent of pick-and-shovel construction workers in California in 1928, and an estimated 75 percent of unskilled construction labor in Texas. As many as twenty-eight thousand Mexicans worked in California industries in the same year.[42] There were also small numbers of migrants who entered the United States not as part of the laboring class, but as middle class and upper-class professionals as the demand for Spanish-speaking services in non-agriculture labor paralleled the boom in agriculture. The overall increase in the demand for agricultural labor during the decade perpetuated the idea that unlimited opportunities existed north of the border. That major employers were opening up spaces for family labor sparked increased interest for family units, especially for families who saw their ability to maintain a patriarchal household eroding.

Twenty-four-year-old Macaria Ávalos had been in Ciudad Juárez with her husband and her one-and-a-half-year-old child for six months with the goal of crossing over to El Paso. It took them four months to walk north from Torreon where they had been working on a ranch and had heard that there was work and money "in abundance" in El Paso. Since they didn't have sufficient money to either enter the United States legally or as "contraband," they stayed in Ciudad Juárez to save enough to make the crossing. At the time of her interview with one of Manuel Gamio's research assistants, she was begging on the street to contribute to the family savings.[43] Macaria's testimony speaks to the allure of US employment, an allure so strong as to induce a family to take their chances on a trek north, despite it leaving them penniless in the process. It also speaks to the physical and the financial cost of uprooting.

As agriculture boomed, federal immigration legislation at mid-decade transformed Mexican migration in profound ways. The most obvious impact of the Immigration Act of 1924, also known as the Johnson-Reed Act, was to heavily curtail European immigration. Mounting protests against the influx of southern and eastern European immigrants resulted in increased restrictions based on an elaborate quota system. The cumulative restrictions against Chinese, Japanese, and now European immigrants opened employment opportunities for Mexicans, who were not subject to numerical visa restrictions. However, that isn't to say that Mexican crossings weren't impacted, for while Mexican migrants would not see numerical restrictions until 1965, the 1924 law made border crossings more prohibitive through visa fees and the initiation of border vigilance. In fact, illegal entries to avoid such requirements resulted in an increase in deportations from 1,751 in 1925 to 15,000 in 1929. As Mae Ngai points out, "more than anything else, the formation of the Border Patrol raised the border."[44]

The law restricted immigration to 155,000 entries per year overall and issued national quotas set at 2 percent of the number of people of each ethnicity present in the United States as of 1890.[45] Immigration legislation was not meant to apply to the Western hemisphere, nor to contain Mexican migrants, much less to interfere with a Southwestern labor system that was dependent on an inflow *and* outflow of Mexican labor. Still, the law kept the sometimes-prohibitive fees that were introduced in 1917 ($10 head tax and $8 visa), established a border patrol, and made it so that anyone who had entered without documentation prior to July 1, 1924, could be deported without consideration of the conditions and the date of their entry. In other words, all migrants who had entered prior to 1924 without documentation—which included those who crossed where there were literally no gates of entry—could be subject to deportation. This not only criminalized many immigrants and migrants, but it did so retroactively. The burden fell not on the state to protect and inspect the border, but rather onto the migrant. Accordingly, border crossers were to have entered through a legal point of entry when an inspector was on duty and to have kept a record of their own entry or ensured that the immigration official correctly noted their entry details and preserved that record.

As pointed out in chapter 1, the Immigration Act of 1917 did present obstacles to Mexican migrants, namely through fees charged and general restrictions based on literacy, the public charge exclusion, as well as a number of other exclusions. Due to World War I-era exemptions offered to Mexican laborers, the 1917 law was applied unevenly but still had the effect of keeping laborers in the United States if they could not afford to pay entry fees for a return trip to the United States.[46] Moreover, as evident from passport requests presented in chapter 1, migrants hoping to cross the border legally still needed to arrange documents, letters of support, and passport photos. The 1924 law shifted visa work to US consular officials within Mexico as opposed to the border. As a result, aspiring migrants would be required to direct their questions to US consuls near where they lived in Mexico prior to travel. Migrants from Jalisco, Michoacán, Colima, and Nayarit would have to submit visa applications and direct their questions to the US Consulate in Guadalajara. There, consuls fielded a range of questions about border crossings, visas, head taxes and other fees associated with migrating, and an increase in questions related to mixed status families.

Crossing the border, was in effect, easy if you were able to read and write, were in good health, and had the money to pay for your visa and head tax. Fernando Manzano Ybarra received confirmation of the basic requirements for entering the United States in a letter from consul McConnico in April 1924.[47] Ybarra, writing from Tenamaxtlán, Jalisco, in what could be characterized as a barely literate letter (he apologized for addressing the consul with no knowledge of orthography), expressed that he and various other men from his town wanted to go to the United States to "lend their services wherever needed." He inquired about requirements to cross the border "without any disturbance," since he had heard about the "many difficulties" associated with going to the United States. A month after receiving information from the consul, Ybarra wrote again conveying that while he didn't think he would have a problem with the requirements, he had been made aware by letters recently sent home that there was now a shortage of work opportunities. He desired a letter of recommendation from the consul so that even if this were true, he could cross without difficulty. The consul reassured him that he should be fine as long as he could fulfill requirements, and added that he should have proof of $50 savings that would support him in the United States while he looked for work. He also confirmed that the only shortages he had knowledge of were in Southern California, and that he should avoid going there. The proof of savings was viewed as a guarantee of Ybarra's future economic standing and of preventing him from becoming a public charge. Interestingly, in this case the consul served as an informal agent of labor redistribution.

With the rise of family migration, a diverse group with varied motivations sought to cross the border. Consuls were inundated with questions which were not always easy to answer. The consul's letter to Ybarra extended tacit support to Ybarra's goal of going to the United States in search of work. Never mind that Ybarra could not read or write well, that he was likely of the lower classes, and almost definitely un- or under-employed in his own country. Even with minimal restrictions in place at the border and propaganda in Mexico dissuading emigrants from leaving, single men still had a reasonable expectation that they would be able to cross. Even if families were increasingly desired by employers in the US, they faced a heavier burden of proof of acceptability at the border, especially because they were likely to include family members not engaged in formal labor and subject to a public charge ruling. Able-bodied men categorically were assumed to be able to support themselves, while women were not.

As the 1924 law shifted more duties to the consuls by having them make initial determinations about migrant visas, the consuls also shared responsibility in determining whether migrants fulfilled requirements. A circular outlining consular duties acknowledged the change, stating, "From a study of its provisions it will be seen at once that the duties, authority and responsibilities of consular officers in connection with the execution of the restrictive immigration policy of the United States are greatly increased by this act."[48] The circular then goes on to outline the changes that would specifically impact consular officials, with at least two being of extreme importance in the case of Mexican immigrants. Consular officials in Mexico and at the border would need to help ensure "A clear distinction between the classes of travelers to the United States to whom passport visas are granted and those who desire to emigrate to the United States to reside permanently and who must obtain consular immigration visas." This meant that consular officials in Guadalajara were tasked with determining which migrants sought only a temporary visit of no more than six months, and those intended to stay for a longer period of time. Visa requirements with set parameters for length of stays clashed with the unpredictable trajectories of migrants. Additionally, consular officials were now responsible for carefully determining whether the potential migrant or immigrant could be denied entry based on a number of exclusionary categories.

The circular also stated that per the 1924 law, "the burden of proof of admissibility to the United States is placed upon the alien seeking admission." The added burden to the migrant meant that even if the (im)migrant was given a visa, they could still be denied entry upon arrival to the United States, which meant that in some cases migrants had to prove their case for admissibility twice. Administratively, it meant that consular officials did not have the last say in a migrant's potential admissibility, and it created room for confusion among both migrants and government officials. The government acknowledged that officials would at times be placed in difficult positions and that "apparent hardships may result to families or groups of aliens." Consular officials constantly wrote petitions and appeals to clarify cases, and in turn, they had to field a host of petitions and appeals from aspiring migrants and migrant family members. The state department and consular service couldn't have fully anticipated the impact that new legislation and added administrative hoops would have on both consular officials and migrants, nor that it would create a unique emotional and social space where representatives of the state and migrant family members would meet to navigate the processes of binational living and migration together.

Due to the requirement for consul-issued visas, a provisional Mexican passport solicited from a state governor was no longer required. The proof of admissibility was no longer a responsibility of Mexican officials. The balance of State-migrant interaction shifted to U.S. officials over Mexican officials except in very specific cases, as will be explored later in the chapter. A Mexican passport no longer did anything to confirm or assure that the migrant would be accepted into the United States upon arrival. Aspiring migrants still obtained letters of recommendation as confirmation of a reputable character; however, approval or recommendation from the Mexican government alone was not enough to counter perceived reasons for exclusion, especially for those deemed likely to become a public charge.

The public charge exclusion was the most important exclusion that governed the border.[49] The public charge exclusion of course applied to immigrants from all countries and was a very clear indication that the US government only wanted immigrants within the nation's boundaries if the balance of capital and labor they contributed outweighed the resources they utilized.[50] By the early 1920s, US immigration officials, US-Mexico border communities, and Mexican families on both sides of the border had already witnessed cyclical repatriations of Mexican migrants. Thus, the wage-earning power and future wage-earning power of a particular immigrant crossing the US-Mexico border became of particular concern. The exclusion law was often applied at the discretion of immigration officials, and along the border, it was applied flexibly enough to allow for temporary labor. Overall, this resulted in a very subjective application of the law. Different immigration officials prior to 1924, and different consular officials after 1924, could make widely different judgements about the potential earning capacity of a migrant and thus their approved entry into the United States. It also meant that officials could be influenced by unequal pressures in making their determinations. The pressure brought on by a US employer that lobbied for the entry of necessary labor was, for example, very different from that of a family member assuring that the migrant in question would be a guaranteed wage earner or that they had family members that would provide completely for their livelihood.[51] Subjective application of the law meant that people of influence, such as diplomats or business partners, could influence and possibly even bribe officials to overlook proof that might otherwise exclude migrants.[52]

Variations in the application of the law were also based on gendered understandings of wage-earning, appropriate head of households, and expectations of family providers. An added provision came into the 1924 law that made subjective determinations more objective, but the law still carried an added burden of proof for migrant families and women. According to the provision, an immigrant who was otherwise admissible could be admitted by the Secretary of Labor "upon giving a bond or putting up a cash deposit, under terms laid down by the Secretary, holding the United States harmless against such alien becoming a public charge." The rule was most likely used to placate US employers who could use the opportunity to sponsor cheap labor, but families could also take advantage of the rule to aid those who were suspected of

> insufficient funds to afford support until arrival at final destination or until employment could be secured; advanced age and no responsible friends or relatives; crippled condition; limited earning power and numerous dependents; a plain intention not to work but to depend on wits and chance for a living; addiction to drink or gambling—these and similar conditions brought out in the course of examination of an applicant would justify refusal of an immigration visa on the grounds that he was likely to become a public charge.[53]

Another form of support to migrants facing the public charge exclusion came in the form of family member affidavits. Single women who were crossing outside of their roles as wives or daughters required a male family member in the United States to confirm that they would not become a public charge.[54]

In 1924, twenty-year-old Andrea Torres was held up at the border by immigration officials and referred to the US consulate at Nogales in order to secure more guarantees against the possibility that she was likely to become a public charge. Because she did not yet have a visa, two separate sets of actions were required for her to enter the United States as a single woman. Despite showing that she had previous work and was intending to seek work as a domestic servant, having $120 dollars in savings, and knowing how to read and write, an affidavit from male family members in the United States saying that she would not become a public charge was required for her entry. The consul at Nogales also sent correspondence to the American consul at Guadalajara requesting letters of recommendation to support her admission into the United States. After securing a letter of support on Andrea's behalf from an American agent at a copper mining company in Ameca, Jalisco, as well as an affidavit signed by her two brothers living in Ray, Arizona, she was admitted into the United States in October of 1920, two months after first arriving at the border. Being a single woman and traveling alone without a male companion made Andrea subject to more scrutiny and required the involvement of two consuls, her two brothers, and additional community references.[55] The fact that an affidavit from her brothers—with no assurance as to their own likelihood of becoming public charges—was required, is another example of patriarchal and gendered border policies. An affidavit from a female family member would not have guaranteed Andrea's entry.[56]

With regard to the public charge exclusion language referenced above, the phrase "limited earning power and numerous dependents" also reveals how immigration legislation could be gendered to exclude women. But even a cash deposit, bond, or affidavit would not be sufficient to counter suspicions of someone whose visual appearance suggested destitution. Furthermore, "limited earning power" lacked a clear explanation. The danger to this course of determination was that racial perceptions and stereotypes equating Mexicans with impoverishment, especially after so many destitute Mexicans had made their way to the United States during the Mexican Revolution, made entry especially difficult. To insure against any hurdles with immigration officers, rejection at the border, and being left stranded without money, migrants and their family members wrote to state officials ahead of their journeys to make sure that they would indeed be admissible.

The greater the size of the family group, including extended family members, the more likely the suspicion of an LPC designation, especially if women and children in the group outnumbered laboring males. Letters written to consular agents in Guadalajara on behalf of family members planning family unit and family chain migration illustrate that migrants were well aware of the challenges of migration during a period of changing exclusions at the border. In November of 1924, Angel Flores temporarily stopped over in Nogales, Sonora, and wrote to his consular district officer in Guadalajara to advise him that he intended to go to Santa Paula, California, accompanied by his brother and wife, asking for "permission necessary at this border in order to proceed."[57] Flores had already worked in the United States for a year before attempting to return to the United States with his relatives. Angel Flores's direct correspondence to the consul at Guadalajara from the border indicates that he had encountered trouble at the border and was told that he needed permission from his consular district. Consul Dwyre replied that Angel must present his case to the consul at Nogales since it was impossible for him to get an immigration visa without applying in person for entry. Either as a result of the change in law since the last time he had crossed, or perhaps because he was accompanied by his brother and wife who had not previously entered the United States, Angel had to initiate a new bureaucratic process with the state. Stricter enforcement of the law meant that Angel's time as a resident in the United States did not exempt him from regularizing his status; strengthened deportation laws required him to do so in an era of increasingly formalized migration requirements.

Angel's case is one of many that illustrates how family unit and chain migration could bring migrants into contact with the state, more so than when males embarked on solo migrations. Adolfo Garcia Gómez's letter, written in October of 1924 from San Luis Obispo, California, states, "Having decided to marry here, and finding that my future wife is there [Guadalajara] I ask that you inform me of the requirements that she needs to start the journey to this country without setback." In this case the consul advised that his fiancée go to the consulate to be "given all the information necessary."[58] Most of the correspondence between migrants and US consuls like Adolfo's was purely informational; however, even as such, these letters reflect immigrants' and migrants' understanding of evolving border and immigration legislation and the gendered aspects of the law as well. Adolfo's future wife would indeed benefit from specific instruction, since engagements, common-law marriages, and even religious marriages (absent a civil marriage) were called into question once migrants arrived at the border.[59] Adolfo and his fiancée were likely aware that announcing an intention to marry in the United States would not be sufficient to prevent migration issues at the border. Even such simple informational requests illustrate the complexities of family migration. Such letters also illustrate the extent to which US consuls could serve as vital allies to migrants as they navigated their binational livelihoods and journeys. The 1920s marked only the beginning of this peculiar relationship between migrant families and consuls abroad.

Consular correspondence throughout the 1920s illustrates how in the middle of the busiest decade ever for Mexican migration, US immigration legislation led to new dilemmas, an increasingly policed border, new migration strategies, and an increased immigrant and migrant selectivity. Labor potential and an intended temporary stay in the country were the most preferable qualities at the gates of entry. Money to cross, health of body and mind, and overall perceived usefulness to the country defined who was admissible. The burden of legal requirements increased, and as a result, so did illegal immigration. An increase of illicit as well as a growing culture of extralegal forgeries, bribes, and corruption marked the borderlands. A treasury official near the Mexican border claimed that 75 percent of inhabitants in Ciudad Juárez were somehow involved in the business of contraband, stating,

> The smuggling of men is enormous. In the public plazas and in all of the centers the smugglers or coyotes go around picking up people to pass them illegally to the American side. They almost always charge upwards of five dollars per person to cross them over. Countless Mexicans pass illegally to the American side because they find it impossible to pay the 18 dollars that they are charged for the visa, the passport, and the head tax.

The consul pointed out that most smugglers were native to the region and thus knew the landscape and how to smuggle men, women, and merchandise.[60] Migrants who had once entered illegally, like Gregoria Ayala, later felt the pressure to pay the eighteen dollars for head tax and visa so that they could re-enter legally. Although she eventually regularized her status upon a subsequent entry, her first entry was facilitated by a coyote who charged her only ten dollars to cross the river, almost halving the cost for legal entry. Gregoria, like many other migrants, entered legally and illegally at various times throughout her life. Even those who had lived in the United States for years and returned to Mexico only for temporary visits were harangued to pay their fees again.[61]

Critically, changes in border and immigration legislation would also impact the families that had become increasingly binational because circular migration throughout the 1920s resulted in families that were composed of both US and Mexican citizens. This would be most clearly revealed during the repatriations of the 1930s when binational families, including US-born children, made up a large percentage of migrants returning to Mexico. Antonia Caldera, for example, had lived in Kansas City from 1916 until 1920 when she returned to Mexico. In 1927, she, along with her husband and four children, migrated to San Antonio on a visitor's visa. Staying on in the United States, she would have two more children, Felipe and Jose. By 1931, she was living in Chicago, where she would board a repatriation train with her husband and six children to Laredo, and then on to her hometown, Puruándiro in Michoacán.[62] Antonia's was one of many families that had migrated throughout the 1920s in a circular fashion, creating a family with mixed citizenship status. Families forging their migrations in the 1920s were truly binational and would encounter a new set of negotiations at the border in whichever direction they travelled. The Baltazar family mentioned in the introduction provides another revealing example of binational migration and a kind of social cartography of Mexican migrant mobility throughout the 1920s. With the husband and wife being born in Guanajuato, their first child being born in the United States, their second being born in Mexico, and then subsequent children being born in cities throughout the United States, we can see the kind of migrant mobility that created families that defied simple national containers.

Notwithstanding the obstacles that first-time migrants faced or the new challenges that experienced border crossers encountered, thousands of Mexicans left their communities throughout the 1920s, and observers on the Mexican side of the border continued to take note of the impact that emigration was having on Mexican communities. Despite various visa and immigration questions directed toward the US consuls, consular duties and field reports focused primarily on business matters and local politics rather than outbound migration. Consular correspondence does reveal, however, that consuls were keenly aware of the growing exodus out of Jalisco. The community impact continued to be reported on in Mexican newspaper reports and editorial laments. Throughout the 1920s, emigration was related to the foremost problems thought to be plaguing the nation including policies regarding labor (article 123), education, and land redistribution.

THE VIEW FROM CENTRAL-WEST MEXICO

Migration in the second half of the decade turned into an uncontrollable force that Mexican officials and communities were forced to reckon with. In

May of 1924 in the "commentaries of the day" section of *El Informador*, an entry simply titled "Emigration" read, "the emigration of Mexican peons who go to the United States is contained by no one. It's a curious phenomenon. At issue is a contagious suggestion that because of being well-paid and happy in some businesses, the recruiter arrives or the letter of some friend who is getting paid a lot of money in Chicago and they leave without listening to reason."[63] The author went on to state that if immigrants had been reasonable, they would have realized that there were still jobs left in Mexico and they would not be foolish enough to just leave their homes on blind faith or lofty promises. After all, there were job opportunities in places like La Laguna where one could earn three pesos daily. The commentary elucidates some of the main features of migration during the 1920s: That migration was an uncontained phenomenon; that the knowledge or rumor of good wages was widespread; and that letters and reports from friends served as a type of informal recruitment that was already operating independently or in concert with more traditional forms of recruitment.

Although Mexico began to see the first signs of real economic growth and hopes of political stability by the mid-1920s, emigration to the United States continued and even became a permanent feature of central-western communities. While increased labor opportunities and the proliferation of family networks across the border contributed to an upturn in migration in 1927, conditions in Mexico also contributed to the outflow. Immigration entries as recorded by the US government show that Mexican immigration in the fiscal years of 1926 and 1927, and 1927 and 1928, surpassed immigration during the earlier part of the decade.[64] Despite government efforts toward nominally and minimally delivering on the promises of the 1917 Constitution, a peaceful transition of power between President Obregón and President Calles, an upturn in the economy within the first two years of Calles's presidency from 1924 to 1926, and a soft de-escalation of violence by providing revolutionary generals with political spoils, many regions in Mexico were still marked with economic and political instability.[65]

The central-west region of Mexico witnessed continued conflagrations throughout the 1920s, and the state of Jalisco, in particular, experienced deep political conflict as evidenced by its twelve governors in ten years. The region was one of the most significant stages for the 1924 De La Huertista rebellion, and increasingly became a hotbed of anti-regime sentiment during the Cristero War. Despite, or perhaps because of, its radical revolutionary and loyal Obregonista governor between 1923 and 1926, many Jaliscienses were caught up in the violence engendered by the radicalism and fanaticism of pro-government partisans on one side and pro-Catholic church interests on the other. As in other parts of central-western Mexico such as Michoacán, the violence that emerged as a result of the Cristero War was as much about the defense of a regional power structure from the overreach of a centralizing state as it was about the defense of Catholicism. And with the state of Jalisco having a particular and historically regional independent streak, the 1920s proved to be an era ripe with anti-government grievances, increased industrialism, rural to urban migration, and contentious agrarianism, all of which provided the backdrop for the largest emigrant exodus seen yet.[66]

Actual land redistributed in Jalisco through policies of agrarian reform was not nearly as substantial as in other areas of Mexico such as Morelos, but some land was redistributed as early as 1915 as a way of ending conflicts between indigenous communities and nearby haciendas. This was done as a means for Carranza to shore up support and cut into Villa's and Zapata's base. These early instances of land redistribution that continued through 1920, and another redistribution under Governor Zuno (1923–1926), gave momentum to groups of *agraristas* and caused concern to large landholders, ranchers, and small landholders alike. Early conflicts between *agraristas* and landholders led to violence in places like Ocotlán, Jalisco, during the first half of the 1920s.[67] The violence and tension that impacted Jalisco strengthened emigration trends that were already in place. Revolutionary promises had been delivered in the form of *ejidos* and land reform for some, but for many in Jalisco, reform policies signaled the demise of local autonomy and the downturn of economic production.

In 1926 the Cristero War engulfed Arandas, part of Los Altos de Jalisco, the region of the state which had already witnessed the sons of businessmen, tailors, and small landholders emigrating since the turn of the century. Sharecroppers and ranch laborers rebelled against the central government in defense of the Catholic Church, culture, and traditional hierarchies of power. *Agraristas* had not gained much traction in towns like Arandas and San José de Gracia in Michoacán, which had already experienced the breakup of large land into smaller units of production through inheritance.[68] But when an attack on religious traditions was paired with *agrarismo*, violence engulfed the center-west in the Cristero War, and Arandanses either emigrated or fought to defend traditional forms of landholding and power.

Paul Taylor documented that some twelve hundred Arandenses emigrated to the United States in the years between 1926 and 1929. The Cristero War hit the region particularly hard. Those Cristeros actively defending the Catholic Church and the local structure of power against the federal troops and agraristas took control of Arandas in 1927. Guerrilla war and an onslaught of federal power and draconian measures to root out Cristero rebels led to destructive violence and terror for the community's inhabitants.[69] Throughout Los Altos de Jalisco in general, the federal government congregated the region's populations into towns as a strategy to more effectively fight against the Cristeros, but this also kept Alteños from working haciendas, thus creating dire circumstances and forcing many to move to other parts of Mexico and especially to the United States.[70]

Taylor's assertion, "Thus, a religious motive became an important incentive to emigration from Arandas" is certainly true, and religious exiles migrated in droves to the United States. In general, though, the economic and social dislocations caused by violence and a disruption to the production of goods led to widespread emigration from the region. In short, the Cristero War accelerated emigration in places where it had already existed. Emigration to the United States had become an increasingly viable option for Mexicans throughout the center-west. In Nogueras, Colima, for example, a sugar hacienda suffered a shortage of workers because their workers had been emigrating to the United States. Rather than look for jobs in surrounding areas during the offseason, workers began to go to the United States. Due to this scarcity, the hacienda was forced to operate at reduced capacity and this created further underemployment. Emigrants began bypassing nearby cities and looked directly to the United States.[71] Other factors that coincided with the Cristero War such as drought, flood, and crop blight continued to provoke the migration of campesinos.[72]

On June 6, 1927, *El Informador* reported yet again on the high number of Mexicans being stranded at the US-Mexico border. While the theme was familiar and had at various times over the past decade prompted officials to try and stem the tide of workers by using newspaper propaganda, the immediacy and seriousness of the problem was conveyed by the fact that the Chamber of Commerce in Nogales, Arizona, had written to the Department of Commerce, Industry, and Mining of Guadalajara, Jalisco to specifically communicate their concerns about the hundreds of workers who had streamed into Nogales, many of them without legal documents. The letter was published in the newspaper so that its warning and suggestions could reach aspiring migrants in Guadalajara. It read, "With the opening of the new rail connection in Guadalajara, the traffic of passengers toward this port has resulted in many people coming from Jalisco to the United States by rail through Nogales. An abnormal number of individuals are now coming from the state of Jalisco to look for work."[73] The Nogales Department of Commerce cautioned migrants to go to the US consulate before leaving Guadalajara. Municipal departments of commerce, not just migration and border officials, were now corresponding about the influx of migrants at the border. Just as in the late 1800s, it was a railroad connection that created a new artery for emigration out of western Mexico, but the pressure had been building for three decades. The issue of proper documentation amidst a changing landscape of entry requirements only worsened conditions along the border. Communities along the border were increasingly drawn into the business of documented and undocumented migration, and communities throughout the interior of Mexico were trying to figure out who to blame and how to stop the exodus.

TAKING NOTICE: FINDING SOMEONE TO BLAME

While material threats of violence and substandard means of living clearly played a role in migration, observers and editorialists in Jalisco were much quicker to blame the increased emigration on post-revolutionary reform and politics regarding land redistribution as opposed to family reunification, binational livelihoods, *enganchadores*, the overwhelming draw of higher wages in the United States, or land tenure issues caused by population pressure and the breaking up of lands due to inheritance. A scarcity of testimonies from migrants who left in the latter half of the 1920s make it difficult to know how much migrants actually attributed their own migrations to politics, versus religious conflicts, family reunification, or sheer economic desperation, but editorials of the era suggest that observers most readily named the post-revolutionary state as the culprit for increasing emigration. Calling out the state (and effectively rendering migrants less agency in their own migrations) became a tool used by opponents of President Calles and laws stemming from the 1917 constitution.

Guadalajara editorials mentioned in chapter 1 revealed that agrarianism sparked by revolutionary governments was seen as the reason for emigration in the early 1920s, but more and more elements of the revolutionary state were called into question by the fiercely partisan observers sharing their views in *El Informador*. The tones taken in the editorials reflect a general dissatisfaction with government and conforms to an overall resistance to federal authority prevalent in Jalisco. Notwithstanding the bias evidenced in such opinion pieces, author arguments provide insight into the broader social changes, political rhetoric of the time, and a shifting economy that caused more Mexicans to pioneer north or join family members abroad.

Conservatives in the region also took issue with post-revolutionary rhetoric directed toward labor interests. One newspaper editorial blamed article 123 of the Mexican constitution for generating labor unrest and ineffective strikes, suggesting that shutting down of factories resulting from these strikes is what caused emigration to the United States.[74] In Jalisco, Governor Zuno's politics threatened traditional paternalistic labor relations.[75] This fell into line with Calles's rhetorical commitment to the increase of wages and allowing of strikes at the national level. While the reality of the situation was that several independent labor unions were bribed and coerced into joining the federally affiliated Confederación Regional Obrera Mexicana (CROM), the Mexican Regional Labor Confederation, and independent labor unions grew increasingly and fiercely controlled in the latter half of the decade, the replacement of traditional labor relations with state-controlled labor relations aroused suspicion from conservative industrialists who faced an erosion of their power.[76] Industrialists in Jalisco had promoted a regional solidarity based on Catholic class fraternity and individualized relationships between industrialists and their employers and balked against any centralizing tendency from Mexico City. Even while national laws, such as the National Federal Labor Law passed in 1929, which sought to enshrine some of the progressive measures of article 123, lacked actual enforcement throughout Mexico, the very idea that revolutionary promises would be deployed from the center without accounting for local and regional power structures gave critics the excuse to blame revolutionary governments for the destabilizing changes they witnessed around them.

Another hallmark reform of the Calles administration which was critiqued and correlated to the emigration of Mexicans was the reform of education. An *El Informador* editorial on September 24, 1926, commented on the increased number of Mexican students enrolled in schools across the Rio Bravo in Texas.[77] The rumor that ten thousand Mexican students (however exaggerated the claim was) were attending school in El Paso prompted the author to cite the education abroad of Mexican students as a potential threat to Mexican nationalism. Emigration was considered a threat to Mexico's future as well as Mexico's present. The reform government's proposals for education became emblematic of a post-revolutionary people's struggle for personal and community autonomy. Education, a most important and noble political priority, and a critically effective tool of propaganda, became a new battle ground for the ideologues. Also, participation in education, as noted by the author of the editorial, was an important measure of freedom that could also impact one's desire to participate or abscond from the national project: "What is to be done about the emigration of students and workers that causes us such harm? In the first place, to grant true educational freedom so that parents might elect the school that is most appropriate for their children following their convictions and beliefs which are completely within their right to express. In the second place, the adults should make life inside the home pleasant."

The call for educational freedom was representative of a reaction toward the federal government's effort to extend more and more power from the center.[78] Along with reforms in education, labor, and the redistribution of land, the Calles administration also created a national bank and nationalized railroads. The federal government's emphasis on bolstering infrastructure through road-building was part of a larger effort to stimulate industrialization and exports. But the slow midcentury economic decline, paired with an increasingly intrusive state, brought on critiques toward the government. In the same article that lamented increased numbers of Mexicans receiving education in the United States, the author pointed out the weakness of an increasingly centralized government and its failures to contain emigration.

> That all of us Mexicans live happily in our land, so that there is prosperity and work for all, it's necessary for our governments to carefully study the idiosyncrasy of the people and their needs. And once they've done so, so as to not contradict the will of the people and to provide necessities as much as possible. If despite that emigration continues, then the Government wouldn't be at all responsible, well they would have done everything they should have.[79]

As articulated by this editorial, emigration reflected the incongruence between state-led reform and the will of the people. The spaces created by the disjuncture between the state and the people, perpetuated by idiosyncratic pueblos and brought into stunning relief by the blunt overreach of the state, resulted in the growth of corporative groups affiliated with government and momentous demands for more reform. That disjuncture shaped the negotiations of those who stayed, but critically also influenced the lives and the trajectories of those who left. The government was now not only expected to appropriately study and know its regions and population, but also to serve its needs in a way fitting its newly reasserted democratic ideals: not to force the will of a tyrant, oligarchies, or regional strongmen, but to absorb and respect the wide-ranging will of its people. The government arguably came to know and provide concessions to some regions over others, and the editorial author from Guadalajara saw Jalisciences as being left out. Again, emigration was framed as a post-revolutionary impulse rather than part of a larger trend of displacement and dispossession that had long marked the center-west.

During the 1927 presidential campaign, an editorialist suggested that the three candidates differed little in their solutions for critical issues such as emigration, stating that they "pass over like hot embers the huge problem that needs to be resolved so that our country does not continue to bleed; so that our wealth does not continue to emigrate, so that the exodus of workers and capitalists is contained."[80] The Mexican public in general did, however, take interest in the emigration problem, and the topic was even the basis of a national student debate contest in July of 1928.[81] While emigration became an increasingly observable phenomenon in the center-west of Mexico, a keen understanding of the dynamics on both sides of the border that were pulling Mexicans into migratory corridors was generally lacking, giving way instead to generalizations and stereotypes about Mexican migrants. Both sending state officials and officials in US destinations underestimated the strong pull of families. Moreover, any easy solution toward the prevention of emigration lacked clarity and none would present itself without understanding that livelihood strategies for many Mexican families were now firmly binational, as were Mexican families.

PREVENTING THE EXODUS

The Mexican Office of Migration only slowly began to involve itself in the active regulation of migrant exodus toward the late 1920s. Initially the Office of Migration was primarily involved with regulating immigration into Mexico, policing for undesirables much in the same way that the US government did, and dealing with the smuggling of unwanted people and untaxed or illegal products into national territory.[82] By March of 1925 the Secretaria de Gobernación had established two new offices of migration in Torreón and Saltillo, both in the state of Coahuila. The creation of these offices revealed the government's acceptance of emigration as it sought to ensure that emigrants complied with the laws of both the US and Mexican governments. But these offices were also specifically created to improve the distribution of migrants to the United States so that critical masses would not overwhelm certain destination cities, subsequently leaving the unemployed vulnerable to repatriation.[83] The two offices of migration would work closely with the Ferrocarriles Nacionales to carry out a policy that had been recommended by Calles in 1923, whereby the sale of second-class train tickets might be sold only to those who had already fulfilled US immigration requirements. This added yet another gate of entry or point of exclusion for migrants making their way up north.[84] The case of Ana Maria Hernández de Cantú demonstrates that migrants instead found ways around such measures.

Ana Maria, along with her two young children, journeyed north and presented herself before Mexican migration agents in Saltillo, Coahuila, to arrange the proper documentation and obtain a pass (alternatively referred to as a ticket or identification card) to cross the border. She was planning on returning to the United States where her husband lived. She had come to Mexico two months prior, probably to pick up her daughter (or perhaps give birth to her) and take her back with her to Austin, Texas. She ran into difficulties when the migration officer told her that she wouldn't have sufficient money to cross, especially with the added cost of a $10 visa for her daughter. He didn't authorize her documents. She ran into further trouble when she couldn't provide the US consul with her daughter's birth certificate, thus failing to get her a passport.

Against the migration agent's suggestion of contacting her husband so he could send more money, Ana Maria instead went back the next day to the migration office without her daughter, explaining that her daughter would no longer be making the trip. With this lie she succeeded in getting a pass for herself and her son and (with her daughter also) boarded a Pullman car heading north. When migrant agent Gustavo Aguila saw her with both children on board the train and realized that he had been "deceived," he forcibly removed the family from the train. Despite Aguila's objections, the train conductor refunded her tickets in full, after being successfully convinced by Ana Maria to do so. The incident led to conflicting opinions between the migration agent and rail employees, which perhaps benefitted Ana Maria in the end. Within two months, she had made it to Austin, Texas, where she actually lodged a formal complaint against the migration agent for poor conduct.[85]

The Mexican government had no real mechanism for preventing emigration, but it also might not have sought to turn off the escape valve. Emigration, after all, would save federal officials from having to intervene in more land

and labor conflicts throughout the country. The community president of Etúcuaro, Michoacán, wrote a letter to his state agriculture committee (which was passed on to the Office of Migration) complaining about the exodus of workers out of his community. He specifically demanded that a neighboring municipality stop giving his community members provisional passes to migrate and suggested that migration agents 875 kilometers away in the state of Nuevo Leon should prevent the crossing of his community members into the United States. He was willing to send a list of names to facilitate this roadblock. The matter was redirected toward the state governor instead; migrant officials had plenty of work in front of them in trying to monitor the stream of migrants at various points on their northward journey. Government officials at various levels passed the responsibility of preventing the northward exodus to other officials. During the 1920s, US employers were winning the contest for Mexican laborers, and the Mexican government, limited in its ability to ameliorate the situation for the Mexican labor contractors and employers, was losing out.

Mexican communities were losing out as well. The commentary section of *El Informador* supplied a witty, yet disparaging remark on what the "feminine exodus" (*éxodo mujeril*) meant to communities. "A newspaper gives the somewhat alarming news that, that through Ciudad Juarez alone, 1000 women are leaving daily to the United States as their destination. Well sir, we are being left without skirts; add that to the fact that due to the fashion of the day, they had already decided to reduce their clothing to the most minimal proportions. We must remedy the exodus of women, because a town of only men is like a stew without salt. Bad with them, but worse without them."[86]

The claim that one thousand women were leaving daily through Ciudad Juárez might have been exaggerated, but was still striking. The exodus of women was clearly alarming and considered inappropriate according to gendered expectations of migration. The author calls for a "remedy," stating that "a town with only men would be like a stew with no salt: bad with women but worse without them." Notwithstanding the misogynistic and disparaging tone, the passage reveals the author's concern over the exodus of women as a threat. And following decades of threats, violence, and disorder, a threat to patriarchy would challenge any vestiges of tradition in the center-west. Likewise, emigration from Arandas was noted as becoming an increasingly more family-oriented affair as one observer reported that "all the cars and buses going to San Francisco Rincón, Guanajuato are going with passengers solely for the purpose of going (to the United States), some with families."[87] While US employers were starting to welcome laborer wives who accompanied laborer husbands, the family and female exodus was drawing concern and shock in sending communities. The full extent and ramifications of the migrant family exodus would not be felt until the Great Depression sent most of them back.

Mexican immigrants and migrants coming to the United States in the 1920s witnessed the expansion of work opportunities, increased border regulation, and the proliferation of social networks. Despite new restrictions at the border and more exclusionary US immigration policy, Mexican legal migration in the 1920s was more than double that of the previous decade. Work opportunities and wages still remained higher in the United States than Mexico, and consular correspondence and migrant testimonies reveal that family networks continued to encourage and facilitate migration. The use of Mexican labor, and specifically Mexican family labor in agriculture, made space for the waves of new migrants and inspired still more to come. Thus, the growth of Mexican communities and social networks in combination with the need for family labor truly defined the 1920s as a decade when a range of migrants with varying social statuses, ages, gender, origins, and destinations made their way across an ever-changing border. The volume of emigrants paired with the new US legislation governing migration and Mexican efforts to prevent border cities from being overwhelmed by migrant traffic made it exceedingly clear that Mexican migrations tested intergovernmental, interregional, and binational cooperation.

The 1920s were also a critical decade for the creation of binational families. Women and children were central to the growth of Mexican-American communities in the United States. They were also regularly crossing the US-Mexico border and thus immigration impacted Mexican communities as well. Moreover, more women were leaving in family units or on their own; sometimes they would return back to their places of origin, or sometimes their journeys would take a multitude of directions and stops. The movement of people out of some communities and into others challenged traditional boundaries and notions of community resources and labor distribution, especially if the presence or absence of migrants was great enough to impact the labor market. But with growing unemployment, threats to community stability by both *agraristas* and *cristeros*, and a slow economic decline beginning in 1926, the exodus could not be stopped. Meanwhile in the United States, in a decade described with terms like "roaring," "boom," and "abundance," Mexican migrants would find themselves on a course of stability and permanence on the one hand, or a course for deportation and disaster on the other. Neither migrants, their family members, nor either government could have imagined the paralyzing effect that the Great Depression would have on Mexican migration to the United States.

PART II

———

Return Flow

FORCING REPATRIATION, KEEPING COMMUNITY

CHAPTER THREE

The Great Depression and
The Great Return

COMING HOME, 1929–1936

IN 1931, DURING THE WORST YEARS of the Great Depression, thousands of Mexican families boarded trains in the United States and headed to their former hometowns in Mexico. The stifling economic crisis compelled migrants to journey south across the border, where they sought reprieve from the insecurity and massive unemployment that struck ferociously at the land of plenty. The reputed abundance found in the City of Angels, and its unincorporated areas, was waning. William Nuñez, a US citizen born in El Paso to Mexican parents, was only eleven when he left his hometown of Belvedere, California. He was one of thousands of children that were swept up in return migration. William's stay in Mexico would be temporary. By 1940, he made his way back to United States, where at the age of twenty, he worked as a "vegetable man" in a hotel kitchen. William's sister worked for a luggage company, and together they supported their elderly parents and the family household that they had been compelled to leave nearly a decade earlier.[1]

We can't be certain of what the train ride from Los Angeles to the Mexican border town of Ciudad Juárez was like for eleven-year-old William Nuñez, how he felt about leaving his home behind, and what he knew, if anything, about the country that would become his new (if temporary) home. Like the other 150 passengers riding the train through Ciudad Juárez on October 22, 1931, he would have to learn how to make a new home on the other side of the border. William's return was just one of many similar journeys taken during an era of economic turmoil and restrictive national border policies.

This chapter examines the era of repatriation from the perspectives of Mexican migrants who struggled through the Great Depression and the welfare and migration officials who negotiated their returns. The term "repatriation" is often associated with the period of Mexican migration between 1930 and 1933, when hundreds of thousands of Mexican immigrants and Mexican-Americans returned to Mexico due to the economic crisis.[2] Repatriations, in fact, continued throughout the 1930s, but this chapter will trace the early repatriations, as they were particularly displacing due to the concerted efforts of US officials to forcibly remove, coerce, or otherwise encourage Mexican citizens and their Mexican-American children to return to Mexico.

Scholars examining this era illustrate how heightened nativism during the United States's economic crisis and strict enforcement of border legislation led to the exclusion and physical removal of hundreds of thousands of Mexicans from the United States. Through excellent works by Abraham Hoffman and George Sanchez we learn about the ways in which Los Angeles city officials and residents responded and reacted to the pressures of the Great Depression. Scholars have depicted how nativism inspired dramatic propaganda campaigns and efforts to uproot Mexican migrants from their homes in Southern California.[3]

What follows is a brief description of Mexican migrant lives during the first years of the Great Depression and an attempt to recognize return migrations of Mexicans and Mexican-Americans to Mexico during the peak year of 1931 as part of both an exceptional moment for some migrant families, and just one episode in the established binational livelihoods of others. Letters from aspiring migrants to consuls and presidents, correspondence between welfare officials in the United States and diplomatic agents abroad, and recorded details of 577 repatriates contained in train manifests, together broaden our understanding of the bidirectional, multigenerational, and diverse nature of migration and repatriation.

Using birthdates indicated on train manifests for multiple family members, I am able to show the circular migrations and binational status of migrant families who had crossed back and forth across the US-Mexico border throughout the 1920s. These records provide evidence that migrant families embarked on international and internal migrations repeatedly and suggest that cross-border movement was part of a broader planned strategy for economic and social livelihood, one defined and determined by migrants themselves, and not always by major historical events.

The migration journeys, as revealed through return train manifests and migrant correspondence, illustrate the broad geographic scope of Mexican migration during the 1920s and 30s, showing migrant trajectories that traverse borderland landscapes and beyond. The Depression disrupted Mexican lives in the United States *and* well-entrenched patterns of family migration and binational living. Through studying this era of bidirectional mobility, the multiple paths and lived experiences of migrant families are revealed.

For William, the journey back to Mexico was not simply a "repatriation," but rather one part of a longer history of binational migration. William's status as a United States citizen allows us to see his journey as just one of many possible cross-border migrations within his own lifetime. His return was not one of legal deportation, but it was a return, nonetheless. His story reminds us of the many children who were either born to Mexican migrant parents while in the United States, or who had made the journey there with their parents during the boom decade of Mexican family migration. Growing opportunities for Mexican migrant families, burgeoning Mexican-American communities, and increased integration into the economic and social fabric of the United States in the 1920s meant that many Mexican migrants faced devastating economic conditions and family separations in the 1930s. While we are able to speculate about the migration routes that William's family undertook, we are left with other questions. Were he and his parents forced to go to Mexico for some reason? Did they choose to take advantage of a subsidized trip back across the border? Was their return trip a response to increasing anti-immigrant sentiment in the 1930s? Were they hoping only to ride out the worst of the economic situation before returning to the United States? Census data reveals several of his family members remained in the United States. The train manifest that lists William's departure with his sister, mother, and father does not reveal that this was only part of his larger family. Census data shows that he had seven other siblings in the Belvedere house. The family owned rather than rented their house. In 1930 William's father, who had worked in construction, was unemployed, but his siblings worked in factories (including macaroni, trunk, and paper factories) while another was a cabinetmaker. William's family managed to retain family ownership throughout the economic crisis and thus William returned to his family home in 1940—a remarkable accomplishment, considering the volume of Mexicans who left the Los Angeles area during the 1930s. Was the return to Mexico a choice of elderly parents who saw a better future for their two youngest children, still of school age, in Mexico, or was it meant to be a chance for their youngest children to get to know their ancestral home now that the violent dislocations of the Mexican Revolution and the Cristero War had subsided?

William's story forces us to ask deeper questions about why people moved across borders and illustrates the diversity of motives and life circumstances that generated long-distance migration. It also reminds us of the diversity of experiences within migrant families. In William's family he was the only sibling born in the United States. In contrast to his eight siblings who were born in the Mexican state of Durango where his parents were also born, William was born in El Paso, Texas. Birthplaces of the children document the migrations of the family. In this case, it appears that the family seemed to make a fairly straightforward migration to Texas in 1916, where William was born, and one more migration to Belvedere, California, by 1930. For other migrants and families, the migrations were many, and the multiple journeys, when taken together, weave a vibrant tapestry of human movement, survival, and adaptation.

The era of return thus illustrates much more than a conflicted era of US border and immigration policy, strained diplomacy, and the potential heartache of uprooting one's life out of desperation—all of which are incredibly important themes of Mexican immigration history, perhaps especially in the 1930s. Deportations, both forced and voluntary, were terribly uprooting, and prompted by anti-foreign and racist sentiment that drove efforts to round up suspected undocumented immigrants for deportation, which in addition to splitting up families had the devastating effect of preventing the legal reentry of deportees into the United States. There were traumatic returns, and family separations, and at least some removals were conducted illegally and in the margins of law. But other return migrations during the Depression fit within a context of established migrant strategies and demonstrate the complexities of Mexican migration. Some migrants left on their own accord, sensing a period of increased hostility, while others embarked on journeys subsidized by both the US and Mexican governments. The era of the *Great Return,* as I refer to it, thus, consisted of multiple and multi-faceted migrations– bidirectional and multidirectional. Migrations were planned but also improvised, governed by familial and labor relationships, and shaped by hospitable environments in some cases and by increasingly antagonistic social landscapes in others.

THE GREAT CRISIS: MEXICANS AND
THE GREAT DEPRESSION

The Great Depression's removal campaigns seemed particularly jarring to the many migrants who had found opportunity and community in the United States during a period of economic boom. The 1930s led to displacement, relocation, and hardship for millions of Mexican migrant families in the

United States and their relatives in Mexico. Economic crisis had initiated what some authors have called "a decade of betrayal" for Mexicans and Mexican-Americans in the United States.[4] Families who had begun to establish their lives in the United States and upon whom US agriculture, mining, and railroad economies depended were now being pressured to leave. Local government officials, immigration restrictionists, and social workers demonized Mexicans for overextending state resources.[5] Economic crisis unleashed discriminatory practices toward foreigners in an environment of heightened nativism. This nativism was not so different from the late-eighteenth-century accusations that German and Irish immigrants were taking American jobs and the late-nineteenth-century prejudices that led to a ban on Chinese laborer immigration.[6] Whereas economic and social dislocation across the US-Mexico border had occurred cyclically for decades, the influx of migrants during the 1920s paired with economic crisis prompted a particularly intense period of anti-immigrant sentiment and immigrant removal efforts during the early 1930s. More employers were hiring only US citizens, and Mexicans were threatened by deportation raids that swept through communities.[7] Some even faced mobs of disgruntled workers who clamored for their return to Mexico.[8]

Even before the stock market crash in the United States, Mexicans experienced difficult living conditions that led to voluntary return migrations. Levels of unemployment in combination with a concerted effort toward immigrant restriction had ensued by 1928. Mexican and US government officials perceiving worsening conditions and, anticipating the further decline in Mexican living standards, began to crack down on surreptitious migration. Debates between representatives of the US government and agricultural interests over immigration restriction had emerged in the mid-twenties. Restrictions of Mexican immigration were staved off for most of the decade because the need for Mexican labor superseded nativist designs. However, a congressional hearing in 1928 on a proposed quota to limit immigration and the 1929 immigration bill, the Undesirable Aliens Act, which made illegal entry a criminal offense, finally had the overall impact of decreasing immigration, increasing return migration, and challenging employers and their use of undocumented and even documented Mexican laborers.[9]

In May of 1928, "grave circumstances" for Mexican workers in the United States were reported and the Mexican government began to consider plans for repatriation. Rumors that troops would be deployed to prevent illegal entry of Mexican workers began to circulate. Additionally, "a multitude of

Mexicans in border communities" were in "terrible conditions due to the absolute lack of work and the many humiliations suffered at the hands of American authorities."[10] Unemployment would go on to grip much of the United States, but economic crisis impacted agricultural areas early and hard. For example, in 1929 growers in California failed to pay $10,000 in wages.[11] Agricultural wages in California agriculture fell from 35 to 14 cents per hour between 1929 and 1933.[12] Those who had skilled jobs moved into agriculture and children dropped out of school to labor with their families. Unemployment in cities displaced workers to agricultural areas and compounded rural job shortages. Migrants living in the Imperial and San Joaquin Valleys who could not afford to buy food had to resort to hunting and eating off the land. Even within agriculture, sharecroppers who might have brought in steadier incomes and maintained greater autonomy than field hands were now forced to work other people's farms in order to survive the Great Depression. All the while, wages and the number of available jobs in rural California were declining precipitously.[13] Likewise, Mexican sharecroppers in Texas faced catastrophe. In 1933, the New Deal's Agricultural Adjustment Act called for the reduction of the cotton crop by 10 million acres (one-fourth of the crop) and led landlords to evict tenants and withhold government checks that were supposed to be distributed to sharecroppers.[14]

City residents, of course, suffered unemployment as well. Los Angeles had an unemployment rate of nearly 10 percent in 1930.[15] Mexicans in cities experienced unemployment even more severely. In Houston, which had better survived the years of economic crisis, Mexican dockworkers, plumbers, and electricians found less work when labor unions preferred and protected their white counterparts.[16] Mexicans in places like South Chicago and Detroit also suffered unemployment, causing them to migrate to other parts of the United States or back to Mexico.[17] In Michigan, for example, Mexicans working in sugar beets were displaced to cities, only to be displaced again from jobs in automobile factories. In November of 1932 alone, five thousand families and single men were deported.[18]

Mexican immigrants dealt with the hardships brought on by the Great Depression in a variety of ways. While some migrants were fortunate enough to determine their own path through tough times by willingly returning to Mexico, waiting out the Depression, or asking for charitable aid, many others were forcibly removed, coerced to return, or legally deported to Mexico. Restricted job access threatened family livelihoods, and in some cases, migrants reached out to representatives of both governments to try and weather the devastation of joblessness and family separation and to navigate exit and return. The stories that follow illustrate the range of migrant fates and strategies during the era of hardship. Correspondence between migrants and government officials illustrate the stifling poverty, the challenges that migrant families faced, and an end to the mobility that so many migrants relied on to build and maintain their cross-border livelihoods.

WELFARE OFFICIALS AND DESERTED MIGRANT WOMEN

Gendered dynamics of migration and labor meant that women who were abandoned during the Great Depression were particularly susceptible to hardship. The turmoil that befell women and children abandoned by a male provider during the economic crisis extended across borders to such a significant extent that consular officials and welfare workers routinely became actors in the conflict resolution of intimate familial relationships. Women were nearly always characterized as victims and men were blamed for shirking their responsibilities as husbands and fathers. A social worker from the Associated Charities of San Francisco lauded one of her clients' attempts to stay afloat during economic hardship: "Mrs. Brust has been making a brave attempt to help herself by doing dressmaking. She has found it impossible, however, to earn enough to support herself and her four children." The family had been provided with "full food relief" for three months and Manuel Brust, the absent father and husband, was seen as the solution to the problem. The social workers asked the American consul to locate Brust in the center-west state of Colima and "find out just what his plans are in regard to his family and why he is making no effort to fulfill his responsibility as a father?" Consul Raleigh Gibson wrote to Brust, telling him that it was "urgent that you take some measure to help your family, and to take on the necessary obligations that are yours as a father and husband." What exactly were Manuel Brust's necessary obligations as a husband? Was he supposed to move his family back to Mexico, or move back to the United States to support his family and rescue them from relying on food relief? Manuel Brust not only understood his duties but took umbrage at the implication that he did not, writing, "Although I have no necessity for you to remind me of the duties I have, given that I know them, I want you to know that I wrote to the Associated Charities of San Francisco, California about how I think to best resolve these difficulties." Several exchanges ensued between the social worker, the consul, and Brust, and it became evident that despite Manuel's attempts to send money to his family, his wife was still having to do her best to keep her family afloat. The social worker stated, "The woman's willingness to cooperate is signified by the fact that last week she went into a home where there were five small children and did all the washing, ironing and cooking and cared for a sick mother and the little ones, in order to make a few cents to help herself out." In the last letter of the exchange, it appeared that Manuel Brust would not be able to satisfy his duties as a provider after all. He wrote to the consul explaining that he was unable to send money due to an illness that prevented him from working, attaching a doctor's note to his letter.

The social worker and consul's indictment of Brust, not to mention their sustained pursuit of him, is striking. We also see that migrants like Mrs. Brust made repeated attempts to make ends meet and that she had difficulty doing so as a woman engaged in poorly paid work. Repatriation, a reality faced by so many migrants during the Depression, was here not seen as the ultimate answer to the resolution of a migrant family's difficulties. The family would remain split across borders in a geographic reversal of assumed migration trends where the male provider attempted to send money and provide for his family in the United States while staying in Mexico. The duty of the husband was to support his wife economically, but not necessarily be by her side; but this was difficult during times of economic hardship. During the 1930s Mexican migrant families had to navigate not only the politics of migration at the border but also had to communicate effectively with representatives of both governments about the intimate politics of family separation and reunification.

ASKING FOR REPATRIATION: LETTERS TO THE MEXICAN PRESIDENT

Migrants stranded in the United States wrote to Mexican officials asking to be repatriated. By 1930, letters from migrants beseeching Presidents Ortiz Rubio, Abelardo Rodríguez, and eventually President Lázaro Cárdenas for repatriation assistance began streaming into the Palacio Nacional. Margarita B. Pérez, writing from Houston, Texas, asked President Rodríguez to be repatriated after her husband found himself without work. Sara Barrón wrote from Gardena, California, asking for help in her repatriation, stating that she had worked as a domestic in the house of the president's father when she was eighteen, but was now living in California having to work to provide for herself after marrying an "hombre vicioso." Maria Zamarripa reported that she had been mistreated simply for being Mexican and needed help repatriating herself and her five kids from Chicago. Maria Dolores Camacho, who supported her children and her elderly mother, had lost her job in Dilley, Texas, but still kept a house that she owned. She wrote to the Mexican president to see if he could arrange that she be given half of the money for her house so that she might use that money to return to Mexico to find a job to support her family. Out of the letter writers above, Camacho actually received a reply from government stating that they would pay for her and her family's rail passes back to Mexico. She wrote a reply thanking the president and letting him know that she would send another telegram to him the day she arrived in Mexico.[19]

Gendered norms for men also shaped their petitions for repatriation assistance. Three men writing to President Ortiz Rubio in 1930 professed themselves to be good men deserving of assistance by claiming that they were patriotic Mexicans who were working in the United States on low wages having "stayed true to the sustenance of their homes." In fact, as workers for the Southern Pacific, they desired to return home to Mexico but found it impossible to make enough money for their return trips.[20] These men found themselves separated from their families who had remained in Mexico, and their initial strategy to work on temporary stints in the United States was no longer viable. Worse, their capacities as providers were compromised by economic crisis. They hoped to find a sympathetic audience in the president, noting the "kindness" that he had demonstrated in his statements to the press.[21] "Anxious" for a solution, the three men looked forward to the day when they would "be free from the enslavement of the land of the dollar."

Jose G. Perez, writing from 306 Tent Alley in Sacramento, California, made a similar appeal to President Abelardo Rodríguez in 1932. He also was unable to send money to his family in Mexico or afford a return trip back due to Mexico due to the "strong crisis." He highlighted his role as a patriarch for his family which consisted of his eighty-seven-year-old father, wife, and three young daughters, who "cry at my absence and lack my work and sustenance." Perhaps because of Perez's effective and sentimental appeal, the office of migration agreed to cover his journey to Aguascalientes if he could get his family to the US-Mexico border on his own account.[22] Commenting on nativist conditions in the United States, Ricardo Frías Beltrán claimed that it had "been nearly impossible to find work for non-citizens." After being pressured to become a citizen by his bosses, he wished instead to return to Mexico, asking for financial assistance to return and a job in Mexico so as to "help provide me with means to return and support my family."[23] For migrants like Frías Beltrán, Maria Camacho, and Manuel Brust, leaving the United States was not the first or only option for surviving the Great Depression.[24] A range of misfortunes befell them including illness, desertion, and language difficulties, which, when combined with economic crisis, meant that they embarked on creative adaptive strategies to support their families.

The role of welfare officials in several of the examples above also reveals, that relief agencies played a significant role in facilitating binational family support networks and attempting to connect migrants in the United States with their families in Mexico. Relief agencies sometimes provided financial assistance to Mexicans so they might stay in the United States. Simultaneously, they were also critical in promoting the repatriation of Mexicans to free up relief rolls for US American citizens. Whether acting benevolently or in service of a more nativist agenda, relief agencies perpetuated what might be the most targeted act of immigrant removal in US history.[25]

REMOVAL AND RETURN

The stories above illustrate the precariousness of migrant livelihoods in the wake of the Mexican migration boom and in the shadow of the economic bust. The unprecedented level of destitution paired with exponential growth in border crossings and binational livelihoods created an environment in which migrants who might not have otherwise interacted with state and local officials were discovered and made themselves discoverable as part of Mexican diaspora in the United States. Many migrants, along with their US-born children, were rounded up and placed on deportation trains, were encouraged to repatriate to Mexico by state and county officials, and sometimes were misled, bullied, or forced into involuntary repatriation. All were at greater risk for deportation, which was the most effective federal strategy to help relief agencies and migrants who felt the acute effects of unemployment and underemployment. Even with increased head taxes and fees for entry during the 1920s, the fluidity of the border, the stretches of unsupervised territory, and the low risk of apprehension still allowed for a number of undocumented crossings. Estimates suggest that as many as 500,000 illegal entries occurred during the 1920s, while only 25,570 apprehensions were made between 1925 and 1930. The Depression transformed this general lack of concern over undocumented crossings into a strong mandate to find migrants who had violated American immigration law. Trains full of families left from Los Angeles, San Diego, San Francisco, and many cities in Texas to the interior of Mexico. Statistics kept on the exodus of Mexicans during the Great Depression are conflicting and are estimates at best, but Balderrama and Rodríguez offer a guess of 1 million.[26]

The struggles of Mexican immigrants and migrants during the Great Depression are often inextricably connected to the dramatic efforts carried out by US federal, and local governments to deport and repatriate Mexican migrants. The deportations and repatriations by far stand out as the most striking feature of this era of Mexican migration. They were not, however, the most salient hardship for all Mexican migrants, especially in those areas that did not witness concerted efforts at removal. Moreover, when repatriation and deportation did happen this was not always an instantaneous event, but rather a process that took time and involved many officials in a multi-step coordination of resources. In some cases, deportation and repatriation consisted of swift action targeting unprepared migrants, but in many other circumstances, Mexicans advocated their own migration solutions to the gripping poverty and stifling unemployment that clamped down so intensely on their mobility. The repatriation and deportation of individuals might be seen either as a culminating event, or as one turning point in a binational migrant's experience.

Focusing narrowly on discrete instances of forced removal and return overlooks longer migrant trajectories including the many strategies used for surviving economic crisis, as well as the uncertainties and range of hardships that migrants endured in the first months and years of the Great Depression. Despite the proliferating social networks and increased economic opportunities achieved during the 1920s, migrants, especially those who arrived in the United States within only a few years of the Depression, still found themselves in precarious living situations. Those who had migrated near the end of Mexico's revolutionary period would have needed to weigh their repatriation carefully against any gains they had made while living in the United States and the future possibilities of returning to their adopted homeland. Returns during the era were sometimes only one part of dynamic life histories and experiences in two countries.

Repatriation and deportation in the early 1930s would go on to impact subsequent waves of entry and return. The heavy logistical burden and cost to both countries for the wide-scale repatriations and the family separations forced a reconsideration of the role that the state played in actively regulating binational labor and migration. While the decade of the 1930s taught the two governments lessons on the bureaucracy of binational migration management, families who lived at the intersection of two countries and two crises— those who had to endure a return or removal as a unified family, who had been forcibly split apart, or who were abandoned by loved ones—had to learn how to negotiate the politics and processes of unexpected exits and returns.

By placing families at the center of analysis for the era of acute crisis, we learn about the intricacies of return migration and the challenges that faced families with varying immigration and citizenship status. Families had become increasingly binational during the 1920s, and not just because they acquired life experiences in two countries but also in terms of citizenship: children were born to Mexican parents living in the United States and their presence challenged strict definitions of immigrant, migrant, citizen, and non-citizen, and general notions of belonging to one nation or the other. Family life cycles and mobility defied increasingly rigid national boundaries. Through the 1920s and subsequent years of economic crisis in the 1930s, Mexican migrants in the United States acquired experiential knowledge of the United States, embarked on binational and intrastate migration, and became all too familiar with their sometimes-precarious position as temporary residents. The threat of removal was very real, and the resultant insecurity inspired the kind of fear that drove hundreds of thousands of migrants back to their homelands.

The return of the prodigal sons and daughters to Mexico—to the nation, to their communities, and to their families—was often fraught with its own challenges. Despite any slow gains that Mexican families and communities might have made since the more tumultuous decades of insurrection and civil war, the influx of so many repatriates into Mexico presented the Mexican State and Mexican families with more mouths to feed. It also presented the Mexican government with the challenges of resettling their migrant citizens. A closer examination of the migrants and families that returned reveals not only the diversity and geographic scope of migrations that they had undertaken in the 1920s, but also illuminates the degree to which migrant families were both Mexican and American.

While some migrants had been removed by legal deportation efforts carried out by the United States government, Mexicans also embarked on the journey back home through their own means and with the sponsorship of the Mexican government. By late 1930 and early 1931 Mexican consuls had started to arrange for discounted rail passes from US cities to the border.[27] Early Mexican efforts to help facilitate the repatriation of Mexicans (such as reduced custom duties) transitioned into more concrete actions that aimed to control and provide for the transportation of repatriates from the border to cities in the interior. With so many migrants congregating in border cities, and with the beginning of county-sponsored trains in the United States, the Mexican government worked with the Mexican National Railways to get free passes and reduced fares to carry migrants the rest of the way home.[28] Depending on whether migrants were receiving aid from welfare agencies, being legally deported at the expense of the US government, or paying for their own travel, migrants had to meet specific requirements to obtain fare reductions sponsored by the Mexican government.

Mexican consuls selected which migrants were eligible for government assistance by conducting "a study of their circumstances, from a legal perspective, to see whether they faced deportation, or from an economic perspective to see if the economic crisis or the lack of personal abilities forced them to leave." After this initial selection was completed a second phase categorized repatriates based on their labor skills to see whether they could work in agriculture, industry, or business upon their return to Mexico.[29]

When the president of the Comisión Honorífica Mexicana, in San Angelo, Texas, wrote to President Ortiz Rubio on behalf of a group of twenty families in dire need of aid and transportation, the Office of Migration took over correspondence and stated that the families would be able to get rail fare from the border to their towns of origin provided that there was proof of indigence from the Office of Migration in Nuevo Laredo, Tamaulipas.[30] It is unclear how consuls were supposed to determine which aspiring repatriates qualified as indigent, but at the very least migrants who could not pay for their return trips home were considered candidates for government-paid train fare. The Mexican government, aware of repeated and circular migrations to the United States, also required proof that migrants have lived continuously in the United States for at least two years to qualify for subsidized travel.

The trains were just one component of efforts in both countries to transport migrants from the United States to Mexico. The journey from the border to the interior of Mexico was the first step in what the Mexican government intended to be a comprehensive plan for the repatriation of their *connacionales*. As early as June 1931, a detailed plan by the Department of Migration chief, Andrés Landa y Piña, outlined how Mexican migrants would be selected to receive aid and be transported by the Mexican government, and how domestic labor conditions could be improved to absorb the entry of repatriates into the work force.[31] A heavy emphasis was placed on making sure that repatriates, and the skills they might have obtained in the United States, could be utilized in Mexico. Repatriates were valued for their experience in agriculture, which is why agricultural colonies became the central focus of repatriation campaigns within Mexico.[32] The Mexican government would receive their citizens and even aid them in their arrival, but also had designs to redistribute returnees according to worker shortages in the country. In short, the Mexican government, much like the US government, envisioned very specific conditions under which repatriates would be sponsored and let back in. Mexico, after all, was dealing with its own labor challenges as the threat of worker unrest was constantly shaping political alignments and the stability of post-revolutionary administrations. In this setting, destitute repatriates were particularly beholden to whomever paid for their transport. They were also subject to migratory paths that were predetermined and regulated for them, as opposed to of their own choosing.

A series of measures were taken to prevent repatriates from threatening labor stability in Mexico. During the economic crisis efforts were made in Mexico to deport foreign workers, a move that opened up opportunities for Mexican repatriates. Furthermore, the "Ley de Trabajo," a law emerging out of the economic crisis, had called for the protection of Mexican workers by regulating the presence of foreign laborers. Specifically, it called for enforcing Article 4 of the Mexican Constitution, which mandated that the percentage of domestic workers in factories would outnumber the percentage of foreign workers by three times. The Office of Migration worked directly with state governors, asking them for help in finding lands for repatriates, and contributing to transportation funds. These efforts were also bolstered by presidential decrees that increased immigrant entry fees and provided a source of revenue to help cover the cost of repatriation. The repatriation of Mexicans was to be an undertaking shared amongst the states and the federal government.

In order to control the flow of repatriates, the Mexican government speci-fied three ports of entry for trains bringing migrants back into the country: Nuevo Laredo, Ciudad Juárez, and Nogales. These border cities were where the majority of Mexicans had first crossed into the United States. The volume of return migration through Nuevo Laredo was especially striking, and in September of 1930 preparations in Nuevo Laredo were made for as many as four thousand Mexicans, including eight hundred families, coming mostly from Karnes, Texas, and nearby counties, to return to Mexico.[33] In January of 1931, a *Los Angeles Times* article reported that, according to Mexican sta-tistics, more people had returned to Mexico through Nuevo Laredo in two weeks than had entered the United States for the previous five months com-bined.[34] Those streaming though Nuevo Laredo were coming from Texas, Illinois, and Colorado, and were headed primarily to Jalisco and Michoacán. The flow and accumulation of migrants at the border city was reported as "abnormally heavy." Migrants would also find themselves stranded on the US side of the border where they would "call on the government for aid in reha-bilitating themselves in Mexico."[35]

Train lists reveal various details about repatriates moving back to Mexico during the height of the Great Depression.[36] Train lists from Laredo include repatriates' occupations and where they lived in the United States, whereas train lists from Nogales and Ciudad Juárez do not reveal such details, but do reveal the birthplace of every repatriate boarding the train. The 577 repatri-ates culled from three train lists for one month in 1931 is a telling sample of the many who returned, and together reveal the diverse nature of migration and repatriation during the Great Depression.

Throughout March of 1931 trains from Nuevo Laredo to central Mexico transported two hundred and fifteen repatriates who "voluntarily" left the United States.[37] When boarding the trains that would take them to their homes in the interior of Mexico, returning migrants provided their names, ages, where they had lived, and the type of employment they held in the United States. Migrants who had documentation of their original entry into the United States were asked about the date of their original crossing. Train manifests also included intended destinations in Mexico as well as vital information that sheds light on the multiple paths and migrations that Mexicans and their US-born children embarked on during the late 1920s and early 1930s.

Notably, a large number of repatriates returning to Mexico through Nuevo Laredo were from northern regions of the Midwest. 40.1 percent of

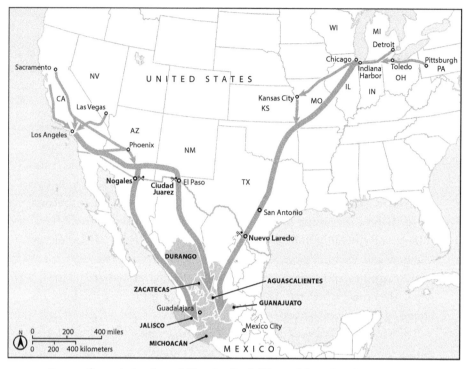

MAP 4. Routes of repatriation through Nogales, Ciudad Juarez, Nuevo Laredo. Map: Ben Pease.

adults leaving through Laredo had previously resided in Texas, but only one-third of them lived, on or near, the border. 24.5 percent of repatriates were leaving the state of Illinois, and of great significance was that all of them (thirty-nine) had previously lived in Chicago. Michigan was the third greatest sending state with 11.3 percent of migrants having previously resided there, mostly in Detroit. A few East Coast states were represented such as New York and Massachusetts, with most East Coast migrants having lived in Pennsylvania. A handful of migrants were making their return trips after living in Missouri and Indiana.[38]

Thus, migrants returning though Laredo had already traveled great distances before embarking on the next phase of their migration and in some cases, they traveled just as far to get to their hometowns in Mexico. The majority of migrants reported that they were returning to the central-west states of Jalisco, Michoacán, and Guanajuato, with 43.5 percent of migrants returning to Guanajuato specifically. Mexican migrants passing through Laredo were in fact returning to the three most significant Mexican sending states of the 1920s. Further, fully 95 percent of migrants who had resided in northern US cities like Chicago and Detroit and states such as Indiana and Pennsylvania were returning to these states.[39] Based on this sample we see a pattern of migration stretching between the central-west Mexican states and northern US states. Not only does this pattern convey the great distance migrants traveled, but it also suggests that traditional sending communities in Mexico were likely the first communities to see their compatriots press farther and farther north of the US-Mexico border. While labor opportunities in northern industries could have certainly beckoned migrants to bypass labor opportunities along the border in the Southwest and Texas, the existence of such strong and exclusive migration patterns between the Mexican west and the US north suggests that established social networks and extended family migrations contributed greatly to such trends. Despite heavy return repatriation during the 1930s, the foundations for binational communities with family members living across borders had been firmly established and the Mexican migrant diaspora existed beyond the traditional geographic definition of the US-Mexico borderlands.

Such long-distance travel was undertaken not only by single and unattached males, although men clearly outnumbered women in return migration through Laredo. Women made up 24 percent of total returning adult migrants, while children of both genders traveling with family members made up another 27 percent. Families with three or more children traveled across long distances from cities such as Indiana Harbor, Kansas City, and Chicago. Antonia Caldera Zavala, for example, was returning from Chicago to Puruándiro, Michoacán, with her husband and her six young children. Antonia had last entered the United States with her husband and four of her children in September of 1927; her two youngest children, Felipe and Jose, were later born in the United States. She had previously lived in Kansas City from 1916 through 1920, returned to Mexico, and in 1927 headed toward San Antonio on a visitor's visa indicating that she would stay in the United States for only ninety days. Four years later she found herself in Chicago during the depths of the Great Depression. From there she would make her journey back to Michoacán where her mother lived. Although the birthplaces for her four eldest children are unknown, her two youngest boys were US citizens and were likely journeying to Mexico for the first time by way of the repatriation trains.

The group returning through Laredo during March of 1931 was a young group, with 98 percent of total repatriates under the age of forty, and 64 percent under the age of thirty. Twenty families with children were repatriating together and 53 of the 215 repatriates were minors. Some families were large, while some consisted of couples traveling with only one child. Focusing on family units reveals a wide age distribution among repatriates, with the eldest repatriate being seventy years old and the youngest only seventeen days.

Romualda Guerrero de Hernández was the mother of the youngest passenger on the Laredo train and her story serves as an example of extended-family migration. She and her husband Anastacio Hernández had been living in San Antonio, Texas. Both originally from Cerrito, San Luis Potosí, they lived in a rented house along with their three children, one of Anastacio's children from a previous marriage, as well as Anastacio's brother and nephew. Romualda, twenty-seven years younger than her husband, gave birth to her daughter Margarita little more than two weeks before packing up her family and returning to Mexico. General farm work had been listed for the men of working age in the household. Romualda's occupation was listed first as "housewife" but later scribbled over and replaced with the word "none" in the 1930 US census.[40] All of her children, including her stepson, had been born in Texas. Her brother-in-law Marcos and his son Angel did not appear to accompany them on the return trip to Mexico.

The Dávalos Rodríguez family reveals yet another picture of family mobility and shows the multigenerational nature of migration. Maria Martínez Vda. de Dávalos was sixty years old when she returned to Mexico from Philadelphia. Her daughter and her four young grandchildren, ages seven, six, four, and three, accompanied her. Her daughter was recently widowed and had been working as a domestic servant in Philadelphia, and Maria's own occupation was listed as "housewife."[41] On the return trip, a relative of her daughter's deceased husband accompanied them. Together they made their way back to Jalisco. If families had migrated separately across the border at different times throughout the 1920s, they often returned in large groups, experiencing their return migrations as extended and multigenerational families. The Betancourt family was another extended family that made the return trip together, in this case with nine members traveling from Eagle Pass, Texas, to Monte de San Nícolas, Guanajuato. This family was composed of four adult sisters with ages ranging from twenty-three to forty-nine, along with one of the sisters' husbands and four young daughters. Forty-nine-year-old Jesús Gonzalez was the only male in the group. While some families migrated as a nuclear unit including a mother, father, and children, these large extended families were common, as were relatives traveling in pairs.

Pairs of relatives were mostly male, while large extended families, like the Betancourts, often included many women.[42]

In addition to family migration, other forms of social migration occurred in which sets of friends without any apparent kinship traveled to Mexico and often returned together. Victoriano Valtierra and Melquiades López, both originally from Guanajuato, worked first in Saginaw, Michigan, and then in Detroit before returning to Mexico. They had each first migrated to the United States at the age of twenty and lived just a couple of houses down from each other as lodgers on N. Washington Avenue in Saginaw. In 1930, both were employed by an auto foundry, and though the census listed each as lodgers living without relatives in the United States, both were married; their wives had likely remained in Mexico.[43]

The majority of migrants traveling to and from the United States were males, but evidence from the Laredo train manifest suggest that many extended families, groups of women, and siblings also returned together. Furthermore, it should not be assumed that young men who migrated alone were unattached. Even if unmarried, migrant males were part of extended family networks that they supported and that supported them either from within Mexico or north of the border. Women traveled alone as well, but not nearly as often as men. Only four women on this manifest returned to Mexico completely on their own without any relatives or children. Four others traveled as single mothers with one child each. All other women traveled with their partners, children, or extended family networks.

The train manifest from Laredo also contains details about the type of labor each returning migrant had performed while in the United States. Seventy-five percent of males were listed as being "jornaleros de campo" or fieldworkers, even if they had lived in places where they were likely engaged in some industrial labor. Only seven of the women who were listed had occupations other than "su hogar," or "her home"; these were a seamstress, cook, laundress, chambermaid, servant, a general employee, and businesswoman. Rail and factory labor were other common occupations for men, while there were also migrants listed with the skilled occupations, such as mechanics and carpenters. Jobs other than fieldworker were most commonly listed for those returning from cities like Detroit and Chicago.

In sum, the largest group of migrants returning to Mexico through Laredo on this train were male agricultural workers, but women and children made up half of those returning. Labor status was likely self-reported and might not have captured the full range of professions and the complexity of migrant livelihoods and labor strategies. Many migrants working in agriculture throughout the Midwest and beyond engaged in seasonal agriculture and would supplement this labor with work in other industries. Informal labor was also likely not captured fully by train manifests. Women's essential but unpaid labor (cooking, childcare, laundry), and their income as small scale or informal market vendors, would be subsumed under the category of housewife. As previously mentioned, listing migrants' labor status would give Mexican officials an idea of the types of jobs repatriates would could perform.

In addition to gender, age, employment, and family status, we also know the dates of arrival to the United States for a subset of Laredo migrants. The overwhelming majority of migrants returning through Laredo had arrived to the United States between 1927 and 1929, with 38 percent of them arriving in 1928. At first glance this suggests that most of these Mexican citizens were very recent arrivals to the United States. Evidence from border crossing records for some of these same migrants, however, reveal that many had repeatedly entered the United States starting as early as 1909. The manifest captured the most recent arrival date, but combined with other data we can see that while stays were often short, they were often also multiple over a long period of time. The frequency of arrivals between 1927 and 1929 coincides with the last big wave of migration before the onset of the Great Depression. Train manifests from Juárez and Nogales, however, point to another wave of Mexican migration to the United States in 1923 and 1924. Migrants hailing from the US West and Southwest generally lived in heavily Mexican US cities like Los Angeles and San Antonio for longer periods of time than those in the Midwest, and like their compatriots returning through Laredo, many of them traveled between the United States and Mexico within family units and supported by social networks.

There are some general similarities between groups of migrants traveling through Laredo, Nogales, and Ciudad Juárez, but there are also notable differences and distinct regional trends. In general, migrants returning through Nogales and Ciudad Juárez were mostly young adults, except for a slightly greater percentage of adults above the age of forty traveling through Ciudad Juárez. A greater percentage of women returned though Nogales and Ciudad Juárez as well. Women made up 35 percent of Nogales migrants and 36.4 percent of Juárez migrants (as compared to 24 percent of those returning through Laredo). Notably, more women over the age of forty also returned through Nogales and Juárez. There were also greater percentages of children traveling in the Juárez and Nogales groups as compared to the Laredo group.

Children accounted for 33.3 percent of total returning migrants through Nogales and 43 precent of those returning through Juárez. Repatriates hailing from Los Angeles to Mexico's interior of Mexico via Nogales and Ciudad Juárez also reveal a strong pattern of return family migration. Of the 120 repatriates leaving through Nogales in October of 1931, 30 repatriates traveled alone while 26 family units traveled together, including 18 families with minors. Of the 242 repatriates leaving through Ciudad Juárez, 45 repatriates traveled alone while 53 groups of families repatriated together, including 39 families with minors.

Migrants returning though Nogales and Juárez were older, included more women and children, and traveled more in family units than their Laredo counterparts. These patterns confirm the presence of more established patterns of migration to the Southwest. Migrants coming back through Laredo from the Midwest and Eastern United States were likely to have more cases of pioneering migrations of individuals rather than families. Growing Mexican-American communities created an environment of support networks for migrant families, and the range of occupational work available for both genders was much wider in the Southwest. Mexican schools and other community organizations were also much more prevalent in the Southwest United States in comparison to the smaller Mexican colonies in the Midwest and Northern cities. There were also distinct regional patterns for those returning through the three different ports of entry and exit that reveal the most common geographic paths of migration.

Whereas migrants returning through Laredo had come from a broad swath of land between the Midwest and Eastern United States, migrants traveling through Juárez and Nogales hailed mostly from the region around Los Angeles. While the majority of these migrants appeared to have lived near Los Angeles before their departure, migrants catching the train there had lived throughout California and the West before returning to Mexico during the era of repatriation. However, like those traveling through Laredo, their journeys from communities across the border and within the United States and then back and forth to Mexico spanned many miles.

A series of tables in the appendix indicates different states of birth for adult migrants. Jalisco, Michoacán, and Guanajuato emerge once again as important sending and receiving states for Mexican migrants throughout the 1920s and 1930s. The key difference is that migrants from central and northern Mexican states were more likely to travel through Juárez, while Mexicans from the western states used the Nogales port for both exit and return. Those traveling through Juárez were overwhelmingly from the states of Zacatecas, Aguascalientes, and Durango. Migrants from the more central-northern states might have taken advantage of government-subsidized rail fare more than those living closer to the border, since they could more easily travel by foot or car back to their hometowns. Train manifests illustrate the truly long journeys that migrants took—especially notable in an era when travel necessitated considerable planning. For example, migrations stretching from northern central Mexico all the way to the west coast of California reflect the lengths to which migrant families went to build their cross-border and regional livelihoods. Such migrations, requiring more money for the longer distances traveled, would have been impacted severely by economic crisis.

When adding information from census records to train manifest records we get a more complete snapshot of migrant occupations prior to their repatriation to Mexico. Many migrants were listed as general laborers, but some specifics indicate that migrants were working on railroads, ranches and farms, in cement mills, and in construction. Jobs for women were harder to uncover for this sample, many again being listed as housewife, but as mentioned in chapter 2, we know that fruit picking, cannery work and work as domestic servants would have been common occupations for migrant women living in Southern California. One woman, Celia de Ortega, who had migrated to the United States in 1913 and lived in New Mexico, then Texas, and then Compton, California, was listed as a soft-drink seller in the 1927 Compton City directory.[44] One of her eldest daughters was employed in a fish cannery. Only Celia and her youngest son returned to Mexico on a train from Juárez in 1931, potentially being separated from her husband and five older children who appear to have remained in the United States.

Train manifests for Nogales and Juárez serve as an invaluable source of information for the birthplaces of migrants and their children. Taken together with details about age, these birthplaces tell us a great deal not only about family composition and structure, but also about the actual geography of Mexican migrations. Tracing the birthplaces of children born to Mexicans in Mexico and the United States sketches out cross-country and binational migrations when migrant voices are otherwise unavailable. Additionally, the birthplaces of children returning to Mexico during October of 1931 confirm and illustrate what scholars of repatriation have previously argued: that the great repatriations of the 1930s did not simply consist of sending Mexican migrants home to Mexico, but actually resulted in a generation of Mexican-American children—US citizens—leaving their birth nation.[45] Lastly, by examining the birthplaces of migrant children, it also becomes clear that Mexican migration was creating binational families with differentiated legal statuses among family members, a phenomenon that would impact and shape Mexican migrations in the future.

Most children who were born to Mexican parents while in the United States were born in California, but the states of Texas, New Mexico, Utah, Nevada, Colorado, Arizona, and Idaho were also all represented in birthplace listings. Sixty-five percent of total children on the Juárez train were born in the United States, while 62.5 percent of children on the Nogales train were American-born. While some children, like William Nuñez, would eventually return to the United States, it is difficult to know how many others returned to their birth country.

The birthplaces listed for children born to Mexican parents provide insight into family settlement. Birthplaces concentrate in Southern California. When examined at a family level, we also see that every family with a child born in the United States would from that point on have to negotiate future border crossings as a binational family with mixed citizenship status. This meant that documenting citizenship, whether Mexican or American, was now more complicated. As will be seen in the following chapter, binational families, especially those undergoing strained marital relationships, faced a host of problems when crossing the border. Whether having to prove child custody claims or evidence of marriage or marriage dissolution, having the right documents would increasingly be necessary as the border tightened during the 1930s. Documents were critical for migrant lives and livelihoods across borders and the lack of proper documents could shape migrations by delaying crossings at the border for days or even months.

Parents and children in migrant families were highly likely to have different citizenship status and citizenship status was also varied among siblings within a family. In fact, families where children were born in different countries and different states provide the most striking evidence for the diverse geographical journeys of migrants throughout the 1920s and the implications for family return migration, separation, and reunification in the 1930s. The journeys also demonstrate how the cycles of life—birth, death, and overall changes in family composition—continued throughout migrations and across borders.

For example, the birthplaces and ages of the Baltazar family, returning on a train to Mexico from Los Angeles via Nogales, provides a possible sketch of the family's migration and also illustrates the mixed citizenship status that

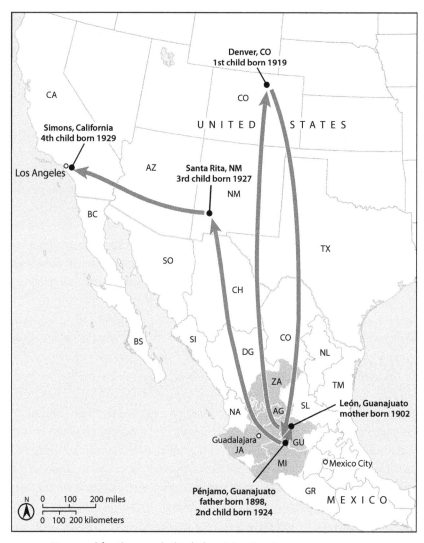

MAP 5. Binational family routes by birthplace. Map: Ben Pease.

often made migrations and return migrations challenging to negotiate. The father was born in Pénjamo, Guanajuato, in 1898, while the mother was born in León, Guanajuato, in 1902. It appears that at some point both parents migrated to Denver, Colorado, whether separately or together. They had their first child in Denver in 1919. This family would already be negotiating the mixed citizenship status of their family after their first child. It appears, however, that the Baltazars did not simply migrate to Denver and stay there, for at some point, at least the mother traveled back to Pénjamo; she had her second child there in 1924. The family moved back to the United States, where in 1927 they had their third child and second daughter in Santa Rita, New Mexico. They migrated once more to Simons, California, a company town and the site of a brickyard that housed a large Mexican community, where sometime between 1927 and 1929 they had their youngest daughter. The train lists do not reveal details about the Baltazar family beyond birthplaces and ages, but what we can see is that this migrant family was composed of both Mexican and US citizens, with children born in three different US cities and one in Mexico. Their return migration during the Depression was just one part of their larger family history of migration.

FAMILY AND WOMEN

Given the lack of records, estimates of total repatriated families are next to impossible to gather, but a bit of context may be gleaned from the statistic that 40,687 children under the age of fourteen left the United States for Mexico during the year 1931, with 8,715 going to Jalisco, Michoacán, and Guanajuato.[46] The 40,687 is likely an underestimate but even then, it lends insight into the number of families who traveled during just one year of repatriations. That many of them were US citizens raises important questions about how Mexican migrants were expected to be temporary, and the degree to which mass repatriation, fueled by the uncertainties of economic crisis and increasing nativism in parts of the United States, perpetuated (sometimes by force) the notion that Mexican migrants were unusually and naturally mobile and were highly expendable.[47] This notion seemed to give both Mexican and US American societies excuses to justify the alternating mass recruitment and removal of Mexicans and their families without regard to the finer details of what that relocation required, the material and psychological impact that it could have, not to mention the reality of the legal complexities that such families posed to rigid frameworks of nationality and citizenship.

As we have already seen, letters to Mexican presidents written during the early years of the crisis illustrate the migrants' creative strategies to resolve their economic struggles. An epistolary tradition of seeking favors and intervention from presidents had long existed in Mexico and was increasingly characterized by language of demand and expectation as well as petition after the Mexican Revolution. With the new spaces created by the revolutionary rhetoric of Mexican nationalism, Mexican citizens would participate in a type of call and response with Mexican leaders in which their promises to uphold the ideals of the Revolution entitled them to an audience with the highest official in the land. Despite residing across the border, migrants also saw this epistolary avenue available to them and articulated their expectations of the Mexican government powerfully throughout the 1930s and 1940s.

In the throes of economic difficulty, having recently lost her husband and finding that a brother in the United States could not support her and two children, Micaela Amador wrote to the Secretary of Government Portes Gil from Las Vegas, Nevada. She was left "without a home, and without money to support her family." Micaela had read in a newspaper that a new school for those who had little money was opening up in Mexico City. In an expression of patriotic lobbying, she explained that she didn't want her children to grow up in the United States but rather in Mexico, so that they would "love their flag and serve their country." She didn't just want to repatriate, she had a plan and attempted to persuade the former president to help her put her plan into action. Like many others who wrote for assistance, she was told to look for financial aid from charitable organizations in the United States to help her get to the border, where the Mexican consular service could then cover her travel expenses into Mexico.[48]

Micaela, a recent widow with a young family and no means of support, was similar to others writing to government officials between 1930 and 1934. Five themes pertaining to family emerge in the letters written during the worst part of the Great Depression: large family size, spousal abandonment, illness, the death of a family member, or being stranded in between their point of departure in the United States and their final destination. All migrants specifically asked for money or "passes" to cross the border, with this latter term usually implying a combination of financial aid and the expediting of legal documents.

The plight of single women is revealed in many of these letters to the president. Emilia Siller Falcon petitioned the president for help on behalf of her sister who had been abandoned in Chicago.[49] If they did not have family in the United States, lone women faced challenging circumstances during economic crises, suffering from decreased work opportunities and reduced access to welfare relief. Tepoxina Pintada Vda. de Ferrer, from San Antonio, showed appreciation for the US "government aid" that she had received over the past year due to her spinal arthritis, and said she "understood why she shouldn't be supported indefinitely." She counted on the president to help her obtain rail tickets to Chiapas, where summer weather might ease her physical pain.[50] While many women left Mexico in the 1920s to reunite with their husbands, two women writing to President Rodríguez in 1934 now hoped to leave the United States to get away from their husbands, including Sara Barrón, mentioned above, as well as another woman who, as part of the fall-out from a fight with her mother-in-law, lost her washing machine, her only means of supporting herself. Both women, whose family circumstances were exacerbated by the hardship of the economic crisis, struggled to provide for themselves and preferred to return to Mexico.[51]

The cases above demonstrate the impacts of economic crisis, repatriation and deportation, and the complicated border crossing requirements for Mexicans families who faced challenging separations and reunifications. Many migrants, whether single or with family members, migrated to the United States and back to Mexico without government assistance or approval; in fact, many migrated beyond the purview of one or both governments altogether. Still, the stories suggest that family migrations, which required planning, legal documents, and financial resources, were a critical feature of Mexican migration in the 1920s and 1930s. Petitions to the Mexican presidents also remind us that repatriation was not a process that began and stopped on the northern side of the US-Mexico border. Mexican officials had to reckon with the sheer mass of repatriates streaming into the country, and the Mexican public had to contend with these returned migrants as well.

As mentioned earlier, border cities such as El Paso/Juárez especially felt the impact of the return exodus of Mexicans, but so did the center-western states. In June of 1931, the Student Federation of Jalisco wrote to President Ortiz Rubio requesting support in transporting *repatriados* out of the capital of Guadalajara, saying that "daily, repatriates from different points in the United States are arriving to this capital in very bad conditions and with their families."[52] The group had been working to provide recently arrived migrants with help and jobs but could not keep up with the influx of people. Those coming back were not all healthy, experienced easily mobile workers. Just as they had been perceived as naturally mobile workers in the United States, migrant families faced similar perceptions back home. But the trains carried many children and families, including the elderly, sick, and poor. While some migrants took advantage of free train tickets to Mexico, others found that they had missed their opportunity for assisted repatriation. Mexican and US funds for repatriation efforts declined over time and migrants would need to plead their cases even more vigorously as the Great

FIGURE 3. Deportees Ana Maria Gonzales, Soledad Zaragoza and Dorothy Barber in a railroad car, Los Angeles, 1935. Photo: *Los Angeles Times* Photographic Archive, Library Special Collections, Charles E. Young Research Library, UCLA.

Depression continued. The logistical challenges of repatriates desiring to repatriate entire families, as opposed to one or two people, would fuel a number of desperate pleas for assistance to top government officials.

In Mexico, private charitable organizations, individuals, and the Mexican government (largely through aid given in the United States by Mexican consuls) all contributed to the transportation of repatriates from the border to the interior of Mexico. Aid societies in Mexico and the Mexican government had provided assistance to repatriated Mexicans in the past on a smaller scale. In May of 1929, even prior to the economic crash, the Mexican Cruz Azul aided those returning to Mexico. The Secretary of Gobernación, per presidential agreement, also declared the government's commitment to helping Mexicans in the United States who needed assistance, doing so "due to the hostilities carried out against them by immigration authorities."[53] In Gómez

Palacio, Durango, charitable ladies' associations provided aid to people returning to their hometowns, what was described as "the interminable caravan of repatriates that continues to pass through this city," composed of families returning from the United States in cars, "very many of which no longer have tires, and in terrible conditions."[54] Hundreds of families arrived on trains to Ciudad Juárez where some were given bread and even money.[55] Repatriates stranded in Monterrey, not having quite enough resources to get to their hometowns, set up "traveling bazaars" where they would sell anything they could to make money they desperately needed after arriving to the city impoverished.[56]

The response was both positive and negative, for where repatriates inundated some cities and stretched resources, other regions welcomed the influx of what was perceived to be a group of repatriates with "modern machines and experience acquired during the time that they worked in the United States."[57] The potential benefits of return migrations would be seen even more favorably during the 1940s and helped propel the binational arrangement for Mexican braceros in the United States. But in the troubled economic times of the 1930s, repatriates were often perceived as a threat to Mexican labor stability. Agents from the Mexican Office of Migration voiced their concern about the concentration of so many unemployed Mexicans living in misery and subject to communist influence. They raised suspicions that repatriates were potential agitators and that together with discontent rail workers were like an "accumulation of gun powder near the tracks, that if not taken seriously, any spark could be dangerous."[58] These fears contrasted the belittling characterizations of repatriates' capacity for political radicalism from a conservative observer in western Mexico: "The emigrant of our country doesn't have the capacity nor the character, nor the conviction to convert himself into a missionary for communism."[59] A range of characterizations attributed to migrants by observers on both sides of the border revealed that throughout the anxious period of economic crisis, repatriates were a wildcard, an unknown, alternatively seen as a financial strain, a financial boon, as politically savvy or as ignorant and ambivalent citizens. In both countries, characterizations of Mexican migrants shifted to fit the purpose of either country's use and tolerance for them. Migrants were often seen as outsiders, with their citizenship and belonging questioned in both countries, leaving them vulnerable to being seen as disposable or second-class citizens. And yet if repatriates were seen as returning with evident savings and something to show for their time in the United States, they might also be perceived as an untapped resource for the Mexican government. One editorialist questioned the real reasons behind the Mexican government's willingness to encourage repatriation: "Do they call on them to rejoin part of the Mexican family, or to leave their money in the cash registers of the office of migration?"[60]

Despite the Mexican government paying 60 percent of train tickets for repatriates enticing them with colonization schemes in underpopulated agricultural areas in need of development, and despite the presidential propaganda that welcomed Mexico's prodigal sons and daughters, it remained to be seen whether Mexican migrants would have a place in the nation, or at the very least, whether Mexico would indeed offer them a better life. It also remained to be seen as to whether FDR's New Deal or Lázaro Cárdenas's post-revolutionary Mexico could provide enough to keep Mexican migrants on one side of the border or the other.

. . .

During the height of the Great Depression, border crossings and migratory livelihoods were marked by deep instability. Central to the history of this troubled and despair-inducing period of migration are stories about family. While the movement of families predating the Great Depression remains largely hidden from the documentary record, the removal and return of migrant families during the early 1930s has always been central to the telling of Mexican migration and hardship during the era. Details about how families actually suffered through the economic crisis and how repatriation was actually carried out emerge from letters written by migrants, train manifests of repatriates, and newspaper reports, and give us more of an understanding about how migrants experienced the period. While excellent studies have provided details on how government officials on each side of the border acted on behalf of migrants during the crisis, a deeper look into migrant lives reveals that repatriation and deportation, return and removal, are only part of broader migration histories. Details about birthplaces of US-born children and Mexican parents reveal the scope and complexity of migration.

The boom period of Mexican migration in the 1920s yielded a rapidly growing migrant population in the United States that then faced enormous challenges as a result of the tightening Mexican-US border. Migrants previously welcomed to vital US agricultural landscapes now faced local efforts toward their removal and witnessed broad propaganda campaigns encouraging them to leave and attempting to convince them that they might be better off in their birth country. Mexican sending communities also felt the impact of the Great Depression as the economic crisis led directly to both the disintegration and reintegration of families. The impact of such dislocations was not simply material for both the migrants and the governments involved, but likely also had a critical psychological impact on migrants and prompted a serious consideration about the place of migrants in the national projects and development of both countries.

After all, this is not just the story about expendable and flexible migrants in a self-regulating binational labor market, but rather a story about binational families with binational livelihoods at stake. Whether migrants boarded repatriation trains or tried to wait out the crisis in the United States, sometimes abandoned by their loved ones, entire families and communities on both sides of the border were affected. Families composed of both men and women, and bicultural if not binational children, were split apart and forced to navigate evolving bureaucracies in order to keep their families together. Children and teenagers born in the United States would "return" to a country they might have never even been to before. Like William Nuñez, some would eventually come back to the United States after many years to take up residence in their native country. Children like William would grow up to be the Mexican-American adults whose lives were shaped by two nations. William spent his formative first eleven years in the United States, his next nine years in Mexico, and his young adulthood in the United States again. Experiences such as these could nominally be characterized by the terms "repatriation" and "deportation" to match the experiences of their parents, but a potentially more insidious process took place that we might call *depatriation*. Despite the years that families spent living and working in the United States, and despite their children having American birth certificates, concerted efforts toward repatriation and deportation by state officials suggested that inclusion was highly conditional. Migrants pushed where they could, and sometimes found that mechanisms for inclusion and exclusion were highly flexible. Federico Camarillo and his wife Cristina Espinosa entered the United States in 1941 with their two US-born daughters (eighteen and fourteen years old). Their purpose: "to reside." They would join Federico's mother. Listed under "Ever in the US" was the answer, "Yes, 1918 until 10/23/31." The binational Camarillos were returning to the United States ten years after their repatriation to Mexico.

For those children and young adults who had spent their first years and perhaps the majority of their lives in the United States, the era of repatriation is better described as an era of removal. For many other migrants, those who chose willingly to board trains as part of a larger binational migration strategy, albeit in an era of extreme pressures, the era might have been characterized as a return. While the return was fraught with challenges, it also signaled a welcoming from a nation that was more ready to receive them and make room for them than it had been in the turbulent revolutionary decades of the past. The inclusion of Mexicans into the Mexican national project, though, was also conditional. Mexicans could not be expelled from their own country, but local observers and government officials questioned the character of such migrants and expected them to contribute to the agricultural development of the country. Mexican migrants, in fact, from the 1930s on, would be met with steep expectations in terms of the knowledge and resources that they brought back to their *patria*.

The displacing first years of the 1930s, however, did not signal the end of the crisis or the end of the repatriations and returns. Beseeching and desperate letters continued to arrive at the National Palace in Mexico City, to the White House in Washington, DC, and to consular representatives of both nations. Migrants continued to communicate their dire circumstances to officials, at times familiarizing themselves with the rhetoric of the New Deal and the Revolutionary Family so as to make more forceful pleas for assistance to one or both nations. They did so with the expectation that, as citizens, they were owed assistance no matter what side of the border they found themselves on. And yet, especially, in cases of intrafamily strife, or of complicated mixed-status migrations, the state had no answer for them. Families who had managed to hold tight in the early years of the Great Depression, either by finding a way to stay in the United States together or leaving together on repatriation trains to Mexico, would fracture and split apart as the economic crisis continued throughout the 1930s.

CHAPTER FOUR

Good Presidents, Bad Husbands, and Dead Fathers

TRIALS OF BINATIONAL LIVING, 1934–1940

Dear Uncle Sam or President,

Hello? I am writing you this letter, asking my country for help to go back. Because we are suffering of hunger. There's eight children, seven born in the state of Iowa. My father, mother and the small baby are of Mexico. When we came the American Consel was suppose[d] to hel[p] us the rest of the road in Mexico. The Mexican Consel didn't help my father the rest of the road. Because we had a car. Then my father had to sell the [car] in which had travel all of the road from Iowa to El Paso, to travel by train to Nochistlan, Zac. Where we are yet suffering of hunger and education. Write me the answer to this address, Nochistlan, Zac.

Yours truly, friend, Nicha Rodriguez[1]

Dear President,

I am writing this letter asking you a great favor which I will tell you in the following. My two sisters and I were born in Mexico (all the family was) as we look back to our childhood days the more it make me to ask you and my sisters beg me to write to you, My President. I think you are wondering what my favor is, well is very simple, My President, that we haven't enough money to go to visit our country for a few months. We come out of school in June and go back September, so My president, can you help us with the train fare please! (My sister is thirteen and the other one sixteen and I am fifteen).

My Dear father is dead and if you only knew what you would do, three girls who want to see their country very, very much and visit their relatives. My Dear President, please don't disappoint us. We will be waiting for your answer.

My President, I know you can help us you are the Father of Our country and that is why I ask you.

I will close my letter dreaming of your answer.

Sincerely your

Nahum Cervantes.

PS. Maybe I am asking too much but I wish I could see you in person and your dear wife.[2]

IN 1936, IOWA-BORN NICHA RODRIGUEZ wrote to President Roosevelt, detailing the events of her family's harrowing repatriation to Mexico. Having traveled the long road from Iowa to El Paso and then to Nochistlán, Zacatecas, Nicha was "suffering of hunger and education" and was appealing to her president for some help to return to her home country. Across the border in the United States, and writing to Mexican President Lázaro Cárdenas in 1939, Nahum Cervantes also appealed to her president for help in returning to her birth country. Nicha and Nahum, two young girls suffering from poverty in a foreign land, with no money to return home, appealed to the highest authorities of their respective nations to help them in their migrations.

Each letter reveals fascinating details about the binational lives that Mexicans and Mexican Americans lived, the ways in which poverty, citizenship, and gender intersected and made for challenging migrations, and the appeals that migrants made to government officials. From Nicha's letter we gain more insight into disruptive repatriations in a time of economic crisis. While Nicha's family had just enough money to begin their journey back to Mexico, they barely had the means to get all the way to their final destination. Although Mexico was home to Nicha's parents, she and her six siblings longed to return to their home in Iowa. She wrote to the person she thought might be able to best assist her: US President Franklin Delano Roosevelt. She was just one of hundreds of thousands of US citizens writing to their beloved President. Whether it was the cult of personality that FDR inspired, or perhaps because no other obvious government official might help with such a plight, Nicha believed that President Roosevelt could help during her family's troubling time.

Nahum, too, saw writing to her nation's top leader as a means to the assistance she needed. Mexican President Lázaro Cárdenas was also heralded as a man of the people, and had made promises to lead Mexico out of an era of crisis and into an era of reform where he could deliver on the promises of the Mexican Revolution. Writing from San Jose, California, fifteen-year-old Nahum wrote to President Cárdenas in English, calling him the father of her country, petitioning him after her own father had died, leaving the family without the resources to return to Mexico for a summer visit. Writing in English to "her" Mexican President, emphasizing her Mexican citizenship, she expressed nostalgia and longing for her birth country. Her father's death and economic crisis had combined to halt the family's return visits to Mexico and the Cervantes girls were now dependent on a benevolent president to pay for their train fare.

Nicha and Nahum were part of a larger group of women, men, and children in binational migrant families who found themselves in dire straits during the latter half of the 1930s. The repatriation and deportation of hundreds of thousands of Mexicans, the increased vigilance and restriction of migration along the US-Mexico border, and the cost of travel were all key factors in prohibiting the previously common circular migration and immigration of US and Mexican citizens across the international border. Women, who already faced many obstacles to entering the United States, found that their ability to use migration as an adaptive strategy was further undercut as the economic crisis wore on.[3] Women who faced the loss of male family members through death, abandonment, and separation were sometimes abused, or found themselves in otherwise dire circumstances, leading them to reach out to the state for help.

This chapter first examines migration and migrant lives in the latter half of the 1930s in Roosevelt's United States and Cárdenas's Mexico. Continuing an analysis of letters written to government officials from last chapter, this chapter focuses particularly on the ways in which women reached out to representatives of the state and revealed private details of their suffering during economic crisis. I show how the intersection of citizenship, poverty, and gender led to bureaucratic complications for both migrants and the state. The economic dislocations of the 1930s could easily seem to render the needs of Mexican migrants marginal to each state; however, by examining migrant correspondence, we can see that migrants did reach out to negotiate and navigate their binational belonging (and sometime their escape). Especially in the face of "bad" or absent fathers and husbands, women reached out to presidents and consular officials in a particularly gendered way. This chapter also continues the story of binational families who had to navigate a more rigidly enforced border with family members of different citizenship statuses.

Migration to the United States from Mexico between 1930 and 1940 drastically declined from the heavy migration of the 1920s.[4] With decreasing job opportunities, the heavy wave of repatriates returning to Mexico, and the increased efforts toward restriction along the border, Mexicans were not as likely to risk the journey. With the onset of the Great Depression in the United States, border agents were encouraged by the US government to be particularly vigilant towards any "undesirables" trying to enter the country, decreasing the number of "aliens" that entered the country between 1930 and

FIGURE 4. Dorothea Lange, "Crossing the international bridge between Juarez, Mexico and El Paso, Texas," May 1937. Photo: Library of Congress, LC-DIG-fsa-8b31944.

1937 by as many as 1,000,000.[5] While Mexican migration to the United States for the period could be described as having more net out-migration than in-migration, or as having being reduced to a "trickle," numerous border crossings still took place and many more were attempted throughout the period.[6] As can be seen through letters to the consul and presidents, Mexicans, and especially Mexican-Americans who had previously been repatriated or who had family members in the United States, still wanted to migrate to reunite with family members.

Although economic recovery started earlier in Mexico than in the United States, Mexico was once again plunged into recession in 1937.[7] With little money to invest in technological improvements, new landholding peasants were at the mercy of irregular rainy seasons, and could not rely on their crops for sustenance with any certainty.[8] State workers such as telegraph and postal employees went through month-long periods without pay, and domestic servants joined with syndicates to negotiate for higher wages.[9] In almost all cases, potential US investors and merchants were discouraged from bringing their money and business to Jalisco by US consular officials, regardless of the particular product they sold or were interested in.[10]

The purchasing power of Jaliscienses was devastated by low wages and steep prices on imports. Imported dried goods in particular were prohibitively expensive. The US consul at Guadalajara reported that "Staple foods such as beans, rice, coffee and garbanzos, used by the natives have increased considerably, although not in the same proportion." He went on to point out, "a housekeeper with 200 pesos per month now finds that she can buy less than she formerly could with only 140 pesos per month."[11] In 1936, the consul estimated that 85 percent of the consular district's population was of the "laboring classes, of whose average wage is not more than 50 cents per day in terms of American currency."[12] In 1936 it cost about $25 US for a rail ticket from Guadalajara to Nogales, Mexico, where migrants would cross over to Nogales, Arizona, then travel by bus to points in the Western United States.[13] As in previous decades, the trip north (and return trips south) required considerable saving and planning.

CONDITIONS IN THE UNITED STATES

Repatriations and deportations in the early 1930s certainly took a toll on many communities and dramatically reduced the number of Mexican residents in the United States, but many other Mexican migrants were able to continue their lives north of the border, albeit often in impoverished circumstances. Mexican migrants were hit particularly hard since it was more difficult for them to obtain various forms of welfare relief, such as access to WPA employment.[14] Mexicans in agriculture had to endure even more challenges when they found themselves without enough resources to follow the crops and cobble together seasons of work. Families waiting for harvest or other employment and lacking the means to travel could be found living in squalid conditions in Hoovervilles, or shantytowns, across California.[15]

Mexican families and their living conditions came increasingly into view as government officials began to take stock of the housing problems caused by a dramatic increase in "migratory workers." The focus was not, however, particularly on Mexican and Mexican American families, as much as it was on the number of destitute families streaming from the Midwest into California. Dust Bowl migrants had begun to replace the Mexicans who had left, and dramatically transformed the composition of agricultural labor in California.[16] White migrant families came to occupy the attention of social reformers, economists, and sociologists. For example, the principal of a migrant school in the San Joaquin Valley reported that Mexican children, as opposed to "new white children" coming in recently from Texas and Oklahoma, at least had shoes, underwear, and coats.[17]

In a 1939 report on housing conditions among migratory workers for the Division of Immigration and Housing in the state of California, Carey McWilliams reported that Mexicans made up 75 percent of sugar beet workers and 40 percent of those working in peaches and hops. While families were the primary working unit in peaches and hops, mostly single men worked in sugar beets, indicating a shift away from the family labor that had predominated for this crop in the 1920s. The Depression caused other demographic shifts, as indicated by the fact that by 1935 white migrant families easily outnumbered Mexican migrant families in the Imperial Valley.[18] The Mexican families that remained in agriculture were primarily those families where heads of household (mostly men) and their spouses were born in Mexico and had come to California in the in the early 1920s or even before. In a survey of California workers, economist Paul S. Taylor and his research team found that "only 17 families out of the total 122 did not come either directly or indirectly from Mexico," meaning that most heads of households were born in Mexico, and that 17 were of Mexican descent but born in the United States. Though the emphasis was placed on the birthplace for heads of households, it was reported that "most of the women were born in Mexico, too." Nearly all of the families (105 of the 110 for which there was a record of their first arrival) had a first entry into the United States before 1930, suggesting that families who had been in the United States longer were the ones most likely to try to weather the Great Depression in place, even under difficult circumstances.[19]

Some families could subsist on agricultural migration year-round, whereas others would have to endure temporary stints of financial assistance. A survey of cotton camps in 1937 reported that out of 150 families only 15 had gone

FIGURE 5. Russell Lee, "Mexican girl [sic], carrot worker, Edinburg, Texas," February 1939. Photo: Library of Congress, LC-USF33–011974-M1.

on welfare relief. One of the families that was interviewed had come to California in 1923. Between 1930 and 1934 they would work in cotton for five or six months, migrate to Tracy to work peas for three months, then to Clarksburg for two months in beets, and finally to San Leandro for work in apricots. The father, mother, maternal grandmother, and oldest son were born in Mexico, with a six-year-old son and a seventeen-day-old daughter born in the United States. The family was reported to have lived in "exceptional standards of comfort and cleanliness."

In contrast to the family described above, another family reportedly lived in a filthy cabin that had been provided rent-free by the grower. The family of eight suffered health problems and one child in particular suffered from a spinal defect, while all were suspected of having tuberculosis. The father worked in cotton in Madera, California, as well as in peas and berries on the coast. The mother and some of the older children also worked from time to time. The family had first arrived in 1921 and returned to Mexico in 1926 for two years. They travelled back to the United States in 1929. At one point they were able to keep three years of continuous residence in Madera County but were splitting time between the coast and the valley during the three years prior to the survey. The family had come to the attention of researchers because of one of their young boys had spinal problems that required surgery in Fresno, California in 1927, and in Guadalajara in 1928. The family had been on relief when the father lost his job, but only for six weeks, which considering the size of the family, low cumulative wages, and health problems, was fairly remarkable.[20]

Some Mexican and Mexican-American families such as this did receive relief through the New Deal. The Federal Emergency Relief Administration and the State Relief Administration of California did not technically bar non-citizens from access to New Deal relief programs; however, when possible, efforts were made to push Mexicans off relief rolls. This was partially accomplished by giving Mexican families less of an allotment of aid than non-Mexican families.[21] Mexicans might also work on WPA projects, unless they were found to be undocumented immigrants, who were barred from the program in 1936. By 1939 non-citizens were fully banned from work on WPA projects.[22]

As will be discussed later in the chapter, families were particularly at risk when a male head of household died or abandoned his family. The chances of getting aid or welfare relief of some kind were, however, greatly enhanced if families had US-born children. Mothers with dependent children had been able to secure various forms of welfare relief throughout the 1930s, and letters from relief agencies such as the Los Angeles County Department of Charities to the Mexican consul at Guadalajara suggest that many of those on public assistance were mothers and children who found themselves in poverty as the result of either the desertion or death of the father. Men were occasionally represented in the letters as well, but only after prolonged unemployment or after an injury or illness.

PETITIONS TO THE PRESIDENT

Despite the increasing nativism that threatened to bar immigrants from relief, the growth in social welfare programs during the New Deal provided hope for millions of immigrants and Americans alike; so too did the charismatic president of the people, Franklin Delano Roosevelt. It was the combination of Roosevelt's personal appeal and New Deal programs that led the public to write three times the number of letters to him than to any previous president.[23] Like Nicha Rodriguez, Rosie Garcia also reached out to the president in 1939 with the hopes that he could help facilitate her return migration to the United States, a letter quoted in full at the beginning of the

Introduction. Rosie recounted her trips back and forth across the border, the death of her father, the chronic illness of her four US-born sisters, the poverty of herself and her husband and their lack of work in Mexico, and her desire for her family to return to the United States. Twenty-one when she wrote this letter to President Roosevelt from the Mexican state of Jalisco, she asked for a passport to her "dear California." In the closing statements of her letter she wrote, "Do your very best to send for us. Answer my letter as soon as you can. . . . I know you can do what we want."[24]

The fact that a young Mexican woman wrote to President Roosevelt asking for him to "send for her" seems incredible, colorful, unlikely, maybe far-fetched, and unique. However, the story she conveys—one of family dislocation, economic hardship, heartache, binational living, and divided patriotism—is emblematic of experiences that many Mexican families faced during the 1920s and 30s. In fact, Rosie Garcia was one of many migrants who petitioned top government officials in both the United States and Mexico for help to relocate family or reunite with relatives across the US-Mexico border. Nicha Rodriguez, along with Rosie Garcia, Antonia Vazquez, and Mary Torres, all wrote to President Roosevelt between 1935 and 1940 asking him if he could aid in their migration to the United States.[25]

Mary C. Enriquez chose a different top official, writing to US Vice President Henry Wallace in December of 1941. Having been encouraged by the Vice President's recent visit to Guadalajara and inspired by a shared Christian faith, Mary described the circumstances that had left her, an American-born woman, stranded in Mexico.

Your Honor, I know you possess a kind heart and I am quite sure that you are a member of the Episcopal Church, so under the Great Power of Our Mighty Lord, in this city there lives a poor American family who begs a hand from you. I am an American, a Public School Teacher graduate from New York. I married a Mexican in that city in 1924, and we have five American children all born there. During the terrible crisis of 1931, my husband who had been living in NY for a period of twelve years, lost his job, and the Public Welfare of New York sent us here, place of birth of my husband. Since that time, we overcome all kind of endurances and bitterness. My husband does not work, for there is no work at all, and my poor children are in the most deplorable situation.[26]

She went on to state, "I want to be repatriated back to New York," stating that she could work as a school teacher if she were to return home. In addition to stating her case, and demonstrating that she could contribute to society upon her return if given the chance, she emphasized not only her poverty but the responsibility owed to her by her home country. "I am an American and I know that my country wouldn't leave us disappear amidst the shadow of hunger and starvation." In an approach that viewed state assistance as an obligation but also welcomed it as a gift, Mary closed her letter with the following statement: "Maybe your decision will be my best Christmas Present, for I am sure I shall have none." Closing with an endearing, if not tragic statement, Mary tried to appeal to the humanity, faith, and generosity of Vice President Wallace.

Seven years earlier, Magdalena E. Ayala sent a similar request to the Mexican President from her home in Alamo, Colorado.[27] Writing to President Cárdenas on Christmas Day of 1934, Magdalena asked him for help in repatriating herself, her husband, and their four children. Magdalena, a school teacher in Mexico prior to her migration, opened her letter by explaining that she had served the Mexican government "in the year 1920, having in my charge a girls' school in Coeneo, Michoacán." Her husband had been out of work for a year and they lacked resources to make the trip south. They had only a car that was in need of repairs and gas, and they asked the president for any assistance he might be able to provide so that they might get back to Mexico. After living in Colorado for nine years and giving birth to three of her four children in the coal mining regions of Del Carbon, Walsenburg, and Rocky Mountain, desperate economic conditions led Magdalena to put faith in the Mexican president. It is unclear if she ever received a response; many letter writers in similar circumstances often did not. Letter writers would either be informed that their correspondence was being forwarded to another department, that they should direct their requests to the nearest Mexican consul in the United States, or told simply that there were no funds for such repatriation efforts.[28] In very rare cases, letter writers were asked for more details in order to facilitate the distribution of rail passes and additional aid.[29]

As with his US American counterpart, more letters from migrants streamed into the Palacio Nacional during Cárdenas's administration than during the administrations before his. Cárdenas cultivated a personalist presidency that attracted an almost celebrity-like following. Mexicans around the country sent letters to Cárdenas, wishing him well, asking for small gifts, and most importantly using the framework of revolutionary reform to deploy their own demands of the government. While in many ways he held a similar appeal to Roosevelt, the context was different: the combination of Cárdenas's populism and charismatic rhetoric promised the return of the ideals fought for in the Mexican Revolution.[30]

Cárdenas, like Roosevelt, was seen as a man who would act on behalf of the people, and the public perceived a kindness in him, and a particular generosity directed toward the poor.[31] Sixty-five-year-old Refugio Espinosa from Laredo, Texas, broke her leg, found herself without money for food, was turned away by a local relief agency, and was neglected by the Mexican consul. At this point she wrote to Cárdenas, telling him that she had heard that he was a "very charitable person who hurts for the poor."[32] Other letter writers, such as Agustin Valle, expressed excitement that was generated around the Cárdenas administration's capacity for reform, telling the president that he desired to "return to my country, to be part of the history of Mexico in its time of reconstruction and sovereignty."[33] Migrants who hoped to return to Mexico employed a combination of what was likely genuine support and patriotic strategy in their letters, frequently heralding Cárdenas's wide-ranging accomplishments. Ricardo Renteria, for example, expressed faith in his government, "in your good person and patrimony, which he had demonstrated toward all of the Republic."[34] Filomena Reyes, originally from Chapala, Jalisco, wrote to the president on behalf of her husband and her children, telling him that he was the only person that could help and that God would repay him if he did so. She and her family wanted to return to Mexico from San Bernardino, California, but didn't have the means to do so.[35] Manuel Salinas wrote from Pueblo, Colorado, not only asking President Cárdenas to be repatriated but also for scholarships for his children.[36]

The approaches and themes of the letters for repatriation were varied. While some professed abject poverty, many offered their services to the state or even suggested ways in which they could contribute or offset the cost of their own repatriations. Flora Guajardo, writing from Corcoran, California, with "East Side Cash Store Box 536" as a return address, wrote to President Cárdenas but assured him that she did not want her repatriation to cost the state. "Seeing as how I find myself very poor and accompanied by all of my family, and I don't want to be a cost to the nation at all, since I can't help, I want to sell the history of my life, if you allow it." Her life story featured the "sacred date of the centenary of independence" and the November 20th call to revolution. It was also a story about a "bad father" and she, as the innocent daughter, would sell the story of her life in exchange for some help from the president. Flora appealed to Cárdenas, asking his forgiveness for her audacity, and counted on his generosity that she "discovered every chance she got to open the newspaper."[37]

In addition to requesting financial and legal assistance in repatriation, migrants and aspiring repatriates also petitioned Cárdenas specifically for lands so that they might establish agricultural colonies. One of the hallmarks of the Cárdenas administration was the redistribution of land. Cárdenas's ambitious agrarian reform efforts, especially his commitment to redistributing land to *ejidatarios* in the first years of his administration, elicited letters from Mexicans around the country who were waiting for access to parcels of land. An *ejido* committee in Oaxaca addressed Cárdenas as follows: "We thus wait for you, fellow citizen President of the Republic, begging once more that they pay attention to just petitions [for land] of the disinherited and needy who struggle to survive at great cost."[38] Like their compatriots in Mexico, emigrant citizens north of the border also made pleas for land. They cited their original lack of land as the reason for their absence from the nation, and hoped to become landholders once they returned.

APPEALS TO MIGRANTS AND
THE POTENTIAL FOR LAND

Courting the nation's lost sons and daughters, President Cárdenas made appeals specifically to emigrant agriculturalists in order to further the political agenda of agrarianism in 1937 and again in 1938.[39] Since the turn of the century, Mexican presidents had acted with patriotic duty to try to bring migrants and repatriates back into the fold of the nation, but Cárdenas's plan for repatriation went beyond the traditional relationship between migrants and the Mexican State. According to varying Mexican press reports, the Cárdenas government was not only willing to provide free transportation, reduce customs fees, and provide work opportunities for repatriates, but would also offer land for those who fulfilled certain requirements. Far from being a welcome return to just anyone who found themselves in dire circumstances in the United States, the program, under the guidance of Manuel Gamio, would privilege the repatriation of those with expertise in agriculture so that they could contribute to Cárdenas's nationalist project.[40] Cárdenas's plans for settling repatriates into agricultural colonies were not merely rhetorical, and groups of repatriates from California and Texas were actually resettled and given land in Chihuahua and Baja California.[41]

Hilario Gonzalez wrote to the president in 1938 from Swink, Colorado, explaining that he and many of his compatriots in the United States wished to repatriate and wanted to know if the president was offering lands for repatriates as stated in the press.[42] Writing from cities in Texas, California, Indiana, and Iowa, Ambrosio Gonzalez, Sabino Alzaga, Luis Navarro, Eugenio Ibarra, and Victoria Valdes were just some of the Mexican migrants in the United States who wrote to President Cárdenas and asked him for repatriation *and* land.[43] It is unknown whether these migrants were chosen to be resettled into agricultural colonies in Mexico, but in 1939 thousands of repatriated families moved to an agricultural colony named after the infamous date of Cárdenas's oil nationalization, 18 de Marzo. The first two years of the Tamaulipas colony were fraught due to a lack of resources, a quick arrival of more families than initially expected, and a year of terrible floods. Those who did not return to Texas within those first couple of years would go on to witness the region prosper as the important cotton producing town of Valle Hermoso.[44]

The act was welcoming toward repatriates but also pragmatic and shrewdly political. Cárdenas very well could have been pushed to act quickly on the invitation made to repatriates in order to counter criticism regarding his policy toward Spanish refugees.[45] Even if the invitation to repatriates to acquire land and to have them settle in agricultural colonies was more political than benevolent, the act signaled a major moment in the history of Mexican migration in which migrants were recognized as a social group that could be brought back into the nation. Migrants who had written to the president used the language of patriotism, rights, and revolutionary promise for the opportunity to reestablish themselves once again as firm members of the nation-state. For many, however, especially children and young adults who lacked basic welfare, politics was of no concern. When letters inundated the presidents, their secretaries, consular officials and welfare advocates, they could offer very little to ameliorate the situations or pay for yet another return migration, this time to the United States. They could only offer suggestions, rather than resources, when reading letters that highlighted the frustrated relocations and interrupted lives straddled across borders.

BINATIONAL FAMILIES REACH OUT TO THE CONSULS

The number of binational families increased during the 1920s, and they faced particular challenges during the era of economic crisis. Binational families, containing family members with different citizenship statuses, had to take extra steps to make sure that they didn't face obstacles at the border. Consular officials became the recipients of many letters from female migrants trying to navigate their family migrations, separations, and reunifications. As discussed earlier, women faced more scrutiny at the border, especially if unaccompanied by a male companion. Because of these complications, letters asking the consul for help in migrating were disproportionately written by women.[46] For Maria del Refugio Gracian de Cervantes and others, the migration and reunion of their binational families required guidance from the US consul and a deeper knowledge of immigration and naturalization policies.[47]

The avalanche of letters written to officials of both nations asking for economic aid and money for repatriation costs continued past the height of the crisis in the early 1930s. Between 1936 and 1940, 175 letters were written to the US consular office at Guadalajara from welfare and relief agencies in the United States.[48] Letters exchanged usually resulted in the consul contacting family members in Mexico who might be able to support their families in the United States. All but a few of the letters were written on behalf of women and their children, and most of these Mexican and Mexican-American women were single mothers who had been widowed or abandoned by their husbands. US-born women made an appearance in these letters as well. In one case, a relief official wrote to a consul in Mexico to ask if the American wife and child of a Mexican man now living there were "returnable."

In 1936, Maria del Refugio was concerned about the "difficulties" she and her binational family might encounter at the border. She was planning on re-migrating to the United States from Mexico as she had been doing over the past several years. She had entered the United States at least twice before, crossing once at the age of twenty with her young daughter to accompany her husband, who labored in the agricultural fields along the central coast of California. She would give birth to her second child in Santa Barbara County before returning to Mexico. Four years later she returned yet again to the United States, this time with two small children and accompanied by her brother. She gave birth to three more daughters in the United States. The family settled in Santa Maria, California, at the time of the 1930 census, when her eldest daughter Isabelle was enrolled in school. In 1936 Maria del Refugio was back in Mexico, now a widow with five daughters to care for. In her past two trips to the United States, she had crossed the border accompanied by a male family member and had enough money to pay the head tax. As a single mother of five children, she asked the consul for any information that might be useful for the successful border crossing of her family.[49]

The consul responded with an informational sheet on visa requirements for her and her Mexican-born daughter. In addition to paying the appropriate fees, she would have to prove that she was capable of supporting herself and her five children as a widow. Without this assurance, she would surely have been refused a visa on account of being categorized as likely to become a public charge.[50] Because she had entered the United States before with no listed occupation, chances of entering again were slim. However, if she could prove that other family members might be able to support her and her five children, she might have entered successfully. The US consul at Guadalajara at least would have to approve or reject her visa application prior to her departure, saving her a trip to the border with her five daughters in tow if she was found ineligible for entry. It is unknown whether she was one of 21 people to have received a visa that year or, if instead, she was one of the 181 who were denied.[51]

Maria del Refugio's migration experience demonstrates how citizenship was intertwined with migration and how binational families faced added difficulties in crossing the border. Her four daughters born in the United States enjoyed citizenship rights and, therefore, the right to cross, while Maria and her eldest daughter did not. Her experience also illustrates that women's circular migration could be jeopardized quite suddenly if they could no longer rely on the support of a male family member. Her correspondence with the consul indicates that it was likely that she had all of her daughters with her in Mexico. The same could not be said for many Mexican parents living in the United States. Vicente Carrillo and Agustina Martinez de García each wrote to the consul from the United States to ask him for advice about their children across the border.

Vicente was among those migrants who wanted to make sure that they had done everything necessary to ensure that their children could join them in the United States. In a letter written to the consul in 1936, he wanted to know what he should do to bring his US-born son across the border to San Francisco, "without having any difficulties with the offices of emigration." He went on to explain, "the boy was born in this country [the United States] and that's why I want to bring him, because I want him to be educated here in the English language." Vicente's son had been living with his grandparents in Guadalajara for the past eight years, but Vicente decided it was time for his son to come back. Agustina also wrote to the consul to have her daughter, whom she had not seen in eleven years, move back to the United States to live with her in Indiana Harbor, just outside of Chicago. Her daughter Angela

Cervantes, meanwhile, had been living with a couple who, according to Agustina, was "very willing" that I have my daughter with me because they are old and cannot assure my daughter anything for the future." Like Vicente Carrillo's son, Angela had been born in the United States. The consul informed both Vicente and Agustina that they would need to send money for travel and be able to establish their children's American citizenship for the successful migrations of their family members.

Agustina sent Angela's proper birth certificate, but Vicente Carrillo only had his son's baptismal certificate. With a civil birth certificate, Angela was able to establish her US citizenship with the Department of State and register as a US citizen with the consul's office. The consul anticipated that she would have no problem crossing the border. Mother and daughter would be reunited. Vicente had reason to be concerned about the difficulties his son might encounter at the border. Although it was up to the discretion of the immigration officer who reviewed the paperwork, baptismal certificates were usually not sufficient proof of citizenship.[52] The Mexican father in the United States and the American-born son in Mexico would remain separated, unless Vicente's son chanced a trip north without the guarantee of entry that his US citizenship should have afforded him. This was a common migrant family experience: the nature of circular migration and seasonal labor made it so that binational families were often separated by distance and circumstance.[53] In fact, a pattern of family separation where mothers and fathers were in the United States while children stayed with family members in Mexico had been established well before the 1920s.[54] Whether parents like Maria were trying to migrate from Mexico with their binational families or whether they were already in the United States and trying to bring their children across the border, like Vicente and Agustina, they realized the necessity of making the appropriate arrangements for the passage of their family members. With so many visas being refused, establishing citizenship was the only guarantee for migration and reunification for these transnational families whose separation was becoming more permanent with the increasing strength of restrictive immigration legislation.[55]

CITIZENSHIP, POVERTY, AND GENDER

On March 8, 1938, Ethel Hinojosa wrote a letter to the US consul at Guadalajara stating, "I am writing these few lines to ask you if you could do us a favor. My husband and I, also our little girls come here to Mexico on the 27th day of January. We thought we could get along better here, but since we came, we have all been sick and find conditions much worse than in the United States."[56] Ethel assured the consul that they could get work on a farm upon their return to the United States if only the consul could provide them with some money for travel. Ethel and her two daughters were born in the United States. Her husband, Charles Hinojosa, was born in Mexico, but had been living in the US since he was two months old. The Hinojosa family was persistent, and Charles wrote to the consul asking for help two months later.[57] In a return letter, the consul suggested that they "endeavor to secure the necessary funds from relatives or friends."[58] They must have had little success. Ethel wrote again in June of 1939 reporting, "In the time we have been here we have gone hungry and my little girls are now barefooted."[59]

The Hinojosa letters suggest that while the family had waited out the worst of the Depression in the United States, by 1938 they took a chance on migrating to Mexico to see if they could find better work opportunities. Charles had worked for the WPA in the United States but decided that he might receive higher wages in Mexico, and believed that he had some property in Mexico.[60] When he returned to Mexico, he found that he "had nothing of value, only papers to an old house that has not been used since the Revolution and has not had any taxes paid on it." The Hinojosas found no support from the US consular office as there were no funds for repatriation of any kind. The Hinojosas, having been "aided by the government" in their migration to Mexico, most likely by means of subsidized train passes from either the American or Mexican government, thought it worth a try to see if they might be helped back, but the US consular service was not repatriating destitute US citizens.

The majority of correspondence at the Guadalajara consulate regarding migration between 1935 and 1940 consisted of these pleas for financial assistance. Barbara Cadena, another US-born woman married to a Mexican man, appealed to the consul wanting help in moving her family to the United States because her children, like Ethel Hinojosa's, were sick.[61] Mabelle Jauregui, also married to a Mexican man, wrote to the consul in 1939 asking for help to move back to the United States stating, "I have sold everything that [is worth] any money to buy food with, and my husband has no chance of getting work." She emphasized that if they could just get back to Jerome, Arizona, they could both easily find work. The consul regretted to inform her "that the government provides no funds for the relief of American citizens residing abroad." To this Mabelle wrote back clarifying that she did not want "relief" abroad, but that she merely wanted assistance to return to her home country. Mabelle did not consider subsidized travel charity and in fact expected it as a service.[62]

Barbara, Ethel, and Mabelle wrote in hopes of getting the passage paid for their entire families, including their Mexican husbands and their Mexican- and US-born children. While Ethel could have potentially crossed by herself, she and her husband hoped to take the journey together. Barbara also wanted her husband to come along, emphasizing that he was the one who would make a living for their family. Mabelle asserted that her husband could not "find enough work to make a home" for them. These wives expected their husbands to provide for them and in the transnational circumstances described above, women hoped to facilitate the migration that would enable their husbands to do so. Men *and* women shared responsibility for family migration strategies; however, the patriarchal order, governed by the husband acting as main provider, was to be maintained whenever possible. Patriarchal family formation was still the goal, even if citizenship, borders, and poverty challenged the norm. Family composition was complex, as were decisions to migrate; citizenship was intricately tied to migration; citizenship and migration shaped migrant gender roles; and wives also played an important role in shaping migration strategies. The three women above were perhaps exceptional, but not because they were US-born women who married Mexicans and chose to move to Mexico; rather they are exceptional because out of all the female letter writers writing to the US consul at Guadalajara between 1936 and 1940, they were the only women who were part of families that remained intact.

SEPARATION AND DESERTION

The pressures of economic uncertainty, the complexities of binational travel across a more rigid border, and the presence of domestic turmoil, broke many migrant families and resulted in disputes between transnational families. Lovenia Chastain de Navarrette and her husband had "talked things over" and decided to go their separate ways under the economic stress. Having been married to her husband for eight years and having moved with him to Mexico for the purpose of visiting her sister-in-law, Lovenia wrote to the consul stating, "he wishes to stay with his folks, and since he cannot afford to support me alone, I have decided to go back to my father."[63] Lovenia had been told (by an unnamed source) "that the American Consulate is to help the Americans stranded in this country." She would have been disappointed by the consul's reply: to seek appropriate funds from her relatives. Her father did not have the resources to pay for her passage either. Lovenia was stranded in Mexico.[64]

Some couples sought their solutions separately, and like Lovenia some women chose to go it alone, or maybe just not with their husbands. Many other migrants, mostly women, faced abandonment by their partners. Consular memos inquiring about whereabouts often listed inquiries by women seeking information on their estranged husbands. Women who were economically and physically stranded because their husbands had abandoned them found themselves trapped in a foreign country and separated from family members who lived on the other side of the border. Abandoned by their husbands, women had even less of a chance to fund migration to their home countries. Mexican and US-American women in both countries wrote directly to the consul to inquire about their deserter husbands, clearly seeking to track them down for economic support. Letters from welfare agencies in the United States reveal the impoverished conditions that Mexican women faced after their husbands abandoned them or died. Social workers asked consular officials in Guadalajara to locate and contact husbands or other family members who might be able to provide a home for their destitute relatives in the United States, thereby lessening the cost of public relief.

ABUSE AND MARITAL DISCORD

For some women the decision, and need, to return to the United States was not a shared decision between husband and wife, and was anything but civil. Theresa Romero wrote to the consul in hopes of escaping her abusive husband and destitute life in Mexico. Theresa was married in 1925 to Efren Romero in Illinois. In 1930 the couple migrated with their two young boys to Jalisco. After seven years in Mexico, Theresa was, in her words, "through putting up with this burden." She was depressed and weak, suffering from emotional and physical abuse from her husband, and missed her life in the United States. She missed white bread, butter, and frankfurters, and she missed her family. She had written to her father telling him that she would go insane if she stayed much longer in Mexico, and begged him to send her money to pay for her train and bus fare. She was even willing to leave her children behind in Mexico. She wrote to her father, "My heart just breaks when I think of the dirty deal this ungrateful wife-beater has given me."[65] Theresa's journey would entail extra-careful planning precisely because she was not just trying to migrate; she was trying to escape.

Theresa's father wrote to the consul and included the letter he had received from Theresa. Eventually Theresa herself wrote to the consul asking for help, until her husband began to intercept her letters. Despite facing death threats and having to leave all but her youngest child behind, Theresa managed to leave her husband after her father had put together sufficient enough funds to pay for her passage. For women like Theresa, US citizenship was not enough to require extraordinary services from the U.S. consul; the poverty of their relatives in times of economic crisis, and their own subordinate and gendered positions in their households, prevented their migration back to the United States.

In another long exchange of correspondence, Mabel Marquez and her relatives in Stillman Valley, Illinois, asked the consul to provide funds for Mabel and her son Melvin to return to the United States. Like Theresa, Mabel's living situation and marital relationship was precarious. Mabel complained that her husband treated her cruelly, threatened to shoot her, lay drunk day after day, and had two other women on the side. She described her situation to her uncle, saying, "We are here in a forest, nothing but trees, no cars, no trains, no shows, nothing here, nothing but murder and drunkards here, shooting at night."[66] In a letter, she advised her mother to tell the consul that whoever came to help her should bring two soldiers so that her husband could not hurt her in her escape.[67]

After initially trying to pass the case off to the consul at San Luis Potosí over a jurisdictional mix-up, the consuls at Guadalajara replied to various letters from Mabel and her relatives, advising them that they would need to provide money for transportation themselves and that because Mabel's home was so far from the city of Guadalajara (three days by horseback), direct communication would "not be practicable for personal issues." The consuls further advised that her family members send any money directly to Mabel once they raised enough. The consuls, either because of the burdensome distance or because of the hassle that such a complicated domestic dispute created, did not offer to facilitate wire transfers, payments to rail companies, or anything of that nature. Mabel did finally leave her husband, fleeing to the house of a friend. Once there, she wrote to the consul yet again to ask for shelter in Guadalajara as she was determined to get to that city and return to Illinois.

Predictably, the consul once again stressed the lack of appropriated funds for Americans in need of relief; he advised her not to come to Guadalajara. At this point the letters stopped; it is unknown whether Mabel and her son Melvin ever made it back to the United States.

These women had little to no recourse for their domestic turmoil. This vulnerability was, in part, due to patriarchal tolerance of spousal abuse (emotional and physical), and, in part, due to their complex binational relationships and transnational status. Who, for example, could do anything about Carmen Kramer de Cavillo's case, in which the money her mother sent her to assist her in traveling back to the United States was "appropriated by her husband"?[68] There was quite simply no protocol. The consul's reply captures this problem: "Whether the husband would permit her to leave without his consent, or permit her to remove the children from this country, of course this office cannot say; nor can it undertake to accept any responsibility in connection with the removal of the wife or children from Mexico."[69]

Women in general, and as part of binational families specifically, were in a nebulous transnational space where the convergence of citizenship, poverty, and gender turned the migration process and survival strategies into personal and jurisdictional quagmires. The cases above provide snapshots into intimate relationships not easily governable by the laws of one nation, let alone two. We also gain a glimpse into the gendered responses to transnational poverty and migration during the 1930s. Women's mobility was more likely to be legally (subject to harsher immigration restrictions), economically (more difficulty in finding wage labor), and physically (as a result of abuse and assault) limited. It is worth asserting that the stories that emerge from the era reveal more discord than harmonious relationships. It is undeniable that abandonment and desertion were common features of the era, and that more women than men appear in the records to have been trapped in a foreign country and separated from family members who lived on the other side of the border. However, as chapter 3 points out, other families were able to endure the trials of the Great Depression as a family unit. In some ways, reflected by the fact that there is any documentary record at all, the cases outlined above are extraordinary, but they also speak to the gendered impacts that members of transnational families experienced during an era of crisis.

As revealed by the correspondence above, consuls came to play a key role as service coordinator, confidant, and counselor for migrant families in an era when no infrastructure, either diplomatic, national, or binational, could attend to the specific issues of binational families and migrant families. Due to the fact that Guadalajara was the commercial center of Western Mexico, consuls primarily dedicated their time towards US state and citizen commercial interests such as investment and trade, but in the era of economic depression, consuls fielded deeply personal petitions from many migrant women and members of divided families. In a meeting for consular officials held in Mexico City in 1937, visa division chief Simmons cautioned that visa cases should be examined, "objectively, fairly, and reasonably, and if necessary exhaustively," and reminded consuls that, "Every immigration visa application represents a human problem and may in some cases have aspects of tragedy."[70]

While the consulate did prioritize issues of trade, business, and the protection of American interests abroad, the consular office also served as a critical hub of transnational migration, a thoroughfare for family communication and perhaps even a place for family conflict mediation. In the 1920s consular correspondence had increased due to shifts in migration policies and increasing binational family migrations, but during the 1930s migrant interactions with consular officials focused more on the extraordinary circumstances caused by financial hardship. Letters shifted from bureaucratic in tone to increasingly more personal. For some migrants like Frank Valadez, who was already in the United States, the US consul acted as a services coordinator by helping to arrange travel accommodations and forward money to relatives living in Mexico. Frank sent money to the consul at Guadalajara and asked him to facilitate cross-border transportation for Mrs. Juana R. Franco and her daughter Rose Marie to the United States. The consul obliged, and for once a mother and her young daughter made the journey north quite smoothly.[71]

The decade of the 1930s was a dynamic era in both the United States and Mexico. Each nation was transformed significantly as governments grew larger and faced rising expectations that they would provide for their people during times of uncertainty. Mexican migrants abroad and US migrants in Mexico fell somewhere in between the extending embrace of the new welfare states. Yet, while stability was created within national units, the border came down on transnational livelihoods with paralyzing force. Some migrants surely managed such difficulties with the help of family networks that stretched across national and transnational spaces. Some of these extended networks could mobilize economic resources, produce correct legal paperwork, or send representatives to extricate their family members from delicate situations. Still, the stories represented above suggest that in the absence of resources for migration and recourse to transnational forms of justice (for none existed for such intimate domestic disputes), many migrants, especially women, were forced to bear their burdens in an isolated fashion. US consuls, relief agency officials, municipal presidents, and even presidents were asked to be arbiters in transnational migration and family life. Welfare officials from both public and private organizations at times established a kind of informal bureaucracy to supplement the state's overburdened resources.[72] With little juridical power, no force of arms, and limited funds, these agents were brought into the spaces of migrant lives that were simultaneously intimate and transnational.

Such stories demand a reconsideration of migrant paths and experiences. These paths were not simply shaped by formal labor and economic motivations, with males at the center and women and children on the periphery. Women, in fact emerge at the center, but so do questions about the duties and responsibilities of migrant husbands and wives, the challenges facing migrant children in multiple-status families, and the ways that tightening borders and increased poverty shaped migrant livelihoods. Questions about the responsibility of governments to their emigrant citizens also emerge and prompt a question as to whether governments responded differently to migrant families than to single migrants, or responded to men differently than women, laborer versus non-laborer emigrants, or temporary versus more permanent migrants.

Migration to the United States during the latter half of the 1930s might aptly be characterized as a slow trickle, but return migration to Mexico was much greater and, while overall migration was less in volume during this era, it was still incredibly significant. The complex family migration patterns and the tensions that were created by the inability of government officials to regulate life cycles, intimate family spaces, and human movement in the first three decades of the twentieth century have been obscured by the more visible and formal histories of the bracero era of the 1940s. The period of crisis, return, and rigidly enforced borders, with binational families enduring family separation and fighting for family reunification, decisively shaped government designs for a more controlled regime of migration. The complexities produced by gender, poverty, and binational families plus the onset of global war gave government officials the opportunity to finally attempt a more overarching regulatory scheme for migrant mobility that had eluded them for decades. In the 1940s, a new migration order would be carved out of old traditions, and a new ideal migrant would emerge. Absent husbands and fathers would be heralded as heroes for their migrations, and families would have to sit on the sidelines of migratory journeys, left just to wait.

PART III

The New Wave

RECRUITING MEN, WOMEN KEEP COMING

CHAPTER FIVE

———

War and a New Migration Order

NATIONS SEEK BRACEROS, WOMEN
MAKE FAMILIES, 1940–1947

Margarita Ramirez de Alvarado, married, Mexican, thirty years old, with the address Calle de Casas Coloradas # 19, Zacatecas, Zac, I state the following: That my husband Mr. Agustin R. Alvarado is in Fresno California contracted under the number 9–6376 for six months, since May 8 of the present year.

I desire that your office give me a pass to be by the side of my husband for the time left for him to complete his contract.

I should clarify that first I directed myself to the Consul of the United States in San Luis Potosí, and he answered by telling me to go to the Secretaría de Trabajo y Previsión Social, to which I went. That Secretaría in a reply numbered 6–4267 on the twentieth of this month, directed me to this office, the Secretaría de Gobernación for the pass. Anticipating that you grant me this request, yours,

Margarita Ramirez de Alvarado[1]

ON AUGUST 7, 1944, the general director of the Office of Population of the Secretaría de Gobernación wrote back to Margarita explaining that he could not grant her the immigration visa she desired: "this Secretary can only authorize the exit of national workers to the United States of America corresponding to the agreement between our country and that nation."

Two years before Margarita wrote the Mexican Farm Labor Program, an agreement by the United States and Mexican federal governments usually referred to as the bracero program, had transformed the nature of Mexican migration. After a turbulent decade of migration in the 1930s, the binational labor arrangement, which would last from 1942 to 1964, provided aspiring migrants with renewed hope. Despite US border policies which had been more rigidly enforced through the 1930s, a new legal channel increased border crossings like never before. However, in a dramatic reversal of family migration trends that were established in the 1920s, the 1940s would usher in an era of new privilege for male migrants and increased limitations on family migration. At first glance, migration during the bracero era harkens back to the pioneering waves at the turn of the century: the seasonal and temporary migration of mostly men recruited by US employers to work primarily in rail and agriculture. However, after decades of social and family migration, the proliferation of binational families, the economic and social integration of women and children into Mexican-American life, and repeated and multi-generational border crossings, the attempts to reorder migration to be only male and only temporary were fraught. Margarita Ramirez de Alvarado was one of the women who found herself caught outside of this new order of sanctioned migration. Migrants were still welcome to attempt a legal entry after having the proper documents, but the preferences for the ideal migrant were clearly set. Women, often wives and mothers, as well as men who did not fit the prototype, fell outside the system as well.

This chapter will examine how Mexican migration proceeded throughout the early1940s. Braceros, aspiring braceros, and their family members wrote thousands of letters to Mexican presidents, governors, and other officials. Through their words we gain an understanding of the conditions propelling migrants to go north, and the ways in which migrants framed their own pleas for bracero contracts within the new context of World War II. In this chapter, I add to the growing scholarship on the program by examining the family-centered petitions that aspiring migrants wrote in order to obtain bracero contracts between 1942 and 1945.[2] While families, and women in particular, were effectively left out and left behind by the bracero program, they were still very much at the heart of bracero-era migrations.[3] Mexican men claimed a right to bracero contracts based on their right, as well as their obligation, to be good patriarchs and provide for their families. Women petitioned government officials on behalf of their male family members for this right as well. With the onset of World War II, emigration through the program was transformed into a patriotic service for Mexico, and men leaving families was merely part of the country's sacrifice for democracy. Integrating the bracero program into my analysis of family migration and how it changed over time illustrates the tension that emerged when a binational state-sanctioned program attempted to reorder migrations that had long been governed by familial and social networks. The state arranged legal migration in very particular ways that ignored binational families, longer migrations, and the consideration that family, whether performing labor alongside their male relatives or not, had always been vital both emotionally and materially to Mexican migrations.

The exclusions written into the program guidelines led to gendered patterns of migration and generated a surge in undocumented migration from the outset, a topic that will be explored in further depth in chapter 6. Women wrote to government officials as soon as the program began, inquiring, just like their male counterparts, as to whether they might also be able to go to the United States. Most women, quickly understanding the new logic of migration, petitioned for bracero contracts on behalf of their husbands. The program, after all, was supposed to help male migrants gain work experience and the means to provide. Temporary labor contracts were meant to strengthen patriarchy by preserving the privilege of household earning for males, but also weakened patriarchy by requiring men to be away from their families. Patriarchal notions of family were bent to fit the reality of the bracero era. Another modernization of patriarchy occurred with regards to migrant families, and this time it was brought on by a different type of revolution.

MEXICO IN THE 1940S

Mexicans living in the 1940s had just lived through the era of Cárdenas and the Revolutionary Family and were now on a course toward Manuel Ávila Camacho's vision of National Unity.[4] The rhetorical shift resulted in real political and economic consequences, the sum of which acted as a counterbalance to the radicalism of expropriation, land redistribution, and the syndicalism of *Cardenismo*. The shift was a reaction to both internal divisions and external challenges. The country, still reeling from the diplomatic consequences of expropriating and nationalizing oil, went from experiencing deep tension with their northern neighbor, to ambiguous neutrality in the lead up to world war. The onset of World War II led to reconciliation, alliance, and mutual support between Mexico and the United States.[5]

A growth in population sparked intense urbanization and fueled state initiatives aimed at rapid production in agriculture and the industrialization and modernization of technology. Ávila Camacho's administration (1940–46), while seeming to rhetorically stay in line with Cárdenas's agrarian policies, favored private property over *ejidos*, or state-regulated communally held land, as the basis for Mexico's agricultural production. A slow neglect of the *ejido* by government programs and a decrease in agricultural credit and technological support lent to *ejidatarios* posed a challenging set of obstacles to Mexican farmers. President Miguel Alemán (1946–52) would move even further from the *ejido* system by reforming laws that amplified small plots and created larger land holdings. Small- and medium-sized property owners were privileged over individual farmers and resources and investments were directed toward export crops. Industrialization was encouraged and *ejidos* were expected to be productive units that would contribute goods to regional and national markets, rather than utilized as a collective good for community subsistence.[6] The overall Mexican population grew from 23.4 million in 1946 to 27.8 million in 1952, while migration to cities led to a growth in urban population from 21.9 percent in 1940 to 31 percent in 1952.[7] In Mexico City, urban factory jobs could not keep up with the population, which ballooned from 1,757,530 in 1940 to 3,050,442 in 1950.[8]

It was within this rapidly changing, urbanizing, and modernizing context that the bracero program promised to deliver much needed wages and capital to Mexican men and their families through a new system of migration. With the onset of World War II and a renewed US growers' demand for imported labor, the US and Mexican governments began to discuss the possibility of a temporary labor program. The wartime context proved to be politically advantageous to the Mexican government, which justified the bracero contracts as a means for Mexico to contribute to the overall war effort. By supplying manpower for production, Mexico would be lending critical support to the Allied forces. A mutually beneficial labor program also fell within the framework of Roosevelt's Good Neighbor policy, first articulated in 1933, but tenuously followed due to tense diplomatic relations during the Cárdenas era.[9]

Even before the United States declared war against the Axis powers, rumors began circulating about the need for Mexican workers to fill labor shortages. By the end of 1941, growers in Texas, Arizona, and California had already begun petitioning for the legalized importation of Mexican workers. They specifically asked for exemptions from immigration laws that barred contract labor.[10] By March, aspiring migrants were writing to the Office of Migration to inquire about the relaxation of border controls. Manuel Yañez, Aurelio Aguirre, and Fidel Carbajal wrote a letter to the Office of Mexican Migration on behalf of themselves and ten families, all of whom lacked work, and were interested in migrating to the United States.[11] According to the US Consul at Guadalajara, "when the first inklings of a possible let down in barriers to workers was mentioned," a constant stream of people came to the consulate. Mexicans were responding to articles like the one published in a Guadalajara newspaper that read "100,000 Mexicans needed to work in the United States." The article described one California senator's plea for Mexican immigrant workers to fill in for the recently interned Japanese agricultural workers.[12]

Mexican families inspired by rumors of worker shortages also trekked north before any formal agreements were announced.[13] Premature migrations swelled populations in cities near the border. After they failed to cross, a group of forty-five men wrote to President Ávila Camacho to ask him to intervene on their behalf after having encountered difficulties with Mexican migration agents. Like so many aspiring migrants before, they turned their pleas directly to the president in hopes of a favorable response. They likely never received a response from Ávila Camacho, for their original letter was passed on to the Governor of Tamaulipas by the Secretaría de Gobernación, urging him to dissuade workers from going to the US.

Like they had in the 1920s, border officials and organizations reported local conditions to government officials in the interior. In a letter written by the National Chamber of Commerce, representatives from Ciudad Juárez described the destitution of failed migrants at the border, stating that even migrants who had worked north of the border returned empty handed. Migrants were "hopeful for the fool's gold that they are offered, but [are] then exploited to the point that they are converted into human waste: they are thrown out without even one morsel of bread in their mouths, with their sick children and their starving women, and at this border have had to find themselves obligated to steal and commit crimes in order to subsist."[14] The dramatically stated case was meant to persuade the Mexican national government to take all necessary steps to prevent laborers from heading north so that Mexico wouldn't face its own shortage of workers. Another primary motivation, though not explicitly stated in the letter, would have been to reduce the number of migrants in border regions causing a strain on resources and infrastructure.

Other organizations and government agencies weighed in on the matter and in April, three months before diplomatic agreements were solidified, Mexico's largest union, the CTM (Confederación de Trabajadores Mexicanos), countered rumors regarding their support of laborers migrating to the United States, stating to the press that they would not permit workers to leave the country during a time of national emergency.[15] They insisted that all Mexicans were needed in the fields and workshops "to intensify national production."

In order to prevent the mass exodus of migrants to the border, government officials issued warnings in the press, asserting that there was no demand for laborers in the United States. Officials urged Mexicans to "pay no attention to invitations made to workers causing them to leave their country, since the best opportunity to ensure their livelihood is in Mexico if they dedicate themselves to the intensification of production."[16] In a reply to aspiring migrants, Carlos A. Gómez, sub-director of the Office of Migration, tried to thwart any premature acknowledgment of such an agreement. First, he flatly denied that such a program existed, thus making it impossible for him to provide help in the matter. He also added that, "reports from the Ministry of Foreign Relations have suggested that the presence of new immigrants in the United States would harm the interests of our co-nationals that are currently residing in the country."[17] In a warning similar to the one made by the Ciudad Juárez Chamber of Commerce, Gómez reminded the letter-writers of the hardships that had befallen many of their compatriots in the past. The xenophobia and racism directed toward Mexicans in the 1930s had left border residents and Mexican officials cautious about any new openings in the channels of migration.

While critics of the program feared a shortage of workers in Mexico, continued poor treatment of Mexicans in the United States, and the congregation of stranded migrants at the border, aspiring braceros actually saw the contracts as insurance against exploitation and an opportunity for a paid passage to and from the United States. In letters, aspiring braceros demonstrated their understanding of migratory work abroad as a way of bringing honor and wages to their country. Despite discouraging propaganda, Mexicans placed hope in the promises of a new and sanctioned era of migration to the United States. The power of the American dream and the promise of successful migrations and binational living strategies—as confirmed by remittances and hopeful tales from friends and family abroad—was too powerful to resist. Completing a stint of work in the United States had become an entrenched pattern of livelihood for many Mexicans. Prior experience in the United States was a major factor in fueling repeated migrations. Mexicans who had already lived and worked north of the border were also making inquiries to government officials about the program.[18] Others, including experienced migrants and new migrants alike, made their way to the border without formalized contracts in hand, in hopes that their services were needed. With its inauguration in August of 1942, the new contract labor program would create formalized criteria for aspiring migrants, attempt to enforce organized selection of workers, and try to mandate a gendered, temporary, legal and ordered process of human migration. Many obtained the coveted contracts, but countless Mexicans did not.

THE PROGRAM

The agricultural program was finally inaugurated when 1,500 Mexican braceros were admitted into the United States on September 29th, 1942, sent to sugar beet farms in five locations in California.[19] Initial contracts were to last six months and could be renewed if agreed to by the laborer and the Mexican government. Wages equal to those which domestic workers received for each region were to be guaranteed, with a minimum of thirty cents per hour, as was the promise that workers would be able to work for at least 75 percent of the days in their contract. A stipulation mandated that 10 percent of the earnings of each worker would be sent back to Mexico and held for the worker by the Banco Nacional de Crédito Agrícola, to ensure that workers and their families would be able to rely on some savings upon their return. Transportation across the border and to work sites would be covered by the employer and a basic minimum standard of housing and services would be provided.[20]

The agreement would undergo revisions that would spell out more strict guaranteed standards of treatment for braceros, raise the minimum wage to reflect increased cost of living, and ensure that if problems occurred between employer and employee, Mexican guest workers would be able to make a case for mediation before being relocated to another work site or sent back to Mexico.[21] Those stipulations worked well enough for each government at the outset of the labor agreement, but the program would undergo a series of negotiations in order for each government to be fully satisfied with the requirements and concessions.[22] Renegotiations were made in 1947, stipulating that employers, rather than the US government, would arrange contracts with the Mexican government, and in 1948, years beyond the conclusion of the war, initiating an entirely new phase of the program. In the 1948 iteration, Mexico was in a disadvantaged position and was no longer able to assure braceros a guaranteed minimum salary per hour or the guarantee of 75 percent days employed for its workers. The most significant characteristic of the new negotiations, however, was the commitment to a more concerted effort toward restricting undocumented immigration. As part of a crackdown, employers who had hired undocumented workers in the past would be banned from participating.[23] During the war years undocumented migration was less visible and less concerning to both governments. However, as the war concluded, more and more waves of undocumented workers were hired by complicit employers. Just as legal migration skyrocketed again with the initiation of the bracero program, undocumented migration skyrocketed as well, leading to a host of problems for the Mexican government and Mexican workers alike. The creation of a legal group of migrants also led to a creation of an *illegal* group of migrants, just as had occurred in the past decades with cumulative immigration requirements and restrictions.[24]

CREATING THE IDEAL MIGRANT

The selection process for bracero contracts reveals the desired characteristics of the ideal Mexican migrant. Aspiring migrants needed to interact with a host of government representatives including those from the US Consulate; the Mexican Ministries of Labor and Foreign Relations; and the Mexican Office of Migration, and could face rejection and dismissal at any step. In a response to brothers from Zacatecas who were interested in becoming braceros, a government official outlined the requirements:

> Each interested applicant should obtain a visa from the North American [US] consulate and should obtain a labor contract authorized by the Ministry of Labor. The Ministry of Foreign Relations also extends a passport which is required for immigration. Furthermore, one would need to complete the legal requirements and follow guidelines of the Office of Migration which requires that all emigrants fifteen years and older obtain a form five card, which costs five dollars, and can be obtained either at this office, or an Office of Population at the port of exit.[25]

Contract centers were first established in Mexico City and eventually were set up in different parts of the country in order to facilitate the process for braceros and employers alike. Aspiring braceros would travel long distances to congregate in stadiums, office buildings, town squares, and sidewalks throughout the country in makeshift camps, where they hoped to be contracted and sent to the United States right away. Government agents representing both countries would be at contract centers to ensure that men fulfilled crucial requirements, and doctors were on hand to ensure a clean bill of health.[26] The US government wanted proof that the workers had experience in manual labor and were free from diseases, while the Mexican government wanted to make sure that men had completed their military service obligation, were not currently employed in other work, and had not been recipients of *ejidos*.[27]

In response to a complaint filed against bracero contractors in Ameca, Jalisco, the municipal president of the town assured the general secretary of the state that enrollees into the program did not own land and were not needed for agriculture. Instead, they were described as "the sons of barbers and potters who don't have established businesses, tailors who have no machine with which to sew, many of them recently married, with skill sets such as shoemaking but not recognized as official shoemakers, or skill sets for other jobs."[28] The municipal president saw no problem in them leaving as braceros, but it was doubtful that representatives of either government would accept them. The government was specifically looking for men experienced in agriculture; the men from Ameca, although not employed, were at disadvantage because they were tradesmen.[29]

Some men who had previous experience working in the United States or who had even lived most of their lives in the United States could not readily obtain contracts. Catarino Escobar Cardona, a Mexican-born man who had lived the majority of his life in the United States, failed to bring legal documents proving that he was eligible to re-enter the United States after having briefly visited Mexico. After a three-year process of trying to prove his legal residency in the United States, US immigration agents were finally satisfied of his legal reentry. However, due to the onset of the bracero program, it was Mexican migration officials that now prevented him from leaving the country as a bracero for failing to satisfy the requirements set out by the program.[30]

A group of fifty men living in Mexico, but born in the United States to Mexican parents, tried to cross the border at Piedras Negras in September of 1942, but were prevented from doing so. US authorities prevented them from going to the United States due to insufficient proof of their birthplace, while Mexican authorities prevented them from entering as contract laborers because they had been personally contacted by an employer, rather than the contract being arranged through the formal procedures of the program.[31] Forty-five men from Nuevo Laredo, Tamaulipas, Mexican by birth, wrote to President Ávila Camacho stating that at various times they had lived in the United States and were now hoping to do so again, since "in our beloved Mexico there is a scarcity of jobs or rather there are no jobs." Having the experience of previously working in the United States provided no guarantee that aspiring migrants would be accepted into the program, however.[32] Binationality of any kind mattered little. The new ideal migrant had to have experience working in agriculture, be hardworking but unemployed, be able-bodied, preferably be single, and be over the age of twenty-one. He was not allowed to have previously been given land by the Mexican government as an *ejidatrio*. Most significantly, if men wanted to obtain a bracero contract they absolutely needed to return to Mexico after their contract was over. While some of those requirements were flexible, especially as the bracero program evolved, the one requirement was not negotiable was that braceros be males.[33]

ASPIRING FEMALE MIGRANTS IN THE BRACERO ERA

Although women in the United States were increasingly entering the labor market to help fill the demand created by the war effort (with many migrant women entering the workforce long before), Mexican women were still expected to serve their country within the boundaries of the nation.[34] Those women who worked outside the home were still expected to take jobs appropriate for their gender. A group of women wrote to President Ávila Camacho on May 12, 1945, to offer their services as nurses in the United States.[35] Their application was forwarded to the Ministry of the Interior, not the Ministry of Labor, an indication that women were not considered for labor contracts abroad even when petitioning within gendered expectations for appropriate labor.

When Elvira Moreno, writing to the president on February 29, 1944, offered to lend her services to the United States and specified that she wanted a contract to work in the fruit packing industries of California, the director of a government employment agency informed her that her request could not be granted. He further explained that this was because "no agreement relative to the contract labor of women existed between the two governments."[36] Despite the growth of fruit-packing industries, especially in California, the high proportion of Mexican women employed in this work, and the increased government contracts given to canneries and packing houses during World War II, the bracero agreements did not take into consideration the need for women migrant laborers.[37] Elvira Moreno was likely just one of many women who knew about these canning opportunities and looked to the bracero program as a way of gaining access to employment.[38] Like other aspiring braceros she was likely in contact with friends and family abroad who would share important news of job openings. In previous decades friends and family would help facilitate their relatives' migration to these jobs; however, aspiring migrants now faced a new set of rules that would structure a new legal and temporary order of migration. In short, government regulations and connections weighed more than social and family connections.

Other women, like Margarita Ramirez de Alvarado mentioned at the outset of this chapter, asked government officials for assistance in joining their husbands in the United States, while still others petitioned the president for themselves, their husbands, and sometimes their extended families. Maria de la Paz Angel, from Guadalajara, wrote to President Ávila Camacho after initially writing to the first lady, to ask for passports for herself and her husband to go to the United States as braceros. Due to poor economic conditions, the couple did not have the money to pay for the cost of travel.[39] Her request was forwarded to the Office of Migration, implying that she and her husband would have to attempt to enter the United States as regular immigrants rather than as sanctioned braceros. Juana Flores de Chavoya, also from Jalisco, wrote to ask the president if her whole family, or at the very least, if her husband, could work in the United States for six months.[40]

Migrants hoping to go to the United States, though not always specifying the need to be part of the program, continued to write for assistance, information, and benevolent intercessions on their behalf just as they had decades before. The era of contract labor, however, influenced the migration process for all migrants and conditioned the responses of government officials in ways they had not before. A group of women wrote to President Alemán pleading for intervention on their behalf with the Office of Migration in Chihuahua. They desired to go to the United States on labor contracts. The president's secretary passed the letter on to the Secretaría de Gobernación, who passed it on to the Office of Migration. This office advised the women not to attempt to cross the border until they had all of their paperwork in order and outlined the requirements for crossing with a valid labor contract "with someone in the United States who desires to use your services." The contract needed to be approved by the Mexican consul of the district to which the women were going and to have a signature of approval from the Secretaría de Relaciones Exteriores. The employer who was contracting the migrants would also have to pay 500 pesos with which to guarantee the cost of repatriation to the worker should they need it.[41] Contractual agreements, in general, were encouraged, as was a strict adherence to the policy of securing money for a migrant's eventual repatriation. The bracero program and emphasis on contractual labor with an expectation of employer responsibility was also a response to the crisis of repatriation and associated costs to the state (both the Mexican and US governments) that ballooned in the 1930s but had antecedents during the repatriations following World War I.

Both governments agreed to a temporary labor program based on their expectations of ideal migrants and migrations. Yet, each government was also attempting to graft bureaucratic requirements and ideal specifications for braceros onto a framework of migration that already included migrants from different sectors of society, of both genders, of a variety of ages, and with a wide range of skills and interests. Moreover, migrants who had previously worked in the United States but now encountered new requirements for their migrations would grow increasingly frustrated. Whether they were migrants who had successfully crossed the border in the past, those who felt they might not pass mandatory medical exams, those unsure of measuring up to other government expectations, or those who relied on meeting a family member near the border to help them get to the other side, many migrants, as in years past, crossed the border on their own and without guarantees—and outside the purview of a formalized migration program. Additionally, the demand to go work in the north simply outnumbered total available contracts. Thousands of aspiring braceros wrote to Mexican presidents to see if they might be one of the chosen few for the new program.

ASPIRING BRACEROS' LETTERS TO THE PRESIDENT

In March of 1943, a group of fifty-three men from Jaripo, Michoacán, sent a telegram to the president of Mexico, asking him for a second time if he could help them get to the United States so that they could look for work. They explained their reasons:

> Well all of us lack our own lands to work, we only work them when those others who do have land are willing to formally contract us. We implore that you order the Ministry of Labor to acknowledge our impoverishment, and hope that the fact that we are unable to come to the capital does not cause difficulty. We know that this is not the time to leave our country but we will return as soon as you order us to, so as to complete our duty as good Mexicans.[42]

The letter captures several themes that can be found in pleas of other aspiring braceros. These themes include: the lack of lands, general impoverishment, the difficulty of transportation, the need to provide for their families, and an acknowledgment of duty and patriotism. What exactly was the duty of a "good Mexican" during World War II? Bracero contracts ironically encouraged the action of emigration—the leaving of one's country as opposed to staying—as a patriotic duty. Migrants, some of whom had been trekking back and forth across the border for years, witnessed a changing paradigm as World War II sparked a dialogue about binational cooperation and introduced new restrictions and new hope in a reformatted era of *sanctioned* migration. Their letters reflect a host of conditions fueling migration in postrevolutionary Mexico and reveal how the desire to provide for family remained a motivating factor for migration in the 1940s.

Migrants who reached out to the president went to great lengths to justify their deservingness of the opportunity to serve their country abroad as providers and soldiers in production. Some went so far as to assert that a bracero contract was owed to them for their prior services as armed revolutionaries who had made sacrifices for the glory of Mexico. Letter writers incorporated the patriarchal right to provide, even if they had to emigrate to do so, into a broader concept of citizenship. Their duties as heads of household and good family patriarchs bound them to implicit contracts with their family to provide sustenance, while international labor agreements bound them to contracts with the United States to provide labor and therefore support for the international cause of democracy. Aspiring migrants had to cleverly justify the necessity to leave their *patria,* while balancing critiques of the current state of affairs in Mexico. Their pleas represented the limits of the national economy while at the same time expressing their loyalty and commitment to elevating the value and honor of their homeland. They had something to offer as provider-citizen-soldiers, but the state also owed them the opportunity to serve.[43]

Letters came in from nearly every state in the republic, letter writers were from different socioeconomic backgrounds, and family members, including women, also wrote on behalf of aspiring braceros. Mexico was in transition, with a centralized government that simultaneously defined itself by, and distanced itself from, the era of revolution with each passing administration. Still, the power and cult of personality of the president that Cárdenas had elevated during the previous administration held through the Ávila Camacho period, and migrants still viewed the president as the final arbiter, intercessor, and benefactor in their quest for bracero contracts.

Mariano Gonzalez wrote to President Ávila Camacho on behalf of himself and fifty other campesinos from Jalisco less than two months after the bracero program officially began. They made the trip north to Tijuana "based on the news from the capital reported in the newspapers assuring that there is a need for workers in the United States."[44] They described themselves as "free" workers—that is, those not belonging to a union—who were simply "looking for the bread of our subsistence." Referencing the labor environment of the time in which politically affiliated corporatist unions dominated many industries, braceros indicating they were "free" signaled to authorities that they were not subject to partisan politics. Not belonging to a union, unfortunately, could also result in their exclusion from employment opportunities; going to the United States could have been one of few options left. They were now stuck at the border with no contracts or resources, and they were forced to sleep on the streets of Tijuana. Letters and telegrams came to the president from other border cities detailing similar circumstances: four hundred men in Mexicali were stranded at the border and needed help returning home; nine hundred migrants, aspiring braceros and their families from the interior, were in Ciudad Juárez, hoping that the president would authorize their crossing into the United States.[45]

Early letters and telegrams to the president suggest, firstly, that those with the resources to do so went directly to the border upon news of contracts being given out, signaling both the expectation of a fairly straightforward crossing, and the intense appeal of a jobs program. Second, as a result of incomplete information and a lack of bureaucratic infrastructure to handle the influx of migrants at the border, many then immediately faced dire circumstances, since the cost of their trips and extended stays at the border depleted the few resources that they had. Letters also reveal a belief that the bracero agreement was connected to the president and that the ability to cross the border was tied to the president's benevolence--making him the ultimate patriarch. The letters also showed that migrants understood and used the rhetoric of a new diplomatic and wartime logic for their appeals, setting their requests against the backdrop of of global politics. Aspiring braceros stranded in Mexicali wrote that "we came to the border with the exclusive purpose of entering the United States to lend our services according to your agreement with the North American Embassy."

Mariano Gonzalez, the man representing the fifty campesinos from Jalisco, suggested that their fate could be sealed with a stroke of the president's pen. Surely if the president made a request to the American authorities, then the group would be let into the country, especially "considering the circumstances of cooperation and the good will that exists because of the

Good Neighbor policy." He closed the letter, "We profess our loyalty and are obligated to your government to give our immediate cooperation in accordance with the circumstances that command it, for we are in a state of war and the country must reclaim its sons."[46]

Aspiring braceros couched their letters to the president in the same language that was being used to attract the support of Mexicans to the allied cause and to the elevation of Mexican honor on a global stage. Letter-writers also attempted to profess loyalty in the context of war, cooperation in the context of diplomacy, while simultaneously articulating a sense of poverty in the context of post-revolutionary Mexico. Aside from any wartime rhetoric, it was most clear that aspiring migrants viewed the program as the solution to unemployment, underemployment, and poverty.

MAKING ENDS MEET IN 1940S MEXICO

Letter writers generally stated that it was a lack of work, lack of land, and poor salaries that led to their desire to go north for a labor contract. Aurelio Hernández from Villa Acuña, Coahuila, near the US-Mexico border, wrote twice to the president citing poor economic circumstances made worse by the fact that goods were being charged for in dollars. He stated, "with each moment it becomes worse and harder for me to support myself and my family."[47] A 1942 survey given to five hundred aspiring braceros by the Ministry of Labor in Mexico City reported that 71.8 percent of them wanted to work in the United States to earn more money, while 14.2 percent wanted to go for "emotional reasons," and 12.4 percent wanted to go in search of adventure.[48] Letters written to the president partially confirm this trend in that the majority of letters, closer to 90 percent, cited the need for higher wages. Only a handful of the five hundred sampled letters for the years 1942 through 1945 mentioned anything such as adventure or education. Qualitative insights revealed through letters also importantly suggest that "emotional or affective reasons" should not be separated, as the Ministry of Labor thought it should, from the need to earn more money. In fact, the most oft-cited reason that braceros mentioned for wanting to leave Mexico for the United States was their inability to sustain their families on their current salaries as the result of lacking permanent employment.

Women's letters to the president asking for bracero contracts for their male family members also illustrate the connection between family life and the economic opportunities afforded to braceros. On January 6, 1944, Castula Guerrero wrote to President Ávila Camacho to ask him for two things. After wishing the president a happy new year, she first asked him if he could give gifts to her young children in honor of it being Three Kings Day. She then asked the president to help facilitate a bracero contract for her husband.[49] Angela Velarde de Madrigal wrote to the President from Mexicali to ask for bracero contracts for herself and for her husband. She cited her husband's low salary and their inability to sustain their four children as a reason for seeking employment opportunities in the United States. For Angela and Castula, the bracero contracts would ensure family subsistence.

A CLAIM FOR RIGHTS

As the war rhetoric quieted down and aspiring braceros began to encounter more and more obstacles in getting contracts, letters began to take a different tone.[50] Whereas initially braceros expressed their loyalty to the president, and their willingness to support the country, the government, and the war effort, aspiring braceros began to characterize the bracero contract less as an opportunity and more as a fundamental right. Over the next few years, the pleas became more explicit and the strategies for obtaining a favorable response became more varied and extreme. Rhetoric of democracy and of rights, a legacy extending from the Mexican Revolution, had been embedded into state petitions and was not new in any way. However, rhetoric about global democracy was internalized to emphasize the need for democracy within Mexico, claiming the right to work as a fundamental right of citizenship. Mexicans had long exercised their constitutional right to leave the country, but aspiring braceros were now claiming their right to leave *through a bracero contract* as a political, moral, and human right.

Where previous letter-writers might have mentioned political support for the president, letters increasingly mentioned having campaigned or performed military service on behalf of the president or a particular general almost as a matter of quid pro quo. While some letter writers were more veiled in their petitions, a group of aspiring braceros from Puebla wrote to the president in March of 1944 asking for contracts.[51] They explained their deservingness by stating, "Well as you might be able to understand, we lack everything needed to sustain our families. Our families who pray that you intervene favorably to our petition—a legal and just petition—considering that we risked our lives in the past presidential campaign in which our current president was elected." How they had risked their lives for the presidential campaign was unclear; this rhetorical flourish could have been more strategy than truth in order to convey the drama of sacrifice.

Veterans and their younger family members from the Revolutionary and Cristero wars also asked for contracts in return for the service they had provided for the country. The president of the Municipal Union of Veterans of the Revolution in Coahuila asked the president to facilitate bracero contracts on behalf of forty families due to the lack of work in the area.[52] Aurelio Segura, the son of a military captain who fought in the Cristero War, also asked for a bracero contract on behalf of himself and his three brothers. He explained that his mother had never been able to obtain a pension after the death of her husband since she lived too far away from the capital. Aurelio implored the president to give him and his family bracero cards, due to the difficult economic situation of the entire family, and in consideration of the services offered during the life of his now deceased father.[53] The program symbolized a way for the government to make good on revolutionary-era debts.

For others, the right to a bracero contract was envisioned more as a natural right, tied directly to the right to work and to provide for their family members. In its most extreme and yet simple elaboration, the right to a bracero contract was connected to the right to be free from hunger, the right not to starve. In post-revolutionary Mexico this right was shaped by politics, the environment, and by overreaching promises of land reform that never quite reached all expectant *campesinos*. Drought, plague, and volcanic ash threatened harvests across Mexico during this period and according to aspiring migrants who wanted to go north just to survive until the next harvest, the land was "dead" and "infertile."[54] Antonia Mora Miraflores wrote to the president complaining that the Banco Ejidal had stopped extending credit, that the governor of Jalisco had done nothing to help campesinos with fields that were "dead," and asked the president to allow laborers in the region go to the United States as braceros.[55] Agricultural un- and under-employment due to poor harvests and environmental disasters had led migrants to work northern harvests for decades, but after the redistribution of lands under President Cárdenas, the problems in the *campo* took on an added political dimension. The land that had been given to campesinos in the 1930s was not giving back to them, and as long as the government kept the Revolution alive in rhetoric, Mexican citizens, including aspiring migrants, would continue to press for revolutionary promises.[56]

The restrictions against *ejiditarios* were especially difficult under these circumstances. A letter to the governor of Jalisco with more than seventy signatories, all from an *ejido* in Santa Rosalía, Jalisco, created by presidential resolution, stated, "they gave us lands that were not cultivatable lands, which has led to a failure for our community." They looked to the governor to resolve the situation: "we ask of you to provide us with a pass to the United States of North America as braceros to remedy our needs and the needs of our families, since we find ourselves without land to work, and without work of any kind."[57] Another letter written by Ismael Torres, president of an *ejido* in La Cienega, Jalisco, commented on the connection between land and emigration: "As you perfectly know our *ejido* in these moments finds itself with land that is of poor quality for harvest; a great number of *ejidatarios* whose land is not producing want to go to the United States as braceros."[58]

Numerous requests for bracero contracts came from those who had received lands but had few resources to make the land productive. Land alone was not enough to sustain Mexican families, as it required capital in terms of financial investment and technology. Some landholdings were also far too small, even in the presence of adequate equipment, to support larger families.[59] An *ejido* commission from Rancho Nuevo de La Cruz, Guanajuato, asked the president for ten bracero contracts for those "who couldn't cultivate their parcels and lacked the resources to sustain their families." Members of the *ejido* commission assured the president that those with contracts would only temporarily leave their *ejidos*.[60] Aspiring migrants with family members who could stay behind and work the *ejido* land sought to justify leaving while still having their family members contribute to the nation—thus serving the nation in both capacities, abroad and domestically.[61] Farmers of small and medium landholdings also needed capital to keep their goods in a market that was dominated by commercialized and "modernized" agriculture. New seed hybrids, fertilizers, and pesticides introduced by the Green Revolution demanded more investment, as did modernized tools, tractors, machines, and parts (many made in the United States).[62] Despite the bracero program requiring agricultural workers, displaced factory workers would also seek contracts. In Santiago, Jalisco, the modernization of textile factories led to the unemployment of many residents and men began leaving as braceros, accompanied by some women as well.[63]

Thus, men who saw themselves as good patriarchs for engaging in military, political, and economic service challenged the government to protect and bolster their households by giving them the opportunity to provide. Women

writing to obtain contracts for male family members used similar justifications. Maria Concepción Armenta de Aguilera from the Valle de Santiago
stressed her poor financial condition and asked the president for his help in
sending her husband Julian to the United States as a bracero.[64] Maria de Jesus
Vda. de la Cruz from Tenamaxtlán, Jalisco, a widow, inquired about a bracero
contract for her brother, while Maria Anguiano Vda. de Hernández, also a
widow, from La Barca, Jalisco, needed help getting her son work as a bracero.[65]
Aurelia Martinez, Concepcion Garcia, and Maria Morales, also from the
Valle de Santiago, Guanajuato, wrote together to the president requesting
bracero contracts for their cousins.[66] Although families were formally excised
from the bracero contracting process, trying to secure contracts through
letter-writing and petitions became a family affair.

The bracero contracts did help some men preserve their roles as family
patriarchs by facilitating short-term economic opportunities and the ability
for some families to gain capital and credit for small business and agricultural
tools and technology, and even greater status in their Mexican communities.[67] However, the overall program was fraught with complications that
often meant minimal savings and also led to long periods of family separations and hardships. Nevertheless, even returned braceros would write again
with their petitions for additional contracts.

By the end of Manuel Ávila Camacho's administration, letters from those
who had already served time as braceros were arriving to the Palacio Nacional.
Some wanted help getting their 10 percent savings, while others, having fin-
ished their contracts, saw the president as an intercessor who could obtain
employment in their home states. The National Alliance of Braceros, representing men who had already served as braceros, petitioned the president for
still more contracts. They wanted to return north, since in Mexico they saw
little promise for continued employment. That braceros created such organizations reflects the ongoing corporatist nature of politics in Mexico and also
the longevity of and sustained interest in the bracero program. Their new
claims, initially couched in the rhetoric of service for the *patria,* and now
claiming rights as revolutionaries, party affiliates, or defenders of democracy,
asked for repeat contracts and continued migration into the United States.
In short, because they had already made the sacrifice of crossing an international border and traveling far from their loved ones, they had earned
the right to serve again so that they might buy land or at have some other
ability to make a living. To preempt the counterargument that there were
jobs to be had in Mexico, they supplied a litany of abuses that employers and

industrialists subjected non-salaried workers to in Mexico City. Also, many returning braceros were campesinos with skills that were increasingly incompatible with an urban labor market. Nor did they make enough money to "buy" rights—an allusion to corrupt schemes that provided contracts through bribes. They demanded the right to provide even if they had to repeatedly leave their country to do so.

The bracero program, designed to supplement the US labor force during war, and to give Mexican men needed jobs and experience which they could utilize upon returning to their country, became a program in which unemployed and underemployed Mexican families placed their hopes for the next twenty years. Even underemployed workers from PEMEX, one of the greatest symbols of revolutionary reform and national sovereignty, petitioned for bracero contracts after work had been completed at the Azcapotzalco oil refinery.[68] In a letter to the Governor of Jalisco, a state that had at various times been blocked from further bracero contracts, Juan Rico Avalos called into question the parameters of Mexican nationalism, including the opportunity for migration, providing for one's family, and building a better Mexico into the fundamental rights of being Mexican.

> We want only work so that we can sustain our children so they can better serve the country. Our voice has been weak, inaudible, and our complaints have been neglected on various occasions when we've asked to emigrate as braceros. Are we not so Mexican like our compatriots from other states who have been given the opportunity to emigrate in search for better possibilities in life?[69]

Rico Avalos centered his plea around the future, not just invoking his children but the children and future of Mexico: "We want a Mexico that is better so that in the near future our children may live happy." But how did the bracero program impact families who were left in Mexico, and not just children and wives, but mothers and sisters?

FAMILY AND FAMILY MIGRATION IN THE BRACERO ERA

While there is some evidence that women and children accompanied braceros during their contracts in the United States, the majority of families affected by the bracero program remained in Mexico while the men on contracts were in the United States. Scholar Ana Elizabeth Rosas shows that as a result of the psychological and economic impacts of separation, wives and children relied on each other when the state took little notice of the families left behind. When mothers and children had to labor in order to make up for the loss of the head of household's wage, and when children had to cope with separation from either one or both parents, teachers in San Martin de Hidalgo, Jalisco, stepped in to try and mediate the hardships experienced in communities affected by the bracero exodus.[70] Some mothers, lacking community support, were much less fortunate. After not hearing from her husband during the year that he had been in the United States, for example, Maria Marrón was forced to leave her two girls at a Guadalajara orphanage in 1946.[71]

As the program continued, presidents received more letters from women desperately inquiring about the whereabouts of their bracero relatives. Trinidad Rojas Andrade wrote to the president in October 1943 after not hearing from her son who had left as a bracero in January of that same year. She had already been in contact with a contracting office that told her he had disappeared from his job in August, after which she went to the president with her plea: "Sir, my son is young, and I find myself desperate, I have written to the Mexican consul but he has not answered me, I want to know about my son, well, for me he is everything, and that is why I write to you, for him, with the hope that my son will be returned to me or that I may learn what became of him."[72] She was not the only mother looking for her son. María Refugio Guzmán de Sandoval asked President Alemán for help in finding her son Rámon, who had been contracted as a bracero the previous year but never reached his destination.[73] Family members of braceros from Tamaulipas wrote to the president after hearing that braceros had been wounded after being shot somewhere near Cedar Creek, Nebraska.[74]

Others inquired about the savings supposedly available to families in Mexico, and in the most tragic of cases, widows whose husbands had died while serving their contracts sought assistance to support their families through owed wages and indemnification. Enriqueta Sánchez de Cuevas wrote to Ávila Camacho asking for her husband's savings after he died in Loray, Nevada, while working for Southern Pacific Railroads. The husbands of Maria Carmen de Garcia, from Zacatecas; Juana Navarrete de Negrete, from Pénjamo, Guanajuato; and Maria de Jesus Ruiz de Sandoval, from Yahualica, Jalisco, all died while on bracero contracts in the United States, and each wrote to the president after attempting to petition another government agency for means of support in the wake of their husbands' deaths.[75]

A telegram sent by Angela Hernandez de Gonzalez to the president captures the widow's desperation.

> I, widow of bracero Margarito Gonzalez Azua, have official copy number 702 consul general Chicago, February 6 sending the Secretaría Relaciones checks for me 107827 and 109593 as social insurance and compensation death of my husband. After reiterating my circumstances before Secretaria Relaciones, they will not send them and finding myself in complete indigence, eight children to whom I give bread, I ask that you attentively order the sending of my checks to the end of aiding me in my desperate situation. Attentively Angela Hernandez Vda. de Gonzalez.[76]

Women dealing with the death of their bracero husbands had to navigate multiple government agencies on both sides of the border, face life without the anticipated crucial income that bracero work would bring, bear witness to their children losing their father, and deal with the loss of their partner in life. Such heart-wrenching losses and separations would continue over the next nineteen years of the bracero program.

·   ·   ·

Letters presented in this chapter add to the history of the bracero program in two important ways. They reveal the strategy and the language which aspiring migrants used with the executives of the state, often shaped by patriarchal expectations of husbands as providers, as they sought to gain (re)entry to the United States. We also gain insight about 1940s Mexico—a Mexico that many aspiring braceros wanted to leave. Even amidst the stabilization of mid-century Mexico and improved economic stability in comparison to previous years, torn by revolution and a global depression, migrants still sought economic remedy in their peregrinations to the north. Combining Mexican revolutionary rhetoric about rights and sacrifice with World War II-era rhetoric of democracy, migrants justified their desires to leave the *patria* in a broader global context while simultaneously commenting on their local realities.

These were often, if not centered, at least articulated as such to the state, around providing for their families. Whereas in the 1920s, observers bemoaned the emigration of Mexican families to the state, in the 1940s it became patriotic for Mexicans to migrate—at least, for Mexican men. Women were left out in that sense. The bracero program allowed Mexican men to reframe their motivations and actions as a way of lending their services to the United States and to Mexico.[77] Rather than being seen as a selfish act of individualism, Mexican migration could now be perceived as service to both countries—a fact that obviously employers and migrants had understood for decades but one that had been curbed by American nativism and Mexican nationalism during the 1930s. The bracero program systematized and legalized temporary binational migratory labor, at least to a degree.[78] The program was conditional and selective and introduced a new expectation of the Mexican migrant, decidedly male and decidedly temporary, set within the context of World War II in an environment rich with the rhetoric of service, rights, and democracy. The program also conditioned the expectations that aspiring migrants, as post-revolutionary Mexicans, had of their *patria* and their *presidente.*

Women were left out of this new migrant ideal and family networks were cut out of the new paradigm of cross-border migrations. Men not fitting the parameters of the new program were also left out. 4.6 million Mexicans did benefit from legal contracts over the course of the program's twenty-two-year period. The bracero program expanded both the opportunity for temporary legal migration and the appeal of northern migration to Mexican communities that hadn't yet experienced international emigration. Throughout the next two decades some fortunate families, especially if they had relatives in the United States, would still be able to participate in straightforward and relatively obstacle-free binational migrations. For them, migrations would continue to be shaped by economic cycles, new border legislation, and life events, and, in the extended bracero era, by the state. But the program that had provided great hope for sanctioned migration, binational cooperation, and bilateral regulation, also ushered forth a new era of vigilance. Gone was the informal border of the 1910s, and the flexible border of the 1920s. Increased desires to migrate paired with increased vigilance at the border formed the basis for the program's other legacy: a surge in illegal immigration. Women, who had been left out and left behind by the formal program, continued to support the migrations of their male family members. But this meant that the families of millions of men would be forced to endure family separations. And they did. That is, until families also began once again to head north, this time on riskier migrations across an increasingly militarized and violent border.

CHAPTER SIX

The Era of Policing

WOMEN BEYOND CONTROL, 1945–1965

IN SPRING OF 1953, a reporter from the *Laredo Times* followed the deportation journey of two hundred braceros from McAllen to Zapata, Texas, where they were to cross over the international bridge back to Mexico. The reporter told the harrowing tale of thirty-six men who were unable to pay for their own transportation after being deported for working illegally in the United States as "wetbacks." They were being forced to carry out the return journey on foot through forty-five miles "of rattlesnake-infested, waterless, uninhabited desert" without food or water. Deporting Mexicans by bussing them to points along the border where they would have to walk miles before reaching the nearest town was reportedly a punishment suggested by a US government official, as a way of discouraging them from returning. By the 1950s it had become quite common for migrants to be deposited across the border only to re-enter the United States again shortly after without documents.

A man who had come to the United States from Michoacán with his wife was one of the men sent to walk to the nearest Mexican city. When asked to explain why he and his wife entered the United States in the first place, he told the reporter, "We could make very little from the crops from our little farm. Often the children were hungry." So, the couple left their children with their paternal grandparents and decided to cross the river after "officials of both countries" had made it difficult for them to enter the United States. Acknowledging that he and his wife's river crossing was illegal, he stated their reasoning for taking the risk: "but we knew, too, that your farmers needed our help. And we had heard how your great chiefs in Washington had what they called the 'Good Neighbor Policy,' and that they called Mexicans their friends and that your country was land of opportunity which welcomed all good people who wanted to work." The wife and husband were able to work only a couple of harvests before they were caught without papers and subsequently taken to a deportation camp. Immigration officials would take his wife to Laredo and deport her there, while he would be made to suffer the forty-five-mile trek as a lesson. "So I gave my wife the little money we had saved. She is somewhere now; maybe on the road between your Laredo and Monterrey. I told her that, God willing, I would meet her there and we would return to our little farm together." The reporter admitted his shock at the "senseless, brutal separation of a man and his wife."[1]

The reporter referred to the practice of requiring deportees to walk long expanses of sparsely inhabited territory during the hot summer months as the "hot-foot lift." Compared to the bus lifts, train lifts, and airlifts that were used in the deportation of undocumented migrants, the reporter found the hot-foot lift to be particularly pernicious. In order to deter migrants, or so-called "repeaters," from coming back to the United States, the US Border Patrol would drop deportees off in locations far from where they had entered or been apprehended so as to disrupt the social networks that could facilitate their return crossing.[2] The reporter's story was particularly effective in demonstrating the crueler aspects of deportation by focusing on the separation of the couple from Michoacán. The poor farmer's quote about the welcoming of Mexicans and mention of the Good Neighbor Policy rings with a tone of irony that the farmer may not have intended. What began as a binational program symbolic of diplomatic cooperation in the face of war had unfolded into a period of disagreement, and ultimately an era of mass deportations that affected millions of migrants and former braceros. The program which was heralded for its commitment to hemispheric solidarity included a forceful crackdown on surreptitious migrations. A trend of illegal immigration had paralleled, and in part been caused by, the legal sanction of labor migration since the inception of the program. Concerted efforts to apprehend and deport migrants took on new dimensions in the 1950s as the intensified regulation of illegal border-crossers served as the counterweight to American critics who claimed that imported Mexican labor led to depressed agricultural wages. Meanwhile, another migration trend was becoming more visible during the 1950s and 1960s as the increased migration of women and children demonstrated that families were migrating alongside their bracero relatives. The overall increase in the migration of women and children, and the increase of undocumented women and children in particular, began to stymie government officials on both sides of the border who were trying desperately to reshape migration into an orderly and temporary movement of male

Mexican laborers only. With their migrations to Mexican border cities and beyond, families challenged narrow expectations of migration and resisted the idea that family separation was a natural and unquestionable cost of participation in the formal program. Migrant women challenged the gendered notion that only men would want to go the United States seeking labor, or be useful laborers once there. Women would increasingly go to the United States and the borderlands, not only to work, but to reunite their families with male relatives. This trend meant that women's migration would equal that of men by the end of the 1970s.

Family migration surged again through both legal and illegal channels. An informal "bracera" movement even began in response to the increased demand for Mexican domestic servants, especially in border cities and especially in Texas.[3] Communities that had not yet witnessed the family or "feminine exodus" would see women migrating north for the first time during the latter years of the bracero period.[4] Increasing urbanization in Mexico would pull more men and women from the countryside first to cities in the interior, then north to border cities, and finally to the United States. Migration routes traced the same well-worn paths of the 1920s; however, the volume of migrants would increase dramatically from levels in the first half of the century. Apprehensions and deportations would also escalate, particularly the apprehensions of women and children. For example, in 1953, 60 percent of border patrol apprehensions in El Paso were of women and children.[5]

This chapter traces the changing nature of Mexican migration during the 1950s and 1960s, when bracero migrations happened alongside other regular migrations, but also alongside undocumented migrations. I argue that despite both governments' attempts to reorder migration as temporary and male, family migrations continued; the result of the governments' actions was that they now often occurred outside sanctioned channels. Due to gendered forms of deportation and detainment, in combination with the increase in voluntary deportation, the removal of women and families was often invisible. I offer here an initial assessment about the gendered dimensions of deportation campaigns such as "Operation Wetback," which reveals that both the US and Mexican governments were aware of the increasing number of family migrations across the border. Recent scholarship on the bracero program importantly explores the impact that bracero migrations had on families who were left behind, and how the gender roles of both women and men were transformed by bracero migrations.[6] I add to this evidence by examining family units that migrated together despite the bracero program's restrictions.

MAP 6. Major ports of entry along the US-Mexico border, 1960. Map: Ben Pease.

What was the role, status, and place of migrant families and migrant women in an industrializing Mexico, a post-war United States, and the ever-changing borderlands? While the bracero program regulated labor network-ing and recruitment to a certain degree, it could not contain the spread of extra-program information about needy employers, preferred worksites, sug-gested labor circuit routes, and smuggling networks. While the program redistributed and managed workers on the US side of the border, its existence created chaos on the southern side; northern Mexican border cities were satu-rated with aspiring braceros and their family members. And if the program was meant to have a controlling and limiting effect on migration patterns, it exploded the demand for migration opportunities across the country, invit-ing exodus communities in the center west to send further generations of family members north and beginning new emigration legacies in central and southern Mexico.

THE CONTINUING DEMAND FOR LABOR

The demand for workers continued due to the increase as irrigation and acre-age opened up for harvest after the war in the United States. By the end of the 1940s, hundreds of thousands of braceros had left Mexico to enter the United States as temporary contract laborers. The program undoubtedly changed the course of Mexican migration throughout the 1940s and continued to do so throughout the 1950s and into the 1960s. Supported by the GI Bill and bolstered by experience in the military, veterans returning from the European and Pacific fronts after World War II would seek educational and labor opportunities that would provide them with more social mobility than prior to their service. In their absence, industrial and agricultural mobilization to help support the war effort and other technological advancements had changed the nation's economy in general, and the nation's rural economy in particular. Mexican braceros continued to stream into the United States on short-term labor contracts in a program retooled to suit the postwar era, an era less defined by the exigencies of binational cooperation agreed to by allies in war and geared instead to the demands of large-scale agribusiness.

The 1950s were marked by the US government abandoning its place as employer of record and carrying out military-named campaigns to remove illegal border-crossers from the country, while agricultural employers continued to hire both approved braceros and undocumented migrants. At the risk of potential exclusion from the program and deportation from the United States, bracero aspirants continued to make haste to the border to plead with officials to obtain contracts. Seasoned braceros returned from the United States to their hometowns, only to make their way back north again. New recruits were eager to get their chance at the coveted contracts despite the widespread circulation of reports about the poor treatment of braceros, bad working environments, and wage scandals. Some braceros, after all, returned with savings to invest in small businesses or small landholdings, along with gifts for any friends and family who might have showed support while they were away.[7] However, despite continued interest in the program by Mexican workers and US employers, the program was embattled by demands for its end as soon as the war concluded. American labor advocates were part of vocal opposition, but so too were various municipal presidents and officials in Mexico. US critics claimed that imported workers with their guaranteed housing, paid transportation, and limited health benefits were prioritized over domestic workers. To Mexican critics, the exodus of vital labor was causing destitution and the decay of social institutions in certain communities. One group from Baja California, for example, pleaded for women to also be allowed to work in the United States, stating that thousands of women were on the verge of resorting to prostitution.[8]

Gone was the rhetoric that hailed Mexican braceros as crucial to the war effort and as US allies in democracy. The debates during the 1950s and 1960s on both sides of the border questioned the need for such laborers and led to discussions that trended toward the commodification of braceros and their labor as material inputs, rather than as thinking and feeling humans. When their humanity was considered at all, it was trumped by the preservation of the integrity and humanity of domestic laborers, domestic farmers, and the American consumer. Braceros' legal status was clearly demarcated: they were *invited* and *temporary* guests, at best. Debates over the need to extend the program, social anxieties about a developing Mexican-American middle class, and the sustained growth of Mexican communities, all forced society to try to understand and define a range of Mexican and Mexican-American identities at the risk of conflating long-term residents with a more feared and supposedly threatening increasingly criminalized "other." The responses to the program from Mexican-American communities were often divided, as evidenced by the fragmented views about immigration held by civil rights groups such as the League of United Latin American Citizens (LULAC) and the GI Forum.[9] The tension between newcomers and long-term residents would be especially pronounced in Texas in the 1950s as the state was removed from the bracero program blacklist and flooded by both sanctioned and unsanctioned workers. For despite the purported gains and stability of the Mexican economy, many Mexicans migrants still viewed binational livelihoods as the best viable option for their families.

INDUSTRIAL DREAMING: MEXICO IN TRANSITION

Contemporary observers and scholars alike often referred to the period between 1940 and 1970 as the "Mexican Miracle" due to the 6 percent annual growth of Mexico's economy. Due in large part to the state-sponsored and subsidized Import Substitution Industrialization (ISI), Mexico's middle class grew, as did their consumption of modern appliances and consumer goods and their hope for upward mobility. However, only a small portion of Mexican citizens benefitted from the so-called "miracle," and even urban middle-class teachers and doctors found themselves desperate for higher wages as state-led development was replaced by neoliberalism.[10] Those living in the Mexican countryside, meanwhile, generally received fewer benefits and suffered greater losses overall. Commercialized agriculture to support growing urban areas led to an increase in landless rural families, from 58 percent in 1940 to 77 percent in 1970.[11]

The modernization and commercialization of agriculture that had its beginnings in the 1940s with help from the Rockefeller Foundation-driven Green Revolution led farmers to increasingly depend on fertilizers, pesticides, and hybrid seed technologies. The new high-yielding and expensive chemical farming challenged farmers who were accustomed to using traditional techniques and made it difficult for them to keep competitively priced goods on the market. It also led to increased reliance on debt, the need for more capital, and migration to the United States.[12] In addition to migrating for purposes of family reunification, *campesinos* found themselves having to migrate for higher wages, for modern implements, or for higher wages to pay for modern implements that would allow them to hold on to their plots of land if they had any.

In the 1950s, the modernization of Mexican agriculture continued to exclude small landowners and create crisis for families raising crops for household consumption. Hydraulic projects dramatically increased irrigable land in cultivation, but also led to the centralization of resources that privileged larger agricultural enterprises. Such projects largely supported the production of monocrop agriculture for export, rather than products for the domestic market.[13] By the 1960s, the use of hybridized seeds further excluded *campesinos* from modernized agricultural systems since seeds required fertilizers, insecticides, access to irrigation, and mechanized technologies for harvesting. The majority of agricultural workers simply did not have the capital to invest in such projects, and by the end of the 1960s there were still only a handful of states where the harvesting was done by tractor rather than the traditional handheld plow. The states benefitting the most from the purchase of tractors and other modern agricultural implements were located in the north of the country where proximity to the border reduced the costs in transportation of US-made machinery. Agriculturalists in the southern states would bear considerably more costs to transport tractors or purchase machine replacement parts.[14] The consolidation of large landholdings increased as agricultural firms began to lease and even extort the best land away from *ejidatarios*.

Families shifted from tenancy to wage-labor, as did families who needed to supplement low-producing parcels with work on other farms or in industry. But as these labor opportunities declined, communities gravitated toward bracero contracts. While some migrants headed to the border immediately at the outset of the program, some communities, even in the top sending state of Jalisco, did not seek contracts until the late 1940s or early 1950s. Up until that point, for example, residents in one southwestern town in the state were able to cobble together livelihoods from limited labor opportunities offered to them by their proximity to Guadalajara. Despite the fact that a large number of families in the region received plots of land in the *reparto,* many families felt the desperation of poverty that came with unproductive lands. Residents of the region had few options for labor, most of which required them to commute to nearby towns where they could participate in tequila, glycerin, and textile production. Others would follow labor opportunities offered to them by the road-building project that connected Guadalajara to the coast. A saving grace came in the form of an increase in Guadalajara's demand for charcoal during the 1940s. Many men were required for deforestation, the burning of wood, and the transportation of goods to the capital. Charcoal production provided jobs until the introduction of propane gas to Guadalajara in 1948. Despite their general poverty, therefore, most of the town's inhabitants found just enough local opportunity that they did not go north during the 1940s; it wasn't until 1951 that the region felt the real impact of the "organized contracting" of braceros.[15]

Meahwhile, a handful of migrants from towns in the region such as Atengo, Juchitlán, Tecolotlán, and Tenamaxtlán traveled north across the border during the first years of the program, but many of them did so initially without contracts. As mentioned in the previous chapter, access to the program was highly dependent on personal relationships and patronage networks, and without a connection to a government representative, aspiring braceros from entire regions were effectively cut off from the program. For example, Jalisciences in this region didn't really begin participating in the program until one of the town's representatives got a job at the bracero contracting center in Irapuato.[16] Undocumented immigration from the region continued after 1951, but now benefiting from personal connections, men were able to legally migrate on multiple contracts, with some arranging legal status for their families as well.[17]

Another study of Jalisco and Michoacán, in two rural and two urban areas, reveals that the bracero program had similar impacts on those regions. Again, a small number of community members migrated to the United States prior to the initiation of the bracero program, but many more left throughout its duration. The program alone did not cause people to leave their communities, but its combination with agricultural modernization and the lack of local labor opportunities contributed to the exodus of migrants.

By the 1970s migration networks were routinized, and seasonal US migration became the "preferred economic strategy" for a number of men and families, especially in the two rural communities. In both communities, residents had received lands as *ejidatarios* but did not have enough money to make their land productive. In one of the rural communities in southern Jalisco, opportunities for employment in vegetable gardens began to disappear as farmers began to focus on the production of the cash crops such as sorghum and alfalfa, which had been increasingly mechanized by the use of threshing machines.[18] Labor contraction pushed more people towards internal and international migration than ever before. While aspiring braceros, some as young as twelve and thirteen, went north with and without contracts during the 1940s, a quarter of the municipalities' population had left for the United States by the 1960s.[19] As men went north, women also left in increasing numbers as part of a growing general trend that resulted in women accounting for 60 percent of internal migrants during the era. In the decade following the bracero program, female migrants also made up 18 percent of total migrants from the community headed to the United States.[20]

Women accompanied their husbands during the last years of the bracero program. In such cases, it was not unusual for families to remain in the United States, use savings to invest in agricultural lands, and then act as absentee landlords while hiring others to cultivate their lands. Braceros who returned to the community even became moneylenders to those who did not have enough capital to cultivate their own lands. The allure for migrants continued through the end of the program depending on local labor developments. After a textile factory intensified the use of machinery, which replaced manual labor and led to the layoff of a thousand workers, migrants went north. Industrial modernization also led to dislocation and emigration. For example, one study reports that "during the late 1940s and 1950s, out-migration from Santiago reached a scale that supported its institutionalization. The process of emigration for work in the United States became commonplace and ultimately, routine."[21] Many migrants who went to the United States without contracts and who were detained or deported settled in the borderlands, where they helped establish migration networks that would help facilitate other migrations from southern Jalisco to California. As scholars commenting on the region state: "The institutionalization of the migrant networks during the Bracero era considerably reduced the costs and risks associated with U.S. migration and made it accessible to everyone, young and old, male and female, poor and rich."[22]

Ejidatarios, who were not supposed to participate in the program, also found a way to do so with the overall goal of using the savings to resurrect their poor-quality lands.[23] Wage laborers who began to see their duties outsourced to machines also hoped to participate in the program. Lastly, workers and residents from semi-urban areas increasingly went north with the specific intention of accruing savings so that they might come back to Mexico to start their own businesses. It was in this way that even urbanized areas like Guadalajara, one of the largest cities in Mexico, were impacted by the program. Emigrants to the United States would leave their towns on the outskirts of Guadalajara and earn enough money to return to set up small shops and businesses in the city, where they benefitted from more consumers and hoped to see their investments gain bigger returns than in their towns of origin.

These trends played out across the country as braceros sought to alleviate a variety of specific hardships with contract earnings.[24] In 1947, Francisco Hernandez from San Luis Potosí wrote to President Alemán to ask for help in getting a bracero contract for the specific purpose of reconciling his debts with the Banco Ejidal, the national bank that gave out loans to *ejidatarios.* Bacilio Guerra wrote from Ciudad Camargo in Chihuahua to say that the lands given to him and his brother were for pasture and not for the cultivation of crops, and to ask for permission to go work in agriculture in the United States.[25] Miners from Michoacán, suffering from "miserable" wages, state workers from the Department of Hydraulic Resources in Tamaulipas, and a philharmonic musician lacking an instrument, were all among the hundreds of letter writers asking President Alemán for bracero contracts well after the initial World War II phase of the program. Women also continued to write on behalf of their loved ones and themselves for the opportunity to migrate to the United States. Maria Heriberta Torres, like Elvira Moreno had in 1944, asked not for a bracero contract, but for official authorization from the president to "lend her services" to a fruit packing plant.[26]

Migration was simply the best alternative for those who faced unemployment, underemployment, and even for those who were turned away in their petitions for land throughout the 1940s, 1950s, and 1960s. Despite this period being heralded as a time of economic miracle and relative political peace, rural land petitioners continued to be met with open repression.[27] When people sought to alleviate their conditions by migrating, the bracero program served as a valuable safety valve for rural governments by decreasing the chances for open clashes over land claims. The program functioned similarly in urban areas as well, as trade workers falling outside of union lines or ostra-cized by union politics also sought temporary reprieve by heading north.[28]

MIGRANT JOURNEYS AND ENTRIES AT THE BORDER

The ending of World War II did little to stem the tide of aspiring braceros headed to the border and to contracting centers in the interior. Moreover, the rigidity with which program requirements were carried out initially was com-promised by a number of logistical problems and also by corruption and graft that immediately began to penetrate every stage of the contracting process.[29] Despite the operation of contracting centers in the interior, the northern Mexican borderlands continued to receive a massive influx of migrants. Alongside migration that was inspired by the bracero program, non-braceros also continued to migrate to the border to visit temporarily, immigrate perma-nently, and reconnect with family or find opportunities outside the formal con-fines of the program. Commuter traffic from Mexico increased in the year after the war, as did temporary visa entries. The number of regular immigrations—that is, the number of Mexicans admitted on immigrant visas—also increased.[30]

The extension of the program was therefore part of an overall increase of migrant entries at the border. By the mid-1940s, some braceros had already been on repeat contracts into the United States.[31] Meanwhile, more and more family members began to join their bracero relatives. The program's postwar continuance announced to all that Mexican workers were still needed in the north, and signaled that to a certain degree, the border was in fact open for business. The border, however, was still mostly governed by existing immigration law that conditioned migrants to fulfill requirements set out by the immigration legislation of years past. With the exception of a few extraordinary moments throughout the late 1940s and 1950s, in which US grower power forcefully opened up the border to satisfy harvest-time interests, braceros had to be processed at bracero centers without exception, while regular migrants and immigrants had to continue to prove that they were not likely to become a public charge and otherwise demonstrate their worthiness to enter the United States. Those wanting to enter who could not satisfy immigration requirements continued to watch for a breakdown in the structures of vigilance and take their chances through risky and unsanc-tioned crossings for employment. Most who tried were confident that they would get work, eventually.

MIGRATING TO THE BORDER:
REGULAR MIGRATIONS

Regular migrations, whether to immigrate, to visit family, or for business or tourism, continued to increase between the 1940s and 1960s. Aspiring migrants who wanted to enter the United States outside of the parameters of the bracero program faced similar requirements to their predecessors in the late 1920s. They had to be literate, not subject to any exclusions based on health or moral character, demonstrate that they were not likely to become a public charge, and were required to pay visa and head taxes. The LPC exclusion was still used to restrict entry during the war and post-war period, with women still being disproportionately excluded for this reason. In order to prevent such a suspicion, women could try to enter on a non-quota immigrant visa carrying letters of support from family members who vouched for their character and assured their financial solvency. Files maintained by the National Catholic Welfare Conference's border representative, Cleofas Calleros, contain many notarized statements from primarily male relatives supporting female family members who wanted to cross on temporary visas to the United States.[32]

Women approaching the border in the 1940s and 50s who didn't fulfill requirements for entry would not be told to go to a bracero contracting center, like their male counterparts; they would just be denied entry. As far as the Mexican government was concerned, women could technically engage in contract labor. When three women from Delicias, Chihuahua, wrote to the president to ask about securing a visa to work in the United States, a migration official who received the forwarded letter wrote back, instructing them that they needed to obtain a Mexican passport, a visa from the United States consulate, and "to present a contract with a person in the United States that desires to utilize your services." The contract was to then be approved by the Mexican consulate in the region where they intended to work, and money for their repatriation would have to be sent to the department of migration to cover the costs of return migration.[33] In other words, contracted labor was possible for women, but not through a formal program and not through a streamlined process. The letter, like the letters written by women during the World War II era, illustrate that women, whether part of a family group or migrating on their own, were also trying to carve a path to the United States. They were working in agriculture, packing houses, and canneries, and perhaps most notably in high numbers as domestic servants.

Although border cities like El Paso had long witnessed the commuter cross-ings of Mexican women employed as domestics, the increase in female migra-tions throughout the 1950s began to command deep concern from Mexican observers. A 1953 article from Guadalajara's *El Informador* titled "Y Ahora, las Braceras," echoed a sentiment from articles written in the 1920s about women participating in the northward exodus, except that it exhibited even more disdain and criticism regarding women who migrated to the United States as domestic servants. The author connected the emigration of women domestics to the bracero program and registers contempt for everyone involved in the process. "Our Good Neighbors aren't satisfied with just tak-ing our Braceros, taking advantage of their services even marrying them off to 'gueras' with blue eyes and fine hair, if allowed, now they want to take our *Braceras*." The author went on, "They want to take our Mexican 'mochachas' to sweep the house, to take care of the 'baby,' and to wash the clothes and the plates, and in sum, they do all of the dirty work entailed in the good conser-vation of their 'homes.'"[34] With a biting sarcastic tone, the author positioned the United States as greedy and insatiable for Mexican labor, which now explicitly included the labor of Mexican women. Employing the familiar rhetoric of the Good Neighbor policy from the previous decade, the author decried the impact that this migration to the United States had on Mexican women. If Mexico was a good neighbor, the United States was not.

Much of the author's contempt, however, was reserved for the women who came back "in complete ruin." The author describes the new attire of female returnees in less than complimentary terms, while also critiquing their new vocabulary, said to include English vulgarities like "gad deme" [goddamn] when they get upset or "maches" [matches] for when they want to smoke. And yet, perhaps the most disdain was reserved for the white men who mar-ried domestic servants and came to Mexico, who get drunk and "attempt to sing Cielito Lindo, and shoot bullets up into the air." The author concluded, "Well, see, our female good neighbors don't even benefit from our Braceras Mexicanas going there," the idea being that if they were not careful, white American women might lose their husbands. In short, the demand for "brac-eras" benefitted no party; not the women who leave only to pick up bad American habits, not the American men who might end up divorcing their wives and marrying one of the maids, and not the women who might have originally thought they would benefit from the Mexican women's services in the first place. The opinion piece is riddled with stereotypes of all parties involved, including the hypothetical white man, "Mr. Smith," described as "un gringazo" dressed in khakis and cowboy boots, who divorces his wife, comes to Mexico with a new wife, and tries to appropriate Mexican customs. The author invoked a classic *malinche* trope: Mexican women would invite white men into Mexico to not only take Mexican women but also Mexican culture.[35] The domestic servants are, significantly, derogatorily depicted as "indias prietas, patas cuadradas y cabellos como de cola de caballo" or as "mixteco-zapoteca." The writer's focus on the indigeneity of the women is striking and can be read either as an attempt to preserve the honor of the "whiter" *tapatia* from condemnation or might reflect the increasing anxiety surrounding urbanization during the period that increasingly brought rural indigenous families into urbanized spaces. What is clear is that the author is speaking to patterns of increasing demand for female migrant labor, and intriguingly chose the term *bracera*. The term "bracero" was used in this area long before the binational bracero program, but the term *bracera,* in this context, is related specifically to the male-only labor program. Women had been migrating for decades to make families and labor in the United States, but the phenomenon was rendered more visible because of the vast and formalized migration of their male counterparts.

In 1953, the *El Paso Herald Post* published the provisions of a proposed "Bracero Maid" contract. This was suggested by the Association for Legalized Domestics, formed in 1953 by American housewives. Vicki Ruiz recounts that "the Association for Legalized Domestics sought the assistance of the Immigration and Naturalization Service (INS) in contracting (legally) the labor of Juárez women." The idea was that, like agricultural labor arrangements prior to and through the bracero program, women migrants would be contracted to specific employers throughout the Southwest, with the clear requirement that the process be legal. In fact, the proposed provisions include involvement of the Immigration and Naturalization Service, the US Consular Service, and the approval of the US Labor Department. A bracero program for maids was never put into effect, and its provisions would have served to bind women to one employer, rendering any women who left poor working conditions subject to losing legal worker status altogether.[36] But legal or not, there was an increased demand for female Mexican labor.

As a border city, El Paso had historically received many migrant domestic servants, and even more border commuters were occupying such jobs throughout the 1940s and 1950s. The bracero program brought with it imaginings of a counterpart female program. Ideas about a how a similar binational program might streamline legal entry for young Mexican women began to circulate as young migrant women became swept up in the concerted efforts to clear out undocumented workers from the borderlands. In August of 1953, four women appeared before a United States District court judge in El Paso for coming into the United States to work illegally as domestics. The women in the case "explained that they were unable to find work in Mexico and had crossed to El Paso in order to support their children." They received a sixty-day suspended sentence and a warning that there would be harsher punishment if they should be caught again. The reason they were brought before the judge in the first place was because they were apprehended as "repeaters." [37] Mexican officials had begun to take notice of the situation as well, and a newspaper report from September of 1953 stated, "They are not only men who clandestinely cross the northern border in search of work, now, following reports sent to officials, it is known that women clandestinely emigrate in search of work in rich American households."[38] The article suggested that once in the United States, the employing families helped arrange their documents for entry. Despite a formal binational labor program and a cooperative understanding between the US and Mexican governments on the necessity to prevent undocumented immigration, the reality on the ground was that both men and women could cross into the United States surreptitiously and could potentially legalize their migrations after entry.

Mexican migrant women laboring in agricultural fields also earned more attention as a consequence of the bracero program. Mexican and Mexican-American families who had not returned to Mexico during the 1930s continued to work in agriculture along migratory circuits throughout the United States. Women, whether part of family units or on their own, found opportunities in the fields. In a 1954 *Los Angeles Times* article that took as its main subject the "current international crisis over the border recruiting of Mexican farm labor," a photograph running down the side of the article showed a young woman with a scarf wrapped around her head, hunched over picking cotton and momentarily looking up to stare off in the distance. The caption reads: "Women, too—Senora Ignacia Jiminez, 22, does a man's work picking cotton for $5 to $10 a day."[39] Whether Ignacia was a Mexican national or had been born in the United States is not clear, but we know that in fact many Mexican-American families worked side by side with Mexican braceros, making the distinction between foreign-born, American-born, or naturalized citizens difficult to discern.

The majority of bracero relatives likely did not follow their male family members, but many did undertake border crossings of their own to join their loved ones. Women and children, without contracts or subsidized transportation, were strongly discouraged from joining their relatives. Family members wouldn't have had as much reason to join men on short contracts, but as more braceros began to migrate on repeat contracts, more family members also began to migrate. Especially when braceros stayed on in the United States beyond their formal contracts, families were motivated to migrate in order to mitigate the hardship of being separated for months or even years. The new designation of a group of braceros known as "specials" increased the presence of family in the borderlands. Specials were braceros who were specifically requested by employers and were given the opportunity to circumvent contracting centers by having their re-contracting paperwork go directly through the Secretaría de Relaciones Exteriores. Population booms in borderland cities tell the partial story of families migrating alongside the braceros. In order to be closer to bracero relatives, many families would come up to settle in border cities such as Mexicali where bracero husbands and fathers could work on US farms to fulfill their contracts but come back across the border to be with their families between contracts.[40]

Families also undertook this strategy as they moved to Ciudad Juárez, again to minimize distance between family members in between contracts, but also as a possible step in a larger plan to establish legal entry into the United States.[41] Ester Duran made the trek with her children, first up to the border city of Mexicali and then to the United States to accompany her husband Federico. At the border, she was asked to show her husband's income tax form, likely provided by the employer for the purpose of supporting Ester's crossing. The form, not so much proving her husband's legality as much as his earnings, proved sufficient to convince border officials that she was admissible for entrance.[42] Of course, not all braceros were able to turn their temporary contracts into an opportunity for their families to move to the United States. Evidence from a growing compendium of oral histories reveals not only that families legally joined their bracero relatives, but also that employers often facilitated and sponsored these migrations.

Margarita Flores, a young girl during the time that her father worked in the United States as a bracero, described her family's reunification as follows: "My father could not be without his family and he sent for us. I don't know what means he used to do it. My mom and I lived in the ranch with my father. The owner of the ranch was very just and grateful for what he [father] did for the ranch, and he offered him a little room in which we lived us three with barely what we needed to survive, but we lived happy because we were together."[43]

For a family to move legally across the border in this era required a good degree of luck, money, and the ability to comply with immigration requirements. In some cases, like those illustrated above, employers helped to regularize the immigration and residency status of braceros and their families, but some families spent years writing to public officials, including the President of Mexico, for a contract or assistance in their migrations. Other families traveled long distances to recruitment centers only to exhaust their economic resources before they could take the journey north. All the while, consular officials of both nations, border officials, and other government representatives urged against family migration, especially due to the overwhelming surge of undocumented migration in the 1950s. But families migrated anyway.

In a letter written in 1954 to then-Senator Lyndon B. Johnson, Rio Grande Valley farmer C. W. Showers wrote of an incident in 1951 on his ranch involving braceros and their families that led to his blacklisting as a bracero employer.

> For the first few days these men were exceptionally good workmen, in fact up until one night they smuggled three of their wives and eight children across the river and established them in our houses where the workmen were staying, and upon my foreman and I finding these families on our premises, and being bound by contract and previously being warned not to permit any Mexican families of the Braceros on our premises, or we would be subject to penalty, contract violated and also would be responsible for anything that might happen to the family. We advised the Braceros that they would have to move their family back to Mexico, and these workmen resented this information very much and states that they brought their familys [sic] across the river to cook for them, and if their families could not stay, then they the workmen would not stay either.[44]

Despite continued attempts by the employers to have the braceros send their families back, the families stayed. The men grew resentful, and began to work less, taking breaks to go back to their camp, and doing their duties poorly, according to the estimation of their employer. Finally, the men stated that they no longer wanted to work, and Showers went through the process of trying to return them to the contract center and follow proper protocol to cancel their contracts. The process proved extensive, requiring inspectors from both nations, including a Mexican consul. In the end, Showers, thinking the ordeal was complete, went away on a business trip only to return and realize that he had been blacklisted from obtaining more braceros. The fallout from the cancelled contracts resulted not only in a loss of $300 US for Showers, but also prevented him from participating in the program for failing to pay the men their guaranteed wages.

After describing the entire event in an attempt to have Senator Johnson intervene on his behalf and restore his ability to contract braceros, he justified his side of the story by stating: "According to Bracero Contract, the workmen violated their contract when they brought their families to our camp and continued to keep them there, and they had no reason to become angry or have ill feeling toward me, because it was necessary that they return their family to Mexico, but one of the workmen continued to tell me that his wife was pregnant and he wanted her Baby borned [sic] in U.S. States." The letter reveals the struggles of a contract labor system devoid of relational considerations. Employers followed the logic set out by the program and in this example Showers, a small-scale employer who lost seven of his eight total laborers, relied on regulations to make his case. The message passed down to Showers was that families were a liability. The bracero was vital but the family had potential for permanent residence, becoming a burden of extra economic cost to the employer, or perhaps a social cost for the United States—a theme evident from congressional hearings regarding the extension of the program, and alluded to by Showers's last comment about the pregnant wife of a bracero. The case is also remarkable as an example of the recourse that braceros had on certain occasions. One wonders whether the braceros could have negotiated a family stay, had Showers realized he might suffer a blacklisting. The fact that the braceros chose to make a claim, and that their claim was attended to, is also surprising, if (as Showers claimed) it was the men who first violated their contracts. Lastly, it is clear and notable that for these particular braceros, family considerations won over keeping paid contracts. Without hearing more from the bracero families themselves, it's difficult to chart out which motivations for keeping the family unit together proved to be the most important. In Showers's rendering of events, the braceros' motivations were nothing if not calculated and came down quite simply to the making of food and the chance at US citizenship for their children. Practical rather than emotional motivations were used to explain the braceros' behavior, but that, surely was only part of the story. Margarita Flores's mother made food for her bracero husband and other workers, but from her recounting we also get the sense that togetherness brought happiness, and that family unity was essential to emotional as well as physical well-being. Male laborer migrants were not atomized beings easily plugged into a labor system, no matter how much the Bracero Program and US employers required or wanted them to be.

MIGRATING TO THE BORDER: BRACEROS

Executing a large-scale migration program moving Mexican men from deep in the interior of Mexico to and around the United States, in a manner pleasing to both the US and Mexican governments, was not an easy undertaking, but by and large, the binational system of labor distribution did what it set out to accomplish: to get large numbers of temporary laborers to specific work sites during peak harvest seasons. The very significant and troubling side effects of the United States's remedy to a shortage of labor, however, were a massive influx of undocumented border crossings, the exploitation that undocumented workers were made to suffer, the displacement of domestic migratory labor workers, the lowering of agricultural wages especially in the US borderlands, and labor shortages and population displacement in Mexico. While workers were indeed moved rather efficiently into the United States, the first part of the journey for Mexican laborers out of their towns, then on to contracting centers, and on to the border, were filled with innumerable challenges.

Successful arrival to and then getting through a contract center in Mexico was an accomplishment of its own, as many braceros had to navigate long distances, corruptive schemes, and humiliating episodes just to be selected for a contract. The minor but ongoing binational tug-of-war over the location of contracting centers meant that these could change from year to year in an attempt to accommodate worker shortages and overages in both the United States and Mexico. The first contracting centers were set up in Mexico City but when bracero *aspirantes* quickly overran the centers there, more centers throughout the nation emerged, primarily in Guadalajara and Irapuato. Throughout the 1940s and 1950s contracting centers were opened up closer to the border as well, in places like Chihuahua and Monterrey, Nuevo Leon. Another significant contracting center was located in Mexicali, Baja

California, but this was closed in 1955 due to both the high numbers of undocumented crossers in the region and also because the influx of aspiring braceros and their families to the region far overran the city's infrastructure.[45] Ciudad Juárez, strongly impacted by population increases since the program began, experienced worsening employment and welfare conditions due to the number of deportees who had been dropped off at the border in the late 1940s and early 1950s.[46] Contracting centers in the interior were also plagued with overcrowding and occasionally corruption as well. A journalist from Irapuato, Guanajuato, wrote in 1955 about the ongoing issues of corruption that were occurring at the Irapuato center, urging its closure. Although best geographically situated for bracero *aspirantes* coming from all across the country, upwards of 50 percent of contracts were given to border state residents, leaving migrants from other states such as Zacatecas or Oaxaca less likely to get contracts. He also insisted that the contract center at Irapuato was the most corrupt of all centers, and was subject to graft where "individuals, many of whom, with the appearance of being honorable people, encourage and protect rufians who steal from the aspiring braceros, offering to intervene so that they might be speedily contracted." He went on to state that they collected up to $200 US from each migrant.[47]

The interior contracting centers operated until 1957, after which they were moved closer to the border again and operated in Empalme, Sonora, Monterrey, Nuevo Leon and Chihuahua, making it difficult once again for braceros from the south of the country to get to centers, and more cost-effective for employers from the United States not to transport workers such long distances.[48] The Empalme contracting center was also the site at which some braceros suffered their worse humiliations, not only being made to strip naked but also to be fumigated and deloused.[49] Being contracted as a bracero certainly carried benefits, but getting into the program was not without its hurdles, especially when there were simply not enough contracts to go around, or when they were prejudicially given to those with political or economic favor. The result was that braceros continued to cross illegally into the United States and employers continued to hire them.

DOCUMENTED AND UNDOCUMENTED

The postwar increase of migration across the US-Mexico border brought with it an increase in vigilance across the border and a concerted binational cooperative effort to prevent the illegal crossings of Mexican migrants.[50] Throughout the war, migrants who crossed without documentation could be caught, detained, potentially jailed, and deported to the United States. For example, in 1944 Felícitas Saavedra Reyes wrote to President Ávila Camacho from Tamaulipas on behalf of her son, who had crossed into the United States without permission and was jailed in Brownsville, Texas, where he escaped and was then turned back over to the sheriff at Brownsville by Mexican authorities. From there he was sent to a detention camp at La Tuna, Texas.[51] As Kelly Lytle Hernández states, "La Tuna was a large borderland prison established to cage Mexico's 'birds of passage' for unlawfully entering the United States."[52] Established in 1932 as a prison farm, La Tuna had quickly turned into an overcrowded prison mostly for Mexicans charged with immigration offenses. Many migrants, especially during the bracero years, would be offered voluntary deportation, but repeat offenders were most likely to be detained in federal detention camps and held on immigration charges. In some cases, migrants would be held in local jails. For example, 1,398 alone were jailed in the El Paso county prison on immigration charges in the year 1945. By and large, jailed migrants stayed for no longer than two or three days, and were then released.[53] According to the 1946 Immigration and Naturalization Service Annual Yearbook, an "acute shortage of detention facilities has sometimes made it necessary to limit the number of aliens who could be arrested and deported in the Mexican border districts." 11,310 Mexican migrants were deported through formal deportation processes that year, 8,080 of them having been deported for entering without inspection; however, 101,945 deportable migrants left voluntarily, and while not all of them were Mexican, 90 percent of apprehensions for the year were made along the Mexican border.[54] Detentions and deportations jumped dramatically in the post-war years with a 44 percent increase in apprehensions occurring between fiscal year 1945 and 1946.[55] By spring of 1947, a Texas official reporting on the number of undocumented crossings asserted that the problem had transitioned from a local problem to a national and international one.[56]

While many migrants were allowed to depart voluntarily, it is important to recall the Undesirable Aliens Act of 1929, passed early in the Great Depression years amid a burst of restrictionist enthusiasm, which criminalized unlawful entry to the United States. If officials proceeded with deportation, a migrant could face a misdemeanor charge, up to a year of jail, and a $1000 US fine. Those who were deported once and then continued to re-enter illegally could be charged with a felony, including up to two years of jail time. In other words, the consequences for unlawful entry were real, and so despite a still-porous border throughout the 1940s, there were risks involved in being apprehended. Elena Moreno de Macias was one woman who was caught in the dragnet of increased vigilance along the border, but also managed to utilize a legal provision to postpone deportation and to eventually regularize her status in the United States. If migrants were found to be deportable, they had two potential options: they could request a change of an order of deportation to one that would allow them to depart voluntarily, or they could apply to suspend their deportation altogether. Elena, with help from the National Catholic Welfare Conference in El Paso, applied for a suspension of deportation based on the fact that "it would be a hardship to deport her in view of the fact that she has three U.S. born children." In 1943, her case was referred to Congress and her deportation was suspended. By 1945 her status had been regularized.[57]

Elena's case was adjudicated in her favor not only because of the hardship that her deportation would cause, but because of other factors that proved her acceptability as a migrant. She had been married to a Mexican citizen who despite entering illegally was able to establish continuous residence since 1923; she also had no police or charity record and "seem[ed] to be well thought of by the neighbors in the neighborhood where they live." With the right assistance and under the right conditions, some migrants, especially those with US-born minor children, were able to contend with the tightened restrictions and increased vigilance. Braceros who had skipped out on their contracts and any migrants who had come to labor in the United States outside of the formal requirements of the bracero program did not find themselves in such favorable conditions—that is, until 1948. The "El Paso Incident of 1948" effectively opened up the border for thousands of undocumented workers to enter into the United States, while Mexico and the United States were undergoing wage disputes over the renegotiation of the program. Rather than denying entry or deporting them, the border patrol either looked the other way or actually assisted in turning the migrants over to employers in the United States so that harvests could still be attended to despite a halting of the program by the Mexican government.[58] As Mae Ngai points out, knowing that their interests would be accommodated anyway, growers had little incentive to contract through the bracero program for workers.[59] Such events at the border would signal to other aspiring braceros that they might be allowed in after all, perpetuating the idea that while a few unlucky migrants might get caught, thousands, if not hundreds of thousands, would get jobs.

The mixed messages regarding legality, illegality, and deportation as a real or false threat would continue with the renegotiated bracero program of 1949. The new agreement would allow for more bracero contracts to be given out with a new key stipulation. Upon reading about the new binational agreement in the newspaper, Miguel Ganoa wrote to President Alemán from Brownsville, stating: "I want you to do the favor of forgiving me for crossing over to Texas to work a few days, well sir, here I send you a little paper in which I read what it says, and I don't think I committed a wrong, since the two nations are united." Attached to the letter was an article from a Spanish-language newspaper about the agreement signed on August 1, 1949. The article specified that its first beneficiaries would be those undocumented migrants that were already in the United States. Thus Miguel, reading the article, correctly saw a chance to legalize his entry. His purpose in writing to the president was to get some kind of written document that he could take to the nearest consul to regularize his status. In case the president could not send him a note, he asked the highest official in the land to inform him of any other job that might be available. 87,220 undocumented workers were regularized as a result of the new agreement, many of whom were immediately given bracero contracts.[60]

While thousands of undocumented Mexicans were regularized, the new agreement did nothing to resolve the issue of continued undocumented immigration. Voluntary departure of deportable aliens increased by 40 percent from the previous year, and 96 percent of total voluntary deportees from the United States left through the southern border ports of Texas and California. Federal jails remained overcrowded and the INS continued to use detention camps at El Centro, Camp Elliot, and Terminal Island in California.[61] In 1950 the Border Patrol apprehended "almost 500,000 deportable aliens." Again, most of those apprehended were given the option to voluntarily depart since, according to the INS Annual Yearbook for that year, "immigration officer personnel was totally inadequate to hold deportation proceedings in any but the most aggravated cases."[62] Repeaters continued to stream into the United States, causing INS officials to propose "that we operate a ship from San Diego to Central Mexico . . . the operation of this plan for even a few months would largely eliminate 'repeaters' who are expelled across the border one day, only to try illegal entry again the next day."[63]

Aspiring migrants who had land and therefore were technically blocked from the program, like Salvador Belmontes Torres from Michoacán, continued to write to the Mexican president to ask him to intercede. Beginning in November of 1949, Salvador wrote repeatedly to President Alemán asking for assistance in either getting to the United States or for assistance in acquiring means for irrigation; he had lost his entire harvest due to the lack of rain, and without the means for farming his parcel of land, he asked the president to "imagine" his necessities and thanked him in advance on behalf of himself and his family for any favors that he might bestow.[64]

Was it the myriad of environmental and political challenges facing agricultural workers in Mexico, the Mexican peso devaluations of 1948, the decline of agricultural worker purchasing power by 47 percent from 1939 to 1947, the continued promise of work to those who could successfully cross the US-Mexico border, the hope that employers would regularize the undocumented status of favored workers, the binational bracero amnesty that was delivered by the agreement of 1949, or the desire to be reunited with loved ones after long periods of separation that kept migrants crossing the US border despite all potential risks?[65] The combination of all of these factors contributed to the tremendous influx of migrants across the border in the 1950s. And while the public focus of Mexican and US officials was, to be sure, on the many Mexican men who were driven to migrate by the promises of the program, the crossings, as well as the detainments and deportations of women and children, were less visible. The program obscured not only the family dynamics that operated alongside it, but also the precarious position that women and children faced with their male laborer relatives in the parallel and increasing current of undocumented migration. The numbers of women and children caught up in deportation campaigns or in the uncertainty of watching one of their relatives be deported was undoubtedly small in comparison to the numbers of men deported. However, private discussions between the two governments reveal the gravity of the influx of undocumented family migration. The public dimensions of undocumented family migration would be felt more powerfully with the border-rattling INS activity known as "Operation Wetback" in 1954, but events taking place in late 1949 would foreshadow a period when each nation grappled with the gendered impacts that detainment and deportation would have on families. Large-scale deportations staggered throughout the waning months of 1949 reveal the degree to which undocumented family migration was taking place. Families had been carrying out undocumented resistance to the new order of migration that had been envisaged by designers of the bracero program, and both governments grew concerned about the optics of resistance and return.

On October 5, 1949, the Mexican ambassador to the United States sent a telegram to the Secretaría de Relaciones Exteriores, communicating that while the status of many braceros had been regularized per the 1949 agreement, the immigration services of the United States had resolved to send back any of their family members who had been residing in the United States illegally, and further, that "a considerable number of deportees would arrive in the coming days to Reynosa and Matamoros."[66] In response, Mexican officials reached out to the US Department of State to insist upon appropriate conditions under which the deportations would be carried out, among them that the deportations would occur over time, rather than all at once, and that families would not be separated from heads of households.

The main objective of the Mexican government was to make sure that repatriations did not occur all at once, "in order to avoid unfavorable reactions from the Mexican public and to avoid creating problems for those involved as well as for border cities." The second request made by the Mexican ambassador was to make known that it was preferable for heads of household to be included in family deportations, because "we believe that for the husband or the father to stay in the United States of America with the rest of the family in Mexico would produce a fracture breaking of the family unit." Thirdly, they urged that a husband and wife or father and children should be in agreement with each other regarding the process of family deportation. Lastly, they expected that the "issue would be examined in a humanitarian fashion resolving each case according to its own merits." The response from Washington was mixed. They agreed to stagger the deportation of families so as to not burden Mexico, but with respect to deportations of family units including the head of household they stated, "it is not felt that this arrangement would be feasible since it would first require the return of workers to the area where their families are illegally residing." The basis given for this line of reasoning was that in negotiations to legalize undocumented workers already in the country, Mexico had insisted that workers be transported to the interior of the United States. In other words, the justification given for the refusal to deport recently legalized workers together with their family members was a logistical and diplomatic one. Rather than admit that employers would be loath to lose some of their recently legalized contract workers, the United States would go forth with deportations that separated families, and the Mexican government would accept this, all on a technicality.

The Department of State went on to deny any possibility of employers or US recruiting center officials being complicit in contracting braceros with families in the United States, stating that no one was aware that workers had families there. "Since it has now come to light, however," the memo noted, "that certain of them did have families in this country, who had also crossed the border in contravention of both Mexican and American laws, it is felt that both Governments should cooperate in bringing about their prompt repatriation. Failure to insist upon the repatriation of the families before the termination of the contract of the head of the family would of course constitute a strong inducement for the worker to remain in the United States or to return thereto illegally." In other words, families would need to be deported immediately so that their recently legalized braceros wouldn't be tempted to stay beyond their newly legal contract terms. Laborers were legalized, families were not, and the priorities of the Department of State were made clear: families had to go.

In the memo's closing we glimpse just how much the balance of power had shifted away from Mexico with regards to the bracero program. The United States, the official wrote, would carry out deportations in a humanitarian fashion and in order to do so the department would ask that the Mexican government "provide temporary housing and transportation to the home of the families in the interior." The memo reiterated that the United States had no desire to break up family units, and that deportations would only happen "where unity has already been broken through voluntary separation by the head of the family." All entities in the United States were absolved of their complicity in a program that separated families, Mexico did what it could to avoid public scandal, and in the end, it was the families alone that were to blame for their contravention of the law; more specifically, family separation was blamed solely on the men who through their decisions sought to "voluntarily break up their family." Little consideration, if any, was given to Mexican underemployment, the historical over-recruiting of Mexican laborers, or the gendered bracero program for the separation of families. An estimated 9,906 people, including 1,288 family units, were deported to Reynosa in the month of October, while 1,148 people, including 300 family groups, were deported to Matamoros. The Mexican ambassador reported that fewer would be deported in the month of November, with an estimated 1,200 migrants *per week* to Reynosa and 800 to Matamoros. These numbers were staggering, to be sure. They also disclose a staggering number of family members who had entered into the United States, supposedly without detection by government officials, in the first place.

The 1948 "El Paso Incident" and the agreement of 1949 were key moments of inflection in a protracted struggle to settle terms that would be beneficial for all parties involved. The bracero program would never satisfy either government's demands and mounting criticism of the program both in Mexico and in the United States would eventually be its undoing. Due to controversy surrounding the program, Mexican migration in general moved more prominently on to the United States's national radar. President Truman, in particular, took an interest in the program as part of his overall interest in the conditions of migratory labor in the United States. In 1950, he established the Commission on Migratory Labor by executive order. The report that emerged from his commission—painstakingly put together through a series of public hearings throughout the country—generally advocated the curtailing of the bracero program and increased protections for domestic migrant workers. Along with the many specific recommendations made to improve the quality of life for these workers, other recommendations included: that a Federal Commission on Migratory Labor be established; that domestic workers be used more effectively, and when needed, supplemented by workers from Hawaii and Puerto Rico rather than foreign labor; and that, since imported foreign labor had decreased domestic agricultural wages, future administration of foreign labor importation should be handled only by the governments involved and that in the United States this should be exclusively done through the INS and the Farm Placement Service.[67] On the topic of illegal immigration, referred to as the "Wetback Invasion" in the report's summary of findings, recommendations included giving the INS the authority to enter places of employment, establishing penalties for "harboring, concealing or transporting illegal aliens," the possibility of fines and imprisonment for employers of undocumented workers, and that the "legalization for employment purposes of aliens illegally in the United States be discontinued and forbidden."[68]

The powerful grower lobby, however, pressured congressional representatives to largely ignore the commission's findings, and instead Congress wrote bills that would extend the program. Eventually 1951's Public Law 78 (also known as the Ellender-Poage Bill) effectively laid the groundwork for the extension of the program for many years to come. Despite Truman's desires to sanction employers of illegal workers, such provisions were not included in the bill. The recommendation to forbid the legalization of undocumented workers was also ignored. The status of illegal workers could be regularized if they had either entered legally on bracero contracts, but they were rendered illegal again by their contract ending, or if they had been in the country for more than five years. The law also stopped short of extending more protections to domestic migrant workers. The Secretary of Labor would have to certify that there was a shortage of labor and that importation of foreign labor would not displace domestic labor, but there were no stipulations for how the Secretary was to determine a shortage or whether braceros had adverse effects on domestic workers.[69]

Congressional debates surrounding both the report of the President's Commission on Migratory Labor and Public Law 78 represented a significant moment not only in the history of the bracero program but also in the broader histories of US agricultural labor relations, border enforcement, and Mexican migration. Concerted efforts by US legislators to understand Mexican migration, both legal and illegal, began in earnest for the purposes of either shoring up grower demands or responding to their constituencies' alarms about migration.[70] The US government proved that it would continue to buckle under grower pressures and keep importing labor, thus preventing the formation of a national farm labor union. Also, a presidential expectation and suggestion to Congress to bolster border enforcement would translate into the eventual imperative to better fund the INS as well as to support border enforcement and migrant deportation campaigns like "Operation Wetback."[71]

A less obvious impact, but one that would be incredibly significant for future Mexican-American communities in the United States, was that the study of migrant workers, both domestic and foreign, would reveal the degree to which Mexican-American families, perhaps only one to two generations removed from their own pioneering migrations to the United States, were involved in domestic migrant work and the deplorable conditions they faced. While government officials were having trouble deciphering the difference between recently arrived immigrants from Mexico and US-born Mexicans, as evidenced by a range of labels used in the congressional hearings, fault lines began to develop within communities made up of both recent migrants and long-established Mexican families who competed for similar job opportunities. These tensions were exacerbated by the new premium placed on legality and citizenship that had developed in the era marked by postwar patriotism and insistence on lawful belonging. Deportation campaigns during the 1950s and the national attention given to them in the press raised the stakes of legality and citizenship even higher.

The events that occurred in 1954 were not so terribly different from the "El Paso Incident" in 1948. The second opening of the border, however, occurred in Mexicali, and it too came as a result of a breakdown of binational negotiations surrounding the terms of the bracero program. As before, a thronging mass of bracero *aspirantes* were congregated at the border, waiting for the Mexican government to find some kind of even footing in a power play with the United States so they might be let in. Like before, US officials threatened to open the border for unilateral contracting of workers, but this time they made the threat public. Unlike in 1948, this time the Mexican government tried to prevent the exodus with military force. A literal tug-of-war ensued over the bodies of Mexican men until terms were finally agreed upon and the program was extended again. Undocumented border crossings had become such a problem that "Operation Cloudburst" was drafted with the goal of using the National Guard and the US military to seal the border. The operation, however, was never approved by President Eisenhower.

The growing attention in US newspapers to the influx of undocumented workers, the pressure on the INS to do something about it, and General Joseph Swing's appointment as INS commissioner proved to be the decisive factor in changing not only how enforcement along the border would look in the future, but also how the bracero program would function in relation to the INS. As Kelly Lytle Hernández points out, the "Operation," despite it being heralded as a type of militarized approach to protecting the border, did not actually result from any dramatic new technologies or military training of border patrol officers. Rather, it consisted of the marshaling of resources and techniques that were already in existence to strategic points along the US-Mexico border and to raids within the interior. And although the press trumpeted a million apprehensions during its run in the summer of 1954, actual apprehensions amounted to a small fraction of that. Numbers were publically inflated as part of an overall message that the era of undocumented immigration across the southern border was over.[72] As S. Deborah Kang notes, pronouncements in the press about what the operation would do and how successful it was were not so unlike the pronouncements that were used in the 1930s to inspire fear in Mexican immigrants so that they might depart voluntarily.[73]

Reports in the press thus set the stage for large-scale deportations. The media's and politicians' criminalization and demonization of Mexican immigrants had been increasing. For example, an article from January 1954, just months prior to the initiation of "Operation Wetback," referred to the problem of undocumented migration as an increasing menace. The California Attorney General justified in advance the sweeping measures about to be enacted, stating that illegal migrants into California would lead to a "grave

social problem involving murder, prostitution, robbery and narcotics infiltra-
tion on a giant scale." The article, titled "Bracero-Wetback Problem Is
Serious," attempted to temper the Attorney General's words by distinguish-
ing between legal and illegal migrants. The reporter suggested that legal
immigrants were under close scrutiny and were not likely associated with
smuggling, but that undocumented immigrants were, and that narcotics
were the biggest smuggling threat of all.[74]

The US public was primed to receive this news of widespread roundups
and deportations. The Mexican government was given advance notice as well
and advised that the Border Patrol would send a thousand deportees through
Nogales. The Mexican government asked for a reduction through that port,
or better yet, for deportations to be carried out directly to the interior, but to
no avail.[75] Even leading Mexican-American civil rights groups such as
LULAC and the GI Forum were made aware of the impending deportations.[76] Publicity given to the targeted sweeps and raids taking place in
California was meant to alert employers throughout the rest of the country,
especially in recalcitrant South Texas, in hopes that they might take appropriate measures—namely to finally fall into line with the bracero program.
So, on June 10 when roadblocks were set up and the twelve-man units swept
through California and Arizona, there were some people who knew what
was coming. However, many thousands of Mexican migrants did not, and
men, women, and children would be snatched from their daily lives, congregated into detainment camps, and then sent back across the border.

Reports from a week into the operation revealed the scope and form of the
southern California apprehensions that would send thousands of braceros
back to Mexico through Mexicali and Nogales. Migrants sent through
Mexicali were mostly rounded up on Imperial Valley farms, while migrants
picked up in the Los Angeles area consisted of agricultural laborers but also
those employed in construction as well as service industries. Articles in the
Los Angeles Times featured the details of numbers detained, the process by
which they would be transported to their homes in Mexico, and the personal
stories of men and families being deported. The main purpose was to point to
the sheer volume of migrants being apprehended, with titles such as "500
Nabbed by Wetback Raiders." Some were sent to Elysian Park in Los Angeles
until they could be bussed through the hot desert and arrive to Nogales where
Mexican immigration officials would then record their names, decipher their
place of origin, and send them on trains to the interior. According to the news
reports, the deportees were mostly men; however, pictures of women and

children accompanied initial reports. One caption of a young woman clutching her baby in her arms read, "YOUNGEST INTERNEE—Ten-month-old Sandra Martinez youngest of hundreds of Mexican nationals rounded up in area, sleeps in arms of mother, Rosario, as they await trip to Elysian Park detention center."[77] Another, with an article the next day about a further 1,259 apprehensions, read, "WISTFUL—Miss Maria Serrano, 21 of Mexico City, nabbed yesterday in Wetback drive, peers sadly from Immigration Service car window. She was deported a month ago, but returned because, 'living was better.'"[78]

Reports were conflicting as to where women and children were being held or sent to, and questions also began to arise about whether the Border Patrol was separating families or deporting them together. One report said there were very few families at Elysian Park and that most women and teen boys had been sent across the border already through Mexicali, while men would be bussed to Nogales. A report from Nogales revealed that in addition to more than a thousand migrants being bused daily to Nogales, some "men had been torn from their homes, wives and children by being caught in the toils of the illegal alien roundup."[79] Either in response to the previous day's reporting or to journalist questions, the director of the INS in Los Angeles, Herman Landon, was careful to state that immigration officers had questioned the migrants to determine whether the men who were apprehended had families. He assured the public that men with women and children were either "released on their own recognizance" or detained at Terminal Island. He went on to state, "If married men have been sent back in the present drive they must have told us they were single."[80] As opposed the deportations that had separated families in 1949 or that separated the young man and his wife via the "hot-foot lift" in 1953, it seemed that during "Operation Wetback" efforts would be made to deport families together. A month later in July of 1954, as border patrol agents were sweeping through the Rio Grande Valley, Harlon Carter, the Border Patrol director for the region, "estimated 10,000 to 15,000 and perhaps as many as 20,000 wetbacks—particularly family groups—have gone back to Mexico voluntarily since the roundup began."[81]

The diffusion of information about the border patrol's "families-together" policy might have prompted some migrants to employ the strategy of assembling "families" out of non-family members in order to take advantage of a gendered and familial approach to deportation. Lytle Hernández points out that INS officials were confronted with migrants joining together to pose as families in order to avoid bus-lift deportations after rumors went around that the INS would not be deporting young children.[82] An INS official reported,

> Attribute to the bus lift the fact that when the wetback grapevine buzzed the news that we were not hauling married couples, every male and female that could do so grabbed an opposite. A great deal of this occurred at the collection point where men and women who had never before set eyes on each other were suddenly man and wife with quickie facts to back up the claim. Sons became their mother's husbands, and the question of ages ceased existence. When it became known that small children were not bus lifted, families loaned, and lend, their children to single wets at the collection point where aliens are separated into bus-lift eligible and non-eligibles. Small children are becoming more prominent in the groups we apprehend.[83]

While gathering in faux family units could present an opportunity for migrants to avoid forced bus-lifts and instead be given the opportunity to depart voluntarily, the strategy still couldn't explain the increase in the number of families being apprehended and deported, and it wouldn't be able to account for the increase in small children within apprehended family units. One front-page headline in Guadalajara's *El Informador* read, "Entire families are being deported from the United States" and confirmed that family units were in fact being removed to Mexico. The article described family migration as part of the second phase of the operation and commented that the families being sent home had lived illegally in Texas for many years. The policy would be for families to be kept together and deported either to Reynosa or sent by ship from Port Isabel, Texas, to Veracruz.[84]

Deportations of families during the late 1950s and 1960s reveal that more families were migrating during the bracero program than previously assumed. Even then, we get only a partial record on the number of women and children leaving during this period, for reasons having to do with the gendered nature of deportation and detainment. The fact is that we know much less about women and children caught up in the federal dragnet due to the fact that they were undocumented twice over: once by way of their crossing without having proper documents, without receiving documentation, without being counted, and then once more by the fact that their apprehensions, their detainment, and deportations were also not documented, and were not counted. Why were the detainments of women and children typically not documented? Quite simply, there was nowhere to keep them for processing. Families were released right back over the border.

FIGURE 6. Couple with children detained in a Mexican immigrant roundup, Los Angeles, 1954. Photo: *Los Angeles Daily News* Negative collection, Library Special Collections, Charles E. Young Research Library, UCLA.

As mentioned at the outset of the chapter, border officials became more concerned with the migration of families, even prior to the concerted efforts of "Operation Wetback," as illustrated by the statistic that 60 percent of border patrol apprehensions in El Paso during the year 1953 were of women and children.[85] As the social and political imperatives for deportation increased over time, the parallel construction of detainment protocols and policies could not keep pace. As a result, by the late 1940s and early 1950s when the prevention of illegal immigration was established as the core counterbalance to the undocumented migration growing out of the restrictions on the legal bracero program, the campaign to increase formal deportations was embarked upon without the infrastructure to carry out the most ambitious deportation schemes. Detention centers and local jails were already overburdened with the influx of male internees, but the presence of women and children in the apprehensions of undocumented migrants complicated issues further. We know from newspaper accounts that at least some families were held at Terminal Island in San Pedro Bay, California; however, it is unclear whether families were also held at other federal detention centers such as the camp at El Centro, California, or Camp Elliott near San Diego. As with much of the farmworker housing throughout the country, barracks-style camps would not have been seen as appropriate housing facilities for families. For similar reasons immigration officers were also not likely to rely on local jails to hold families waiting for deportation proceedings or even voluntary deportations.

Finding appropriate detention options along the border for the temporary housing of women awaiting deportation was not new. Historically, women who entered illegally were only detained if they had committed criminal acts. According to correspondence between the District Director of Immigration Services at El Paso and inspectors in Nogales in 1929, women were only detained when "cases were so flagrant that it was inadvisable to accord them the voluntary departure privilege."[86] Women were also likely subject to detainment for formal deportation proceedings if they were repeat offenders. Twenty-one-year-old Maria Serrano, reported on in the *Los Angeles Times* as the "wistful" woman being detained in a Nogales detention camp awaiting transportation to the Mexican interior, would have been likely facing formal deportation since she was a "repeater." Similarly, the four women working as domestic servants were brought before a judge in 1953 because they had repeatedly entered the United States without papers. In short, women would only be detained if they were charged with or convicted of a crime, if they had consistently flouted the law by entering illegally, or if they were waiting to be deported with their entire families.[87]

Voluntary return was the most likely option given to women and children, and the lack of records attesting to their detainment reflects the gendered nature of deportation rather than the actual number of undocumented women and children living in the United States. We do know that when women and children were kept overnight temporarily at the federal detainment camp in

McAllen, Texas, they stayed in a special section. The camp kept around 160 beds for women and children along with 840 beds for men. According to a report from the Chief of the Border Patrol section of San Antonio, children were only detained if their mothers were also there. Rather than be subject to bus lifts that would take them miles away from where they might have entered, women and children would be kept for one night at most. They would then be taken back across the border, often without a formal statement to immigration officials.[88]

The gendered dimensions of "Operation Wetback" have yet to be studied in great detail, but nevertheless are important for understanding how gendered immigrant surveillance, detainment, and deportation strategies would unfold in the future. On the surface "Operation Wetback" seemed to effectively curtail the number of apprehensions of undocumented migrants. However, Lytle Hernandez points out that the Border Patrol's shift in strategy back to two-man patrol units after the operation, as opposed to the twelve-man strike forces during the operation, reduced border patrol agents' capacity to make apprehensions, thus giving the overall appearance that undocumented immigration had declined. The greatest accomplishment of the campaign might have been to sell the public on the notion that the United States's southern border was effectively sealed.[89] Despite the Border Patrol's claims to victory, however, undocumented immigration and smuggling, in particular, continued to be a concern and a threat to US domestic agricultural labor. The bracero program, though reworked and reestablished for the foreseeable future, also continued to be a contentious issue.

KEEPING THE BRACERO PROGRAM ALIVE

The program, now guided by Public Law 78, had to be discussed every couple of years in order to stay on the books and to keep budgetary extensions in support of the continued importation of Mexican workers. The driving questions that lay at the heart of whether to extend the bracero program were as follows: Whether or not there was an actual labor shortage? Whether domestic laborers would do the work that braceros were doing? And whether mechanization or other changes in agriculture might eventually lead to the termination of the program?

Of key concern was whether the importation of foreign workers was displacing American workers from agricultural labor. The Secretary of Labor, as well as worker organizations, desired a stronger commitment to protecting domestic labor, insisting that domestic workers be afforded the same benefits as imported workers. The 1955 congressional discussions thus focused on the "comparability" between domestic and foreign workers. From these discussions we see how employers and government officials imagined the braceros as different from agricultural laborers in the United States.

It cannot be underestimated that testimonies provided to congressional officials were undoubtedly given with the purpose and goal of showing overwhelming support for the extension of the program. Thus, it would be understandable that when asked whether there was a shortage of labor, employers would emphatically suggest that there was indeed a shortage. Experts testifying for congressional hearings would argue for the extension of the program, offering a resounding consensus among participants that there was undoubtedly a shortage of farm labor. The statement of shortage, however, was probed further by congressional officials who brought up time and again that there were in fact numbers of unemployed people throughout the country either residing in or living near regions of employer shortage. Employers explained that the presence of unemployed workers in the area from other industries did not automatically yield workers for agriculture. In the first place, many employers found that not every worker was willing to do "stoop labor"; others reported that workers would stay on for a very short period of time before becoming dissatisfied with the type of work or seeking better wages elsewhere and moving on.[90] Earl M. Hughes from the United States Department of Agriculture explained further that there were "inadequate supplies of domestic workers able and willing to accept short-term, intermittent employment."[91]

This line of questioning usually went further into the topic of motivations, and why domestic workers would not do such work. Freedom was the answer. One respondent stated:

Again, well-meaning persons say 'why do we need to import Mexican nationals when there are thousands of unemployed citizens in the United States?' The answer is simply that this is a free country. Any man is free to work where he pleases. An idle auto worker in Detroit will not come to New Mexico to pick cotton and perform other stoop labor. In the first place, he doesn't want to, in the second place, he doesn't know how to do that kind of work; and in the third place he couldn't stand to work in the summer and fall heat of southern New Mexico and other border states. Therefore, he stays in Detroit. Only a totalitarian government can load its citizens into a truck and command them to work where they do not want to go.[92]

In the Cold War era anything resembling totalitarianism would need to be avoided at all costs. And yet Mexican nationals, by the nature of their contract, were bound to one employer at a time and thus their legality was circumscribed by remaining with the employer, at the farm or ranchland where they were assigned. Upon stepping beyond such bounds they could be determined to be illegally present in the United States and liable to deportation.[93] Advocates for the continuation of Public Law 78, in short, saw that a captive labor force was necessary for short-term, intermittent, stoop labor. Opponents of the program were quick to recognize the exploitative effects of the program on domestic and foreign workers alike, but the grower lobby remained powerful. The belief that somehow Mexican laborers would be the best candidates for such jobs was based on a number of myths that had existed for decades. One such myth was that braceros were *solos,* and that it was preferable to import *solos* under the premise that they were highly mobile and without affective social and family attachments. By hiring Mexican *solos,* employers could help preserve the integrity of domestic farmworker families.

During the proceedings of the 1955 Farm Labor congressional discussions, Matt Triggs, Assistant Legislative Director of the American Farm Bureau Federation, spoke to the distinctive characteristics of domestic workers and imported foreign workers:

> I think this concept of identical comparability can be carried to a ridiculous extreme. There are some basic differences between the nature of employment of Mexican workers and domestic workers. In the first place, most Mexican workers are single men or at least they come up here as one man. They live in camps or barracks. Most logical domestic workers, most migratory workers are family people. The accommodations that they need are entirely different.[94]

What makes this statement so interesting is that Triggs did acknowledge the subtlety between a "single" man and those who migrated "as one man." He implicitly acknowledged that the men that came to fulfill the temporary labor needs of the United States might have families but thought, or at least wanted to pretend, that they migrated alone. The housing of entire families would call for different arrangements that would become a burden for the employer, and unlike the 1920s when family labor was seen as a beneficial, cost effective, and stabilizing force for male laborers, the considerations that would need to be made for domestic and migrant families of the 1950s were now beyond what employers were willing to provide. Most compelling is Triggs's observation that the most likely ("logical") domestic migrant workers would by contrast with Mexicans be "family people." The comment on one hand half-acknowledged Mexican workers potentially having family ties in Mexico, and on the other underplayed the importance of bracero family relationships in contrast to those of domestic workers. Imagining these laborers as single males functioned as a critical step in stripping them of their relational identities and seeing them as commodities, or interchangeable cogs in the greater agribusiness machine who could be slotted into barrack beds at night. It also further erased women and children from public view.

Braceros' perceived singleness, however, could as also be seen as a social threat. An exchange between Triggs and Congressman Harlan Hagen, who represented a district near San Francisco, revealed a potential social issue with foreign labor. Hagen turned the conversation from growers' labor needs to welfare agencies' fears in a statement rife with negative assumptions about Mexican laborers.

> I want to point out that I come from a farm area and even in these areas, in fact, this influx of foreign labor, whether it be illegal or legal, is not exactly popular in this community. I mean you take these imported Mexican laborers, males, they get acquainted with the local female population and will have a youngster that we cannot enforce the liability of the male parent for, and the caseload on the agency goes up, for example.

Hagen asked Triggs to evaluate whether the costs of such potential impacts outweighs the benefit of the program:

> MR. HAGEN: . . . I come from California. We have experience in importing foreign workers of various kinds. For example, the Filipino community in California which is kind of a rare specimen because apparently they did not let them import any Filipino females and there have been some kind of a minor social problem there not because of the character of the Filipino people necessarily but because of the situation they were in.
>   Do you think that in all fairness the burden of proof is on the advocates for this program?
> MR. TRIGGS: No question about that.
> MR. HAGEN: They should be willing to come in periodically and justify the continuance of the program?

MR. TRIGGS: Well, first, as to this social situation. It is a difficult problem. But is it not a fact that the social problem that is created by bringing
single men from Mexico [is] considerably less serious than the social
problem that is created by having domestic migratory workers, families,
and so on, that travel around the United States? I think the Mexican
program does serve this purpose too.[95]

Triggs essentially argues that any potential "social problems," used here as a
code for sexual relations between single Mexican men and American women
and especially those that result in children, would be less severe than uprooting domestic families. The bracero program was thus related directly to the
preservation of the stability of American farm families. Splitting up or
uprooting domestic families was to be avoided at all costs. The preservation
of the integrity and family unity of US American families was privileged over
the family unity of Mexican braceros.

It would be up to the opponents of the program, like Andrew McLellan
from the Texas State Federation of Labor, AFL, to point out the exploitative
elements of the program in its current version that endangered both domestic
and bracero families. Aside from pointing out the large numbers of Texan
migrant workers who were displaced by bracero labor, he also called attention
to the graft at the Mexican contracting centers that resulted in braceros
spending large amounts of money just be able to earn a shot at a contract.
Pointing out how the situation impacted Mexican border cities, he called
attention to Baja California's governor having to siphon off money from
public works programs to shelter campesinos, referring also to Mexico's
alarm at the population shifts caused by families moving to the northern
border so that braceros could visit them over the weekend.[96] The indefatiga-
ble labor organizer Ernesto Galarza, in one of his many appearances before
Congress, testified yet again to call for an end to the program and to ask the
subcommittee to "examine, to X-ray this composite heap of festering evils
because they are there."[97] However, Congress would go on to hear testimony
from a range of advocates for, and opponents to, the bracero program, and
they would go on to extend the program yet again, until finally they decided
to let the program expire at the end of 1964.

Throughout the late 1950s and into the 1960s the combination of imported
labor and an increase in mechanization began to squeeze out US families
from agriculture and led to oppressive rural poverty. Hearings before the
House of Representatives in 1963 repeated many of the pros and the cons
related to the importation of braceros, but the theme of mechanization

becoming a possible substitute for foreign labor was especially prevalent.[98] Mechanization in the harvesting of cotton and sugar beets, and also in vegetable crops like onions and carrots, had dramatically reduced the number of workers necessary. By the 1960s talk of the threat of undocumented labor had declined and concern had now shifted to the danger that employer-sponsored green card holders might pose to domestic labor. The issue of housing once again reemerged and proposals on behalf of migrant families in the United States suggested that if domestic families were to engage in this kind of farm work that they should at least have appropriate accommodations.[99] The construction of barracks to house single men reproduced a cycle in which domestic migratory families could not find appropriate accommodations and thus could not fill advertised positions; this was then misconstrued as a presumed worker shortage, which would then lead to the continued importation of bracero single men. The pressure of groups advocating for domestic farm labor accommodation and protections undoubtedly contributed to the ending of the program, but mechanization also effectively reduced the number of outspoken growers who had pressured Congress to keep the program running since the 1940s. The final winning argument had to do with the now decades-long claim of wage depression, but in the 1960s this was most elaborately defined as a fundamental positioning of the bracero *solo* laborer against the domestic migrant agricultural family. In many regions these domestic families were Mexican-American, most likely the recent descendants of immigrants themselves. The irony of the bracero program was that it separated Mexican families in order to protect American families. The tragedy was then that the program caused fault lines within Mexican and Mexican-American communities already battling exploitative labor conditions, regardless of their legal status.

By the conclusion of the program, despite the fact that Mexican families had been crossing the border for decades and that many Mexican-American families with American-born children were increasingly brought into view through the official documentary record of the United States, the Mexican migrant and Mexican immigrant were still coded as male. Several myths, assumptions, and justifications about migration persisted and were even elaborated on by the conclusion of the program: the Mexican was still seen as migratory and temporary, and courtesy of border enforcement campaigns were re-written as illegal and of questionable belonging. The imagined Mexican laborer could survive on very low wages, and was either a *solo* male, or a man who chose to leave his family, perhaps a man who didn't need his family. A Mexican *solo* was very fortunate, for his earnings meant he and his family, if he had one back home, would benefit from the golden age of capitalism even if their home country was still struggling to enter this arena. Lastly, except for a few instances when the numbers of deportable families were too high, and thus the social cost of family separation in public view was also too high, Mexican family separation across borders was normalized, justified, and even expected.

EPILOGUE

Fit to Be Migrants

UNDOCUMENTING LIVES, 1965–1986

You probably have a little girl of your own down there, just as
pretty as her. Have you sent anything to her lately. She needs
many things to become a fine woman. How long is it since you
sent the last check home?[1]

THESE WERE WORDS SPOKEN TO HUNDREDS of braceros working in
Yolo County, California in July of 1961 during the waning years of the
bracero program, by "wandering messenger" Carlos Fradera Brunet. Brunet,
a former radio announcer commissioned by the Mexican government,
traveled throughout California, Arizona, and Texas in an effort to remind
Mexican men of their homeland. Depicted in the US press as an educational
mission and a program for boosting morale, "Saludos de La Patria," Brunet's
one-man show, traveled the Southwest projecting images of home, distribut-
ing Mexican newspapers, and giving out everything from savings tips to ciga-
rettes to thousands of braceros working in the fields.[2] "I try to remind them
that the country is proud of them, that the country hasn't forgotten them,"
Brunet told newspaper reporters.

In the nineteenth year of the program's existence Mexican men living and
working at great distances from their families and hometowns were being
reminded of their nation's pride in them and of their patriarchal duties to
their families and communities. They were also being given advice on what
types of merchandise to buy, what items would be allowed through customs
upon their return to Mexico, and how to save some of their hard-earned
dollars. Calls for the program's end throughout the 1960s, paired with
the increase in agricultural mechanization, made it a matter of time
before bracero contracts would be terminated once and for all. Mexico
would be faced with welcoming back, reintegrating, and reabsorbing the
hundreds of thousands of braceros who had up until then been living binational lives.

This would not, as this book has made clear, be the first time that Mexico would be receiving repatriated migrants back into the fold of the nation. Circular migrations and periods of repatriation had occurred repeatedly over the course of seventy-five years by the time the bracero program was terminated. The program was only one aspect of the collective waves of migration that occurred from 1890 to 1965. Mexican migrants across these decades had created a type of transnational and binational *patria* that was no longer reserved for adventurers and the desperate. The contours of community could now extend along narrow swaths of land marked by train stops and bus stations, familiar towns, and family homes, across a border and back again.

The bracero program did, however, decidedly change the nature of sanctioned migration, family migration, and *expected* migration. The expectation and justification of family separation as a necessary part of a binational system of labor was now fully entrenched. The creation of binational families was an undeniable legacy of decades-long social and labor migration, but the bracero program had the overall effect of splitting up families up . . . at least until they came together again. Migrations during the bracero era continued the legacy of emigration for Mexican communities, further ingraining the cross-border alternative for future generations of Mexican families, while also introducing it to new communities for the first time, particularly those in rural areas where agricultural livelihoods became less and less sustainable.[3] Social networks and employer contacts proliferated, while braceros gained experiential knowledge in the US agricultural system, with some forging connections that would grant them status as "specials." With such status, migrants could gain legal permanent residency and then facilitate the sponsorship of families. Others mastered the agricultural circuits, learning the routes, farms, and crops that they might be able to rely on again when they returned to the United States with their families. Whether they were sanctioned or unsanctioned, and detained or not, would depend a great deal on chance, timing, and the number and position of border patrol personnel along the border. After the bracero program, families would reassert themselves as migrant recruiters, agents, support systems, and route experts. A movement that began in earnest in the 1920s and that was at times described as an exodus spread across the country in the 1940s and 1950s. In the 1960s and 1970s it would become ever more deeply rooted and continue for the rest of the century

The patterns that played out in in the late 1890s and early 1900s in regions like Los Altos de Jalisco and parts of Michoacán would play out over and over again in new regions of Mexico for the rest of the century. Migration would start with a few individuals temporarily migrating to nearby cities, then further, eventually crossing the border north and drawing more families into circular migration until either, by choice or tightening border restrictions, members of extended families might find themselves stranded in different countries. Women, children, and the elderly all participated in journeys northward, sometimes with the expectation that they would return and sometimes not. Despite a bolstered vigilance and removal regime in the United States and the purported economic "miracle" in Mexico during the 1960s, Mexican immigration increased, and despite the attempt to reshape the movement to be only male and only solo, family migration persisted.

THE ENDING OF THE BRACERO PROGRAM

As early as 1961, the bracero program had begun to decline for various reasons. Primary among them was the fact that farmers were being made to pay hourly wages to bracero laborers as opposed to the piece rates (for example, per bushel picked) that tended to have the effect of keeping labor costs down for employers.[4] Rather than employ braceros, farmers could easily turn to the undocumented workers who were circumventing bracero contracting and other legal migration processes. If either the farmer or the worker felt the risk of undocumented migration too high, Public Law 414, a law providing the option to legalize work status, could be used. The Immigration and Nationality Act of 1952, also known as the McCarran-Walter Act, contained definitions for non-immigrants that included workers who came temporarily to the country to perform jobs under special circumstances. Thus even prior to the formal termination of the bracero program, a parallel system of legal temporary labor was established. Bracero contract labor that was subject to mandatory hourly wages simply began to lose its appeal.

The hourly wage is also what drove mechanization. Farmers in Texas cotton finally shifted toward mechanization after a seventy-cent hourly minimum was mandated for braceros.[5] In California, the Secretary of Labor's 1962 mandate that piece rates for cotton should yield a minimum rate of a dollar an hour for braceros also inspired a move toward mechanization in cotton. Employer fears of decreased availability of "foreign workers" prompted "experimental mechanization in vegetable and melon harvesting." And yet another law regulating a minimum wage for women and children in apricot work led to the use of mechanical apricot cutters.[6] This meant that even as women and children over twelve were looked at as a possible reserve pool of labor in the post-bracero era, agricultural hourly and daily wage increases, legislated with a consideration of increasing living expenses, continued to push farmers either toward mechanization when they could afford it, or the hiring of undocumented workers when they could not. The pattern of acquiring cheaply paid labor from Mexico had been set for half a century; the shift toward a high percentage of the labor pool being undocumented occurred alongside, and especially, in the aftermath of the bracero program. In the end, mechanization would not fulfill expectations of decreasing reliance on a foreign labor pool. In places like California, according to Juan Vicente Palerm and José Ignacio Urquiola, "Facing soaring costs of production and stagnant farm values, many California farmers abandoned low-value mechanized crops in favor of high-value, labor intensive specialty crops and, in the process, substantially increased labor demands."[7]

While this shift in production was occurring north of the border, Mexico's "Green Revolution," in its pursuit of high-yielding crops, also spurred a shift to labor-saving production. High-yielding labor-saving production, coupled with Mexico's dramatic population explosion, plus continued demand for agricultural labor in the United States, further entrenched urban and northward migration. Facing a decline of opportunities in rural areas and then also in urban areas, Mexican migrations, both internal and international, became more frequent, more undocumented, and more female. The shift to a higher number of female cross-border migrants would occur most noticeably during the 1970s but the precedent for exodus was already being set out during the latter decades of the "Mexican Miracle."

At the termination of the bracero program, braceros and their families made their way back to a country that was experiencing its largest-ever sustained increase in GDP. A rising GDP, among other economic indicators, gave the government the basis to claim tremendous growth, but the bounty of those years was not ultimately distributed evenly through society. Instead, widening disparities and unsustainable protectionist mechanisms would eventually lead to economic decline in 1971 and economic disaster by 1982.[8] In a time of national economic prosperity, and purported and perceived political stability, migrants were still streaming out of the nation to join other family members and to earn money elsewhere to better facilitate their families' lives in Mexico.[9] The overall national economic progress did little to make the century-long escape valve less attractive. Those excluded from the

"Miracle" still fought rural and urban battles against the government or traveled north.

For its part, Mexico unintentionally created one demographic shift in an effort to stop another by creating the Border Industrialization Program in 1965. Rather than promote jobs for now unemployed braceros returning across the US-Mexico border, the program resulted in northward internal migration within Mexico. Instead of employing men, the newly built manufacturing plants along the US-Mexico border drew women into their ranks. Women, mostly young and single, participated in rural to urban migration within Mexico for decades, and became the majority of internal migrants between 1960 and 1980.[10] In the 1970s the percentage of economically active women in the border cities of Juárez and Tijuana increased as the *maquiladora* industry came to restructure borderland economies.[11] Like men in the 1910s who migrated to Northern Mexico for mining and cotton and then continued to the United States, women seeking higher wages and better working environments were just miles away from opportunities across the border, increasing as a percentage of the total international migration stream.[12] Commuters also became a significant part of the migration stream, and took advantage of a new legal category which allowed them to cross daily for work in the United States. While maintaining united households, women's necessity for higher wages pulled them away from their families, stretching binational families further apart.

Changes to US immigration policy also created new cross-border dynamics. During the height of the civil rights movement, new immigration legislation in the United States revised the decades-old national quota system. Like the Johnson-Reed Act in 1924, the Immigration and Nationality Act (the Hart-Celler Act) of 1965 was designed with European immigration in mind rather than with any specific attention to the US-Mexico border, and yet the law would go on to have profound impacts on Mexican and Latin American immigration to the United States. The act shaped Mexican migration in two major ways. First, in an attempt to craft immigration legislation that was theoretically more equal, immigration caps would now be applied to the Western Hemisphere. In what Mae Ngai describes as an eleventh-hour decision, legislators included numerical quotas for Western Hemisphere countries, thus reversing a decades-old policy of numerically unlimited immigration from Mexico. The Pan-Americanism that previously facilitated migration from Latin American countries and US business interests in Latin America was replaced by a liberal critique against immigration restriction that urged formal equality among sending nations. This was paired with a concern expressed by conservative senators about Latin America's population growth and the possible resulting increase of Latin American migration to the United States.[13] For Latin America, the hemispheric quota "represented a 40-percent reduction from pre-1965 levels."[14] For Mexico, the change in law meant that within just years of the temporary labor program that had welcomed 450,000 Mexican guest workers annually (not to mention any other resident visas issued during the bracero era), starting in 1976 only 20,000 annual resident visas would be given to immigrants hailing from Mexico.[15] The most immediate impact of the hemispheric 120,000-person ceiling that went into effect by 1968 was that deportations of undocumented Mexican migrants jumped by 40 percent, to 151,000, and by 1976 deportations had climbed to 781,000 persons.[16] The Hart-Celler Act had brought promise for some migrants and peril to others.

The second major impact of the Hart-Celler act on Mexican immigration was the preference given to relatives of US citizens to immigrate to the United States. Visas given to spouses and children of US citizens and residents were not subject to the quotas imposed by the new law. So, while the act effectively rendered those unable to acquire visas due to the numerical cap illegal, the law also made room for more legal immigration of Mexican families. The principle of family reunification expressed in the 1965 act was not designed with Mexican families in mind. Rather, legislators were thinking of US servicemembers abroad who had married foreigners and were hoping to bring their families back to the United States. The unintended consequence of this part of the law was the dramatic increase not only of Latin American immigration but also of Asian immigration. Increasing legal immigration of Mexican families would beget even more migration, especially as more Mexican migrants sought to gain citizenship through the naturalization process rather than remain in the country as legal permanent residents.[17]

While legal immigration skyrocketed due to changes in immigration law, undocumented Mexican immigration drew much of US government officials' and media focus throughout the 1970s. Although not a major concern throughout the 1960s due to a host of other domestic issues, discussions surrounding illegal immigration increasingly employed militarized metaphors and referred to Mexican immigration as an invasion. Aside from the real increase in undocumented entries, immigration scholars point out that prior to the 1970s, "owing to the Bracero Program . . . the lion's share of the migration was temporary and circular and hence invisible to citizens."[18] Thus, the more visible permanent immigration and more notable rise in illegal immigration brought attention to Mexican border crossings like never before. Ngai notes that "The Hart-Celler Act furthered the trend begun in 1920s that placed questions of territoriality, border control and abstract categories of status at the center of immigration law. That shift in the law's center of gravity naturalized the construction of 'illegal aliens' and, increasingly, of illegal aliens as Mexican." Government officials would ratchet up defenses along the border based on the threat of illegal immigration irrespective of actual immigrant entries according to what Douglas Massey and Karen Pren refer to as an "enforcement loop."[19] The overall effect of the shift in US immigration policy, along with the ending of the bracero program, was that Mexican immigration became more visible and more illegal at the same time. Meanwhile, the history of legal Mexican migration, particularly of Mexican families prior to 1965, including regular circular migrations, faded into the background. There was little room in the public imagination for binational families, Mexican legal migration, or the historical contributions of Mexican immigrants to the United States, with the new paradigm set in place.

The emigration of women and children had been a concern in some regions like the center-west of Mexico since the 1920s. But by the 1970s, it was undeniable that women were an increasing portion of those migrating to the United States and anthropologists and sociologists began to take note. In general, the role of women in agricultural regions and rural migration began to command more scholarly attention, as did the understanding that the plight of rural families in Mexico was deeply intertwined with the story of migration to the United States.[20] As towns in Mexico began to empty out more and more, local observers as well as Mexican academics began to investigate the social impacts of such migrations. What stood out clearly was that men still made up the majority of Mexican migrants, but that women were increasingly leaving as well, either alongside or independent from male relatives. Different patterns of migration emerged across the country, varying even within those subregions of the center-west that had a long tradition of emigration. Many of these communities developed a patttern of "relay migration," where fathers would work in the United States when their children were young, until young men were old enough to take their place in the familial migration strategy.[21] In cases where migrants had landholdings and used binational migration to subsidize agricultural efforts, women often stayed behind; notably, those who did go, for example from a town

Rafael Alarcón studied in Northeastern Michoacán, entered into the United States legally.[22]

As mentioned in the previous chapter, however, women began to make up more of the total numbers of undocumented migrants to the United States as well. Tracing the prevalence of undocumented migrations by women, much like correctly estimating undocumented migrations of total immigrants, is difficult and incomplete, especially since most estimates are based on apprehensions. A study commissioned by the Department of Labor's Employment and Training Administration conducted in 1976 suggested potential reasons for the undercounting of undocumented female migrants in particular, stating that among other reasons women, who were disproportionately turned away at ports of entry, were not included in statistics for attempted migration since they were not considered to be "apprehended." The authors further pointed out the fact that no overnight detention facilities existed for women at the time of the study, meaning that it was impossible to question, interview, and even numerically document migrant women who had crossed the border illegally in the same way that studies had done for undocumented male migrants.[23] It's also worth noting that interviews with apprehended men would also not likely yield a full picture of their familial status or indicate the presence of women and children accompanying them at all, considering that if apprehended they would most likely report that they were single.[24]

However, considering the increase of women who were now legally migrating out of Mexican towns, facilitated by the 1965 immigration law, as well as those who entered independently of that law; those who had travelled to northern Mexico for *maquila* work and then across the border for higher paying jobs; the increased number of commuter migrants, including a significant portion of women; and the overall increase of undocumented migrants, among whom women were in all likelihood drastically undercounted for the reasons listed above, we see that female migrants had come to account for a significant portion of crossings to the United States from Mexico by the 1980s. Traditional sending regions like Los Altos de Jalisco and the Bajío Zamorano in Michoacán that had sent their earliest migrants in the 1890s were now fully enveloped in migration networks, but the migration process was also developing with a quickening pace out of newer sending regions like the Mixtec highlands of Oaxaca.[25] The agricultural and industrial expansion in Northern Mexico paired with the aftermath of the bracero program was a watershed moment that led even larger numbers of migrants, both documented and undocumented, and increasingly female, to congregate along Mexico's northern frontier and cross into the United States. Another watershed moment in a history of watershed moments in Mexican migration occurred in the 1980s when Mexico was thrown into economic crisis.

The prosperity of mid-century proved a mirage by the 1970s and 1980s when Mexico's external debt soared just as oil prices plummeted. Peso devaluations, the nationalization of Mexico's banking system, and austerity measures taken to pay off international loans led to inflation, unemployment, and a severe curtailment in public spending. The 1980s would be marked by economic crisis just as lawmakers in the United States were drawing up yet another set of plans for immigration reform.[26] Since the Carter administration, Congress had been debating a move towards a comprehensive immigration plan that would be centered on three main goals: penalizing employers for hiring undocumented workers, shoring up personnel and vigilance systems along the US Mexico border, and providing a path to citizenship for undocumented migrants who were residents of the United States. Congress could not agree to the specifics of such legislation until 1986 when the Immigration Reform and Control Act of 1986 was passed.[27] The legislation would also foreshadow decades of policy at the US-Mexico border calling for comprehensive immigration reform that addressed legal immigration and militarized border enforcement, while increasing the severity of punishment against undocumented border-crossers. It would also facilitate the entry of yet more women. Prior to the 1986 law, women constituted nearly 50 percent of legal migration and constituted around 25 percent of undocumented immigration. Subsequently, the participation of women in undocumented migration increased to at least one-third of total undocumented migrants.[28]

Indigenous and female migrants came to dominate the new migrations, and contemporary observers began to focus on issues such as transnational mothers, spousal abandonment, domestic violence, poverty, migrant health, and transformed gender relations within migrant and immigrant households.[29] The scale of female and family migration was unprecedented, but as the stories I have told in this book of women leaving and making their lives in two countries through the early decades of the twentieth century show, family migration was nothing new.

The developments surrounding Mexican migration over the last half century take up a considerable amount of scholarly attention for good reason. Migration, after all, is consistently contemporary: an ongoing phenomenon that every four to six years takes center stage in many political debates. Social workers, teachers, and health-care workers spend considerable effort trying to understand migrant needs. Politicians build platforms on their plans for amnesty, restriction, drivers' licenses, and walls. Some employers lobby Congress for special worker visas, some see no need, some are apathetic. Scholars debate migrant assimilation, Americanization, cultural pluralism, and cultural relativism. Family members invite other relatives to join them or find themselves contemplating a return to their homelands. And migrants and immigrants keep coming to the United States from all regions of the world and for a variety of reasons. While the scale of these global migrations might be vastly different from the scale of migration in the early 1900s, many core issues remain.

The stories of migrants from the early 1920s illustrate how Mexican migration has evolved over time in relation to border policies, economic expansion and contraction, social pressures, and a range of state interventions (or non-interventions). The Mexican migrants of the early 1900s carved their multiple journeys during a period when nations were defining nationhood, and were doing so across borders that became more physical and less conceptual over time. In the United States, the degree to which Mexican migrants or their US-born Mexican children would ever be fully accepted as citizens with equal rights was still to be determined. In Mexico, citizenship was being redefined in the throes and aftermath of the Mexican Revolution and the Cristero War. In places like Jalisco and the rest of the center-west, Mexicans faced competing visions of nationalism and were skeptical of political power that emerged from Mexico City. Many of their routes, after all, led north, and it is worth asking whether, or at which point, many Mexican communities had more economic and social ties across the border to the north than they did to the national capital.

As this book has shown, while mostly men traveled as pioneer migrants during the first decades of the northerly cross-border migration, relatives began to migrate quickly thereafter, and local observers and migration officials began to recognize that "even the women were leaving." The early twentieth century was not only a period of dramatic transformation for each nation, but it was also a period of transformation within the family and of gender roles. First, migration was not only relegated to Mexican males, and second, formal wage labor was no longer relegated to only male migrants. Women were immigrating to be with relatives but also to provide for themselves and their families. With few women's voices available it is difficult to know exactly how gender dynamics changed within families and specifically how patriarchy changed in the early decades of the twentieth century, but the fact that women were also leaving their communities, and not just to the nearest city but across an international border, indicates shifts in society that would increasingly challenge the traditional hierarchies within families and communities. That, is of course, if men could not reconstruct their version of patriarchy in quite the same way a world away from home. The 1930s, filled with turmoil and separations, was one such era, in which the hope for a more traditionally defined version of family and more unified vision of family migration was challenged. Paralyzing economic conditions stranded families across borders and began to regularize the experiences and expectations of migrant families living apart—and not just in ways that cut through families where the male breadwinner stayed on one side of the border while the others remained at home. Evidence from the latter half of the 1930s demonstrates the multiple obstacles for women who encountered separation from their male partners for one reason or another. The fact that consular officials and even presidents were called on to resolve financial and familial problems speaks to both the expected paternalism (and expected benevolence) of the state, and to the fact that family migration and reunification was a goal mostly realized in times of economic prosperity. Migration and repatriation during the Great Depression reveal the fragility of the family unit and fraught reunifications.

From this point on, while some families with enough means were able to migrate together or migrate easily to reunite with their loved ones, many families would need to make difficult decisions regarding who would go and who would stay, knowing full well that if times were hard, relatives might not be able to return for a very long time. If the bracero program tried to regularize migration, make it more temporary and more male, it succeeded, but only for a brief time. Indeed, the fact that more than 4 million men participated in the program does represent a significant social reengineering of human migration, temporary as it might have been. But a history of circular migration led to binational families and binational families led to continued migration. Family migration would again prevail as women and children kept migrating, albeit in a more restrictive environment. Letters from female family members of braceros reveal many problems with the program, including the problem of being left behind, but as with other letters written to government officials, the letters most importantly reveal a language of petition and a bold assertion that migrant families and families of migrants deserved the attention, respect, and rights of any ordinary citizen in Mexico.

Migrant letters joined the chorus of other letters streaming into the Palacio Nacional. Migrants and their families pleaded their cases as best they could for assistance, for savings due, for the opportunity to provide for their families, and for the right to be heard, just as other groups made their claims in post-revolutionary Mexico.

When examining Mexican migration and migration experiences through the words of those who migrated we see a much more detailed picture of transitory, bidirectional, and repeated migration, binational living, and cross-border experiences. We see migrants as part of families and communities, with evolving life plans, strategies, and dreams, rather than just a nameless mass of people who exist between two nations. Migrants made their lives in two nations. Migrants interacted with the state—two states, in fact—and negotiated and navigated their cross-border livelihoods through a range of societal transformations. And of course, we see women. We see pioneering Mexican women who embarked on migrations by themselves, with their children, or with their families, and see that they have been doing so for more than one hundred years. The wide variety of family and personal circumstances, the importance of life cycles, and the rich family histories of cross-border living, produced an enduring legacy of migration that simply would not be contained, regulated, reordered, or fit into a logic of labor and commodities. Migration was, and always will be, unpredictably human.

APPENDIX

The following tables reflect statistics gathered from the manifests of three repatriation trains boarded at Laredo, Juárez, and Nogales in 1931 ("Repatriados que voluntariamente regresar al pais," INAMI 1–161–1931–189).

TABLE 1 Previous State of Residence for Those Returning
Through Nuevo Laredo

State	Number of Migrants
Texas	65
Illinois	39
Michigan	18
Missouri	11
Pennsylvania	10
Indiana	7
Kansas	3
Wisconsin	2
Ohio	1
Oklahoma	1
New York	1
Massachusetts	1

TABLE 2 States of Return for Those Returning through Nuevo Laredo

State	Number of Migrants
Guanajuato	60
Michoacán	41
Jalisco	37

TABLE 3 Geographic Region of Return for Those Returning through Nuevo Laredo

Region	Number of Migrants
Center-West	138
Center and Southern	19
North	1

TABLE 4 Gender Breakdown of Those Returning through Nuevo Laredo

	Men		Women	
Age	Number	Percent	Number	Percent
21–30	76	77.6%	22	22.4%
31–40	32	74.4%	11	25.6%
41–50	5	71.4%	2	28.6%
51–60	5	83.3%	1	16.7%
61–70	0	0	1	100%

TABLE 5 Date of Arrival to the United States for Three Subsets of Repatriates

Year	Laredo	Juárez	Nogales
1908		1	1
1909		1	
1910			
1911			
1912			
1913		1	1
1914		3	3
1915		3	1
1916		2	2
1917			2
1918			2
1919		2	3
1920		5	3
1921		2	3
1922		1	2
1923	1	3	6
1924		5	
1925			3
1926	3	4	3
1927	13	4	1
1928	19	6	1
1929	15	1	2
1930	1	1	
1931	1		
Total	40	43	39

TABLE 6 Breakdown by Age and Gender of Migrants Returning through Laredo, Nogales and Juárez

	Laredo			Nogales			Juárez		
	Gender	Number	Percentage	Gender	Number	Percentage	Gender	Number	Percentage
21–30	women	22	22.4%	women	9	34.6%	women	25	45.5%
	men	76	77.6%	men	17	65.4%	men	30	54.5%
	total	98		total	26		total	55	
31–40	women	11	25.6%	women	7	30.4%	women	11	26.2%
	men	32	74.4%	men	16	69.6%	men	31	73.8%
	total	43		total	23		total	42	
41–50	women	2	28.6%	women	4	44.4%	women	3	17.6%
	men	5	71.4%	men	5	55.6%	men	14	82.4%
	total	7		total	9		total	17	
51–60	women	1	16.7%	women	3	60%	women	8	53.3%
	men	5	83.3%	men	2	40%	men	7	46.7%
	total	6		total	5		total	15	
61–70	women	1	100%	women	1	25%	women	1	33.3%
	men	0	0%	men	3	75%	men	2	66.7%
	total	1		total	4		total	3	

TABLE 7 State of Birth for Those Traveling through Juárez

Region	State	Number of Migrants
Central-West	Jalisco	24
	Michoacán	11
	Guanajuato	12
Northwest	Sinaloa	1
	Sonora	2
	Nayarit	1
North	Zacatecas	23
	Aguascalientes	22
	Durango	26
	Chihuahua	8
	Coahuila	5
	Nuevo León	1

Other Localities: San Luis Potosí (2); Mexico DF (1); Querétaro (1); Los Angeles, CA (1)

TABLE 8 US-born Children returning through Nogales

Birthplace	Number of Migrants
Los Angeles, California	3
Santa Ana, California	3
Downy, California	3
Venice, California	2
Salt Lake City, Utah	2
Santa Monica, California	2
Simons, California	1
Fresno, California	1
La Habra, California	1
Simons, California	1
Huntington, California	1
El Monte, California	1
Jerome, Arizona	1
El Paso, Texas	1
Blackfoot, Idaho	1
Santa Rita, New Mexico	1
Denver, Colorado	1

NOTE: Tables compiled by author, "Repatriados que voluntariamente regresar al pais," INAMI 1–161–1931–189.

TABLE 9 US-Born Children Returning through Juárez

Birthplace	Number of Migrants
Los Angeles, California	15
Santa Paula, California	4
San Pedro, California	4
Santa Barbara, California	4
Huntington, California	4
Sacramento, California	4
Terminal, California	3
Tehachapi, California	3
Colton, California	3
Glendora, California	2
El Rio, California	2
Ventura, California	2
La Habra, California	2
Santa Monica, California	1
Whittier, California	1
Alamitos, California	1
Sloan, Nevada	3
Las Vegas, Nevada	2
Arden, Nevada	2
Nevada	1
Herle, New Mexico	1
Carrizozo, New Mexico	1
La Union, New Mexico	1
El Paso, Texas	1
Utah	1

NOTES

INTRODUCTION

1. Letter from Rosie Garcia to President Roosevelt, April 29, 1939, Box 22, file no. 310, U.S. Department of State, Records of the Foreign Service Posts of the Department of State, 1788–ca. 1991, General Records, compiled 1936–1949, RG 84, NARA.

2. Most studies of transnational Mexican and US American families begin with 1965 as a departure date for their analysis for various reasons. The Immigration and Nationality Act of 1965 (the Hart-Celler Act) is recognized for removing country quotas and facilitating family reunification through family member restriction exemptions. It coincided with the end of the bracero program, an increase in illegal immigration, and a notable increase in female migration from Mexico. These changes in migration patterns, in addition to the increased attention given to Mexican-American communities through the farm workers' movement and Chicana/o scholarship, led to a sociological focus on family. However, few studies extended an analysis of family migration and binational families prior to the bracero contract era. Key studies documenting post-1965 family migration are Douglas Massey et al., *Return to Aztlan: The Social Process of International Migration from Western Mexico* (Berkeley: University of California Press, 1987); Pierrette Hondagneu-Sotelo, *Gendered Transitions: Mexican Experiences of Immigration* (Berkeley: University of California Press, 1994); Denise A. Segura and Patricia Zavella, *Women and Migration in the U.S.-Mexico Borderlands: A Reader* (Durham, NC: Duke University Press, 2007); Tamar Diana Wilson, *Women's Migration Networks in Mexico and Beyond* (Albuquerque: University of New Mexico Press, 2001); Lynn Stephen, *Transborder Lives: Indigenous Oaxacans in Mexico, California and Oregon,* (Durham, NC: Duke University Press, 2007). Key studies that include a discussion of family migration include George J. Sanchez, *Becoming Mexican American: Ethnicity, Culture, and Identity in Chicano Los Angeles, 1900–1945* (New York: Oxford University Press, 1993); Robert R. Alvarez, *Familia: Migration and Adaptation in Baja and Alta California* (Berkeley: University of California Press, 1987); Mario T.

García, *Desert Immigrants: The Mexicans of El Paso, 1880–1920* (New Haven, CT: Yale University Press, 1981).

3. David Montejano, *Anglos and Mexicans in the Making of Texas, 1836–1986* (Austin: University of Texas Press, 1987); Ben Heber Johnson, *Revolution in Texas: How a Forgotten Rebellion and Its Bloody Suppression Turned Mexicans into Americans* (New Haven, CT: Yale University Press, 2003); Monica Muñoz Martinez, *The Injustice Never Leaves You: Anti-Mexican Violence in Texas* (Cambridge, MA: Harvard University Press, 2008); Samuel Truett, *Fugitive Landscapes: The Forgotten History of the U.S.-Mexico Borderlands* (New Haven, CT: Yale University Press, 2006).

4. For important scholarship on the transitory populations of Mexican borderland communities, which also focus on gender and labor, see Sonia Hernández, *Working Women into the Borderlands* (College Stations: Texas A&M University Press, 2014); Verónica Castillo-Muñoz, *The Other California: Land, Identity and Politics on the Mexican Borderlands* (Oakland: University of California Press, 2017); Verónica Castillo-Muñoz "Intermarriage and the Making of a Multicultural Society in the Baja California Borderlands: Gender, Race and Intermarriage in Borderlands," in *Red and Yellow, Black and Brown: Decentering Whiteness in Mixed Race Studies*, ed. Joanne L. Rondilla, et al. (New Jersey: Rutgers University Press, 2017); Julian Lim, *Porous Borders: Multiracial Migrations and the Law in the U.S.-Mexico Borderlands* (Chapel Hill: The University of North Carolina Press, 2017).

5. Sanchez, *Becoming Mexican American*; García, *Desert Immigrants*.

6. A pair of key studies by Mark Reisler and Lawrence Cardoso in the late 1970s built upon the early works of Taylor, Gamio, and McWilliams to historicize the early decades of Mexican migration to the United States. Reisler contributed an assessment of US government and labor union sources, and Cardoso specifically incorporated an analysis of historical transformations and perspectives toward emigration in Mexico. Both works focus primarily on laborers. See Mark Reisler, *By the Sweat of Their Brow: Mexican Immigrant Labor in the United States, 1900–1940* (Green Port, CT: Greenwood Press, 1976); Lawrence Cardoso, *Mexican Emigration to the United States, 1897–1931* (Tucson: University of Arizona Press, 1980).

7. For more on the early rationale for the use of Mexican labor in the United States, particularly with regards to how employers deployed the prototype of the "temporary" Mexican laborer to calm fears about the social impact of Mexican migration, see David G. Gutiérrez, *Walls and Mirrors: Mexican Americans, Mexican Immigrants and the Politics of Ethnicity* (Berkeley: University of California Press, 1995), 46–51. See Cardoso, *Mexican Immigration*, chapter 7, for the evolution of restriction efforts which resulted from a combination of labor union efforts and political efforts undergirded by eugenic arguments about the supposed racial inferiority of Mexicans that were circulating in the 1920s. Restriction debates continued throughout the 1920s, and though Mexican immigration to the United States would escape restriction by quota under the 1924 Immigration and Nationality Act, and the proposed House Resolution known as the Box Bill in 1927 ultimately failed, Mexican visas were significantly reduced.

8. Statement of S.P. Frisselle, United States Congress, House Committee on Immigration and Naturalization, *Seasonal Agricultural Laborers from Mexico, Hearings before the Committee on Immigration and Naturalization, House of Representatives, Sixty-Ninth Congress, First Session* (Washington: Government Printing Office, 1926), 5–27.

9. Other important scholarship on Mexican migration with particular attention to labor includes Zaragosa Vargas, *Proletarians of the North: A History of Mexican Industrial Workers in Detroit and the Midwest, 1917–1933* (Berkeley: University of California Press, 1993). Exceptional studies incorporating analysis of families and labor and families in labor include Monica Perales, *Smeltertown: Making and Remembering a Southwest Border Community* (Chapel Hill: University of North Carolina Press, 2010); Matt García, *A World of Their Own: Race, Labor, and Citrus in the Making of Greater Los Angeles, 1900–1970* (Chapel Hill: University of North Carolina Press, 2002); Michael Innis-Jiménez, *Steel Barrio: The Great Mexican Migration to South Chicago* (New York: NYU Press, 2013); Devra Weber, *Dark Sweat, White Gold: California Farm Workers, Cotton, and the New Deal* (Berkeley: University of California Press, 1996).

10. Massey et al., *Return to Aztlán*, 3–6.

11. For the latter see Julia G. Young, *Mexican Exodus: Emigrants, Exiles and Refugees of the Cristero War* (New York: Oxford University Press, 2019).

12. Circular migration and immigration are not terms that are mutually exclusive but I will use the term "circular migration" to describe instances in which people repeatedly migrate between the United States and Mexico. I will use the term "immigration" when describing the process by which people seek to live in the United States permanently. I describe people as immigrants only when the evidence clearly suggests that they wanted to establish permanent residence in the United States; for all others, who represent the majority of my cases, I use the term "migrant".

13. The stories of the migrants mentioned here are woven throughout subsequent chapters but were culled from a number of archival sources including consular correspondence with welfare officials in the United States, letters to Mexican and US presidents, correspondence of US and Mexican migration officials, and repatriation train manifests.

14. For more on the bracero experience see Deborah Cohen, *Braceros: Migrant Citizens and Transnational Subjects in the Postwar United States and Mexico* (Berkeley: University of California Press, 2011); Michael Snodgrass, "The Bracero Program, 1942–1964," in *Beyond La Frontera: The History of Mexico-U.S. Migration*, ed. Mark Overmyer-Velázquez (New York: Oxford University Press, 2011); Mireya Loza, *Defiant Braceros: How Migrant Workers Fought for Racial, Sexual, and Political Freedom* (Chapel Hill: University of North Carolina Press), 2016. It's important to note that men defying these parameters increasingly participated in the bracero program due to political favoritism and widespread corruption; see chapters 5 and 6.

15. Ana Elizabeth Rosas, *Abrazando el Espíritu: Bracero Families Confront the U.S.-Mexico Border,* (Berkeley: University of California Press, 2014).

16. Joseph and Daniela Spenser, *In from the Cold: Latin America's New Encounter with the Cold War* (Durham, NC: Duke University Press, 2008).

17. For a classic collection on post-revolutionary state formation in Mexico see Gill Joseph and Daniel Nugent, *Everyday Forms of State Formation: Revolution and the Negotiation of Rule in Modern Mexico* (Durham, NC: Duke University Press, 1994).

18. For historical works that address patriarchal households in Mexico, see Ana María Alonso, "Rationalizing Patriarchy: Gender, Domestic Violence, and Law in Mexico," *Identities* 2, no. 1–2 (1995): 29–47; essays by Elizabeth Dore, Maxine Molyneux, Mary Kay Vaughan, and Ann Varley in Elizabeth Dore and Maxine Molyneux, eds., *Hidden Histories of Gender and The State in Latin America* (Durham, NC: Duke University Press 2000); Steve J. Stern, *The Secret History of Gender: Women, Men, and Power in Late Colonial Mexico* (Chapel Hill: University of North Carolina Press, 1995); John Tutino, *The Mexican Heartland: How Communities Shaped Capitalism, a Nation, and World History, 1500–2000* (Princeton, NJ: Princeton University Press, 2018). For a view of patriarchal relations within migrant households see Hondagneu-Sotelo, *Gendered Transitions*.

19. Mary Kay Vaughan, "Modernizing Patriarchy: State Policies, Rural Households, and Women in Mexico, 1930–1940," in *Hidden Histories of Gender and The State in Latin America*, ed. Elizabeth Dore and Maxine Molyneux (Durham, NC: Duke University Press 2000).

20. For more on the way local conditions in the borderlands impacted border policy see S. Deborah Kang, *The INS on the Line: Making Immigration Law on the US-Mexico Border, 1917–1954* (New York: Oxford University Press, 2017).

21. Mae Ngai, *Impossible Subjects Impossible Subjects: Illegal Aliens and the Making of Modern America* (Princeton, NJ: Princeton University Press, 2004); Kelly Lytle Hernández, *Migra! A History of the U.S. Border Patrol* (Berkeley: University of California Press, 2010); Kang, *The INS on the Line*.

22. Dierdre Moloney, "Women, Sexual Morality and Economic Dependency in Early Deportation Policy," *Journal of Women's History* 18, no. 2 (2006): 95–122; Donna Gabaccia, *From the Other Side: Women, Gender and Immigrant Life in the U.S., 1820–1996* (Indiana University Press, 1995); Margot Canaday, *The Straight State: Sexuality and Citizenship in Twentieth-Century America* (Princeton, NJ: Princeton University Press), 2010.

23. Ann Varley, "Women and the Home in Mexican Family Law," in *Hidden Histories of Gender and The State in Latin America*, ed. Elizabeth Dore and Maxine Molyneux (Durham, NC: Duke University Press, 2000), 242.

24. Vaughan, "Modernizing Patriarchy," 199.

25. See Weber, *Dark Sweat, White Gold,* for cotton; García, *A World of Their Own*, for citrus.

26. Exceptional works that take Mexican migrant women as central subjects include Mario García, "The Chicana in American History: The Mexican Women of El Paso, 1880–1920: A Case Study," *Pacific Historical Review* 49, no. 2 (1980): 315–37; George Sanchez, "'Go after the women': Americanization and the Mexican Immi-

grant Woman, 1915–1929," in *Mothers & Motherhood: Readings in American History*, ed. Rima D. Apple and Janet Lynne Golden (Columbus: Ohio State University Press, 1997); works by Vicki Ruiz including "By the Day or the Week: Mexicana Domestic Workers in El Paso," in *Women on the U.S.-Mexico Border Responses to Change*," ed. Vicki L. Ruiz and Susan Tiano (Winchester, MA: Allen & Unwin, 1987) and *From Out of the Shadows: Mexican Women in Twentieth Century America*, 10th anniversary ed. (New York: Oxford University Press, 2008); Ramón and Trisha Arredondo, *Maria's Journey* (Indianapolis: Indiana Historical Society Press, 2010).

27. See, for example, the essays in John Tutino, ed., *Mexico and Mexicans in the Making of the United States* (Austin: University of Texas Press, 2012), as well as many of the other sources in these notes.

28. Julie M. Weise, *Corazón De Dixie: Mexicanos in the U.S. South Since 1910* (Chapel Hill: University of North Carolina Press, 2015); George J. Sánchez, *Boyle Heights: How a Los Angeles Neighborhood Became the Future of American Democracy* (Oakland: University of California Press, 2021); Jerry Gonzalez, *In Search of the Mexican Beverly Hills: Latino Suburbanization in Postwar Los Angeles* (New Brunswick, NJ: Rutgers University Press, 2018); Lim, *Porous Borders*.

29. For a recent example, see Miroslava Chávez-García, *Migrant Longing: Letter Writing Across the U.S.-Mexico Borderlands* (Chapel Hill: University of North Carolina Press, 2018).

30. Camille Guerín-Gonzales, *Mexican Workers and American Dreams: Immigration, Repatriation and California Farm Labor, 1900–1930* (New Brunswick, NJ: Rutgers University Press, 1994), 6–7.

CHAPTER ONE: "AND THEY GO SILENTLY"

1. Passport application for Elena G. Viuda de Arroyo, AHJ G-8–1920, Box 54.

2. Passport application for Rodolfo de Luna, AHJ G-8–1920, Box 53. Emphasis original.

3. Passport application for Micaela Carranza, AHJ G-8–1920, Box 53.

4. For pre-1920 migration descriptions inclusive of family migrations see Sanchez, *Becoming Mexican-American*; Alvarez, *Familia*; García, *Desert Immigrants*; Cardoso, *Mexican Emigration*.

5. For works on gendered experiences and the migration for the period, and specifically at the border, see Martha Gardner, *Qualities of a Citizen: Women, Immigration, and Citizenship, 1870–1965* (Princeton, NJ: Princeton University Press, 2005).

6. Manuel Gamio, *The Mexican Immigrant: His Life Story* (Chicago: University of Chicago Press, 1931); Manuel Gamio, *Mexican Immigration to the United States* (Chicago: University of Chicago Press, 1930); Paul Schuster Taylor, *Mexican Labor in the United States* (New York: Arno Press, 1970); Paul Schuster Taylor, *A Spanish-Mexican Peasant Community: Arandas in Jalisco, Mexico* (Berkeley: University of California Press, 1933). For other work on early communities see García, *Desert*

Immigrants; Sanchez, *Becoming Mexican American*; Albert Camarillo, *Chicanos in a Changing Society: From Mexican Pueblos to American Barrios in Santa Barbara and Southern California, 1848–1930* (Cambridge, MA: Harvard University Press, 1979); Reisler, *By the Sweat of Their Brow*; Cardoso, *Mexican Emigration;* Fernando Saúl Alanis Enciso, *El Primer Programa Bracero y El Gobierno De México, 1917–1918* (San Luis Potosí: Colegio de San Luis, 1999).

7. Ann R. Gabbert, "Prostitution and Moral Reform in the Borderlands: El Paso, 1890–1920," *Journal of the History of Sexuality* 12, no. 4 (2003): 575–604.

8. Mario Aldana Rendón, *Del reyismo al nuevo orden constitucional, 1910–1917* (Guadalajara: Universidad de Guadalajara, 1987).

9. Paul Friedrich, *Agrarian Revolt in a Mexican Village* (Chicago: University of Chicago Press, 1977), 45–49.

10. Álvaro Ochoa S., "Arrieros, jornaleros, braceros y migrantes (1894–1934)," in *Emigrantes del Occidente* (Mexico: Consejo Nacional para la Cultura y los Artes, 1990) in *Movimientos de población en el occidente de México,* eds. Thomas Calvo and Gustavo López (Zamora: El Colegio de Michoacán, 1988), 24–26; José Alfredo Uribe Salas, "Enganchados y emigrantes en el occidente de Michoacán," in the same volume, p. 43.

11. Salas, "Enganchados y Emigrantes," 52. This same logic about families domesticating men and keeping men tied to certain work locations would operate for certain industries and agricultural sectors within the United States as well; see below.

12. John Tutino, *From Insurrection to Revolution in Mexico: Social Bases of Agrarian Violence, 1750–1940* (Princeton, NJ: Princeton University Press, 1986), 302–3.

13. In considering whether the Carrancista administration actively supported emigration as a safety valve for labor unrest, Alanis Enciso finds no concrete evidence that the executive government encouraged international immigration, but rather argues that government-funded mobilization of workers from the interior to better job markets in northern Mexico and along the border unintentionally contributed to the exodus of Mexican workers to the United States (*El Primer Programa Bracero*, 85–89).

14. Casey Walsh, *Building the Borderlands: A Transnational History of Irrigated Cotton Along the Mexico-Texas Border* (College Station: Texas A&M University Press, 2008), 32.

15. Tutino, *From Insurrection to Revolution in Mexico,* 303.

16. Camarillo, *Chicanos in a Changing Society*, 87.

17. Camarillo, *Chicanos in a Changing Society*, chapter 4, especially 90–96.

18. John Hart, *Empire and Revolution: The Americans in Mexico since the Civil War* (Berkeley: University of California Press, 2002), 106–9.

19. Carey McWilliams, *North from Mexico: The Spanish-Speaking People of the United States.* (New York: Greenwood Press, 1968), 167. For more on the Chinese Exclusion Act, see Erika Lee, *At America's Gates: Chinese Immigration During the Exclusion Era, 1882–1943* (Chapel Hill: University of North Carolina Press, 2017).

20. Camarillo, *Chicanos in a Changing Society,* 97.

21. McWilliams, *North from Mexico,* 168.

22. Reisler, *By the Sweat of Their Brow*, 3.

23. Rachel St. John, *Line in the Sand: A History of the Western U.S.-Mexico Border* (Princeton, NJ: Princeton University Press, 2011).

24. García, "The Chicana in American History"; Gabbert, "Prostitution and Moral Reform in the Borderlands"; Alexandra Minna Stern, "Buildings, Boundaries, and Blood: Medicalization and Nation-Building on the U.S.-Mexico Border, 1910–1930," *The Hispanic American Historical Review* 79, no. 1 (1999): 41–81. For more on borderlands and the border see St. John, *A Line in the Sand;* Truett, *Fugitive Landscapes;* Katherine Benton-Cohen, *Borderline Americans: Racial Division and Labor War in the Arizona Borderlands* (Cambridge: Harvard University Press, 2009).

25. Daniel D. Arreola, "The Mexican American Cultural Capital," *Geographical Review* 77, no. 1 (1987): 22–24.

26. Lim, *Porous Border*, 43. For immigrant entries to El Paso, see Oscar Martinez, *Border Boom Town: Ciudad Juárez since 1848* (Austin: University of Texas Press, 1975), 35.

27. García, *Desert Immigrants,* 38.

28. Interview with Cleofas Calleros by Oscar Martinez, 1972, "Interview no. 157," Institute of Oral History, University of Texas at El Paso, transcript, 4.

29. Interview with Cleofas Calleros by Oscar Martinez, 1972.

30. Innis-Jiménez, *Steel Barrio*, 33.

31. McWilliams, *North from Mexico,* 169.

32. See Reisler, *By the Sweat of their Brow,* 8–9, and especially chapter 1, for a discussion of labor contractors' practices. More often than not, costs for transportation, food, and basic necessities would be taken from their wages, thus creating indebtedness.

33. Álvaro Ochoa, *Viajes De Michoacanos Al Norte* (Zamora: Colegio de Michoacán, 1998).

34. Moisés González Navarro, "Los braceros en el Porfiriato," *Estudios Agrarios: Revista de la Procuraduría Agraria: México: Procuraduría Agraria* (2010), 14.

35. Álvaro Ochoa S., "Arrieros, jornaleros," 27; "Advertencia del gobierno mexicano a los braceros sobre las condiciones difíciles de trabajo en tierras norteamericanas, 1904," Archivo Municipal de Zamora, Ramo de Gobernación, published in *Emigrantes del Occidente,* 75.

36. See Álvaro Ochoa S., "Arrieros, jornaleros," and Uribe Salas, "Enganchados y emigrantes"; and Victor Clark, "Mexican Labor in the United States" (from Department of Commerce and Labor, Bureau of Labor Bulletin No. 78, Washington, DC, 1908, in Taylor, *Mexican Labor in the United States,* for increase in migration. Friedrich Katz describes the challenges faced by Mexican semi-agricultural and industrial workers who were confronted by "constant insecurity" caused by cyclical fluctuations in "Labor Conditions on Haciendas in Porfirian Mexico: Some Trends and Tendencies," *The Hispanic American Historical Review* 54, no. 1 (1974): 35.

37. González Navarro, "Los braceros en el Porfiriato," 11–12.

38. Friedrich Katz, *The Secret War in Mexico* (Chicago: University of Chicago Press, 1981), 15, 31.

39. Moisés González Navarro, *Los Extranjeros en México y Los Mexicanos en El Extranjero, 1921–1970* (Mexico City: El Colegio de México, 1994), 3:194.

40. For more on early Mexican emigration see Cardoso, *Mexican Emigration*; chapter 3 in particular provides a comprehensive analysis of migration during the Mexican Revolution and World War I. On Mexican labor conditions in the Southwest see Reisler, *By the Sweat of Their Brow*. For more on Mexican labor and immigrant and migrant lives in the United States see Taylor, *Mexican Labor in the United States*; Gamio, *Mexican Immigration to the United States*; Gamio, *The Mexican Immigrant*.

41. Susie S. Porter, *Working Women in Mexico City: Public Discourse and Material Conditions, 1879–1931* (Tucson: University of Arizona Press, 2003), 5–6.

42. Enrique Cárdenas Sánchez, *El largo curso de la economía mexicana: De 1780 a nuestros días* (Mexico City: El Colegio de México, 2015), 314–15.

43. For examples of migrants leaving because of the violence of the Mexican Revolution and to avoid conscription see testimonies in Manuel Gamio, *The Life Story of the Mexican Immigrant: Autobiographic Documents Collected by Manuel Gamio* (New York: Dover Publications, 1971), 4, 61, 96, 153, 195, 217.

44. Leonor Salazar to Lazaro Cárdenas, AGN RP-LCR 549.5.

45. Yolanda Chavez Leyva, "'I go to fight for social justice': Children as Revolutionaries in the Mexican Revolution, 1910–1920," *Peace & Change* 23, no. 4 (October 1998): 423–40.

46. George H. Estes, "Internment of Mexican Troops," *Infantry Journal* 11 (1915): 751–52.

47. Estes, "Internment of Mexican Troops," 765. For the impact of Mexican immigrants and refugees on El Paso during Mexico's revolutionary conflict, see García, *Desert Immigrants*, 40–46.

48. "News Briefs—New American Citizens," *Los Angeles Times*, February 12, 1915.

49. "Refugee Horde Called Danger," *Los Angeles Times*, April 4, 1916.

50. See Stern, "Buildings, Boundaries, and Blood." For increasing associations and cultural representations held by public officials toward Mexicans depicting them as disease carriers, see chapter 2 of Natalia Molina, *Fit to Be Citizens: Public Health and Race in Los Angeles, 1879–1939* (Berkeley: University of California Press, 2006). See also John McKiernan-González, *Fevered Measures: Public Health and Race at the Texas-Mexico Border, 1848–1942* (Durham, NC: Duke University Press, 2012), and Heather M. Sinclair, "White Plague, Mexican Menace," *Pacific Historical Review* 85, no. 4 (November 2016): 475–505.

51. J. Blaine Gwin, the Secretary of Associated Charities in El Paso, Texas, noted the trend of Mexicans returning after 1915 in "Immigration Along our Southwest Border," *Annals of the American Academy of Political and Social Science* 93 (1921): 126–130.

52. Fernando Saúl Alanís Enciso, "Nos Vamos Al Norte: La Emigración de San Luis Potosí a los Estados Unidos Entre 1920–1940," *Migraciones Internacionales* 2, no. 4 (2004): 71–72.

53. Cardoso, *Mexican Immigration;* Reisler, *By the Sweat of Their Brow;* Alanís Enciso, *El Primer Programa Bracero.*

54. Alanís Enciso, *El Primer Programa Bracero,* 66–69.

55. Alanís Enciso, *El Primer Programa Bracero,* 26–32.

56. "200 Mexican Families From El Paso to Work in Idaho," *El Paso Herald Post,* March 19, 1918.

57. *El Informador,* June 30, 1918.

58. *El Informador,* August 26, 1920.

59. "Los Mexicanos Que Emigran han sido victimas de los explotadores Americanos," *El Informador,* August 30, 1920.

60. "Aviso," *El Informador,* April 9, 1918.

61. Yolanda Chávez Leyva finds that family reunification was a strong motivation for the migration of children during the Mexican Revolution, especially for those who were poor and orphaned, and points out "intergenerational reliance" as a means of child survival. See "Cruzando La Linea: Engendering the History of Border Mexican Children during the Early Twentieth Century," in *Memories and Migrations: Mapping Boricua and Chicana Histories,* ed. Vicki L. Ruiz and John R. Chávez (Champaign-Urbana: University of Illinois Press, 2008), 71–92.

62. Reisler, *By the Sweat of their Brow,* 29–36, 38.

63. Moloney, "Women, Sexual Morality, and Economic Dependence."

64. Kang, *The INS on the Line,* 19–25

65. For examples of passport announcements in the press see *El Informador,* February 18, 1920, and October 16, 1920. Lawrence Cardoso suggests that the effort to dissuade Mexican migrants from going to the border by publicizing harsh conditions in the United States and the difficulties crossing the border was actually part of the Carranza administration's policies toward regulating emigration during the period ("Labor Emigration to the Southwest, 1916–1920: Mexican Attitudes and Policy," *Southwest Historical Quarterly* 79, no. 4 [1976]: 400–16). He argues that this propaganda campaign (of course some of the abuses suffered and difficulties at the border were true) was part of a two-step effort toward preventing and regulating emigration. The other part of the policy was to bolster the protection of workers abroad through the work of consuls. This may be the period, as Cardoso suggests, that set the basis for future policy toward emigration. However, as a "policy," it seems that the measures taken were not significantly different from previous efforts to stymie emigration, nor is there enough evidence to suggest that the measures taken were outlined, regulated, mandated, and funded by a centralized authority. For an example of the articles published to dissuade migration in regional papers see "Aumenta La Emigración de Braceros Mexicanos a Los Edos. Unidos," *El Informador,* February 14, 1920, http://hemeroteca.informador.com.mx, accessed October 25, 2020. Aspiring migrants also would have read about border-crossing conditions and the availability of jobs in the United States in Mexican newspapers. Attributing influence to local print sources assumes a certain level of literacy within sending communities that is difficult to calculate, but letters written to Mexican presidents in the 1930s and 1940s do show that migrants cited specific newspaper articles for

their information regarding migration requirements. See chapters 3 and 4 for examples.

66. Álvaro, *Viajes De Michoacanos Al Norte*; Gamio, *The Mexican Immigrant*.

67. Jamie Tamayo, *Jalisco: Desde La Revolución, Los movimientos sociales 1917–1929*, vol. 1 (Guadalajara: Universidad de Guadalajara, 1988); "Revista de Los Estados: Michoacán," *El Informador*, March 19, 1920.

68. *El Informador*, October 16, 1920. For warnings about scam artists see *El Informador*, February 18, 1920.

69. Passports were considered provisional until they received a visa from a Mexican consular official.

70. Letter to the Secretariat of Gobernación from migration inspector F. Felix, June 24, 1926, INAMI 4–161–1926–12, p. 74.

71. Some specify their intended final destination down to the street and neighborhood, while others simply state the need to go to the United States. Twenty-eight listed the United States without specifying their destination. Seven did not state destination.

72. Sanchez, *Becoming Mexican American*, 65, 90; Arreola, "The Mexican American Cultural Capital," 23. For the number of Mexicans in San Antonio see Sanchez, *Becoming Mexican American*, 65.

73. The next five cities indicated were Chicago (nine applicants), Toledo, Ohio (seven), Dallas, Texas (seven), New York (seven), and Pueblo, Colorado (five).

74. For more on the early Mexican and Mexican-American populations of Illinois see Gabriela Arredondo, *Mexican Chicago: Race, Identity and Nation, 1916–39* (Champaign-Urbana: University of Illinois Press, 2008); Innis-Jiménez, *Steel Barrio*; Arredondo and Arredondo, *Maria's Journey*.

75. AHJ, G-8, Box 54.

76. Gamio, *The Mexican Immigrant*.

77. Other family-related reasons for travel by men were specified as "visiting or seeing family" which accounted for 6 percent (11 of 183 specified), and "making family arrangements", which accounted for 15 percent (27 of 183 specified). The language used in these cases conveys that trips were meant to be of a shorter duration and that temporary migration or permanent immigration was not the goal of such trips.

78. AHJ G-8–1920, Box 54.

79. AHJ G-8–1920, Boxes 53 and 54. 40 percent specifically requested passports for the purpose of reuniting with families and a further 20 percent of passport requests cited family reasons as well as other reasons. The 40 percent of requests that made no mention of family listed commercial interests, work, study, and recreation as the main purpose for their journey.

80. Hondagneu-Sotelo, *Gendered Transitions*, 38–39.

81. Segura and Zavela, *Women and Migration*; Jorge Durand, Douglas S. Massey, and René M. Zenteno, "Mexican Immigration to the United States: Continuities and Changes," *Latin American Research Review* 36, no. 1 (2001): 107–27; Massey et al., *Return to Aztlan*.

82. AHJ G-8–1920, Box 55.

83. A San Luis Potosí consul commented specifically that after a review of passport applicants in 1918, nearly all had friends assuring them of "good treatment in the United States." See Consul Cornelius Ferris to Consul Lansing, March 11, 1920, File 811.504/203, RG 59, NARA, reprinted in Cardoso, "Labor Emigration," 408.

84. *El Informador*, May 28, 1918; July 2, 1918; July 11, 1918.

85. *El Informador*, September 20, 1920.

86. *El Informador*, February 29, 1920.

87. *El Informador*, although tending to lean conservative, was known for staying fairly objective in its reporting. Rather than extend critiques toward the government or church, it tended to focus more on global events, in large part due to its original patronage and subscription by French and American colonies of Guadalajara. Ironically, despite the commentary from above which shows so much disdain for Obregón, the newspaper departed from its more neutral political stance during the era by promoting Luis Castellanos y Tapia for Governor and Obregón for president. See Enrique E. Sánchez Ruíz, "Apuntes para Una Historia de la Prensa en Guadalajara," *Comunicación y Sociedad, 4–5* (1989).

88. Tamayo, *Jalisco*, 150–62.

89. The exodus was noted again in newspaper reports, like one from San Martín de Hidalgo, Jalisco in February, reporting that a large number of braceros were looking for jobs in the North (*El Informador*, February 26, 1923).

90. "Los Que Se Van," *El Informador,* December 10, 1922.

91. See Muñoz Martinez, *The Injustice Never Leaves You.*

92. As cited in Jurgen Buchenau, *The Last Caudillo: Álvaro Obregón and the Mexican Revolution* (Hoboken, NJ: Wiley Blackwell, 2011), 101.

93. "Resumen de las ultimas noticias de la prensa de Mexico que llega hoy," *El Informador,* July 16, 1920.

94. "Pueblo Vacio," *El Informador,* November 10, 1920.

95. "Se Garantizaran Los Intereses de Los Mexicanos Que sean enganchados," *El Informador*, November 10, 1921.

96. According to Lawrence Cardoso one million dollars was spent on an estimated fifty thousand repatriations ("La Repatriacíon De Braceros En Época De Obregón—1920–1923," *Historia Mexicana* 26, no. 4 [1977]: 589).

97. *El Informador,* March 12, 1922.

98. "Sección editorial," *El Informador,* July 12, 1920.

CHAPTER TWO: FROM REVOLUTION TO EXODUS

Epigraph: PSTP, Carton 1, Folder 26, "Corridos 1931–1932."

1. For a classic work on the Cristero War see Jean Meyer, *La Cristiada* (Mexico City: Siglo Veintiuno Editores), 1970. For the impact of the Cristero War on Mexican emigration and Mexican emigrants in the United States, see Young, *Mexican Exodus.*

2. For an excellent example of the extensive literature on Americanization see Sanchez, "'Go after the women.'"

3. The numbers increased from 219,004 between 1910 and 1920 to 459,287 between 1920 and 1930. Statistics from "Indicadores de la Migración en México," INEGI 1985, table 4, pg. 125, in Luis Miguel Rionda Ramírez, *Y jalaron pa'l norte..: Migración, agrarismo y agricultura en un pueblo michoacano: Copándaro de Jiménez* (Mexico D.F.: Instituto Nacional de Antropología e Historia, 1992), 81. US and Mexican government statistics used by Paul Taylor reveal a similar trend despite the chronic differences between numbers gathered on each side. For the period 1920–1928 US statistics measured 579,031 arrivals (up from 247,846 between 1910 and 1920) and Mexican statistics counted 446,392 (up from 298,266 between 1910 and 1920). See Taylor, *Mexican Labor in the United States* 1:241. The half a million migrants (give or take) entering the United States from Mexico during the decade only reflects those whom entered legally. Lawrence Cardoso suggests that around a hundred thousand Mexican immigrants entered off the books yearly during the 1920s (*Mexican Emigration*, 94). Mae Ngai also found that around one hundred thousand undocumented Mexicans arrived yearly during this period, but found that an average of 62,000 came in legally per year (*Impossible Subjects*, 131).

4. Interview with Juana Martínez by Luis Felipe Recinos, Los Angeles, CA, April 6, 1927, in Devra Weber, Roberto Melville, and Juan Vicente Palerm, eds., *El Inmigrante Mexicano: La Historia De Su Vida: Entrevistas Completas, 1926–1927* (Mexico DF: Secretaria de Gobernacion, 2002), 277–88.

5. Massey et al., *Return to Aztlan*, 46–47.

6. Interview with Isabel González by Louis Felipe Recinos, Ciudad Juárez, Chihuahua and El Paso, Texas, March 15, 1927 in Weber, Melville, and Palerm, *El Inmigrante Mexicano*, 255.

7. See Matt García, *A World of Their Own;* Perales, *Smeltertown*; Mario Garcia, *Desert Immigrants;* Oscar Martinez, *Ciudad Juárez: Saga of a Legendary Border City* (Tucson: University of Arizona Press, 2018)

8. Mark Reisler, "The Mexican Immigrant in the Chicago Area during the 1920s," *Journal of the Illinois State Historical Society* 66 (1973): 144–58; Taylor, *Mexican Labor in the United States*, 2:82–95.

9. See chapter 3 for an extensive discussion of return migrations documented by train manifests.

10. Sanchez, *Becoming Mexican American*, 67–69.

11. Sanchez, *Becoming Mexican American*, 188–206.

12. As Mario García points out, the majority of Mexican-born women in El Paso worked as laundresses or domestic servants in El Paso, but some also worked in garment industries, cigar factories, or as store clerks (*Desert Immigrants*, 76–79). Mexican women worked in the garment industries of both Texas and the United States; see Rosalinda M. González, "Chicanas and Mexican Immigrant Families 1920–1940: Women's Subordination and Family Exploitation," in *Decades of Discontent: The Women's Movement, 1920–1940*, ed. Lois Schart and Joan M. Jenson (Westport, CT: Greenwood Press, 1983), 68–71.

13. Sanchez, *Becoming Mexican American*, 66.

14. Interview with Señora Cruz Loera de Torres by Manuel Gamio (n.d.), in Weber, Melville, and Palerm, *El Inmigrante Mexicano*, 230–32; US Census, 1930.

15. See Taylor, *Mexican Immigration*, 23, 24.

16. Reisler, *By the Sweat of Their Brow*, 78.

17. Reisler, *By the Sweat of Their Brow*, 78; D. Weber, *Dark Sweat, White Gold*, 23. According to Taylor the California Alien Land Law of 1920 and then a federal law of 1923 led to the decline of Japanese landownership and overall number of Japanese laborers in California agriculture, as well as the number of Japanese who had previously leased land for truck crops such as melon and lettuce. When Japanese lessees were forced out merchant companies would sublease small parcels of land from growers to produce a system that Taylor describes as, "in effect, large scale agriculture upon a leasing rather than an ownership basis" (*Mexican Labor in the United States*, 1:4–6, 32).

18. Reisler, *By the Sweat of Their Brow*, 78.

19. Taylor, *Mexican Labor in the United States*, 1:17.

20. D. Weber, *Dark Sweat, White Gold*, 20–35. Despite the difficulty that small landowners might have had in acquiring enough capital to maintain cotton farming and invest in technological equipment, Weber suggests that government interest came from the increase in profits to the public utility sector that would come from increased reliance on irrigation needed for cotton.

21. D. Weber, *Dark Sweat, White Gold*, 21.

22. See Jim Norris, *North for the Harvest: Mexican Workers, Growers, and the Sugar Beet Industry* (St. Paul: Minnesota Historical Press, 2009) for the Red River Valley. Sugar beet production was also prominent in California; see Frank P. Barajas, *Curious Unions: Mexican American Workers and Resistance in Oxnard, California, 1898–1961* (Lincoln, NE: University of Nebraska Press, 2012).

23. Taylor, *Mexican Labor in the United States*, 1:108–9.

24. Prior to the restriction to European immigration, employers began to prefer Mexican workers for their perceived docility and reluctance to participate in strikes. See Mark Reisler, "Always the Laborer, Never the Citizen: Anglo Perceptions of the Mexican Immigrant during the 1920s," in *Between Two Worlds: Mexican Immigrants in the United States*, ed. David G. Gutierrez (Wilmington, DE: Scholarly Resources, 1996). Perceived docility was likely due to the deportable status of those who had previously arrived undetected and undocumented and who were less likely to strike, especially after deportation became a more important feature of US immigration policy after 1924. Examples of employer comments and preference can be found in both volumes of Taylor's *Mexican Labor in the United States* and also in D. Weber, *Dark Sweat, White Gold*; Reisler, *By the Sweat of Their Brow*.

25. Taylor, *Mexican Labor in the United States*, 1:323.

26. Taylor, *Mexican Labor in the United States*, 1:132.

27. Taylor, *Mexican Labor in the United States*, 1:131.

28. Taylor, *Mexican Labor in the United States*, 1:134.

29. Taylor, *Mexican Labor in the United States*, 1:139.

30. American Beet Sugar Company, Carton 10, Folder 38, PTSP.

31. D. Weber, *Dark Sweat, White Gold*, 64.

32. Neil Foley, *The White Scourge: Mexicans, Blacks, and Poor Whites in Texas Cotton Culture* (Berkeley: University of California Press, 1997), 42.

33. Taylor, *Mexican Labor in the United States*, 1:7; D. Weber, *Dark Sweat, White Gold*, 35.

34. *Solos* were single men not considered attached to family groups (Taylor, *Mexican Labor in the United States*, 1:139).

35. Matt García, *A World of Their Own*, 42.

36. Reisler, *By the Sweat of Their Brow*, 88.

37. Taylor, *A Spanish-Mexican Peasant Community*, 41.

38. Labor shortage versus labor over-supply. Reisler points out that the definitions for labor shortage were inconsistent, suggesting that growers consistently complained about labor shortages when they felt like harvesting crops in the quickest, most profitable manner, whereas other perspectives, such as that from the Department of Agriculture, judged that there was a chronic oversupply of labor during the 1920s (*By the Sweat of Their Brow*, 82).

39. Douglas Monroy, *Rebirth: Mexican Los Angeles From the Great Migration to the Great Depression* (Berkeley: University of California Press, 1999), 120–21.

40. Mario García, *Desert Immigrants*, 75–59. One study in the 1930s actually suggested that 40 percent of Mexican women worked in domestic service where only 21.2 percent worked in agriculture. However, the numbers are not disaggregated into categories of Mexican-born and US-born Mexicans. See González, "Chicanas and Mexican Immigrant Families 1920–1940," 67.

41. Massey et al., *Return to Atzlán*, 46–47.

42. Reisler, *By the Sweat of Their Brow*, 97.

43. Interview with Macaria Ávalos by Luis Felipe Recinos, Ciudad Juárez, March 1927, in Weber, Melville, and Palerm, *El Inmigrante Mexicano*, 242.

44. Ngai, *Impossible Subjects*, 7, 66–70.

45. Ngai, *Impossible Subjects*, 23.

46. Sanchez, *Becoming Mexican American*, 59.

47. Consul McConnico to Fernando Manzano Ybarra, April 1924, "Department of State U.S. Consulate, Guadalajara, Mexico. 1896–1977 (Most Recent)," Series: United States Consular Records for Guadalajara, Mexico, 1896–1935, Volume 74, file no. 811.11, RG 84, NARA.

48. Department of State, "Admissions of Aliens into the United States," General INS. Consular No. 926- Diplomatic Serial No. 273. June 13, 1924. Received by American Consulate in Guadalajara, Mexico June 25th, 1924 to the Diplomatic Officers of the United States, U.S. Consulate, Guadalajara, Series 1896–1935, Volume 87, file no. 855, RG 84, NARA.

49. The excludable categories of political affiliation were very critical during the armed phase of the Revolution, as was the contract labor exclusion at various points during the first two decades of the twentieth century, but during the 1920s, especially as Mexican labor restrictionists lost their battle to incorporate Mexican

immigrants into the quota system, the strict application of the "likely to become a public charge" exclusion was encouraged so that those entering the United States as laborers could at the very minimum pay for the return back to their countries in the event of a shortage of labor opportunities. It is clear that various employers in the United States were able to have influence via the application of the LPC exclusion.

50. Furthermore, as Martha Gardner points out, "'Likely to become a public charge,' or 'LPC' in the parlance of immigration officials, denoted not only current poverty but potential poverty" (*The Qualities of a Citizen*, 87).

51. It is worth noting that family members at times vouched as employers of their migrant family members.

52. Although I have yet to find a case where a person of influence tried to prevent another person's migration, the possibility exists that the subjective nature of the law could allow for that as well. While the concept of political patronage and favorable labor contracts and migration status does not present itself clearly until the bracero contract era, it is worth considering, especially during the Obregón and Calles period, as patronage politics was forging a number of political alliances, that Mexican politicians could influence Mexican and US immigration officials.

53. "Admission of Aliens into the United States," General Ins. Consular No. 926 Diplomatic Serial No. 273 June 13 1924. Issued by the Department of state & received by the American Consulate in Guadalajara, Mexico June 25th 1924. U.S. Consulate, Guadalajara, Series 1896–1935, Volume 92, RG 84, NARA.

54. Gardner, *Qualities of a Citizen*, 94.

55. Correspondence between consuls at Guadalajara and Nogales regarding Andrea Torres, U.S. Consulate, Guadalajara, Series 1896–1935, Volume 88, file no. 811.11 RG 84, NARA.

56. Gardner, *Qualities of a Citizen*, 94 and chapter 5.

57. Correspondence between consuls at Guadalajara and Nogales regarding Angel Flores, U.S. Consulate, Guadalajara, Series 1896–1935, Volume 90, RG 84, NARA.

58. Correspondence between consuls at Guadalajara and Nogales regarding Adolfo Garcia Gómez, U.S. Consulate, Guadalajara, Series 1896–1935, Volume 90, RG 84, NARA.

59. Gardner, *Qualities of a Citizen*, 34–35.

60. Interview with Andrés Morán by Luis Felipe Recinos, Chihuahua, March 8, 1927, in Weber, Melville, and Palerm, *El Inmigrante Mexicano*, 236.

61. See interview with Señor Sandoval by Luis Felipe Recinos (n.d.), and interview with Gregoria Ayala by Luis Felipe Recinos (n.d.), in Weber, Melville, and Palerm, *El Inmigrante Mexicano*, 160–61 and 184–86.

62. Train lists from Archivo Histórico de Inmigración, 22 de Octubre LA 1931 via Nogales, 22 de Octubre LA 1931 via Juárez, "Repatriados que voluntariamente regresar al pais" Laredo a Mexico, March 1931, INAMI 1–161–1931–189.

63. *El Informador,* May 13, 1924.

64. 1926–1927: 66,766 equaling 19.9 percent of total admitted; 1927–1928: 57,765 equaling 18.8 percent of total admitted. In actual numbers these years were similar

to 1923 and 1924 but made up less of total immigrants into the United States. See State of California, *Governor C.C. Young's Mexican Fact-Finding Committee, Mexicans in California* (San Francisco: California Department of Industrial Relations, 1930), 20.

65. Cárdenas Sánchez, *El largo curso*, 379–80.

66. José María Muriá, *Breve Historia de Jalisco* (Mexico City: El Colegio de Mexico, 2000), 155–64; Susan M. Gauss, *Made in Mexico: Regions, Nation, and the State in The Rise of Mexican Industrialism, 1920s–1940s* (University Park: Pennsylvania State University Press, 2010), 55–61.

67. Tamayo, *Jalisco*, 162. More research is needed to bear out a direct connection between pre-Cristero violence and emigration in the region, but it is worth noting that Ocotlán was one of the most notable emigrant-sending regions in 1920 as revealed through passport applications (see chapter 1).

68. Although there are similarities between San José de Gracia and Arandas with regard to land tenure patterns, ranching, and roles in the Cristero wars, a key difference is that Arandas had been sending emigrants to the United States for decades, whereas San José de Gracia did not experience emigration until after the Cristero wars.

69. Taylor, *A Spanish-Mexican Peasant Community*, 37–40.

70. See David Fitzgerald, *A Nation of Emigrants: How Mexico Manages its Migration* (Berkeley: University of California Press, 2009), 43; Young, *Mexican Exodus*.

71. "Faltan Braceros en el Estado," *El Informador*, February 12, 1925.

72. "Se anuncia la inauguracion del Ferrocarril sud-pacifico para el domingo 17 de los corrientes," *El Informador*, April 9, 1927; "Corespondencia de Arrandas: 30% de las cosechas se perdió," *El Informador*, January 6, 1926.

73. "Muchos Mexicanos sufren Miseria en EE.UU.," *El Informador*, Guadalajara, Jalisco, June 6, 1927. Trains connecting Guadalajara directly to Nogales began running April 17, 1927, less than two months before the noticeable increase in migrants as indicated by the Nogales Department of Commerce.

74. *El Informador*, March 17, 1925. See Kevin Middlebrook, *The Paradox of Revolution: Labor, The State and Authoritarianism in Mexico* (Baltimore, MD: Johns Hopkins University Press, 1995), 48–49.

75. Gauss, *Made in Mexico*, chapter 2.

76. Middlebrook, *The Paradox of Revolution*, 90–93.

77. *El Informador*, September 24, 1926.

78. See Mary Kay Vaughan, *Cultural Politics in Revolution: Teachers, Schools and Peasants in Mexico, 1930–1940* (Tucson: University of Arizona Press, 1987), for a description of the contested educational programs of the Cardenista period and the ways in which communities used state rhetoric to advocate for local demands related to education.

79. *El Informador*, September 24, 1926.

80. *El Informador*, July 11, 1927.

81. *El Informador*, July 5, 1928: "la gente culta y conocedora del ambiente laborista en los Estados Unidos."

82. *El Informador*, November 3, 1925.

83. *El Informador,* March 3, 1925: "Serán creadas dos nuevas agencias de migración."

84. González Navarro, *Los Extranjeros en México,* 3:292.

85. "Asunto: Participa que bajo a la Sra. Ana Maria Hernández de Cantu del tren en que viajaba por no tener documentación para emigrar," November 11, 1925, INAMI 4–353–2–1925–5A.

86. *El Informador,* February 2, 1927. The original is difficult to translate due to the author's use of double entendre, so I give it in full here: "Un periódico da la noticia un tanto cuanto alarmante de que solamente por Ciudad Juárez, están saliendo mil mujeres diariamente con destino a Los Estados Unidos. Pues señor nos estamos sin faldas; y eso que ya ella se habían quedado antes por efecto de la moda actual, que ha reducido tal incremento a sus mínimas proporciones. Hay que poner remedio al éxodo de mujeres; por que un pueblo de puros hombres seria un puchero sin sal. Mal con ellas, peor sin ellas."

87. *El Informador,* April 4, 1927.

CHAPTER THREE: THE GREAT DEPRESSION AND THE GREAT RETURN

1. "Repatriados que voluntariamente regresar al pais," INAMI 1–161–1931–189. Biographical data compiled by author from Fifteenth Census of the United States, 1930 (Washington, DC: National Archives and Records Administration, 1930), Belvedere, Los Angeles, California; Roll: 123; Page: 4B; Enumeration District: 0818; Image: 738.0; FHL microfilm: 2339858. United States of America, Bureau of the Census, accessed through Ancestry.com.

2. Abraham Hoffman, in his landmark study of Mexican repatriation in Los Angeles, estimated that a total of 500,000 were repatriated and deported (*Unwanted Mexican-Americans in the Great Depression: Repatriation Pressures 1929–1939* [Tucson: University of Arizona Press, 1974]). Francisco Balderrama and Raymond Rodriguez estimate that 1 million Mexicans returned to Mexico from the United States in the 1930s (*Decade of Betrayal. Mexican Repatriation in the 1930s* [Albuquerque: New Mexico University Press, 2006]).

3. Hoffman, *Unwanted Mexican-Americans in the Great Depression*; Sanchez, *Becoming Mexican American.* For more works on repatriation see Fernando Saúl Alanís Enciso, *Que se queden allá: El Gobierno de México y la repatriación de mexicanos en Estados Unidos (1934–1940)* (Tijuana: El Colegio de La Frontera, 2007); Mercedes Carreras, *Los Mexicanos Que Devolvió La Crisis, 1929–1932* (Tlatelolco, México: Secretaría de Relaciones Exteriores, 1974); Guérin-Gonzalez, *Mexican Workers and American Dreams.*

4. Balderrama and Rodriguez, *Decade of Betrayal.*

5. For details on immigration restrictionists and their concern regarding the fecundity of Mexican women and the fear that they relied disproportionately on welfare see Molina, *Fit to be Citizens?,* 141–50. Balderrama and Rodriguez describe

how certain community organizations like the National Club of America for Americans Inc. tracked the cost of welfare spending on "aliens" and pressured county officials in Los Angeles to prohibit relief spending on Mexicans (*Decade of Betrayal*, 94–99).

6. See Erika Lee, *America for Americans: A History of Xenophobia in the United States* (New York, NY: Basic Books, 2019).

7. Balderrama and Rodríguez, *Decade of Betrayal*, 90, 120–21.

8. Balderrama and Rodríguez, *Decade of Betrayal*, 73–78.

9. Hoffman, *Unwanted Mexican Americans*; Hernandez, *Migra!*, 92; Matt García, *A World of Their Own*, 87; Cardoso, *Mexican Emigration to the United States*, 139–43.

10. *El Informador*, May 19, 1928.

11. D. Weber, *Dark Sweat, White Gold*, 77.

12. Sanchez, *Becoming Mexican American*, 210.

13. D. Weber, *Dark Sweat, White Gold*, 76–77.

14. Foley, *The White Scourge*, 166.

15. Sanchez, *Becoming Mexican American*, 210–11.

16. Arnoldo de León, *Ethnicity in the Sunbelt: A History of Mexican Americans in Housto,* (Houston: University of Houston, 1989), 47.

17. Innis-Jiménez, *Steel Barrio*, 138.

18. Rudolph Valier Alvarado and Sonya Yvette Slate Alvarado, *Mexicans and Mexican Americans in Michigan* (East Lansing: Michigan University State Press 2003), 27–28.

19. Letter from Margarita B. Perez, 244.1/10; letter from Sara Barron, 244.1/75; letter from Maria E. Zamarripa 244.1/55; letter from Maria Dolores Camacho, 244.1/81; in Ramo Presidentes Abelardo Rodríguez (ALR), AGN-RP-ALR.

20. Transcribed letter in letter to Sec. de Agricultura and Sec. de Industria Comercio y Trabajo from the Office of Migration, July 17, 1930, 3–356–1930–94, INAMI. Census data on Luis Narvaez stated that he had arrived in 1923, and that in April of 1930, only two months prior to his letter to the President, he had been living in a rail car along with other Mexican laborers. 1923 was likely his first entrance into the United States, after which subsequent migrations were made.

21. Mexicans, had, in fact, been invited to return to their homelands and encouraged to do so by consuls abroad. Records do not indicate whether these three men actually returned to Mexico as they originally hoped.

22. Letter to the President from Jose Perez, October 31, 1932, 4/356/1173, INAMI; AGN-RP-ALR 244.1/3.

23. Letter to President Abelardo Rodríguez from Ricardo Frías Beltrán, 1933, AGN-RP-ALR 241/4.

24. For discussions on repatriation, Americanization, and identity see Arredondo, *Mexican Chicago*; Perales, *Smeltertown*.

25. Sanchez actually suggests that a decline in percentage of relief cases—from 21 percent in 1929 to 16 percent in 1930—occurred rather than an increase in dependence on aid (*Becoming Mexican American*, 107).

26. Balderrama and Rodríguez, *Decade of Betrayal*, 151.

27. Hoffman, *Unwanted Mexican-Americans in the Great Depression*, 85.

28. Carreras, *Los Mexicanos Que Devolvió La Crisis*, 90; Hoffman, *Unwanted Mexican-Americans in the Great Depression*, 87. County-sponsored trains began leaving Los Angeles in March, 1931.

29. "Plan para la repatriación de connacionales," INAMI 4–356–1931–338.

30. Letter from President of Comisión Honorífica Mexicana, San Angelo, Texas, December 1931, INAMI 4–356–1931–603.

31. "Plan para la repatriación de connacionales," INAMI 4–356–1931–338.

32. For repatriates and colonization efforts see Alanis Encisco *Que se queden allá*; Carreras, *Los Mexicanos Que Devolvió La Crisis*.

33. "Thousands of Mexicans Will Go Back Home," *Los Angeles Times*, October 1, 1931.

34. 1635 between December 16 and December 30.

35. "Exodus of Mexicans Runs High: Nuevo Laredo Returns in Brief Period Pass Entry Totals for Five Months," *Los Angeles Times*, January 10, 1931.

36. Train lists, 22 de Octobre LA 1931 via Nogales, 22 de Octobre LA 1931 via Juárez, "Repatriados que voluntariamente regresar al pais," Laredo a Mexico, March 1931, INAMI 1–161–1931–189.

37. "Repatriados que voluntariamente regresar al pais," Laredo a Mexico, March 1931, INAMI 1–161–1931–189.

38. 159 adults had their previous location of residence indicated (see appendix for more information). Top return-migrant sending states included: Texas (65), Illinois (39), Michigan (18), Missouri (11), Pennsylvania (10), Indiana (7).

39. Out of the seventy-four migrants returning from Illinois, Michigan, Pennsylvania, and Indiana, four returned to Mexico City, three of whom resided in Philadelphia.

40. Fifteenth Census of the United States, 1930. Washington, DC: National Archives and Records Administration, 1930. *Precinct 4, Bexar, Texas;* Roll: *2298;* Page: *15B;* Enumeration District: *0164;* Image: *958.0;* FHL microfilm: *2342032* United States of America, Bureau of the Census, accessed through Ancestry.com.

41. "Repatriados que voluntariamente regresar al pais," Laredo a Mexico, March 1931, INAMI 1–161–1931–189.

42. "Repatriados que voluntariamente regresar al pais," Laredo a Mexico, March 1931, INAMI 1–161–1931–189.

43. Fifteenth Census of the United States, 1930, Washington, DC: National Archives and Records Administration, 1930. Census Place: *Saginaw, Michigan;* Roll: *1021;* Page: *16B;* Enumeration District: *0027;* Image: *990.0;* FHL microfilm: *2340756* for Victor Valtierra, Year: *1930;* Census Place: *Saginaw, Michigan;* Roll: *1021;* Page: *14A;* Enumeration District: *0027;* Image: *985.0;* FHL microfilm: *2340756,* for Melquiades López. United States of America, Bureau of the Census, accessed through Ancestry.com.

44. *Watts-Compton City Directory 1927–1928* (Los Angeles: Los Angeles Directory Co.); U.S. City Directories, 1822–1989, https://www.ancestry.com/search /collections/2469.

45. For US-born children who were sent back, see Hoffman, *Unwanted Mexican-Americans In the Great Depression*, 94–96. Balderrama and Rodríguez suggest that up to 60 percent of total Mexican repatriates were American-born (*Decade of Betrayal*, 330).

46. "Repatriados registrados en el país durante el año de 1931, con expresión de las Entidades Federativas donde fueron a radicarse y grupos de edad hasta 14 años," June 25th, 1932, Departamento de la Estadística Nacional, INAMI 4–350–1930–448.

47. As Katherine Benton-Cohen shows, the Dillingham Commission, the US commission tasked with studying immigration from 1907–1910, had not viewed Mexicans as a threat to American labor because they were expected to return to Mexico after short stays of duration ("Other Immigrants: Mexicans and the Dillingham Commission of 1907–1911," *Journal of American Ethnic History* 30, no. 2 (2011): 33–57.

48. Letter to Emilio Portes Gil from Micaela B. de Amador, February 27, 1930, INAMI 4–356–1930–89.

49. AGN-RP-ALR, Box 25 244.1/66.

50. AGN-RP-ALR, Box 25, 244.1/89.

51. AGN-RP-ALR, Box 25, 244.1/75, 244.1/89.

52. Letter to Mexican President Ortiz Rubio from Student Federation of Jalisco, June 26, 1931, INAMI 4–356–1931–332.

53. "Se Modifica La Ley Box en E.U. en favor de Los Mexicanos," *El Informador,* May 24, 1929.

54. "Por Gomez Palacios Siguen Pasando Numerosas Repatriados," *El Informador,* December 19, 1930.

55. "Dio principio repatriación de Mexicanos," *El Informador,* January 12, 1931.

56. "Todo lo que traen consigo los repatriados lo están malbaratando," *El Informador,* November 12, 1931.

57. "Serán poderoso factor los Braceros Deportados para el Resurgimiento de la agricultura," *El Informador,* February 12, 1930.

58. April 22, 1931, Nogales, "Informe de la Visita practicada a a la Delegación del Servicio de Emigración Inspector Ramon Tirado," INAMI 4 161–1931–173.

59. "El Fantasma Migratorio," *El Informador,* June 6, 1933.

60. "Una remora para la repatriación," *El Informador,* February 24, 1930.

CHAPTER FOUR: GOOD PRESIDENTS, BAD
HUSBANDS, AND DEAD FATHERS

1. Unless otherwise indicated, correspondence is quoted exactly as written. Nicha Rodriguez, 1936, "Department of State U.S. Consulate, Guadalajara, Mexico. 1896–1977 (Most Recent)," Box 3, file no. 310, U.S. Department of State, Records of the Foreign Service Posts of the Department of State, 1788- ca. 1991, RG 84, NARA.

2. Letter to Lázaro Cárdenas from Nahum Cervantes, May 1939, AGN, Ramo Presidentes, Fondo Lázaro Cárdenas del Rio (AGN-RP-LCR) Box 549.5/74.

3. See Gardner, *The Qualities of a Citizen.*

4. 66,526 immigration and non-immigration visas were issued to persons born in Mexico for the years 1926–1927, after which the issuance of immigration visas dropped precipitously. Ten years later, for the years 1935 and 1936, only 1,427 visas were given. See Statistical Report of Immigration and Non-Immigration Visas for Year July 1, 1935 to June 30, 1936, U.S. Consulate, Guadalajara, Box 6, file no. 811.11, RG 84, NARA.

5. Immigration and Visa Discussions at the Consular Conference, Mexico City, October 9–15, 1937, U.S. Consulate, Guadalajara, Box 9, file. no. 811.11., RG 84, NARA.

6. Cardoso, *Mexican Emigration to the United States*, 148.

7. Mexico's industrial sector actually grew significantly from 1926 to 1940, but it doesn't appear to have brought significant benefits to the majority of the Mexican population. See Enrique Cárdenas, *La Industrialización Mexicana Durante La Gran Depresión* (El Colegio De Mexico: Mexico DF, 1987), 32–55.

8. Political and Economic reports July 1939-December 1939, U.S. Consulate, Guadalajara, Box 25 file no. 800, section titled *Agrarian*, RG 84, NARA.

9. Political and Economic reports July 1939-December 1939, section titled Domestic Servants, July 1, 1939 Report; section titled postal and telegraph workers, August 1, 1939, Report, U.S. Consulate, Guadalajara, Box 25 file no. 800, RG 84, NARA.

10. A number of US companies wrote to the consul seeking information on the market conditions for products including jewelry, tobacco, cotton clothing, gas stoves, radios, and cars. See U.S. Consulate, Guadalajara, Box 7 file no. 867; 1937 Box 13 File no. 866.12, RG 84, NARA.

11. Political and economic reports July 1939-December 1939, U.S. Consulate, Guadalajara, Box 25 file no. 800, RG 84, NARA. See especially October 2, 1939, *Cost of Living.*

12. Letter from US Vice Consul Norris S. Haselton to The Drell Manufacturing Novelty Company, July 14, 1936, U.S. Consulate, Guadalajara, Box 7, 867.4, RG 84, NARA.

13. Correspondence between US consul and Frank Valadez, 1936, U.S. Consulate, Guadalajara ,Box 3, file no. 310, RG 84, NARA.

14. Cybelle Fox, *Three Worlds of Relief: Race, Immigration and the American Welfare State from the Progressive Era to the New Deal* (Princeton, NJ: Princeton University Press, 2012), 215.

15. "Memorandum on Housing Conditions among migratory workers in California," PTSP.

16. In reality these migrants from Oklahoma, Texas, and much of the midwestern plains came in droves to California not only because of the extreme drought that contributed to the Dust Bowl. The Great Depression, with its decreasing crop prices, and subsidized programs that actually encouraged farmers to take their lands out of cultivation, hit the rural Southwest particularly hard. The movement west by these white migrants (including white collar, blue collar and farmers) had its origins prior

to the 1930s and was largely facilitated by family connections; however, the particular migrants who settled in the central valleys of California were a particularly destitute group hoping to take advantages of higher wages, year-round farming, and California social relief. See James Gregory, *American Exodus: The Dust Bowl Migration and Okie Culture in California.* (New York: Oxford University Press, 1989).

17. "A study of 132 families in CA cotton camps. Medical Care"; "A Study of the Health of 1000 children of Migratory Agricultural Laborers in California," UC Berkeley Bancroft Library Manuscripts Collection, BANC MSS 84/38c, Carton 15 Folder 51, PTSP.

18. White migrant families = 1837; Mexican families = 130. See "Memorandum on Housing Conditions among migratory workers in California," UC Berkeley Bancroft Library Manuscripts Collection, BANC MSS 84/38c, PTSP.

19. "Survey of California Workers," UC Berkeley Bancroft Library Manuscripts Collection, BANC MSS 84/38c, Carton 15, folder 35, PTSP.

20. "A study of 132 families in CA cotton camps. Medical Care"; "A Study of the Health of 1000 children of Migratory Agricultural Laborers in California," UC Berkeley Bancroft Library Manuscripts Collection, BANC MSS 84/38c, Carton 15 Folder 51, PTSP.

21. Stephanie Lewthwaite, *Race, Place and Reform in Mexican Los Angeles: A Transnational Perspective* (Tucson: University of Arizona Press, 2009), 162–63.

22. C. Fox, *Three Worlds of Relief,* 215. Mexican Americans in the United States also benefited from FSA housing initiatives; see Verónica Martínez-Matsuda, *Migrant Citizenship: Race, Rights, and Reform in the U.S. Farm Labor Camp Program* (Philadelphia: University of Pennsylvania Press, 2020).

23. Robert Cohen, *Dear Mrs. Roosevelt: Letters from Children of the Great Depression* (Chapel Hill: University of North Carolina Press, 2002), 5.

24. Letter from Rosie Garcia to President Roosevelt, April 29, 1939, U.S. Consulate, Guadalajara, Box 22, file no. 310, RG 84, NARA.

25. Nicha Rodriguez, 1936, Box 3, file no. 310; Rosie Garcia, 1939, Box 22, file no. 310; Antonia Vasquez, 1939, Box 22, file no. 310; Marry Torres, 1936, file no. 811.11; all U.S. Consulate, Guadalajara, RG 84, NARA. These letters were written to the White House and then forwarded to the US consular office at Guadalajara. US consuls were responsible for writing responses to inform letter-writers that there were no funds to pay for the migration of US or Mexican citizens to the United States. One other letter to the president surfaced in these files and was written by David Fernandez who wrote to the president asking for help in re-entering the country after he had been deported and had since been turned away at the border; see U.S. Consulate, Guadalajara, Box 12, file no. 811.11, RG 84, NARA.

26. Letter From Mary C. Enriquez to Vice President Henry Wallace, December 6, 1941, Box 28, file No. 310, RG 84, NARA.

27. Letter to President Cárdenas from Magdalena E. Ayala, AGN-RP-LCR 549.5/22.

28. For an example of letter directing migrants to the consul see letter to Jesus Suárez from Manuel Gamio, AGN-RP-LCR, 549.69. Señora J. Márquez de Edwards

Vda. de Alonso, writing from Seeley, California, in 1938, was told that due to budgetary constraints she would not receive aid for her repatriation but that perhaps aid could be granted the following year (AGN-RP-LCR, 549.5/133).

29. Such was the case for Victor Sandoval who wrote from Nogales, Sonora, in 1939 to ask the president for rail passes for his sister and her children from San Pedro, California, to Aguascalientes. Sandoval had actually previously secured rail passes for himself and eight other family members from Chula Vista to Mexico in 1935 (AGN-RP-LCR, 549.5/43).

30. Federal programs directed specifically towards mothers and children emerged in Mexico in the 1940s and 1950s, and the Secretaría de Asistencia Publica was created in 1937 just a few years after the New Deal programs in the United States. See Nichole Sanders, *Gender and Welfare in Mexico: The Consolidation of a Post-Revolutionary State* (University Park: Pennsylvania State University Press, 2012). The 1917 Mexican Constitution did include elements of social welfare, including articles which gave the state control over benevolent organizations and established a public health authority (10). In one sense this can be interpreted as a fairly progressive move, but given the increased authority conferred to the state, this was more likely a direct attack on social welfare offered by religious institutions.

31. For more on Cárdenas's appeal to popular sectors in Mexican society, see Alan Knight, "Cardenismo: Juggernaugt or Jalopy?," *Journal of Latin American Studies* 26, no. 1 (1994): 80–81; Amelia Kiddle and Maria Muñoz, eds., *Populism in Twentieth Century Mexico: The Presidencies of Lázaro Cárdenas and Luis Echeverría* (Tucson: University of Arizona Press, 2010).

32. Letter to Cárdenas from Refugio Espinoza, April 14, 1938, AGN-RP-LCR 549.5/69.

33. Letter to Cárdenas from Agustin Valle, July 7, 1939, AGN-RP-LCR 549.5/170. Valle was no doubt referring to Cárdenas's nationalization of oil.

34. Letter to President Cárdenas from Ricardo Renteria, March 18, 1938, AGN-RP-LCR 549.5/74.

35. Letter to President Cárdenas from Filomena Reyes, AGN-RP-LRC 549.9/134.

36. Letter to Cárdenas from Manuel Salinas, AGN-RP-LRC 549.5/33.

37. Letter to Cárdenas from Flora N. Guajardo, April 14, 1938, AGN-LCR 549.5/74. Flora wrote specifically that she learned of President Cárdenas's generosity through reading the "periodicos Lozano." This refers to the Spanish-language newspapers started by Ignacio Lozano, a Mexican who fled to Texas during the Mexican Revolution and who started "La Prensa" in San Antonio and "La Opiñon" in Los Angeles. These were the most widely read Mexican newspapers during the time. See Mario T. García, "La Frontera: The Border as Symbol and Reality in Mexican-American Thought," *Mexican Studies/Estudios Mexicanos* 1, no. 2 (1985): 197–99.

38. As cited in Lynn Stephen, *Zapata Lives!: Histories and Cultural Politics in Southern Mexico* (Berkeley: University of California Press, 2002), 57.

39. Alanís Enciso, *Que se Quedan*, 151, 160.

40. Alanís Enciso, *Que se Quedan*, 151–55.

41. Alanís Enciso, *Que se Quedan*, 161–63. In November of 1938 Cárdenas's plan for repatriation was formalized and government resources were used to provide for the repatriation and colonization of hundreds of Mexican families.

42. Letter to President Cárdenas from Hilario González, February 22, 1938, AGN-RP-LRC 549.5/88.

43. Fernando Gonzalez, AGN-RP-LRC 549.5/108; Victoria Valdes, AGN-RP-LRC 549.5/113; Eugenio Ibarra, AGN-RP-LRC 549.5/146; Luis Navarro, AGN-RP-LRC 549.5/160; Ambrosio Gonzalez, AGN-RP-LRC 549.5/169; Sabino Alzaga, AGN-RP-LRC 549.5/168.

44. For more on the repatriates and colonization see Alanís Enciso, *Que se Quedan*, including chapter 7 on the Colonia "18 de Marzo." Additionally, for the story of Doña Elisa who arrived to the colony as a girl with her parents who repatriated from Texas see Walsh, *Building the Borderlands* (1–3); Walsh also gives another detailed description of the repatriation to the Rio Bravo delta (136–53).

45. Fernando Saul Alanis Enciso, "The Repatriation of Mexicans from the United States and Mexican Nationalism, 1929–1940," in *Beyond La Frontera: The History of Mexico-U.S. Migration*, ed. Mark Overmyer-Velázquez (New York: Oxford University Press, 2011), 69–70.

46. Four out of five letter-writers writing to the consul at Guadalajara between 1936 and 1940 were women.

47. See Maria del Refugio Gracian de Cervantes, Box 2, no. 130; Otilia R. Haro 130.7 H; Angela Cervantes 130.7 C; Vicente Carrillo, 130, letter from Irma Wagner 1938, Box 15, file no. 130, U.S. Consulate, Guadalajara, RG 84, NARA.

48. Twenty-eight welfare cases in 1936; forty-seven in 1937; twenty-nine in 1938; twenty-seven in 1939; forty-four in 1940.

49. Correspondence between Maria del Refugio Gracian de Cervantes and the US consul, U.S. Consulate, Guadalajara, Box 2, no. 130, RG 84, NARA. 1930 US Census, Border Crossing Manifest 1920, Border Crossing Manifest 1924, General Records of the Immigration and Naturalization Service, RG 85, NARA, accessed through Ancestry.com. Consuls left no indication or specific criteria for explaining the refusal of visas for particular cases. It can be assumed that during this period the majority of refusals were based on the LPC exclusion (see chapter 2).

50. According to discussions held at the consular conference on immigration in Mexico City, the public charge clause was responsible for 95 percent of visa refusals. See Immigration and Visa Discussions at the Consular Conference, Mexico City, October 9–15, 1937, U.S. Consulate, Guadalajara, Box 9, file. no. 811.11. p. 8, RG 84, NARA.

51. Summary of Business for the Consular Branch of the American Foreign Service at Guadalajara, Quarterly Reports for 1936, U.S. Consulate, Guadalajara, 1936, Box 2, file no. 130, RG 84, NARA.

52. See the following cases for examples of citizenship denied on presenting baptismal certificates alone: Correspondence between Louise S. Lopez and the consul, U.S. Consulate, Guadalajara, 1938, Box 15, file no. 130, RG 84, NARA; and correspondence between Jose Cervantes and the consul, 1938, Box 15, file no. 130, RG 84, NARA.

53. Letter to U.S. Consul from Vicente Carrillo, February 24, 1936; letter to Vicente Carrillo from U.S Consul George H. Winters, February 28, 1936, U.S. Consulate, Guadalajara, Box 2, file no. 130, RG 84, NARA.

54. Laredo, Texas Board of Inquiry (Transcripts), Children Under 16, without Parents, Mexicans, 1919, Casefile 54281/36G, Records of the Immigration and Naturalization Service, Series A: Subject Correspondence Files, Part 2: Mexican Immigration 1906–1930, NARA.

55. The lack of correct paperwork could be prohibitive in establishing citizenship but even with the right paperwork citizenship was unstable, and the potential for migration back and forth across the US-Mexico border reduced. Guillermo Warden hoped to establish his citizenship through his American father, but because he had been born out of wedlock, the consul reported back to him that it was doubtful that he would ever be able to gain US citizenship through his father. Correspondence between William Warden and US consul George H Winters, U.S. Consulate, Guadalajara, Box 2, file no. 130, RG 84, NARA.

56. Letter from Ethel Hinojosa to the US consul at Guadalajara, March 9, 1938, U.S. Consulate, Guadalajara, Box 16, file no. 310, RG 84, NARA.

57. Letter to the consul from Charles Hinojosa, April 28, 1938, U.S. Consulate, Guadalajara, Box 16, file no. 130, RG 84, NARA.

58. Letter to Ethel Hinojosa from consul Geonare H. Winters, March 11, 1938, U.S. Consulate, Guadalajara , Box 16, file no. 130, RG 84, NARA.

59. Letter to the consul from Ethel Hinojosa, June 8, 1939, U.S. Consulate, Guadalajara, Box 22, file no. 310, RG 84, NARA.

60. It is quite possible that Charles had lost his job provided by the New Deal's WPA, since by 1937 the WPA had started to reduce WPA relief projects in places such as California's San Joaquin Valley. See D. Weber, *Dark Sweat, White Gold*, 167–71.

61. Letter from Barbara Cadena to the consul, March 27, 1940, U.S. Consulate, Guadalajara, Box 28, file no. 130, RG 84, NARA.

62. Correspondence between US consul and Mabelle Jauregui, 1940, U.S. Consulate, Guadalajara, Box, 28, file no. 130, RG 84, NARA.

63. Lovenia opened her letter to the consul, "I am an American girl, born January 22, 1913 in Emma, Illinois." At the time of writing, she was twenty-five years old, and it appears that she did not have any children of her own. Her appeal to the consul is particularly interesting because she identifies herself as a girl, not a woman, and clearly suggests that she desires to go back to her father. This could of course be because she truly did see herself as young girl and defined herself still in relation to her father, having not yet given birth to her own children, but her use of such language could also be suggestive of her making an appeal to the consul on the basis of her youth, perhaps trying to elucidate more sympathy. In any case, her letter is striking because Lovenia's wellbeing is grounded in a patriarchal paternal order that places women in the care of their husbands or of fathers. More information on this particular case is needed (there are only two letters exchanged) to speculate about how Lovenia might have viewed the consul in light of this system of protective

patriarchy. In general, it seems that women might have purposefully constructed appeals around this notion of protective patriarchy in order to make a better case to the consul, attributing personal responsibility to consuls as substitute patriarchs.

64. Letter from US Consul to Lovenia Chastain de Navarrete, August 8, 1938, U.S. Consulate, Guadalajara, Box 16 file no. 310, RG 84, NARA.

65. Letter from Theresa Romero to her father, May 16, 1937, U.S. Consulate, Guadalajara, Box 9, file no. 310, RG 84, NARA.

66. Letter from Mabel to her uncle, April 22, 1936, U.S. Consulate, Guadalajara, Box 3, file no. 310, RG 84, NARA.

67. Mabel also had to communicate with the consul and her family using the address of a friend in town once her husband became suspicious of her writing letters to the American consul.

68. Letter from Predicanda Kramer to US Consul, January 31, 1939, U.S. Consulate, Guadalajara, Box 22, file no. 310, RG 84, NARA.

69. Letter from Consul M.L. Stafford to Predicanda Kremer, February 7, 1939, U.S. Consulate, Guadalajara, Box 16, file no. 310, RG 84, NARA.

70. Circular no. 97, "Immigration and Visa Discussions at the Consular Conference, Mexico City, October 9–15, 1937," 3, U.S. Consulate, Guadalajara, Box 9, file no. 811.11, RG 84, NARA.

71. Correspondence between consul and Frank Valadez, 1936, U.S. Consulate, Guadalajara, Box 3, file no. 310, RG 84, NARA.

72. See for example the work of Cleofas Calleros, Director of Immigration Services for the National Catholic Welfare Conference in El Paso. Case files for thousands of border-crossers held in the Cleofas Calleros Papers at the Sonnichsen Special Collections library at the University of El Paso reveal a para-state bureaucracy operating in the borderlands throughout the first half of the twentieth century.

CHAPTER FIVE: WAR AND A NEW MIGRATION ORDER

1. Letter from Margarita Ramirez de Alvarado to the Secretaría de Gobernación, n.d.; Letter from Director Gonzalo Aguirre Beltrán to Margarita Ramirez de Alvarado, August 7, 1944, INAMI 4–357–0–1944–6241.

2. Various scholarly assessments of the program offer insight into the benefits and negative consequences at the individual, family, and state level, as well as whether it stands as a viable model for temporary labor programs. Most recently, works have incorporated bracero testimonies to find out whether the bracero program was good or bad for braceros. The ultimate conclusion seems to be that it was both. The program and the lived experiences of braceros were not homogenous, but dictated by regional politics, social standing, labor status, position in the family, and responsibilities to community. Works based on oral testimonies complicate arguments that characterize the binational program primarily as exploitative and victimizing. See Ernesto Galarza, *Strangers in Our Fields* (Washington, DC: United States

Section, Joint United States-Mexico Trade Union Committee, 1956); Gilbert Gonzalez, *Guest Workers or Colonized Labor? Mexican Labor Migration to the United States* (London: Routledge, 2006); D. Cohen, *Braceros*; Snodgrass, "The Bracero Program"; Ana Elizabeth Rosas, "Flexible Families: Bracero Families' Lives Across Cultures, Communities, and Countries, 1942–1964" (PhD diss., University of Southern California, 2006).

3. See, in particular, Rosas, *Abrazando El Espíritu.*

4. The concept of the Revolutionary Family carried multiple meanings. In a political sense, the Revolutionary Family was a concept that sought to present a united front of power at the center. It was a way of distancing post-revolutionary powerholders from the factional infighting that took place during the 1920s, and a concept that would legitimize the PNR through the 1930s. Scholars who incorporate gender into their historical analysis of the period see the Revolutionary Family more literally and, following Mary Kay Vaughan's concept of modernizing patriarchy, suggest that the roles of the Revolutionary Family and revolutionary family members were defined by the state and prescribed gendered forms of contributing to the nation. I incorporate it here to reinforce the shift away from using the rhetoric of revolution to the rhetoric of unity—a rhetorical shift from left to moderate but also one from national to international. For Revolutionary Family as political, see Thomas Benjamin, "Rebuilding the Nation," in *The Oxford History of Mexico,* ed. Michael C. Meyer and William H. Beezley (New York: Oxford University Press, 2000), 467; Thomas Benjamin, *La Revolución: Mexico's Great Revolution as Memory, Myth, and History* (Austin: University of Texas Press, 2000), 68; see also newspaper editorials in *El Informador,* March 1929. For the Revolutionary Family as prescriptive family norm see Ann S. Blum, *Domestic Economies: Family, Work, and Welfare in Mexico City, 1884–1943* (Lincoln: University of Nebraska Press, 2009), and Ann S. Blum, "Breaking and Making Families: Adoption and Public Welfare, Mexico City, 1938–1942" in *Sex in Revolution: Gender, Politics, and Power in Modern Mexico,* ed. Jocelyn Olcott (Durham, NC: Duke University Press, 2006). See also Vaughan, "Modernizing Patriarchy"; D. Cohen, *Braceros,* 33.

5. Blanca Torres Ramírez, *Mexico en La Segunda Guerra Mundial* (Mexico: El Colegio De Mexico), 1979.

6. Luis Medina, *Del Cardenismo al avilacamachismo* (Mexico DF: El Colegio de México, 1978), 231–43; Blanca Torres Ramírez, *Hacia la utopía industrial* (Mexico DF: El Colegio de México, 1979), 57–60.

7. Torres Ramírez, *Hacia la utopia industrial,* 52.

8. Gauss, *Made in Mexico,* 108.

9. For more on the nationalization and expropriation of Mexican petroleum during the Cárdenas era and the delicate negotiations with the Roosevelt administration, see Adolfo Gilly, *El Cardenismo: una utopía Mexicana* (Mexico, DF: Mexico: Ediciones Era, 2001).

10. Don Mitchell, *They Saved the Crops: Labor, Landscape, and the Struggle Over Industrial Farming in Bracero-Era California* (Athens: University of Georgia Press, 2012), 22; Ngai, *Impossible Subjects,* 137.

11. "Braceros Mexicanos," letter to the Department of Migration from Manuel Yanez, March 4, 1942, INAMI 4–357–1–1936–81.

12. "Piden Cien Mil Mexicanos Para Que Trabajan en E.U.," *El Informador,* April 13, 1942.

13. "No los dejarán ir a los E.U.," *El Informador,* April 23, 1942.

14. "Braceros Mexicanos," letter to Miguel Aleman, Secretaria de Gobernación, from Confederaciones Camaras Nacionales de Comercio e Industria, June 1942, INAMI 4–357–1–1936–81.

15. "Que no Vayan a los EE. UU," *El Informador,* April 17, 1942.

16. "No hay demanda de Mexicanos en los EE.UU," *El Informador*, July 14, 1942.

17. "Braceros Mexicanos," letter to the Department of Migration from Manuel Yanez, March 4, 1942; letter to Manuel Yanez from associate director Carlos A. Gomez, March 10, 1942, INAMI 4–357–1–1936–81.

18. Letter to president Avila Camacho from Jose de Jesus Cervantes, n.d., INAMI 4–357–1936–81.

19. *Los Angeles Times,* September 23, 1942; Robert C. Jones, "Los Braceros Mexicanos en Estados Unidos," in Jorge Durand, ed., *Las Miradas Mexicana y Estadounidense: Antología (1945–1964)* (México: Miguel Ángel Porrúa, 2007), 91. Fall of 1942 would mark the formal initiation of the agricultural bracero program. The much-less-studied railroad bracero program began in 1943 and only lasted for the duration of the war (with last contracts expiring in 1946). The railroad bracero program was much smaller in terms of number of contracts given out in comparison to those given to agricultural workers even within the same time period. Contract centers were in San Luis Potosí, Queretaro, and Mexico City. The requirements for participation in the program were very much the same, with the exception of railroad workers going through an additional screening to assess their level of skill. See Barbara A. Driscoll, *Tracks North: The Railroad Bracero Program of World War II* (Austin: University of Texas Press, 1999). Also see Torres, *Hacia la Utopía Industrial,* 237.

20. Luis Fernández del Campo, director of Secretaría del Trabajo y Previsión Social, "Los Braceros," 1946, in Durand, *Braceros,* 165, 166.

21. del Campo, "Los Braceros," in Durand, *Braceros,* 167–68.

22. Durand, *Braceros.*

23. Durand, *Braceros,* 239–42.

24. See Ngai, *Impossible Subjects,* 6, for more on the idea of "illegal alienage" being a product of positive law.

25. "Braceros Mexicanos," letter from Alfonso Garcia to Ochoa brothers, August 18, 1942, INAMI 4–357–1–1936–81.

26. Snodgrass, "The Bracero Program," 90. For a description of the selection process see D. Cohen, *Braceros,* 91–93.

27. As discussed in previous chapters, land reform and the distribution of *ejidos* had been cited by contemporaries as a force that drove migrants out in the 1920s and enticed migrants back to Mexico in the 1930s. The exclusion of *ejidatarios* from bracero contracts reflects the broader and more pronounced government expecta-

tions that those who had received *ejidos* in the Cárdenas period were dutifully bound to work them to the exclusion of taking on other forms of wage-labor.

28. AHJ G-8–1946, Box 11, file no. 240/6 2088.

29. It is worth noting regarding the statement above from the municipal president that shoemakers were "not recognized as official shoemakers" that union politics were often at play in communities where employment was contingent on becoming a union member.

30. Letter to the Secretaria de Gobernación's Office of Migration from Benito Garza, Chief of Piedras Negras Office of Population in Coahuila, August 1942, INAMI 4–357–1–1932–38.

31. Telegram to the Secretaria de Gobernación from Benito Garza Villareal, Director General of Population at Piedras Negras, Coahuila, September 19, 1942, INAMI 4–357–1–1932–28.

32. "Braceros Mexicanos," INAMI 4–357–1–1936–81.

33. Although it is quite possible that women might have tried to pass for men to get bracero contracts, I have found no evidence that this happened. Other requirements for braceros might be circumvented by potentially using false documents to lie about age or occupation, and it's very likely that officials might have looked in the other direction altogether with regards to some of the requirements. However, the medical inspection, which often required aspiring braceros to take off all of their clothes, would have likely prevented any women from making the attempt.

34. At a certain point in negotiations leading up to the final and formalized agreement, the inclusion of women and children must have been debated, as illustrated by a study carried out by the Ministry of Labor in 1946 titled *Los Braceros*, reprinted in Durand, *Braceros,* 162. See González Navarro, *Los Extranjeros en México*, vol. 3. Deborah Cohen suggests that women and children were not included in contracts because their inclusion was feared to lead to the permanent settlement of braceros (*Braceros,* 22).

35. Letter to the President from Carmen G. de Terches, M. Rodriguez Neri, and others, AGN-RP-MAC 546.6/120–1, box 793. For various discussions on the tension around women's proper role in labor see Jocelyn Olcott, Mary Kay Vaughan, and Gabriela Cano, eds., *Sex in Revolution: Gender, Politics, and Power in Modern Mexico* (Durham, NC: Duke University Press, 2007.

36. Letter from Director Luis Fernandez del Campo to Elvira Moreno, March 9, 1944, AGN-RP-MAC 546.6/120–1, box 793/

37. Vicki Ruiz, *Cannery Women, Cannery Lives: Mexican Women, Unionization, and the California Food Processing Industry, 1930–1950* (Albuquerque: University of New Mexico Press, 1987), 23–26, 80.

38. Maria Heriberta Torres, for example, wrote to President Aleman after the war ended in 1948 and asked for authorization to offer her services as a fruit packer; see AGN-RP-MAV 546.6/1–8, box 0593.

39. Letter from Maria de la Paz Angel, AGN-RP-MAC 546.6/120–8, box 793.

40. Letter from Juana Flores de Chavoya, August 1, 1944, AGN-RP-MAC 546.6/120–3, box 793.

41. Letter to Maria de la Paz Rios Rodríguez from Arcadio Ojeda Garcia, Chief of the Department of Migration, January 21, 1948, AGN-RP-MAV 546.6/1–7, box 594.

42. Telegram to the President from J. Jesus Guerrero etc., Zapata, Michoacán, March 30 1943, AGN-RP-MAC 546.6/120, box 793.

43. As will be demonstrated later in the chapter, aspiring braceros were versed in the war rhetoric of the times and relied on their previous military and militia experience to conjure up the image of the soldier continuing his duty for his country. Based on oral history interviews, historian Michael Snodgrass also finds that veteran braceros continued to see themselves as "soldiers of peace" ("The Bracero Program," 79).

44. Correograma from Mariano Gonzalez to President, September 23, 1942, AGN-RP-MAC 546.6/120–1, box 793.

45. Telegram from Alfredo Rodriguez Romo to President, August 22, 1942; telegram from Luis Mendoza to President, August 24, 1942. Both in AGN-RP-MAC 546.6/120–1, box 793.

46. Correograma from Mariano Gonzalez to President, September 23, 1942, AGN-RP-MAC 546.6/120–1, box 793.

47. Letter from Aurelio Hernandez to Octavio Diaz de Leon, secretary to the president, February 11, 1943, Villa Acuña, AGN-RP-MAC 546.6/120–9, box 795.

48. Luis Fernández del Campo, director de Previsión Social de la Secretaría de Trabajo, 1946, "Los Braceros," in Durand, Braceros, 189. 1.60 percent wanted to go under the category "educarse," but the study authors suggest that those offering this as a motivation were exceptional cases who had actually mentioned one of the other three motivations as well.

49. Abstract of letter from Castula Guerrero to President Ávila Camacho, AGN-RP-MAC 546.6/120–1, box 0793.

50. This was due to an insufficient supply and over-demand of contracts; some were sold and resold in corruptive schemes, and some states were blocked entirely by quotas.

51. For an example of "more veiled" see Jose Santana S. and others, Mexicali, May 13, 1943; Luis Sanchez, Ciudad Juárez, July 23, 1943; both in AGN-RP-MAC 546.6/120, box 793. The letter from Puebla is from Francisco Pérez etc. to the President, March 14, 1944, Moyotzingo, Puebla, AGN-RP-MAC 546.6/120, box 793.

52. Letter to the President from Sabino Pantoja, President of the Municipal Union of the Veterans for the Revolution, Nueva Rosita, Coahuila, August 7, 1943, AGN-RP-MAC 546.6/120, box 793.

53. Letter to Ávila-Camacho from Aurelio Ureña Segura, January 2, 1945, AGN-RP-MAC 546.6/120–5.

54. Telegram from Salvador Tiscareño to President, March 22, 1945, AGN-RP-MAC 546.6/120–5.

55. Abstract of letter to the President from Antonia Mora Miraflores, March 13, 1945, AGN-RP-MAC 546.6/120–5.

56. Letter writers from Guanajuato emphasized ruinous plant diseases and drought; those from Michoacán emphasized volcanic ash; those from Querétaro,

Jalisco and Zacatecas also mentioned drought as the reason for poor harvests. See AGN-RP-MAC 120.

57. AHJ G-8–1946, Box 11, file no.240/6.

58. AHJ G-8–1946, Box 11, file no.240/6.

59. For a discussion about the parcelization of land, family sustenance, and its connection to emigration see Luis González y González, *San Jose de Gracia: Mexican Village in Transition* (Austin: University of Texas Press, 1972), 205–6.

60. Abstract of letter from Jesus Cervantes to President, AGN-RP-MAC 546.6/120–10.

61. Letter from Natividad Amaro to President, December 6, 1944, AGN-RP-MAC 546.6/120–10.

62. Angus Wright, *The Death of Ramón González: The Modern Agricultural Dilemma* (Austin: University of Texas Press, 2005), 171–88.

63. Massey et al., *Return to Aztlan*, 89–91.

64. Abstract of letter from Maria Concepción Armenta de Aguilera, May 15, 1946, AGN-RP-MAC 546.6/120–8, box 793.

65. Letter from Maria de de Jesus Vda. de la Cruz to Ávila-Camacho, AGN-RP-MAC 546.6/120–5 box 793; letter from Maria Anguiano Vda. de Hernandez to Ávila-Camacho, AGN-RP-MAC 546.6/120–8, box 793.

66. Abstract of Letter from Aurelia Martinez, Concepción Garcia, and Maria Morales to Ávila-Camacho, May 5, 1945, AGN-RP-MAC 546.6/120–5, box 793.

67. For example, Massey et al. found that the bracero program especially gave *ejidatarios* a source of investment capital and independence from moneylenders who had come to dominate economic life in Chamitlán, Michoacán, after 1930s agrarian reform. A similar scenario occurred in Altamira, Jalisco, where bracero earnings facilitated farming that *ejidatarios* had previously been too poor to initiate (*Return to Aztlan,* 55, 72–76).

68. Letter to President Aleman from Francisco Estudillo, representing five hundred workers, AGN-RP-MAV 546.6/1–8.

69. Letter from Juan Rico Avalos to Governor Marcelino Garcia Barragan, AHJ G-8–1946, Box 12, file no. 240/6 849.

70. Ana Elizabeth Rosas, "Breaking the Silence: Mexican Children and Women's Confrontation of Bracero Family Separation, 1942–64," *Gender & History* 22, no. 2 (2011).

71. Letter to State Government from Lucia Navarro de Perez, Hospicio Cabañas August 14, 1946 Re: Maria Marrón, AHJ 205 (28)/10; Letter to State Government from Lucia Navarro de Perez, Hospicio Cabañas, October 1, 1946 Re: Mercedes Alvarez, AHJ G-8–1946, Box 8, file no. 205(16)/1.

72. Letter to consul general of Mexico, Los Angeles, California, from Secretary of Protection, Ministry of Foreign Relations, AGN-RP-MAC 546.6/120–3.

73. Letter to President Manuel Alemán Valdez from María Refugio Guzmán de Sandoval, July 29, 1947, AGN-RP-MAC 546.6/1–31, box 593.

74. Letter to Ávila Camacho from Ramona Avalos, Bertha Marquez and others, August 7, 1945, AGN-RP-MAC 546.6/120–8, box 795.

75. Abstract of Letter to Ávila Camacho from Maria Carmen de Garcia, January, 25, 1946, AGN-RP-MAC 546.6/120–31, box 795; abstract of Letter to Ávila Camacho from Juana Navarrete de Negrete, March 12, 1945, AGN-RP-MAC 546.6/120–8, box 795; abstract of Letter to Ávila Camacho from Maria de Jesus Ruiz de Sandoval, June 26, 1945, AGN-RP-MAC 546.6/120–12, box 794.

76. Telegram to President from Angela Hernandez Vda. de Gonzalez, April 26, 1945, AGN-RP-MAC 120–23, box 795.

77. Letter to the President from Abel Martinez Luba, Acámbaro Guanajuato, May 5, 1943, AGN-RP-MAC 546.6/120, folder 1, box 794.

78. A temporary labor program had operated during World War I but was regional in scope and not sanctioned by either federal government.

CHAPTER SIX: THE ERA OF POLICING

1. Clipping from the *Laredo Times*, June 5, 1953, #1554–3, SRE.

2. Lytle Hernández, *Migra!*, 134.

3. Gardner, *Qualities of a Citizen*, 210–11.

4. Massey et al., *Return to Aztlán*.

5. Lytle Hernández, *Migra!*, 135.

6. Rosas, *Abrazando el Espíritu*; Loza, *Defiant Braceros*; Nicole M. Guidotti-Hernández, *Archiving Mexican Masculinities in Diaspora* (Durham, NC: Duke University Press, 2021).

7. D. Cohen, *Braceros*, 184–87.

8. Letter to Ruiz Cortines from Grupo San Luis, Union of Residents from the State of Baja California, November 6, 1956, ARC 548.1/124, no. 26515, cited in D. Cohen, *Braceros*, 83.

9. See Gutiérrez, *Walls and Mirrors*.

10. Louise E. Walker, *Waking from the Dream: Mexico's Middle Classes after 1968* (Stanford, CA: Stanford University Press, 2013).

11. Massey et al., *Return to Aztlán*, 43.

12. Wright, *The Death of Ramón González*, 171–87.

13. María Rodríguez Batista, "El reparto agrario en Jalisco: dos administraciones poscardenistas, 1940–1952," in *Desarrollo rural en Jalisco: Contradicciones y perspectivas*, ed. Sergio Alcántara Ferrer and Enrique Sánchez Ruiz (Guadalajara: Colegio de Jalisco, 1985), 49.

14. Julio Moguel, *Historia de la Cuestión Agraria Mexicana: La época de oro y el principio de la crisis de la agricultura Mexicana: 1950–1970* (Mexico DF: Siglo xxi editors, 1988).

15. Victor Manuel Castillo Girón, *Sólo Dios y El Norte: Migración a Estados Unidos y desarrollo en una region de Jalisco* (Guadalajara: Universidad de Guadalajara, 1995), 88–93.

16. Irapuato was still over 300 kilometers away, but what mattered was the personal connection that could facilitate the entry into the program.

17. Castillo Girón, *Solo Dios y El Norte,* 99.

18. This region is referenced to as Altamira in Massey, et al., *Return to Aztlán,* but scholars gave studied communities fictional names in order to protect any undocumented immigrants that had left from the region throughout the rest of the twentieth century.

19. Massey, et al., *Return to Aztlán*, 55.

20. Massey, et. al., *Return to Aztlán,* 59. For an example of the migration of women from Irapuato, Guanajuato to Mexico City, see Patricia Arias, "La Migración Femenina en Dos Modelos de desarrollo: 1940–1970," in *Relaciones de género y transformaciones agrarias: estudios sobre el campo mexicano,* ed. Soledad González Montes y Vania Salles (Mexico City, MX: El Colegio de Mexico, 1995).

21. Massey, et al., *Return to Aztlán*, 91–92.

22. Massey, et al., *Return to Aztlán,* 61.

23. Massey, et al., *Return to Aztlán,* 57–58.

24. See D. Cohen, *Braceros,* for an in-depth examination of braceros and aspiring braceros from Durango.

25. AGN-RP-MAV 546.6/1–23; AGN-RP-MAV 546.6/1–7, box 593; AGN-RP-MAV 546.6/1–15; AGN-RP-MAV 546.6/1–27.

26. AGN-RP-MAV 546.6/1–8.

27. Rodríguez Batista, "El reparto agrario en Jalisco," 55. See also Tanalis Padilla, *Rural Resistance in the Land of Zapata: The Jaramillista Movement and the Myth of the Pax-Priísta, 1940–1962* (Durham, NC: Duke University Press, 2008) and Elisa Servín, "Reclaiming Revolution in Light of the 'Mexican Miracle': Celestino Gasca and the Federacionistas Leales Insurrection of 1961," *The Americas* 66, no. 4 (April 2010): 527–57.

28. Letter to Manuel Ávila Camacho from Santiago Fontaner and Tranquilo Hernández, MAC 546.6/120–21.

29. See Durand, *Braceros,* chapter 3, for examples of corruptive schemes early on in the program.

30. The Annual Report of the Immigration and Naturalization Services for fiscal years 1943–1944 and 1945–1946 shows an increase in commuters, from 77,094 to 114,986; an increase in immigrants admitted, from 6,399 to 6,805; and in nonimmigrant entries, from 2,440 to 5,628.

31. One sample study of a sending region, Jalisco, found that 73 of 102 braceros had made more than one trip to the United States and that the average number of trips back to the United States was 4.2. See Douglas S. Massey and Zai Liang, "The Long-Term Consequences of a Temporary Worker Program: The US Bracero Experience," *Population Research and Policy Review* 8, no. 3 (September 1989): 209.

32. See, for example, the cases of Irma Ligia Almuina and Maria Lopez-Gonzalez, MS 231, Box 12, Folder 5, CCP.

33. Letter to Srita. Ma. De la Paz Rios Rodriguez from Arcadio Ojeda Garcia, Department of Migrations, January 21, 1948, AGN-RP-MAV 546.6/1–7.

34. "Y Ahora, las Braceras," *El Informador,* November 15, 1953. Original text: "No contentos nuestros Buenos vecinos con llevarse a nuestros braceros. Cuyos

Buenos servicios aprovechan hasta para casarlos con una guera de ojos azules y cabellos de jilote, si se dejan, ahora quieren llevarse a nuestras braceras."

35. Sandra Messinger Cypess, "'Mother' Malinche And Allegories Of Gender, Ethnicity And National Identity In Mexico," in *Feminism, Nation And Myth: La Malinche,* ed. Rolando Romero and Amanda Nolacea Harris (Houston, TX: Arte Publico Press, 2005), 19–27.

36. See Ruiz, "By the Day or the Week," 65–67.

37. "Mexican Domestics Problem in El Paso," *New York Times,* August 30, 1953.

38. "También Pasan Ilegalmente," *El Informador,* September 20, 1953.

39. *Los Angeles Times,* February 7, 1954.

40. Castillo-Muñoz, *The Other California,* 102–5.

41. Martínez, *Ciudad Juárez,* 111.

42. Interview with Federico Navarro Duran by Mireya Loza, 2006, "Interview no. 1303," Institute of Oral History, University of Texas at El Paso.

43. Original text: "Mi padre no pudo estar mas sin su familia y nos mando a traer a mi madre y a mi, desconozco los medios en como lo hizo verdad. Mi madre y yo venimos a vivir en el rancho con mi padre. El dueño del rancho era muy justo y agradecido por lo que hacia para el en el rancho y le ofrecio un cuartito en el cual vivimos los tres con apenas lo necesario para vivir, pero vivamos felices porque estabamos todos juntos." Interview with Margarita Flores by Mireya Loza, 2008, "Interview no. 1100," Institute of Oral History, University of Texas at El Paso.

44. General Records of the Department of Labor, Office of the Secretary, Subject files of Secretary James P. Mitchell, RG 174, NARA.

45. José Lázaro Salinas, "La emigración de braceros. Visión objetiva de un problema mexicano," 1955, in Durand, *Braceros,* 300.

46. Martínez, *Ciudad Juárez,* 112.

47. Lázaro Salinas, "La emigración de braceros," in Durand, *Braceros,* 300–2.

48. Gloria R. Vargas y Campos, "El Problema del Bracero Mexicano," in Durand, *Braceros,* 423.

49. See for example the testimony given in an interview with Jesus Rivera L. by Perla Guerrero, 2006, "Interview no. 1178," Institute of Oral History, University of Texas at El Paso.

50. See Lytle Hernández, *Migra!,* for a description of cooperation in what she terms as the "corridors of cross-border migration control." Collaborative efforts began as early as 1945 (126–27).

51. MAC 546.6/120–1.

52. Kelly Lytle Hernández, *City of Inmates: Conquest, Rebellion, and the Rise of Human Caging, 1771–1965* (Chapel Hill: University of North Carolina Press, 2017).

53. Books 35–38, Immigration U.S. Prisoners in El Paso County Records MS 132, Sonnichsen Special Collection, University of Texas at El Paso, El Paso Texas.

54. Annual Report of the Immigration and Naturalization Services, U.S. Department of State, Philadelphia, Pennsylvania for Fiscal Year Ended June 30, 1946, 9.

55. INS, *Annual Report 1946,* 28.

56. Ngai, *Impossible Subjects,* 148.

57. MS 173, National Catholic Welfare Conference, Case files 1905–1958, Box 33, UTEP-Special Collections. The INS Annual Report of 1943 reads, "The act of June 1942 provides that the Attorney General may suspend the deportation of an alien who is deportable on grounds other than criminal, immoral, or subversive, or because of physical or mental defects, and who has been proven to be of good moral character, if he finds that such deportation would result in serious economic detriment to a citizen or legally resident alien who is the spouse, parent, or minor child of the deportable alien."

58. See Lytle Hernandez, *Migra!*, 136–37; Martínez, *Ciudad Juárez*, 112; Ngai, *Impossible Subjects*, 153.

59. Ngai, *Impossible Subjects*, 153.

60. Mitchell, *They Saved the Crops*, 138.

61. *INS Annual Report*, 1949.

62. *INS Annual Report*, 1950, 2.

63. *INS Annual Report*, 1950, 2.

64. MAV 546.6/1–25.

65. Paul Gillingham and Benjamin T. Smith, *Dictablanda: Politics, Work, and Culture in Mexico, 1938–1968* (Durham, NC: Duke University Press, 2014), 12.

66. This and other correspondence cited in the next several paragraphs can be found in File 1454/2, Papers of Rafael Colina Riquelme, Mexican Ambassador to the United States, SRE.

67. The commission urged that before resorting to foreign labor in the future, workers might be brought in from Puerto Rico and Hawaii. See *The Recommendations of the President's Commission on Migratory Labor,* by Maurice J. Tobin, Secretary, U.S. Department of Labor, and William L. Connolly, Director, Bureau of Labor Standards, April 1952, https://oac.cdlib.org/ark:/28722/bk0003z5t83/?brand = oac4, accessed July 2019.

68. *The Recommendations of the President's Commission on Migratory Labor*; Robert S. Robinson, "Taking the Fair Deal to the Fields: Truman's Commission on Migratory Labor, Public Law 78, and the Bracero Program, 1950–1952," *Agricultural History* 84, no. 3 (2010): 381–402.

69. Mitchell, *They Saved the Crops*, 193–97.

70. This of course, is not to say that this was the first time that government officials showed this interest historically, and in fact debates over the program echoed earlier debates over proposed immigration restriction in the 1920s.

71. Kang, *The INS on the Line*, 139.

72. Lytle Hernández, *Migra!*, 189–90.

73. Kang, *The INS on the Line*, 158.

74. "Bracero-Wetback Problem Is Serious," *Los Angeles Times*, January 28, 1954.

75. Lytle Hernández, *Migra!*, 186.

76. Lytle Hernández, *Migra!*, 192.

77. "500 Nabbed by LA Wetback Raiders," *Los Angeles Times*, June 18, 1954.

78. "1259 More Wetbacks Reported in a Single Day," *Los Angeles Times*, June 19, 1954.

79. "Wetbacks Herded at Nogales Camp," *The Los Angeles Times,* June 20, 1954.

80. "10 Bus Loads of Mexicans Leave L.A.," *The Los Angeles Times,* June 21, 1954.

81. "Family Groups Gone Back Voluntarily," *The Los Angeles Times,* July 18, 1954. The article also remarked on the requests for five thousand braceros that had been made to the Hidalgo contracting center. So, while eight thousand men were reportedly picked up in forty-eight hours, many would in fact turn around to become legalized braceros, thereby giving South Texas employers a backdoor option to prevent losing their laborers. This process would not work in exactly the same way for the many migrants, especially around the Los Angeles, who were not agricultural workers and were working in different industries at the time of their apprehension.

82. Lytle Hernández, *Migra!,* 136.

83. "Report experts compiled from Patrol Inspectors in the McAllen sectors," from inspector WF Kelly to the District Director of San Antonio, June 1, 1953. Entry 9, File 56364/43SWpt3, RG 85, NARA I.

84. "Familias Enteras Están Siendo Deportados de E.U.," *El Informador,* August 6, 1954.

85. Lytle Hernández, *Migra!,* 135.

86. Letter to District Director of Immigration Service at El Paso Texas from Office of Inspector at Nogales Arizona, November 30, 1929, file 55610/160, RG 85, NARA.

87. In the first decades of the twentieth century, a suspicion of loose morals or prostitution might also have meant detention for women, even if they had not been convicted.

88. "Report on" from inspector WF Kelly to the District Director of San Antonio, June 1, 1953. Entry 9, File 56364/43SWpt3, RG 85, NARA I.

89. Lytle Hernandez, *Migra!,* 189–90.

90. See United States Congress, House Committee on Agriculture, *Mexican Farm Labor Program: Hearings before the Subcommittee on Equipment, Supplies, and Manpower on H. R. 3822* (Washington, DC: Government Printing Office, 1955), testimony of Matt Triggs, Assistant Legislative Director, American Farm Bureau Federation, 56- 57.

91. See United States Congress, *Mexican Farm Labor Program: Hearings,* testimony of Earl M. Hughes, administrator, commodity stabilization service, United States Department of Agriculture, 53.

92. United States Congress, *Mexican Farm Labor Program: Hearings,* testimony of W. P. Thorpe, Director, New Mexico Farm and Livestock Bureau, Relative to H.R. 3822, 86.

93. United States Congress, *Mexican Farm Labor Program: Hearings,* testimony of Matt Triggs, Assistant Legislative Director, American Farm Bureau Federation, 60.

94. United States Congress, *Mexican Farm Labor Program: Hearings,* testimony of Matt Triggs, Assistant Legislative Director, American Farm Bureau Federation, 60.

95. United States Congress, *Mexican Farm Labor Program: Hearings,* testimony of Matt Triggs, Assistant Legislative Director, American Farm Bureau Federation, 60–62.

96. United States Congress, *Mexican Farm Labor Program: Hearings*, testimony of Andrew C. McLellan, 168.

97. United States Congress, *Mexican Farm Labor Program: Hearings*, testimony of Ernesto Galarza, 180.

98. United States Congress, *Mexican Farm Labor Program: Hearings*.

99. United States Congress, *Mexican Farm Labor Program: Hearings*, 11–12.

EPILOGUE: FIT TO BE MIGRANTS

1. "Wandering Messenger Brings Note of Warmth, Patriotism to Braceros," *The Sacramento Bee,* Sunday July 23, 1961, clipping in D234, 12:3, RRC.

2. Jacqueline Stanton, "Men reminded of homeland," *Appeal Democrat,* Marysville/Yuba City, CA, July 24, 1961, clipping in D234, 12:3, RRC.

3. For a detailed example of how this took place in the Valle de Santiago, Guanajuato, see Juan Vicente Palerm and José Ignacio Urquiola, "A Binational System of Agricultural Production: The Case of the Mexican Bajío and California," in *Mexico and the United States, Neighbors in Crisis: Proceedings from the Conference, Neighbors Crisis, a Call for Joint Solutions, February 1989,* ed. Daniel G. Aldrich and Lorenzo Meyer (San Bernardino, CA: Borgo Press, 1993).

4. "The Mexican Bracero: Will He Ever Come Back to Texas?," *The Odessa American,* September 5, 1965; "Mechanization & Other Labor-Saving Trends," *California Annual Farm Labor Report 1962* (California: State Department of Employment, 1963); both in D-234 12:3, RRC.

5. John Weber, *From South Texas to the Nation: The Exploitation of Mexican Labor in the Twentieth Century* (Chapel Hill: University of North Carolina Press, 2015), 214; "The Mexican Bracero: Will He Ever Come Back to Texas?"

6. "Mechanization & Other Labor-Saving Trends"; "Minors, Women Can be Paid on Piecework Basis," *The Sacramento Bee,* June 24, 1962.

7. Palerm and Urquiola, "A Binational System of Agricultural Production."

8. Cárdenas Sánchez, *El largo curso de la economía mexicana,* 575–93.

9. Louise Walker suggests that rather than analyzing the degree of relative political stability in the period known as the Pax Porfirista, it is more important to realize the degree to which PRI politicians and others believed in a narrative of economic prosperity and mid-century stability. "It may be true that this dream never existed in reality, but stability is often a state of mind, and in the early 1970s a perceived stability began to unravel" (*Waking from the Dream*, 9).

10. Lourdes Arizpe, "Introduccion," in *Población y Trabajo en contextos regionales,* ed. Gail Mummert (Zamora, Michoacán: El Colegio de Michoacán, 1990), 11.

11. Rodolfo Cruz Pineiro, "Mercados de Trabajo y migración en la frontera norte: Tijuana, Ciudad Juárez y Nuevo Laredo," *Frontera Norte* 2, núm. 4 (Jul-Dic 1990): 67.

12. Norma Iglesias Prieto, *Beautiful Flowers of the Maquiladora* (Austin: University of Texas Press, 1997).

13. Ngai, *Impossible Subjects,* 257–58.

14. Ngai, *Impossible Subjects,* 261.

15. Douglas S. Massey and Karen A. Pren, "Unintended Consequences of U.S. Immigration Policy: Explaining the Post-1965 Surge from Latin America," *Population and Development Review* 38, no. 1 (March 2012): 4.

16. Ngai, *Impossible Subjects,* 261.

17. For a discussion on naturalization trends, especially after Immigration Reform and Control Act of 1986, see Massey and Pren, "Unintended Consequences."

18. Massey and Pren, "Unintended Consequences," 1.

19. Massey and Pren, "Unintended Consequences," 13.

20. See Lourdes Arizpe, *Migración, Etnismo y Cambio Economico: Un Estudio Sobre Migrantes campesinos a la ciudad de México* (Mexico City: El Colegio de Mexico, 1978). Also showcasing the importance of social networks in rural to urban migration (in this case, Mexico City), see Larisa Adler Lomnitz, *Networks and Marginality: Life in a Mexican Shantytown* (New York: Academic Press, 1977). For an early study examining Mexican migrant women's acculturation to the United States, see Margarita B. Melville, "Mexican Women Adapt to Migration," *The International Migration Review* 12, no. 2 (1978): 225–35.

21. Lourdes Arizpe, "The Rural Exodus in Mexico and the Mexican Migration to the United States," *The International Migration Review* 15, no. 4 (1981): 641.

22. Rafael Alarcón, "El Proceso de 'Norteñizacion': Impacto de la migración internacional en Chavinda, Michoacán," in *Movimientos de población en el occidente de México* (Zamora: El Colegio de Michoacán, 1988), 337–58 .

23. David S. North, Marion F. Houstoun, and United States Employment and Training Administration, *The Characteristics and Role of Illegal Aliens in the U.S. Labor Market: An Exploratory Study* (Washington, DC: New TransCentury Foundation/Linton, 1976), 69–73.

24. Melville, "Mexican Women Adapt," 229.

25. Oaxacan migrants had first migrated as a result of agricultural expansion in Mexico's northern states, namely Sinaloa, Sonora, and Baja California in the 1950s. By the end of the 1970s seasonal migrations from Oaxaca to Northern Mexico extended into California, Oregon, and Washington. For more on indigenous migrants see Jonathan Fox, "Indigenous Mexican Migrants," in *Beyond La Frontera: The History of Mexico-U.S. Migration,* ed. Mark Overmyer-Velázquez (New York: Oxford University Press, 2011). For more on Mixtec migrant women to Tijuana, see Laura Velasco Ortiz, "Women, Migration, and Household Survival Strategies: Mixtec Women in Tijuana," in *Women and Migration in the U.S.-Mexico Borderlands: A Reader,* ed. Denise A. Segura and Patricia Zavella (Durham, NC: Duke University Press, 2007). See also Stephen, *Transborder Lives.*

26. Cárdenas Sánchez, *El Largo Curso,* chapter 11.

27. Oscar Martínez, "Migration and the Border, 1965–1985," in *Beyond La Frontera: The History of Mexico-U.S. Migration,* ed. Mark Overmyer-Velázquez (New York: Oxford University Press), 112–13.

28. Douglas S. Massey, Jorge Durand, and Nolan J. Malone, *Beyond Smoke and Mirrors: Mexican Immigration in an Era of Economic Integration* (New York, NY: Russel Sage Foundation), 134. Melville suggests that women made up to 50 percent of undocumented migration ("Mexican Women Adapt to Migration"). See also Katherine Donato, "Current Trends and Patterns of Female Migration: Evidence from Mexico," *The International Migration Review* 27, no. 4 (Winter, 1993): 748–71.

29. Lourdes Baezconde-Garbanati and V. Nelly Salgado de Snyder, "Mexican Immigrant Women: A Selected Bibliography," *Hispanic Journal of Behavioral Sciences* 8, no. 3 (1987): 331–58.

BIBLIOGRAPHY

ARCHIVES

AGN Archivo General de la Nación, Mexico City
INAMI Archivo Histórico del Instituto Nacional de Migración, Mexico City
SRE Archivo Histórico del Secretaría de Relaciones Exteriores, Mexico City
AHJ Archivo Histórico del Estado de Jalisco, Guadalajara
CCP Cleofas Calleros Papers at C.L. Sonnichsen, Special Collections Department of the University of Texas at El Paso Library
PSTP Paul Schuster Taylor Papers, BANC MSS 84/38 c, The Bancroft Library, University of California–Berkeley.
RG 84 Records of Foreign Service Posts of the Department of State
RRC Raymond Roth Collection, Special Collections Department, University of California–Davis Library.
NARA National Archives Records Administration, Washington, DC, and College Park, MD.

NEWSPAPERS

El Informador (Guadalajara, Mexico)
El Paso Herald Post
The Los Angeles Times
New York Times
The Sacramento Bee

PRINTED SOURCES

Aldana Rendón, Mario. *Jalisco Desde La Revolucíon: Del reyismo al nuevo orden constitucional, 1910–1917*. Guadalajara: Universidad de Guadalajara, 1987.

Alonso, Ana Maria. "Rationalizing Patriarchy: Gender, Domestic Violence,and Law in Mexico." *Identities* 2, no. 1–2 (1995): 29–47.

Alvarado, Rudolph Valier, and Sonya Yvette Slate Alvarado. *Mexicans and Mexican Americans in Michigan.* East Lansing: Michigan University State Press 2003.

Alvarez, Robert C. *Familia: Migration and Adaptation in Baja and Alta California.* Berkeley: University of California Press, 1987.

Alanís Enciso, Fernando Saúl. *Que se Quedan: El Gobierno de México y la repatriación de mexicanos en Estados Unidos (1934–1940).* Tijuana: El Colegio de la Frontera Norte, 2007.

———. "Nos Vamos Al Norte: La Emigración de San Luis Potosí a los Estados Unidos Entre 1920–1940." *Migraciones Internacionales* 2, no. 4 (2004): 66–94.

———. *El Primer Programa Bracero y El Gobierno De México, 1917–1918.* San Luis Potosí: Colegio de San Luis, 1999.

———. "The Repatriation of Mexicans from the United States and Mexican Nationalism, 1929–1940." In *Beyond La Frontera: The History of Mexico-U.S. Migration*, edited by Mark Overmyer-Velázquez, 51–78. New York: Oxford University Press, 2011.

Alarcón, Rafael. "El Proceso de 'Norteñizacion': Impacto de la migración internacional en Chavinda, Michoacán." In *Movimientos de población en el occidente de México,* edited by Thomas Calvo and Gustavo López, 337–58. Zamora: El Colegio de Michoacán, 1988.

Arias, Patricia. "La Migración Femenina en Dos Modelos de desarrollo: 1940–1970." In *Relaciones de género y transformaciones estudios sobre el campo mexicano*, edited by Soledad González Montes y Vania Salles, 223–54. Mexico City: El Colegio de Mexico, 1995.

Arizpe, Lourdes. "Introduccion." In *Población y Trabajo en contextos regionales,* edited by Gail Mummert, 11–15. Zamora, Michoacán: El Colegio de Michoacán, 1990.

———. *Migración, Etnismo y Cambio Economico: Un Estudio Sobre Migrantes campesinos a la ciudad de México.* Mexico City: El Colegio de Mexico, 1978.

———. "The Rural Exodus in Mexico and the Mexican Migration to the United States." *International Migration Review* 15, no. 4 (1981): 626–49.

Arredondo, Gabriela. *Mexican Chicago: Race, Identity and Nation, 1916–39.* Champaign-Urbana: University of Illinois Press, 2008.

Arredondo, Ramón and Trisha. *Maria's Journey.* Indianapolis: Indiana Historical Society, 2010.

Arreola, Daniel D. "The Mexican American Cultural Capital." *Geographical Review* 77, no. 1 (1987): 17–34.

Baezconde-Garbanati, Lourdes, and V. Nelly Salgado de Snyder. "Mexican Immigrant Women: A Selected Bibliography." *Hispanic Journal of Behavioral Sciences* 8, no. 3 (1987): 331–58.

Barajas, Frank P. *Curious Unions: Mexican American Workers and Resistance in Oxnard, California, 1898–1961.* Lincoln: University of Nebraska Press, 2012.

Balderrama, Francisco, and Raymond Rodríguez. *Decade of Betrayal: Mexican Repatriation in the 1930s.* Albuquerque: New Mexico University Press, 2006.

Benjamin, Thomas. *La Revolucion: Mexico's Great Revolution as Memory, Myth, and History*. Austin: University of Texas Press, 2000.

———. "Rebuilding the Nation." In *The Oxford History of Mexico,* edited by Michael C. Meyer, and William H. Beezley. New York: Oxford University Press, 2000.

Benton-Cohen, Katherine. "Other Immigrants: Mexicans and the Dillingham Commission of 1907–1911." *Journal of American Ethnic History* 30, no. 2 (2011): 33–57.

———. *Borderline Americans: Racial Division and Labor War in the Arizona Borderlands*. Cambridge, MA: Harvard University Press, 2009.

Blum, Ann S. *Domestic Economies: Family, Work, and Welfare in Mexico City, 1884–1943*. Lincoln: University of Nebraska Press, 2009.

———. "Breaking and Making Families: Adoption and Public Welfare, Mexico City, 1938–1942." In *Sex in Revolution: Gender, Politics, and Power in Modern Mexico,* edited by Jocelyn Olcott, Mary Kay Vaughn, and Gabriela Cano, 127–46. Durham, NC: Duke University Press, 2007.

Buchenau, Jurgen. *The Last Caudillo: Álvaro Obregón and the Mexican Revolution*. Hoboken, NJ: Wiley Blackwell, 2011.

———. *Plutarco Elías Calles and the Mexican Revolution*. New York: Crown and Littlefield, 2007.

Calvo, Thomas and Gustavo López, eds. *Movimientos de población en el occidente de México*. Zamora: El Colegio de Michoacán, 1988.

Camarillo, Albert. *Chicanos in a Changing Society: From Mexican Pueblos to American Barrios in Santa Barbara and Southern California, 1848–1930*. Cambridge, MA: Harvard University Press, 1979.

Canaday, Margot. *The Straight State: Sexuality and Citizenship in Twentieth-Century America*. Princeton, NJ: Princeton University Press, 2010.

Cárdenas, Enrique. *La Industrialización Mexicana Durante La Gran Depresión*. Mexico D.F.: El Colegio De Mexico, 1987.

Cárdenas Sánchez, Enrique. *El largo curso de la economía mexicana: De 1780 a nuestros dias*. Mexico City: El Colegio de México, 2015.

Cardoso, Lawrence. *Mexican Emigration to the United States, 1897–1931*. Tucson: University of Arizona Press, 1980.

———. "La Repatriacíon De Braceros En Época De Obregón—1920–1923." *Historia Mexicana* 26, no. 4 (1977): 576–95.

———. "Labor Emigration to the Southwest, 1916–1920: Mexican Attitudes and Policy." *Southwest Historical Quarterly* 79, no. 4 (1976): 400–16.

Carreras, Mercedes. *Los Mexicanos Que Devolvió La Crisis, 1929–1932*. Tlatelolco, México: Secretaría de Relaciones Exteriores, 1974.

Castillo Girón, Victor Manuel. *Sólo Dios y El Norte: Migración a Estados Unidos y desarrollo en una region de Jalisco*. Guadalajara: Universidad de Guadalajara, 1995.

Castillo-Muñoz, Veronica. "Intermarriage and the Making of a Multicultural Society in the Baja California Borderlands: Gender, Race and Intermarriage in Borderlands." In *Red and Yellow, Black and Brown: Decentering Whiteness in Mixed*

Race Studies, edited by Joanne L. Rondilla, et al., 49–70. New Jersey: Rutgers University Press, 2017.

———. *The Other California: Land, Identity and Politics on the Mexican Borderlands*. Berkeley: University of California Press, 2016.

Chávez-García, Miroslava. *Migrant Longing: Letter Writing Across the U.S.-Mexico Borderlands*. Chapel Hill: University of North Carolina Press, 2018.

Cohen, Deborah. *Braceros: Migrant Citizens and Transnational Subjects in the Postwar United States and Mexico*. Berkeley: University of California Press, 2011.

Cohen, Robert. *Dear Mrs. Roosevelt Letters from Children of the Great Depression*. Chapel Hill: University of North Carolina Press, 2002.

Cruz Pineiro, Rodolfo. "Mercados de Trabajo y migración en la frontera norte: Tijuana, Ciudad Juárez y Nuevo Laredo." *Frontera Norte* 2, núm. 4 (Jul-Dic, 1990): 62–93.

Cypess, Sandra Messinger. "'Mother' Malinche And Allegories Of Gender, Ethnicity And National Identity In Mexico." In *Feminism, Nation And Myth: La Malinche*, edited by Rolando Romero and Amanda Nolacea Harris, 19–27. Houston, TX: Arte Publico Press, 2005.

Donato, Katherine. "Current Trends and Patterns of Female Migration: Evidence from Mexico." *The International Migration Review*: 27, no. 4 (Winter, 1993): 748–71.

Dore, Elizabeth, and Maxine Molyneux, eds. *Hidden Histories of Gender and The State in Latin America*. Durham: Duke University Press, 2000.

Driscoll, Barbara A. *Tracks North: The Railroad Bracero Program of World War II*. Austin: University of Texas Press, 1999.

Durand, Jorge. *Braceros: Las Miradas Mexicana y Estadounidense: Antología (1945–1964)*. México: Miguel Ángel Porrúa, 2007.

Durand, Jorge, Douglas S. Massey, and René M. Zenteno. "Mexican Immigration to the United States: Continuities and Changes." *Latin American Research Review* 36, no. 1 (2001): 107–27.

Estes, George H. "Internment of Mexican Troops." *Infantry Journal* 11 (1915).

Fitzgerald, David. *A Nation of Emigrants: How Mexico Manages its Migration*. Berkeley: University of California Press, 2009.

Friedrich, Paul. *Agrarian Revolt in a Mexican Village*. Chicago: University of Chicago Press, 1977.

Foley, Neil. *The White Scourge: Mexicans, Blacks, and Poor Whites in Texas Cotton Culture*. Berkeley: University of California Press, 1997.

Fox, Cybelle. *Three Worlds of Relief: Race, Immigration and the American Welfare State from the Progressive Era to the New Deal*. Princeton, NJ: Princeton University Press, 2012.

Fox, Jonathan. "Indigenous Mexican Migrants." In *Beyond La Frontera: The History of Mexico-U.S. Migration*, edited by Mark Overmyer-Velázquez, 161–78. New York: Oxford University Press, 2011.

Gabbert, Ann R. "Prostitution and Moral Reform in the Borderlands: El Paso, 1890–1920." *Journal of the History of Sexuality* 12, no. 4 (2003): 575–604.

Gamio, Manuel. *The Life Story of the Mexican Immigrant: Autobiographic Documents Collected by Manuel Gamio*. New York: Dover Publications, 1971.

———. *The Mexican Immigrant: His Life Story*. Chicago: University of Chicago Press, 1931.

———. *Mexican Immigration to the United States*. Chicago: University of Chicago Press, 1930.

Gabaccia, Donna. *From the Other Side: Women, Gender and Immigrant Life in the U.S., 1820–1996*. Bloomington: Indiana University Press, 1995.

Galarza, Ernesto. *Strangers in our Fields*. Washington, DC: United States Section, Joint United States-Mexico Trade Union Committee, 1956.

García, Mario T. "La Frontera: The Border as Symbol and Reality in Mexican-American Thought." *Mexican Studies/Estudios Mexicanos* 1, no. 2 (1985): 195–225.

———. *Desert Immigrants: The Mexicans of El Paso, 1880–1920*. New Haven, CT: Yale University Press, 1981.

———. "The Chicana in American History: The Mexican Women of El Paso, 1880–1920: A Case Study." *Pacific Historical Review* 4, no. 2 (1980): 315–37.

García, Matt. *A World of Their Own: Race, Labor, and Citrus in the Making of Greater Los Angeles, 1900–1970*. Chapel Hill: University of North Carolina Press, 2002.

Gardner, Martha. *The Qualities of a Citizen: Women, Immigration, and Citizenship, 1870–1965*. Princeton, NJ: Princeton University Press, 2005.

Gauss, Susan M. *Made in Mexico: Regions, Nation, and the State in The Rise of Mexican Industrialism, 1920s-1940s*. University Park: Pennsylvania State University Press, 2010.

Gillingham, Paul, and Benjamin T. Smith. *Dictablanda: Politics, Work, and Culture in Mexico, 1938–1968*. Durham: Duke University Press, 2014.

Gilly, Adolfo. *El Cardenismo: una utopía Mexicana*. Mexico, D.F.: Mexico: Ediciones Era, 2001.

Gregory, James. *American Exodus: The Dust Bowl Migration and Okie Culture in California*. New York: Oxford University Press, 1989.

Gonzalez, Gilbert. *Guest Workers or Colonized Labor? Mexican Labor Migration to the United States*. London: Routledge, 2006.

González, Rosalinda M. "Chicanas and Mexican Immigrant Families 1920–1940: Women's Subordination and Family Exploitation." In *Decades of Discontent: The Women's Movement, 1920–1940*, edited by Lois Schart and Joan M. Jenson, 59–84. Westport, CT: Greenwood Press, 1983.

González, Jerry. *In Search of the Mexican Beverly Hills: Latino Suburbanization in Postwar Los Angeles*. New Brunswick, NJ: Rutgers University Press, 2018.

González Navarro, Moisés. "Los braceros en el Porfiriato." *Estudios Agrarios: Revista de la Procuraduría Agraria: México: Procuraduría Agraria* (2010): 9–26.

———. *Los Extranjeros en México y Los Mexicanos en El Extranjero, 1921–1970*. Vols. 2 and 3. Mexico, D.F.: El Colegio de México, 1994.

González y González, Luis. *San Jose de Gracia: Mexican Village in Transition*. Austin: University of Texas Press, 1972.

Guerín-Gonzáles, Camille. *Mexican Workers and American Dreams: Immigration, Repatriation and California Farm Labor, 1900–1939.* New Brunswick, NJ: Rutgers University Press, 1994.

Guidotti-Hernández, Nicole M. *Archiving Mexican Masculinities in Diaspora.* Durham, NC: Duke University Press, 2021.

Gutiérrez, David. *Walls and Mirrors: Mexican Americans, Mexican Immigrants, and the Politics of Ethnicity.* Berkeley: University of California Press, 1995.

Gwin, J. Blaine. "Immigration Along our Southwest Border." *Annals of the American Academy of Political and Social Science* 93 (1921): 126–30.

Hart, John. *Empire and Revolution: The Americans in Mexico Since the Civil War.* Berkeley: University of California Press, 2002.

Hernández, Sonia. *Working Women Into the Borderlands.* College Station: Texas A&M University Press, 2014.

Hoffman, Abraham. *Unwanted Mexican-Americans in the Great Depression: Repatriation Pressures 1929–1939.* Tucson: University of Arizona Press, 1974.

Hondagneu-Sotelo, Pierrette. *Gendered Transitions: Mexican Experiences of Immigration.* Berkeley: University of California Press, 1994.

Iglesias Prieto, Norma. *Beautiful Flowers of the Maquiladora.* Austin: University of Texas Press, 1997.

Immigration and Naturalization Service. *Annual.* Washington, DC: Government Printing Office, 1920–1960.

Johnson, Ben Heber. *Revolution in Texas: How a Forgotten Rebellion and Its Bloody Suppression Turned Mexicans into Americans.* New Haven, CT: Yale University Press, 2003.

Joseph, Gilbert M., and Daniel Nugent. *Everyday Forms of State Formation: Revolution and the Negotiation of Rule in Modern Mexico.* Durham, NC: Duke University Press, 1994.

Innis-Jiménez, Michael. *Steel Barrio: The Great Mexican Migration to South Chicago.* New York: New York University Press, 2013.

Kang, S. Deborah. *The INS on the Line: Making Immigration Law on the US-Mexico Border, 1917–1954.* New York: Oxford University Press, 2017.

Katz, Friedrich. *The Secret War in Mexico.* Chicago: University of Chicago Press, 1981.

———. "Labor Conditions on Haciendas in Porfirian Mexico: Some Trends and Tendencies." *The Hispanic American Historical Review* 54, no. 1 (1974): 1–47.

Kiddle, Amelia, and Maria Muñoz, eds. *Populism in Twentieth Century Mexico: The Presidencies of Lázaro Cárdenas and Luis Echeverría.* Tucson: University of Arizona Press: 2010.

Knight, Alan. "Cardenismo: Juggernaut or Jalopy?" *Journal of Latin American Studies* 26, no. 1 (1994): 73–107.

Lee, Erika. *America for Americans: A History of Xenophobia in the United States.* New York, NY: Basic Books, 2019.

———. *At America's Gates: Chinese Immigration During the Exclusion Era, 1882–1943.* Chapel Hill: University of North Carolina Press, 2003.

de León, Arnoldo. *Ethnicity in the Sunbelt: A History of Mexican Americans in Houston*. Houston, TX: University of Houston, 1989.

Leyva, Yolanda Chávez. "Cruzando La Linea: Engendering the History of Border Mexican Children during the Early Twentieth Century." In *Memories and Migrations: Mapping Boricua and Chicana Histories*, edited by Vicki L. Ruiz and John R. Chávez, 71–92. Champaign-Urbana: University of Illinois Press, 2008.

———. "'I go to fight for social justice': Children as Revolutionaries in the Mexican Revolution, 1910–1920." *Peace & Change* 23, no. 4 (October 1998): 423–40.

Lim, Julian. *Porous Borders: Multiracial Migrations and the Law in the U.S.-Mexico Borderlands*. Chapel Hill: University of North Carolina Press, 2017.

Lewthwaite, Stephanie. *Race, Place and Reform in Mexican Los Angeles: A Transnational Perspective*. Tucson: University of Arizona Press, 2009.

Lomnitz, Larisa Adler. *Networks and Marginality: Life in a Mexican Shantytown*. New York: Academic Press, 1977.

Loza, Mireya. *Defiant Braceros: How Migrant Workers Fought for Racial, Sexual, and Political Freedom*. Chapel Hill: The University of North Carolina Press, 2016.

Lytle Hernández, Kelly. *Migra!: A History of the U.S. Border Patrol*. Berkeley: University of California Press, 2010.

———. *City of Inmates: Conquest, Rebellion, and the Rise of Human Caging in Los Angeles, 1771–1965. Justice, Power, and Politics*. Chapel Hill: University of North Carolina Press, 2017.

Massey, Douglas, Rafael Alarcon, Jorge Durand, and Humberto Gonzalez. *Return to Aztlan: The Social Process of International Migration from Western Mexico*. Berkeley: University of California Press, 1987.

McKiernan-González, John. *Fevered Measures: Public Health and Race at the Texas-Mexico Border, 1848–1942*. Durham, NC: Duke University Press, 2012.

Martínez, Oscar. *Border Boom Town: Ciudad Juárez since 1848*. Austin: University of Texas Press, 1975.

———. *Ciudad Juárez: Saga of a Legendary Border City*. Tucson: University of Arizona Press, 2018.

———. "Migration and the Border, 1965–1985." In *Beyond La Frontera: The History of Mexico-U.S. Migration,* edited by Mark Overmyer-Velázquez, 103–21. New York: Oxford University Press, 2011.

Martínez-Matsuda, Verónica. *Migrant Citizenship: Race, Rights, and Reform in the U.S. Farm Labor Camp Program*. Philadelphia: University of Pennsylvania Press, 2020.

Massey, Douglas S., Jorge Durand, and Nolan J. Malone. *Beyond Smoke and Mirrors: Mexican Immigration in an Era of Economic Integration*. New York, NY: Russell Sage Foundation, 2002.

Massey, Douglas S., and Zai Liang. "The Long-Term Consequences of a Temporary Worker Program: The US Bracero Experience." *Population Research and Policy Review* 8, no. 3 (September 1989): 199–226.

Massey, Douglas S., and Karen A. Pren. "Unintended Consequences of U.S. Immigration Policy: Explaining the Post-1965 Surge from Latin America." *Population and Development Review* 38, no. 1 (March 2012): 1–29.

McWilliams, Carey. *Ill Fares the Land*. Boston: Little, Brown and Company, 1942.
———. *North from Mexico: The Spanish-Speaking People of the United States*. New York: Greenwood Press, 1968.
Medina, Luis. *Del Cardenismo al avilacamachismo*. Mexico D.F.: El Colegio de México, 1978.
Melville, Margarita B. "Mexican Women Adapt to Migration." *The International Migration Review* 12, no. 2 (1978): 225–35.
Meyer, Jean. *La Cristiada*. Mexico City: Siglo Veintiuno Editores, 1970.
Middlebrook, Kevin. *The Paradox of Revolution: Labor, The State and Authoritarianism in Mexico*. Baltimore, MD: Johns Hopkins University Press, 1995.
Mitchell, Don. *They Saved the Crops: Labor, Landscape, and the Struggle over Industrial Farming in Bracero-Era California*. Athens: University of Georgia Press, 2012.
Moguel, Julio. *Historia de la Cuestión Agraria Mexicana: La época de oro y el principio de la crisis de la agricultura Mexicana: 1950–1970*. Mexico: Siglo xxi editors, 1988.
Molina, Natalia. *Fit to Be Citizens: Public Health and Race in Los Angeles, 1879–1939*. Berkeley: University of California Press, 2006.
Moloney, Dierdre. "Women, Sexual Morality and Economic Dependency in Early Deportation Policy." *Journal of Women's History* 18, no. 2 (2006): 95–122.
Monroy, Douglas. *Rebirth: Mexican Los Angeles From the Great Migration to the Great Depression*. Berkeley: University of California Press, 1999.
Montejano, David. *Anglos and Mexicans in the Making of Texas, 1836–1986*. Austin: University of Texas Press, 1987.
Muñoz Martinez, Monica. *The Injustice Never Leaves You: Anti-Mexican Violence in Texas*. Cambridge, MA: Harvard University Press, 2008.
Muriá, José María. *Breve Historia de Jalisco*. Mexico City: El Colegio de Mexico, 2000.
Ngai, Mae. *Impossible Subjects: Illegal Aliens and the Making of Modern America*. Princeton, NJ: Princeton University Press, 2004.
Norris, Jim. *North for the Harvest: Mexican Workers, Growers, and the Sugar Beet Industry*. St. Paul: Minnesota Historical Press, 2009.
North, David S., Marion F. Houstoun, and United States Employment and Training Administration. *The Characteristics and Role of Illegal Aliens in the U.S. Labor Market: An Exploratory Study*. Washington, DC: New TransCentury Foundation/Linton, 1976.
Ochoa, Álvaro. *Viajes De Michoacanos Al Norte*. Zamora: Colegio de Michoacán, 1998.
Olcott, Jocelyn, Mary Kay Vaughn, and Gabriela Cano, eds. *Sex in Revolution: Gender, Politics, and Power in Modern Mexico*. Durham, NC: Duke University Press, 2007.
Overmeyer-Velázquez, Mark, ed. *Beyond La Frontera: The History of Mexico-U.S. Migration*. New York: Oxford University Press, 2011.
Padilla, Tanalis. *Rural Resistance in the Land of Zapata: The Jaramillista Movement and the Myth of the Pax-Priísta, 1940–1962*. Durham, NC: Duke University Press, 2008.

Palerm, Juan Vicente, and José Ignacio Urquiola. "A Binational System of Agricultural Production: The Case of the Mexican Bajío and California." In *Mexico and the United States, Neighbors in Crisis: Proceedings from the Conference, Neighbors Crisis, a Call for Joint Solutions, February 1989,* edited by Daniel G. Aldrich and Lorenzo Meyer, 311–67. San Bernardino, CA: Borgo Press, 1993.

Perales, Monica. *Smeltertown: Making and Remembering a Southwest Border Community.* Chapel Hill: University of North Carolina Press, 2010.

Porter, Susie S. *Working Women in Mexico City: Public Discourse and Material Conditions, 1879–1931.* Tucson: University of Arizona Press, 2003.

Reisler, Mark. *By the Sweat of Their Brow: Mexican Immigrant Labor in the United States, 1900–1940.* Green Port, CT: Greenwood Press, 1976.

———. "Always the Laborer, Never the Citizen: Anglo Perceptions of the Mexican Immigrant during the 1920s." In *Between Two Worlds: Mexican Immigrants in the United States,* edited by David G. Gutierrez, 23–44. Wilmington, DE: Scholarly Resources, 1996.

———. "The Mexican Immigrant in the Chicago Area during the 1920s." *Journal of the Illinois State Historical Society* 66 (1973): 144–58.

Rionda Ramírez, Luis Miguel. *Y jalaron pa'l norte..: Migración, agrarismo y agricultura en un pueblo michoacano: Copándaro de Jiménez.* Zamora: El Colegio de Michoacán, 1992.

Robinson, Robert S. "Taking the Fair Deal to the Fields: Truman's Commission on Migratory Labor, Public Law 78, and the Bracero Program, 1950–1952." *Agricultural History* 84, no. 3 (2010): 381–402.

Rodríguez Batista, María. "El reparto agrario en Jalisco: dos administraciones poscardenistas, 1940–1952." In *Desarrollo rural en Jalisco: Contradicciones y perspectivas,* edited by Sergio Alcántara Ferrer and Enrique Sánchez Ruiz. Guadalajara: Colegio de Jalisco, 1985.

Rosas, Ana Elizabeth. *Abrazando el Espíritu: Bracero Families Confront the U.S.-Mexico Border.* Berkeley: University of California Press, 2011.

———. "Breaking the Silence: Mexican Children and Women's Confrontation of Bracero Family Separation, 1942–64." *Gender & History* 22, no. 2 (2011): 382–400.

———. "Flexible Families: Bracero Families' Lives Across Cultures, Communities, and Countries, 1942–1964." PhD diss., University of Southern California, 2006.

Ruiz, Vicki. *Cannery Women, Cannery Lives: Mexican Women, Unionization, and the California Food Processing Industry, 1930–1950.* Albuquerque: University of New Mexico Press, 1987.

———. "By the Day or the Week: Mexicana Domestic Workers in El Paso." In *Women on the U.S.-Mexico Border: Responses to Change,* edited by Vicki L. Ruiz and Susan Tiano, 61–76. Winchester, MA: Allen & Unwin, 1987.

———. *From Out of the Shadows: Mexican Women in Twentieth-Century America.* 10th anniversary ed. New York: Oxford University Press, 2008.

St. John, Rachel. *Line in the Sand: A History of the Western U.S.-Mexico Border.* Princeton, NJ: Princeton University Press, 2011.

Sánchez, George J. *Becoming Mexican American: Ethnicity, Culture, and Identity in Chicano Los Angeles, 1900–1945*. New York: Oxford University Press, 1993.

———. *Boyle Heights: How a Los Angeles Neighborhood Became the Future of American Democracy*. Oakland: University of California Press, 2021.

———. "'Go after the women': Americanization and the Mexican Immigrant Woman, 1915–1929." In *Mothers & Motherhood: Readings in American History*, edited by Rima D. Apple and Janet Lynne Golden, 475–94. Columbus: Ohio State University Press, 1997.

Sánchez Ruíz, Enrique E. "Apuntes para Una Historia de la Prensa en Guadalajara." *Comunicación y Sociedad* 4–5 (1989): 10–38.

Sanders, Nichole. *Gender and Welfare in Mexico: The Consolidation of a Post-Revolutionary State*. University Park: Pennsylvania State University Press, 2012.

Segura, Denise A., and Patricia Zavella, eds. *Women and Migration in the U.S.-Mexico Borderlands: A Reader*. Durham, NC: Duke University Press, 2007.

Servín, Elisa. "Reclaiming Revolution in Light of the 'Mexican Miracle': Celestino Gasca and the Federacionistas Leales Insurrection of 1961." *The Americas* 66, no. 4 (April 2010): 527–57.

Sinclair, Heather M. "White Plague, Mexican Menace." *Pacific Historical Review* 85, no. 4 (November 2016): 474–505.

Snodgrass, Michael. "The Bracero Program, 1942–1964." In *Beyond La Frontera: The History of Mexico-U.S. Migration*, edited by Mark Overmyer-Velázquez, 79–102. New York: Oxford University Press, 2011.

Spenser, Joseph and Daniela. *In from the Cold: Latin America's New Encounter with the Cold War*. Durham, NC: Duke University Press, 2008.

State of California. *Governor C.C. Young's Mexican Fact-Finding Committee, Mexicans in California*. San Francisco: California Department of Industrial Relations, 1930.

Stephen, Lynn. *Transborder Lives: Indigenous Oaxacans in Mexico, California and Oregon*. Durham, NC: Duke University Press, 2007.

———. *Zapata Lives!: Histories and Cultural Politics in Southern Mexico*. Berkeley: University of California Press, 2002.

Stern, Alexandra Minna. "Buildings, Boundaries, and Blood: Medicalization and Nation-Building on the U.S.-Mexico Border, 1910–1930." *The Hispanic American Historical Review* 79, no. 1 (1999): 41–81.

Stern, Steve J. *The Secret History of Gender: Women, Men, and Power in Late Colonial Mexico*. Chapel Hill: University of North Carolina Press, 1995.

Tamayo, Jaime. *Jalisco: Desde la Revolución: Los movimientos sociales 1917–1929*. Guadalajara: Universidad de Guadalajara, 1988.

Taylor, Paul Schuster. *A Spanish-Mexican Peasant Community: Arandas in Jalisco, Mexico*. Berkeley: University of California Press, 1933.

———. *Mexican Labor in the United States*. 2 vols. New York: Arno Press, 1970.

Torres Ramírez, Blanca. *Hacia la Utopía Industrial*. Mexico: El Colegio De Mexico, 1979.

———. *Mexico en La Segunda Guerra Mundial*. Mexico: El Colegio De Mexico, 1979.

Truett, Samuel. *Fugitive Landscapes: The Forgotten History of the U.S.-Mexico Borderlands*. New Haven, CT: Yale University Press, 2006.

Tutino, John. *From Insurrection to Revolution in Mexico: Social Bases of Agrarian Violence, 1750–1940*. Princeton, NJ: Princeton University Press, 1986.

———. *The Mexican Heartland: How Communities Shaped Capitalism, a Nation, and World History, 1500–2000*. Princeton, NJ: Princeton University Press, 2018.

———, ed. *Mexico and Mexicans in the Making of the United States*. Austin: University of Texas Press, 2012.

United States Congress. House Committee on Immigration and Naturalization. *Hearings before the Committee on Immigration and Naturalization, House of Representatives, Sixty-Ninth Congress, First Session*. 16 vols. Washington, DC: Government Printing Office, 1926.

United States Congress. House Committee on Agriculture. *Mexican Farm Labor Program. Hearings before the Subcommittee on Equipment, Supplies, and Manpower on H. R. 3822*. Washington, DC: Government Printing Office, 1955.

Vargas, Zaragosa. *Proletarians of the North: A History of Mexican Industrial Workers in Detroit and the Midwest, 1917–1933*. Berkeley: University of California Press, 1993.

Vaughan, Mary Kay. *Cultural Politics in Revolution: Teachers, Schools and Peasants in Mexico, 1930–1940*. Tucson: University of Arizona Press, 1987.

———. "Modernizing Patriarchy: State Policies, Rural Households, and Women in Mexico, 1930–1940." In *Hidden Histories of Gender and the State in Latin America*, edited by Elizabeth Dore and Maxine Molyneux, 194–214. Durham, NC: Duke University Press, 2000.

Varley, Ann. "Women and the Home in Mexican Family Law." In *Hidden Histories of Gender and The State in Latin America*, edited by Elizabeth Dore and Maxine Molyneux, 238–61. Durham, NC: Duke University Press, 2000.

Velasco Ortiz, Laura. "Women, Migration, and Household Survival Strategies: Mixtec Women in Tijuana." In *Women and Migration in the U.S.-Mexico Borderlands: A Reader*, edited by Denise A. Segura and Patricia Zavella, 341–59. Durham, NC: Duke University Press, 2007.

Walker, Louise. *Waking from the Dream: Mexico's Middle Classes After 1968*. Stanford, CA: Stanford University Press, 2013.

Walsh, Casey. *Building the Borderlands: A Transnational History of Irrigated Cotton Along the Mexico-Texas Border*. College Station: Texas A&M University Press, 2008.

Weber, Devra. *Dark Sweat, White Gold: California Farm Workers, Cotton, and the New Deal*. Berkeley: University of California Press, 1996.

Weber, Devra, Roberto Melville, and Juan Vicente Palerm, eds. *Manuel Gamio El Inmigrante Mexicano: La Historia De Su Vida: Entrevistas Completas, 1926–1927*. Mexico DF: Secretaria De Gobernacion, 2002.

Weber, John. *From South Texas to the Nation: The Exploitation of Mexican Labor in the Twentieth Century*. Chapel Hill: University of North Carolina Press, 2015.

Weise, Julie M. *Corazón De Dixie: Mexicanos in the U.S. South Since 1910*. Chapel Hill: University of North Carolina Press, 2015.

Wilson, Tamar Diana. *Women's Migration Networks in Mexico and Beyond.* Albuquerque: University of New Mexico Press, 2001.

Wright, Angus. *The Death of Ramón González: The Modern Agricultural Dilemma.* Austin: University of Texas Press, 2005.

Young, Julia Grace Darling. *Mexican Exodus: Emigrants, Exiles, and Refugees of the Cristero War.* New York: Oxford University Press, 2015.

INDEX

Note: Page numbers in italics indicate illustrative material.

abandonment, spousal, 97–99, 116, 130,
  140–41
abuse: of migrant laborers, 40, 41–42, 45,
  46, 153, 237n32; sexual violence, 37–38;
  spousal, 141–43. *See also* violence
African Americans, Great Migration of,
  63, 64
Agricultural Adjustment Act (1933, US), 96
agriculture, Mexican: and drought, 165, 195,
  260–61n56; labor shortages, 54, 80, 86,
  104, 153–54; land privatization, 27–30,
  151–52, 178; land redistribution and
  ejido system, 54–55, 79, 134–35, 151–52,
  157, 158, 165–66, 180, 181, 258–59n27;
  modernization and mechanization, 166,
  177–81, 216
agriculture, US: boom in Southwest during
  1920s, 63–67; and drought, 251n16;
  family labor as central to, 59, 63;
  impacted by Great Depression, 96, 128;
  labor shortages, 41, 42, 152, 207; modernization and mechanization, 176,
  210–11, 215–16. *See also* bracero program; labor migration
Aguascalientes, 112
Aguila, Gustavo, 85
Aguirre, Aurelio, 152
aid, financial. *See* financial assistance and
  welfare
Alanís Enciso, Fernando Saúl, 39, 40,
  236n13

Alarcón, Rafael, 6, 220
Alemán, Miguel, 152, 159, 169, 181, 194–95,
  259n38
Allende, Teresa Brizuela, 51
Alonso, Señora J. Márquez de Edwards
  Vda. de, 252–53n28
Alvarado, Margarita Ramirez de, 149, 159
Alzaga, Sabino, 135
Amador, Micaela, 116
Andrade, Trinidad Rojas, 169
Angel, Maria de la Paz, 159
Arandas, Los Altos de Jalisco, 48, 79–80,
  246n68
Arizona: borderland population growth,
  34; deportation operations in, 201;
  family labor in, 66; labor exemption
  petitions, 152; rail connection in, 31,
  80–81, 127
Arizona Cotton Growers Association, 66
Armenta de Aguilera, Maria Concepción,
  167
Arroyo, Elena G. Viuda de, 23, 24, 25
Asian immigrants, 31, 63, 64, 69, 243n17
Association for Legalized Domestics, 185
Ávalos, Macaria, 68
Ayala, Gregoria, 76
Ayala, Magdalena E., 132

Baja California, 134, 210. *See also* Mexicali
Balderrama, Francisco, 247n2, 247–48n5,
  250n45

Baltazar family, 8, 77, 113–15
Barber, Dorothy, *118*
La Barca, Jalisco, 48
Barrón, Sara, 98–99, 117
Benton-Cohen, Katherine, 250n47
Betancourt family, 108–9
binational families: and bracero program, 157, 211; created through circular migration, 76–77, 214; deportation dynamics, 193, 199; diversity of experiences, 7–9, 93–94; and proof of citizenship, 138, 157, 255n55; repatriation dynamics, 102, 107–9, 112–15, *114*, 121–22, 123–25, 131–32, 135–38, 140–43; US anxieties about, 38–39, 177, 189, 209
border enforcement, US: detention facilities, 192, 194, 205–6, 220; formation of, 69; hot-foot lift practice, 173; Operation Wetback, 13, 200–206; and troop deployment, 95; uneven regulation of, 12–13, 26, 73, 193. *See also* deportation; illegal/undocumented migration
Border Industrialization Program (Mexico), 217
borderland communities: bracero families in, 187–88; formation of, overview, 4–5, 7, 11–12; labor transformations during Porfiriato, 30–34; major ports of entry for migrants, *60*, *175*; Mexican consul advocacy for migrant laborers, 42; population growth, 34, 61, 187, 191; as refuge from revolutionary violence, 37, 38–39. *See also* family networks
Box Bill (1927, US), 232n7
boxcar settlements, 34
bracero program: overview, 9–10, 149–51, 170–71; claimed as right, 164–68; contract agreements, 155, 159–60, 167, 188–89, 194; contracting centers, 190–91; criticism of, 153–54, 176–77, 184–85, 198, 206–7, 209–11; domestic service program proposal, 185–86; end of, 210, 211, 213, 215; family dimension, 149, 168–70, 173, 174, 187–90, 196–97, 201–6, *204*, 214; ideal migrants for, 156–58, 208–9; and illegal immigration, 155–56, 193–94, 196, 198–99, 266n81; and industrialization in Mexico, 151,

152, 177–81, 216; and mechanization in United States, 210–11, 215–16; patriarchal rhetoric, 161, 163–64, 166–67, 168; patriotic rhetoric, 160–63, 164–65, 260n43; postwar continuance of, 175–76, 182, 207, 210; railroad division, 258n19; scholarship on, 174, 256n2; "specials" designation, 187, 214; and wartime labor demands, 152–53; women excluded from, 158–59, 176, 259nn33–34
Brunet, Carlos Fradera, 213
Brust, Manuel, 97–98

Cadena, Barbara, 139
Caldera, Antonia Zavala, 77, 107
California: agricultural boom during 1920s, 63–64; agricultural impact of Great Depression, 96, 128, 251–52n16; agricultural mechanization during bracero era, 215, 216; agricultural transition during nineteenth century, 30–31; deportation operations in, 201, 205; illegal migration into, 200–201; labor exemption petitions, 152; relief agencies in, 130; as top destination for passport applications, 48. *See also specific cities*
California Alien Land Law (1920), 243n17
Calleros, Cleofas, 34, 183, 256n72
Calles, Plutarco Elías, 78, 81–83, 85
Camacho, Manuel Ávila: agrarian reform, 151–52; migrant letters to, 153, 157, 158, 159, 160–65, 167, 169–70, 192; presidential campaign, 9
Camacho, Maria Dolores, 99
Camarillo, Albert, 30–31, 62
Camarillo, Federico, 121
canneries and fruit-packing industry, 68, 158, 181, 259n38
Cantú, Ana Maria Hernández de, 85
Carbajal, Fidel, 152
Cárdenas, Lázaro: agrarian reform, 134–35, 165; cult of personality, 132, 161; migrant letters to, 8, 37, 98, 123–24, 132–35
Cardona, Catarino Escobar, 157
Cardoso, Lawrence, 40, 232n6, 239n65, 242n3
Carranza, Micaela, 23–24, 26
Carranza, Venustiano, 44, 79

economy *(continued)*
    post-revolutionary era, 54–55, 79, 134–35, 151–52, 157, 158, 165–66, 180, 181, 258–59n27; perceived stability *vs.* decline in 1970s and 1980s, 216, 221, 267n9; privatization during bracero era, 151–52, 178; privatization during Porfiriato, 27–30; recovery from Great Depression, 126; repatriates as threat to labor stability, 104, 119; and socio-political instability during post-revolutionary era, 55, 60–61, 78–80; in traditional migration history, 2, 3, 4. *See also* agriculture, Mexican; industrialization, Mexican
economy, US: Great Depression, overview, 91–97; panic of 1907, 36; post-WWII, 176; wartime labor demands, 40, 41, 42, 53–54, 152–53. *See also* agriculture, US; industrialization, US
editorials. *See* press
education. *See* schools
Eisenhower, Dwight D., 200
ejido system and land redistribution, 54–55, 79, 134–35, 151–52, 157, 158, 165–66, 180, 181, 258–59n27
Ellender-Poage Bill (1951, US; Public Law 78), 198–99, 206, 208
El Paso, Texas: detention facilities in, 192; domestic service in, 185–86; illegal migration through, 193; immigration procedure in, 46; labor recruitment in, 31; open border in, 193; population and demographics, 34, 62; schools for migrants in, 82; as top destination for passport applications, 48
El Paso Herald Post (newspaper), 41, 185
emigration. *See* immigration/emigration legislation, Mexican
Empalme, Sonora, 191
enganchadores (recruiters), 35, 42, 61
Enriquez, Mary C., 131–32
Espinosa, Cristina, 121
Espinosa, Refugio, 133
European immigrants, 63, 64, 69, 217

Falcon, Emilia Siller, 116
family-centered migration: defined, 2–4; and public charge exclusion, 71, 73,

74–75, 137; revolutionary-era rise of, 38, 44–45, 239n61; scholarship on, 3, 231n2. *See also* binational families
family labor: during bracero era, 186; as central to US agriculture, 59, 63; demographic shifts during Great Depression, 128; employer preference for, 6, 12, 14, 63, 65–67, 68; as migration phenomenon, overview, 4–5, 6–7, 14; mixed work opportunities, 61–63; railroad camps, 34; survival during Great Depression, 128–30
family networks: deportation hot-foot lift as disruption to, 173; establishment of foundational, during pioneering era, 25, 31, 48; as informal labor recruitment, 78, 158–59, 179, 180, 214; navigation of border-crossing process through, 45–46, 61, 214; significance for migration, overview, 3, 6, 9
family reunification: during bracero era, 187–90, 214; as constant factor driving migration, 2–4, 9; as passport application motivation, 23, 24, 25, 47, 48–51, 240n77, 240n79; through 1965 immigration law, 218; through repatriation, 99–100, 137–38
family separation: in bracero program stipulations, 149, 168–70, 174, 214; deportations, 173, 196–97, 201–6, *204*; and preservation of US American families, 208–9, 210; spousal abandonment, 97–99, 116, 130, 140–41
"family stage" migrations, 51–52
Farm Placement Service (US), 198
Fernandez, David, 252n25
Ferrer, Tepoxina Pintada Vda. de, 116–17
financial assistance and welfare: from employers, for transportation costs, 30, 65, 66, 155, 159; from Mexican government, during bracero era, 159, 160, 253n30; from Mexican government, during Great Depression, 56–57, 98–100, 103–4, 112, 116–19, 120, 123–24, 130–33, 134–35, 138–40, 253nn28–29; from US government, during Great Depression, 97–98, 100, 116, 127, 128–32, 138–40, 141, 143, 145, 248n5, 248n25, 252n25, 253nn28–29

immigrants, as term, 233n12
Immigration Act (1917, US), 40, 43, 69–70
Immigration and Nationality Act (1924, US; Johnson-Reed Act), 69–76, 232n7
Immigration and Nationality Act (1952, US; McCarran-Walter Act), 215
Immigration and Nationality Act (1965, US; Hart-Celler Act), 217–18, 219, 231n2
Immigration and Naturalization Service (INS), 185, 194, 198, 199, 200. *See also* Operation Wetback
immigration/emigration legislation, Mexican: Border Industrialization Program, 217; contract labor regulation, 40–42, 56–57; establishment of offices of migration, 84–85; restriction of foreign workers, 104. *See also* bracero program; consuls, Mexican; passports; repatriation
immigration legislation, US: exemptions for Mexican laborers, 40, 44, 45, 70, 152; Good Neighbor Policy, 152, 163, 172, 173, 184; head taxes, 26, 40, 69, 76; literacy tests, 40, 44; public charge exclusion, 70, 71, 72–74, 137, 183, 244–45nn49–50; restriction debates and discourse, 5–6, 12, 95, 198–99, 207–10, 232n7; restriction of Asian immigrants, 31, 63, 64, 69, 243n17; restriction of European immigrants, 63, 64, 69, 217; restriction of Western Hemisphere immigration, 217–18; uneven application of, 72–73. *See also* border enforcement, US; bracero program; consuls, US; deportation; illegal/undocumented migration; passports; visas
Immigration Reform and Control Act (1986, US), 221
industrialization, Mexican: agricultural mechanization, 166, 177–81, 216; during bracero-era Mexico, 151, 152, 177–81, 216; during post-revolutionary era, 83, 251n7
industrialization, US: agricultural mechanization, 176, 210–11, 215–16; labor demands during 1920s, 61, 68. *See also* railroads
El Informador (newspaper): on contract labor abuse, 41–42; on education

reform, 82; on family deportations, 203; on mass emigration, 54, 56, 78, 80, 83, 86, 184–85; objective reporting, 241n87; passport requirement notice, 43
INS (Immigration and Naturalization Service), 185, 194, 198, 199, 200. *See also* Operation Wetback
Irapuato, Guanajuato, 190, 191

jails and detention facilities, 192, 194, 205–6, 220
Jalisco: and bracero program, 179–80, 190, 263n31; economic recession during 1930s, 127; emigrant exodus from, 29, 41, 48, 54, 55, 56, 57, 59, 77, 79–81; land tenure changes and redistribution in, 27–29, 54–55, 79, 166; map, *28*; political instability during 1920s, 78–80; repatriation to, 106–7, 111, 115. *See also* *specific cities*
Japanese immigrants, 64, 69, 243n17
Jauregui, Mabelle, 139–40
Jiminez, Ignacia, 186
Johnson, Lyndon B., 188, 189
Johnson-Reed Act (1924, US), 69–76, 232n7

Kang, Deborah, 200
Katz, Friedrich, 237n36

labor migration: and demographic shifts, 64, 128, 217; vs. domestic laborers in United States, 198, 199, 206–8, 211; vs. domestic labor shortages in Mexico, 54, 80, 86, 153–54; employer preference for married vs. single laborers, 14, 65, 66, 208–9, 211–12; employer preference for Mexican laborers, 64, 207, 208, 243n24; and invitation, 12; Mexican regulation of contracts during revolutionary/post-revolutionary era, 40–42, 56–57; mixed work opportunities, 61–63, 68, 109–10, 112, 242n12; permanent vs. temporary settlement, 5–6, 39–40, 61, 66, 71, 115, 177, 250n47; during Porfiriato, 27–30; and Public Law 78, 198–99, 206, 208; and Public Law 414, 215; railroad construction and maintenance, 29–30, 31,

to apply for, 23–26, 45, 47, 48–51, 240n77, 240n79; provisional, 46, 72, 240n69; requirements and procedures for obtaining, 43, 44, 46, 47, 72; top destinations for applications, 48, *49*, 240n73. *See also* visas

patriarchy: in bracero program rhetoric, 161, 163–64, 166–67, 168; and familial poverty, 1, 98–100, 123, 128–30, 131–33, 138–43, 169–70; and gendered dependency assumptions, 13–14, 24–25, 26, 44, 51, 52–53, 71, 73–74, 137, 142, 143, 183, 255–56n63; and gendered dimensions of deportation, 193, 201–6, 220; heads of household, death of, 1, 63, 123, 131, 136–37, 165, 169–70; heads of household, obligations as providers, 97–98, 99–100, 140, 161, 166–67, 168; heads of household, place in family deportations, 196–97, 202–3; and Mexican presidency, 162; modernization in Mexico, 13, 257n4; and spousal abandonment, 97–99, 116, 130, 140–41; and spousal abuse, 141–43; women's exodus from Mexico as threat to, 56, 86, 184–85. *See also* gendered roles; men; women

patriotic and nationalist rhetoric, 116, 131, 133, 135, 160–63, 164–65, 260n43

patronage politics, 73, 245n52

Pérez, Dámos, 48

Pérez, Francisco, 9

Perez, Jose G., 99

Pérez, Margarita B., 98

policies. *See* immigration/emigration legislation, Mexican; immigration legislation, US

Porfiriato: economic decline and revolution, 36; land tenure changes during, 27–30; railroad industrialization during, 31–35

Portes Gil, Emilio, 116

poverty: familial, 1, 98–100, 123, 128–30, 131–33, 138–43, 169–70; and public charge exclusion, 70, 71, 72–74, 137, 183, 244–45nn49–50; and racial stereotypes, 74; and repatriation subsidy qualification, 103. *See also* financial

assistance and welfare; unemployment and underemployment

Pren, Karen, 219

press, Mexican: contract labor abuse criticism, 41–42, 239n65; deportation reports, 203; employment announcements, 41, 42, 153; Lozano newspapers, 253n37; mass emigration concerns, 54, 55, 56, 77, 78, 81, 83, 153–54, 184–85, 186, 239n65; post-revolutionary political criticism, 54–55, 81–84

press, US: deportation reports, 172–73, 200–202; mixed citizenship status concerns, 38; public health concerns, 39

prisons and detention facilities, 192, 194, 205–6, 220

public charge exclusion, 70, 71, 72–74, 137, 183, 244–45nn49–50

Public Law 78 (1951, US; Ellender-Poage Bill), 198–99, 206, 208

Public Law 414 (1952, US), 215

racial discourse: nativism, 5, 92, 95, 130; perceived docility of Mexican laborers, 243n24; and poverty stereotypes, 74; public health concerns, 39; and restriction debates, 95, 232n7; "social problem" concerns, 200–201, 209–10; white American stereotypes, 184–85

railroads: and boxcar labor camps, 34; bracero program division, 258n19; construction and maintenance jobs for migrants, 29–30, 31, 34–35; facilitation of migration to United States, 29, 36, *37*, 61, 80–81, 85; facilitation of return migration to Mexico, 103, 105–6, *106*, *118*; routes and connections, *32–33*

ranching industry, 30, 31, 35, 54, 188

refugees: of Cristero War, 79–80; of Mexican Revolution, 36–39, *37*

regulations. *See* immigration/emigration legislation, Mexican; immigration legislation, US

Reisler, Mark, 40, 232n6

relief. *See* financial assistance and welfare

religious conflict, Cristero War (1926–29), 58, 78–80

Renteria, Ricardo, 133

repatriation: in bracero program, 159–60, 213; in context of longer migrant trajectories, 101–2, 214; during panic of 1907, 36

repatriation, during Great Depression: ambivalence toward, in Mexico, 119–20, 122; binational family dynamics, 102, 107–9, 112–15, *114*, 121–22, 123–25, 131–32, 135–38, 140–43; demographics and statistics, 105–11, 112, 115, 247n2, 250n45; government financial assistance for, 56–57, 98–100, 103–4, 112, 116–19, 120, 123–24, 130–33, 134–35, 138–40, 253nn28–29; and job placement in Mexico, 104, 110, 119, 134–35; patterns of long-distance travel, 105–7, *106*, 112; as phenomenon, 91–94, 121–22; ports of entry, 105, 110–12

return migration. *See* deportation; repatriation

reunification. *See* family reunification; family separation

Revolutionary Family rhetoric (Mexico), 151, 257n4

Reyes, Felícitas Saavedra, 192

Reyes, Filomena, 133

Reynosa, Rafael, 48

Rico Avalos, Juan, 168

Rodríguez, Abelardo, 98, 99, 117

Rodriguez, Nicha, 123, 124, 131

Rodriguez, Raymond, 247n2, 247–48n5, 250n45

Romero, Efren, 141–42

Romero, Theresa, 141–42

Roosevelt, Franklin D., 1, 8, 123–24, 130–31

Rosas, Ana Elizabeth, 169

Rosas, Jose Rivera, 41

Ruiz, Leocadia, 23

Ruiz, Vicki, 185

Ruiz de Sandoval, Maria de Jesus, 169

Salinas, Manuel, 133

San Antonio, Texas: labor recruitment in, 42; population and demographics, 34, 48, 61, 62; as top destination for passport applications, 48

Sánchez, George, 4, 62, 92, 248n25

Sandoval, Victor, 253n29

San Francisco, California, 48

San José de Gracia, Michoacán, 79, 246n68

Santa Barbara, California, 30, 31

Santa Fe Railroad, 31, *32–33*, 34

schools: for migrants, 62, 82; post-revolutionary reform in Mexico, 82–83

Segura, Aurelio, 165

separation. *See* family reunification; family separation

Serrano, Maria, 202, 205

Showers, C. W., 188–89

Silliman, John R., 43

Silva, Antonio, 51

smuggling and smugglers, 76, 201. *See also* illegal/undocumented migration

Snodgrass, Michael, 260n43

social workers, 97–98. *See also* financial assistance and welfare

Sonora, 191. *See also* Nogales

South Pacific Railroad, 31

Southwest United States. *See specific states and cities*

specials (braceros designation), 187, 214

spousal abandonment, 97–99, 116, 130, 140–41

spousal abuse, 141–43

sugar beet production: impacted by Great Depression, 128; mechanization, 211; periods of expansion, 41, 63, 64, 67; preference for family labor, 65

Swing, Joseph, 200

Tamaulipas, 105–6, 109–11

Taylor, Paul Schuster, 5, 25, 45, 65, 67, 79–80, 128, 232n6, 242n3, 242n12

Texas: agricultural mechanization in, 215; bracero program in, 177, 266n81; detention facilities in, 192, 206; and Great Depression, 96; labor exemption petitions, 152; as top destination for passport applications, 48. *See also specific cities*

Torres, Andrea, 73–74

Torres, Dolores, 66

Torres, Ismael, 166

Torres, Maria Heriberta, 181, 259n38

Torres, Mary, 131
Torres, Salvador Belmontes, 194–95
Torres, Señora Cruz Loera de, 62–63
trains. *See* railroads
Triggs, Matt, 208–9
Truman, Harry S., 198
Tucson, Arizona, 34
La Tuna detention camp, 192
Tutino, John, 30

Undesirable Aliens Act (1929, US), 95, 192
undocumented migration. *See* illegal/ undocumented migration
unemployment and underemployment: and industrialization, 166, 215–16; labor migration driven by, 1, 55, 131, 140, 158, 163, 167, 168, 172, 178–81; and labor shortages, 54, 207; and over-recruitment, 67; rates during Great Depression, 96; repatriation driven by, 91, 98, 100
unions. *See* labor unions
United States government: financial assistance for migrants, 97–98, 100, 116, 127, 128–32, 138–40, 141, 143, 145, 248n5, 248n25, 252n25, 253nn28–29; migrant letters of petition to, 1, 8, 97–98, 123–24, 130–32, 135–44, 252n25. *See also* bracero program; consuls, US; economy, US; immigration legislation, US
urbanization, 27–29, 151, 152, 185
Urquiola, José Ignacio, 216

Valadez, Frank, 144
Valdes, Victoria, 135
Valle, Agustin, 133
Valtierra, Victoriano, 109
Vaughan, Mary Kay, 257n4
Vazquez, Antonia, 131
Villa, Pancho, 38, 79
violence: Cristero War, 79–80; Mexican Revolution, 36–39, *37*. *See also* abuse
visas: for families of US citizens, 218; and gendered dependency assumptions, 73–74; prohibitive fees, 69, 76, 85; and

provisional passports, 46, 72, 240n69; requirements and procedures for obtaining, 70–76, 183; rise in admissions during bracero era, 182. *See also* passports
voluntary deportation, 192, 193, 194, 202, 205

wages: in bracero program, 155, 215; and Great Depression, 96; and labor unions, 82; and mechanization, 215–16; and over-recruitment, 67
Walker, Louise, 267n9
Wallace, Henry, 131–32
Walsh, Casey, 30
Warden, Guillermo, 255n55
welfare. *See* financial assistance and welfare
women: absence in traditional migration history, 2, 3, 14, 20; age for adult *vs.* adolescent classification, 44; bracero program, exclusion from, 158–59, 176, 259nn33–34; bracero program, letters of petition, 159, 163–64, 166–67, 169–70, 181; dependency assumptions, 13–14, 24–25, 26, 44, 51, 52–53, 73–74, 137, 142, 143, 183, 255–56n63; deportation dynamics, 193, 201–6, 220; employer expectations of, in family labor unit, 65, 66; exodus from Mexico as threat to patriarchy, 56, 86, 184–85; family stage migration of, 51–52; financial assistance during bracero era, 159, 169–70; financial assistance during Great Depression, 97–99, 116–17, 123–24, 130–33, 139–40, 141–43; independent migration of, 23, 26, 73–74, 109, 136–37, 141–43, 158–59, 174, 183–86, 219–21; in lens of family-centered migration, 6–7; morality concerns, 13, 176, 266n87; occupational variety, 31, 62, 68, 109–10, 112, 242n12, 244n40; repatriation dynamics, 61, 98–99, 107, 108, 109, 110, 116–17, 123–24, 130–33, 135–43; rural to urban migration within Mexico, 36, 217; sexual violence against, 37–38. *See also* gendered roles; men; patriarchy

Founded in 1893,
UNIVERSITY OF CALIFORNIA PRESS
publishes bold, progressive books and journals
on topics in the arts, humanities, social sciences,
and natural sciences—with a focus on social
justice issues—that inspire thought and action
among readers worldwide.

The UC PRESS FOUNDATION
raises funds to uphold the press's vital role
as an independent, nonprofit publisher, and
receives philanthropic support from a wide
range of individuals and institutions—and from
committed readers like you. To learn more, visit
ucpress.edu/supportus.